Stanley Henry M.

Through the Dark Continent

Stanley Henry M.

Through the Dark Continent

ISBN/EAN: 9783744760089

Printed in Europe, USA, Canada, Australia, Japan

Cover: Foto ©Andreas Hilbeck / pixelio.de

More available books at **www.hansebooks.com**

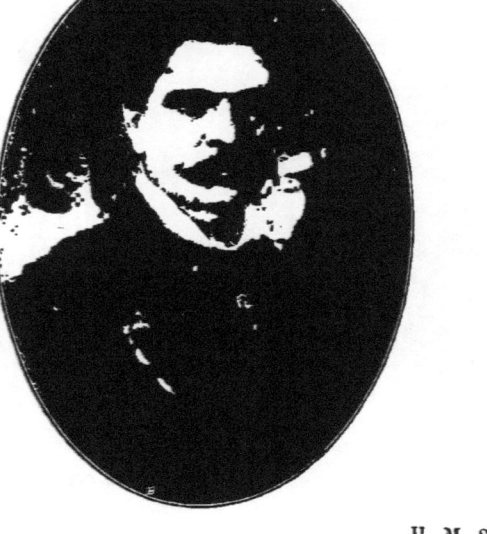

TAKEN BEFORE HIS DEPARTURE, 1874.

H. M. STANLEY.

TAKEN ON HIS EMERGING FROM AFRICA, 1877.

[*Frontispiece.*

THROUGH THE DARK CONTINENT

OR

THE SOURCES OF THE NILE AROUND THE GREAT LAKES OF EQUATORIAL AFRICA AND DOWN THE LIVINGSTONE RIVER TO THE ATLANTIC OCEAN

BY

HENRY M. STANLEY

AUTHOR OF "IN DARKEST AFRICA," "HOW I FOUND LIVINGSTONE," "MY KALULU," ETC.

MAP AND ILLUSTRATIONS

WITH A NEW PREFACE BY THE AUTHOR, WRITTEN FOR THIS EDITION.

VOL. II.

LONDON: GEORGE NEWNES, LIMITED
SOUTHAMPTON STREET, STRAND
1899

CONTENTS.

CHAPTER I.

PAGE

Ujiji, its scenery, residents, market, and vicinity—Arab rivals—The circumnavigation of the Tanganika—Commander Cameron and the outflowing Lukuga—The encroaching waters—The legend of the Lake—Evening 1

CHAPTER II.

The *Lady Alice* afloat again—Her mate and crew—Anxiety on her behalf—On hallowed ground—Unwelcome visitors: in the haunts of the Ruga-Ruga—The aborigines' last retreat—A scene of blood—The robbers of the Lake, and their tutelary spirits—A geological problem: were there once two lakes?—Rising waters—The abode of the genii—A storm—Forest fires—At the mouth of Cameron's "outlet"—The Lukuga creek 11

CHAPTER III.

Back in camp—An epidemic of small-pox—Panic of desertion—Kalulu's disloyalty—Livingstone's lenience—Imaginary terrors—Hairdressing *ad absurdum*—Ruanga's opinion of white men—A village sketch—The villagers of Uhombo—*In puris naturalibus*—A touch of human nature—On Livingstone's traces—What is there in feathers?—The Manyema: their life and manners—Our ass astonishes the natives—Bloodless wars—Nicknames—A tribe with beards but no wives—The confluence of the Luama and the Livingstone 48

CHAPTER IV.

At a swinging pace—Tippu-Tib, the Arab trader—News of Cameron and his difficulties—The river that flows North for ever—In Dwarf-land, fighting the dwarfs—Tippu-Tib's conditions—Friends in council—Heads or tails—Kalulu's accident at Nyangwé—Its residents and market—A muster of the Expedition 73

CHAPTER V.

PAGE

Tippu-Tib's henchmen—In the primeval forest, a wilderness of trees—Primitive furniture—Our sufferings in the pagans' forest—Tippu-Tib breaks down—A village blacksmith—Soko skulls; the missing link—Professor Huxley's opinion thereof—THE LIVINGSTONE—A day dream—The road to the ocean—Timid counsels—"The Wasambye!"—"Ooh-hu! ooh-hu!"—Successful diplomacy 98

CHAPTER VI.

"Mama, the Wasambye!"—The fight in the Ruiki—The lost found—Dangerous disobedience—In the nick of time—A savage captive—Music hath charms—In the haunts of Nature—A town of one street—Deserted villages—Organizing a hospital—An island wasted by lightning—"The people of the filed teeth"—Primitive salt-making—Hostages captured—At close quarters—Raining arrows—"Bo-bo, bo-bo, bo-bo-o-o-oh!"—A desperate affair and opportune reinforcements—Cutting the canoes adrift—Tippu-Tib deserts me—My appeal to the "sea children"—Christmas Day among the cannibals—"Victory or death!" 122

CHAPTER VII.

Farewell to Tippu-Tib—Attacked from both banks—The fat savage makes a bad shot at me—In the home of the elephants—Insect life—In covert—The Lowwa river—A storm on the river—New Year's day—Bullets against spears—"Sennenneh!"—Tempting the female mind—The reward of a good deed—A river armada: crocodile boats—Betwixt cataracts and cannibals 153

CHAPTER VIII.

Fighting betimes—Blazing a path—We take an island by storm—A desperate dilemma—Road-making under fire—A miraculous escape—A terrible march—Peace by stratagem—Below the Fifth Cataract—Our cannibal captives—Fighting the Wana-Rukura—The Wana-Rukura islanders—Approaching the Seventh Cataract—A deserted island—The Seventh Cataract of the Stanley Falls—The first of the Cataracts—Clear of the Stanley Falls 174

CHAPTER IX.

Again in open water—Frank Pocock feels the position—The Mburra or Yaryembi—A running fight—"Ya-Mariwa! Ya-Mariwa!"—Our tactics of capture—Monster spears—Growing weary of fighting for life—The power of laughter—Fish creeks—A wasp swarm of canoes—Another invincible armada—A village of ivory—Relics of cannibal feasts—The Wellé of Schweinfurth—Hunted to despair—Their "meat" escapes the cannibals—Wild nature—Among friendly natives—The Congo! 200

CHAPTER X.

PAGE

High art in tattooing—Suspicious friendliness—Friends or foes?—A treacherous attack—The fauna of the Livingstone—Among the "Houyhnyms"—The "Yaha-ha has"—Frank's courage and narrow escape—Our fight with the Bangala—The mirage on the river—The great tributary of the Livingstone—Among friends 222

CHAPTER XI.

Running the gauntlet—Kindly solitudes—Amina's death—The humanizing effects of trade apparent—"The most plausible rogue of all Africa"—The king of Chumbiri; his hospitality, wives, possessions, and cunning—Making up a language—Pythons—The Ibari Nkutu or the Kwango—Treacherous guides—The Stanley Pool—Chief Itsi of Ntamo—We have to give up our big goat—River observations . . 241

CHAPTER XII.

The struggle with the river renewed—Passing the "Father"—In the "Cauldron"—Poor Kalulu!—Soudi's strange adventures—At the "Whirlpool Narrows"—Lady Alice Rapids—Our escape from death —"Isles of Eden"—Thieves amongst us—The Inkisi Falls—The canoes dragged over the mountain—Trade along the Livingstone—Ulcers and entozoa—An artful compound 260

CHAPTER XIII.

Glorious timber—Cutting canoes—Frank suffers from ulcers—The episode of the fetished axe—Rain-gauge readings—The rise of the river—"Goee-goees"—The *Lady Alice* breached for the first time—A painful discovery: Uledi's theft—His trial and release—The burning of Shakespeare—The bees of Massassa—Local superstitions—Frank's cheery character 283

CHAPTER XIV.

Leaving Mowa—The whirling pools of Mowa—The *Jason* swept over the falls—The "Little Master" drowned—Too brave!—"Ah, Uledi, had you but saved him!"—The sympathy of the savages 305

CHAPTER XV.

Mutiny in the camp—Again among the cataracts—Frank's body found—The fall of the Edwin Arnold river—Tired out!—Wholesale desertion —More cataracts—"Good-bye, my brother; nothing can save you!" —Rushing blindly on—Saved again!—The *Jason* found . . . 317

CHAPTER XVI.

PAGE

Final warnings against theft—Humiliating a protectionist—Kindly tribes—Five of the Expedition abandoned to slavery for theft—Safeni goes mad from joy—Goaded to crime—Ali Kiboga's adventures—The cataract of Isangila—Only five marches from white faces!—Staunch to the death—Rum—My appeal to Embomma—The forlorn hope—The "powerful man" insults us—Struggling on—"We are saved, thank God!"—"Enough now; fall to"—My letter of thanks—Approaching civilization—Amongst whites; Boma—The Atlantic Ocean 328

CONCLUSION.

Kabinda—San Paulo de Loanda—Simon's Bay—Cape Town—Natal—Zanzibar—Joy of the returned—The martyrs to geography—Reverie—Laus Deo! 362

INDEX . 375

LIST OF ILLUSTRATIONS.

FULL-PAGE ILLUSTRATIONS.

SMALLER ILLUSTRATIONS.

UJIJI, LOOKING NORTH FROM THE MARKET-PLACE, VIEWED FROM THE ROOF OF OUR TEMBÉ AT UJIJI.

(From a photograph by the Author.)

[*To face page* 1.

THROUGH THE DARK CONTINENT.

CHAPTER I.

Ujiji, its scenery, residents, markets, and vicinity—Arab rivals—The circumnavigation of the Tanganika—Commander Cameron and the outflowing Lukuga—The encroaching waters—The legend of the Lake—Evening.

June.—The best view of Ujiji is to be obtained from the flat roof of one of the Arab tembés or houses. A photograph which I took of the view north from my tembé, which fronted the market-place, embraced the square and conical huts of the Wangwana, Wanyamwezi, and Arab slaves, the Guinea palms from the golden-coloured nuts of which the Wajiji obtain the palm-oil, the banana and plantain groves, with here and there a graceful papaw-tree rising amongst them, and, beyond, the dark green woods which line the shore and are preserved for shade by the fishermen.

South of the market-place are the tembés of the Arabs, solid, spacious, flat-roofed structures, built of clay, with broad, cool verandahs fronting the public roads. Palms and papaws, pomegranates and plantains, raise graceful branch and frond above them, in pleasing contrast to the grey-brown walls, enclosures and houses.

The port of Ujiji is divided into two districts—Ugoy, occupied by the Arabs, and Kawelé, inhabited by the Wangwana, slaves, and natives. The market-place is in Ugoy, in an open space which has been lately contracted to about 1200 square yards. In 1871 it was nearly 3000 square yards. On the beach before the market-place are drawn up the huge Arab canoes, which, purchased in Goma on the western shore, have had their gunwales raised up with heavy teak planking. The largest canoe, belonging to Sheikh Abdullah bin Suliman, is 48 feet long, 9 feet in the beam, and 5 feet high, with a poop for the Nakhuda (captain), and a small forecastle.

Sheikh Abdullah, by assuming the air of an opulent ship-owner, has offended the vanity of the governor, Muini Kheri, who owns nine canoes. Abdullah christened his "big ship" by some very proud name: the governor nicknamed it the *Lazy*. The Arabs and Wajiji, by the way, all give names to their canoes.

The hum and bustle of the market-place, filled with a miscellaneous concourse of representatives from many tribes, woke me up at early dawn. Curious to see the first market-place we had come to since leaving Kagehyi, I dressed myself and sauntered amongst the buyers and sellers and idlers.

A NATIVE OF RUA WHO WAS A VISITOR AT UJIJI.

Here we behold all the wealth of the Tanganika shores. The Wajiji, who are sharp, clever traders, having observed that the Wangwana purchased their supplies of sweet potatoes, yams, sugar-cane, ground-nuts, oil-nuts, palm-oil and palm-wine, butter, and pombé, to retail them at enormous profits to their countrymen, have raised their prices on some things a hundred per cent. over what they were when I was in Ujiji last. This has caused the Wangwana and slaves to groan in spirit, for the Arabs are unable to dole out to them rations in proportion to the prices now demanded. The governor, supplied by the Mutwaré of the lake district of Ujiji, will not interfere, though frequently implored to do so, and, consequently, there are frequent fights, when the Wangwana rush on the natives with clubs, in much the same manner as the apprentices of London used to rush to the rescue or succour of one of their bands.

Except the Wajiji, who have become rich in cloths, the rural natives retain the primitive dress worn by the Wazinja, Wazongora, Wanyambu, Wanya-Ruanda, Kishakka, Wanyoro, and Wanya-Nkori, Wasui, Watusi, Wahha, Warundi, and Wazigé, namely, a dressed goatskin covering the loins, and hanging down to within six inches above the knees, with long depending tags of the same material. All these tribes are related to each other, and their language shows only slight differences in dialect. Moreover, many of those inhabiting the countries contiguousto Unyamwezi and Uganda have lost those special characteristics which distinguish the pure unmixed stock from the less favoured and less refined types of Africans.

Uhha daily sends to the market of Ujiji its mtama, grain (millet), sesamum, beans, fowls, goats, and broad-tailed sheep, butter, and sometimes oxen; Urundi, its goats, sheep, oxen, butter, palm-oil and palm-nuts, fowls, bananas, and plantains; Uzigé—now and then only—its oxen and palm-oil; Uvira, its iron, in wire of all sizes, bracelets, and anklets; Ubwari, its cassava or manioc, dried, and enormous quantities of grain, Dogara or whitebait, and dried fish; Uvinza, its salt; Uguha, its goats and sheep, and grain, especially Indian corn; rural Wajiji bring their buttermilk, groundnuts, sweet potatoes, tomatoes, bananas and plantains, yams, beans, vetches, garden herbs, melons, cucumbers, sugar-cane, palm-wine, palm-nuts, palm-oil, goats, sheep, bullocks, eggs, fowls, and earthenware; the lake-coast Wajiji bring their slaves, whitebait, fresh fish, ivory, baskets, nets, spears, bows and arrows; the Wangwana and Arab slaves bring slaves, fuel, ivory, wild fruit, eggs, rice, sugar-cane, and honey from the Ukaranga forest.

The currency employed consists of cloths, blue "Kaniki," white sheeting "Merikani" from Massachusetts' mills, striped or barred prints, or checks, blue or red, from Manchester, Muscat, or Cutch, and beads, principally "Sofi," which are like black-and-white clay-pipe stems broken into pieces half an inch long. One piece is called a *Masaro*, and is the lowest piece of currency that will purchase anything. The Sofi beads are strung in strings of twenty Masaro, which is then called a *Khetć*, and is sufficient to purchase rations for two days for a slave, but suffices the freeman or Mgwana but one day. The red beads, called Sami-sami, the Mutunda, small blue, brown, and white, will also readily be bartered in the market for provisions, but a discount will be charged on them, as the established and universal currency with all classes of natives attending the market is the Sofi.

The prices at the market in 1876 were as follows:—

	Sheeting cloths of 4 yards long.
Ivory per lb.	1
1 goat	2
1 sheep	1½
12 fowls	1½
1 bullock	10
1 potful—equal to 3 gallons—of wine	2
1 " " " " of palm oil	4
60 lbs. of grain—Mtama	1
90 lbs. " Indian corn	1
½-gal. potful of honey in the comb	1
1 slave boy between 10 and 13 years old	16
1 " girl " " "	50 to 80
1 " " " 13 and 18 "	80 to 200
1 " woman " 18 " 30 "	80 to 130
1 " " " 30 " 50 "	10 to 40
1 " boy " 13 " 18 "	16 to 50
1 " man " 18 " 50 "	10 to 50

The country of Ujiji extends between the Liuché river, along the Tanganika, north to the Mshala river, which gives it a length of forty-five miles. The former river separates it from Ukaranga on the south, while the latter river acts as a boundary between it and Urundi. As Ujiji is said to border upon Uguru, a district of Uhha, it may be said to have a breadth of twenty miles. Thus the area of Ujiji is not above nine hundred square miles. The Mtemi, or king, is called Mgassa, who entertains a superstitious fear of the lake. His residence is in a valley amongst the mountains bordering upon Uguru, and he believes that in the hour he looks upon the lake he dies. This superstitious fear may have some connection with the Legend of the Lake, which I shall give later.

I should estimate the population of the country to be very fairly given at forty to the square mile, which will make it 36,000 souls. The Liuché valley is comparatively populous, and the port of Ujiji—consisting of Ugoy and Kawelé districts—has alone a population of 3000. Kigoma and Kasimbu are other districts patronised by Arabs and Wangwana.

The Wajiji are a brave tribe, and of very independent spirit, but not quarrelsome. When the moderate fee demanded by the Mutwaré of Ugoy, Kawelé, and Kasimbu is paid, the stranger has the liberty of settling in any part of the district, and as an excellent understanding exists between the Mutwaré and the Arab governor, Muini Kheri, there is no fear of ill-usage. The Mgwana or the Mjiji applying to either of them is certain of receiving fair justice, and graver cases are submitted to an international commission of Arabs and Wajiji elders, because it is perfectly understood by both parties that many moneyed interests would be injured if open hostilities were commenced.

The Wajiji are the most expert canoemen of all the tribes around the Tanganika. They have visited every country, and seem to know each headland, creek, bay, and river. Sometimes they meet with rough treatment, but they are as a rule so clever, wide-awake, prudent, commercially politic, and saperior in tact, that only downright treachery can entrap them to death. They have so many friends also that they soon become informed of danger, and dangerous places are tabooed.

The governor of the Arab colony of Ujiji, having been an old friend, was, as may be supposed, courteous and hospitable to me, and Mohammed bin Gharib, who was so good to Livingstone between Marungu and Ujiji, as far as Manyema, did his best to show me friendly attention. Such luxuries as sweetmeats, wheaten bread, rice, and milk were supplied so freely by Muini Kheri and Sheikh Mohammed that both Frank and myself began to increase rapidly in weight.

Judging from their rotundity of body, it may fairly be said that both the friends enjoy life. The governor is of vast girth, and Mohammed weighs probably only two stone less. The preceding governor, Mohammed bin Sali, was also of ample circumference, from which I conclude that the climate of Ujiji agrees with the Arab constitution. It certainly did not suit mine while I was with Livingstone, for I was punished with remittent and intermittent fever of such severe type and virulence that in three months I was reduced in weight to seven stone!

Muini Kheri's whole wealth consists of about 120 slaves, male and female, eighty guns, eighty frasilah of ivory, two tembés, or houses, a wheat and rice field, nine canoes with oars and sails, forty head of cattle, twenty goats, thirty bales of cloth, and twenty sacks of beads, 350 lbs. of brass wire, and 200 lbs. of iron wire, all of which, appraised in the Ujiji market, might perhaps realise 18,000 dollars. His friend Mohammed is probably worth 3000 dollars only! Sultan bin Kassim may estimate the value of his property at 10,000 dollars, Abdullah bin Suliman, the owner of the *Great Eastern* of Lake Tanganika, at 15,000 dollars. Other Arabs of Ujiji may be rated at from 100 to 3000 dollars.

Sheikh Mohammed bin Gharib is the owner of the finest house. It is about 100 feet long by 25 feet in width and 14 feet in height. A broad verandah, 10 feet wide and 40 feet long, runs along a portion of the front, and affords ample space for the accommodation of his visitors on the luxurious carpets. The building is constructed of sun-dried brick plastered over neatly with clay. The great door is a credit to his carpenter and his latticed windows are a marvel to the primitive native trader from Uhha or Uvinza. The courtyard behind the house contains the huts of the slaves, kitchens, and cow-house.

By his Arab friends Sheikh Mohammed bin Gharib is regarded as an enterprising man, a good friend, but too liberal to his slaves, for which reason they say he is on the verge of bankruptcy. He is so much in debt that he has no credit at Zanzibar.

There is a good deal of jealousy between the Arabs of Ujiji, which sometimes breaks out into bloodshed. When Sayid bin Habib enters Ujiji trouble is not far off. The son of Habib has a large number of slaves, and there are some fiery souls amongst them, who resent the least disparagement of their master. A bitter reproach is soon followed by a vengeful blow, and then the retainers and the chiefs of the Montagues and Capulets issue forth with clubs, spears, and guns, and Ujiji is all in an uproar, not to be quieted until the respective friends of the two rivals carry them bodily away to their houses. On Arabs, Wangwana, and slaves alike I saw the scars of feuds.

Abdullah bin Suliman and his partisans are settled in Kasimbu, because Muini Kheri's hot-headed young Arab relations, Bana Mokombé and Muini Hassan, are for ever endangering the peace by their insolence. The feud began by a slave of Abdullah's having attempted to stab Bana Makombé, because the haughty young Arab had spurned him once with his foot. Only a few drops of the bluest blood from the aristocracy of Sa'adani were drawn in the happily abortive attempt, but the aristocrats mustered in force. The coast Arabs residing at Kigoma advanced towards Ujiji with 300 guns, and called upon the governor to arm, to avenge the blood that had been shed. The governor, however, called upon the Mutwaré, and the Wajiji swarmed by the hundreds to attack Abdullah bin Suliman. Fortunately Abdullah was prudent, and met them with only a few men. But though he mildly expostulated with them that it was a drunken slave who was the cause, he was condemned to lose his right hand, from which fate, however, he was saved by the governor relenting and demanding instead the head of the murderous slave.

It will be manifest, then, that the safety of a European at Ujiji would be but precarious. Any of his people, inspired by pombé or native wine, might, at any moment, in drunken fury, mortally wound an Arab or Mswahili of the coast, the result of which would be that the European would either have to forfeit all his goods or his life, or decamp with his people immediately to save himself.

Life in Ujiji begins soon after dawn, and, except on moonlight nights, no one is abroad after sunset. With the Arabs—to whom years are as days to Europeans it is a languid existence, mostly spent in gossip, the interchange of dignified visits, ceremonies of prayer, an hour or two of barter, and small household affairs.

There were no letters for either Frank or myself after our seventeen months' travels around and through the lake regions. From Kagehyi, on Lake Victoria, I had despatched messages to Sayid bin Salim, governor of Unyanyembé, praying him to send all letters addressed to me to Muini Kheri, governor of Ujiji, promising him a noble reward. Not that I was sure that I should pass by Ujiji, but I knew that, if I arrived at Nyangwé, I should be able to send a force of twenty men to Muini Kheri for my letters. Though Sayid bin Salim had over twelve months' time to comply with my moderate request, not a scrap or word of news or greeting refreshed us after the long blank interval! Both of us, having eagerly looked forward with certainty to receiving a bagful of letters, were therefore much disappointed.

As I was about to circumnavigate the Tanganika with my boat, and would probably be absent two or three months, I thought there might still be a chance of obtaining them, before setting out westward, by despatching messengers to Unyanyembé. Announcing my intentions to the governor, I obtained a promise that he would collect other men, as he and several Arabs at Ujiji were also anxious to communicate with their friends. Manwa Sera therefore selected five of the most trustworthy men, the Arabs also selected five of their confidential slaves, and the ten men started for Unyanyembé on the 3rd of June.*

Before departing on the voyage of circumnavigation of Lake Tanganika, many affairs had to be provided for, such as the well-being of the Expedition during my absence, distribution of sufficient rations, provisioning for the cruise, the engagement of guides, &c.

The two guides I obtained for the lake were Para, who had accompanied Cameron in March and April 1874, and Ruango, who accompanied Livingstone and myself in December 1871 to the north end of Lake Tanganika.

The most interesting point connected with this lake was its outlet. Before starting from Zanzibar, I had heard that Cameron had discovered the outlet to Lake Tanganika in the Lukuga river, which ran through Uguha to the west, and was therefore an affluent of Livingstone's great river.

In Commander Cameron's book, vol. i. p. 305, the following sentences, bearing upon what he personally saw of the Lukuga, are found:

"In company with the chief, I went four or five miles down the river, until navigation was rendered impossible, owing to the masses of floating vegetation. Here the depth was 3 fathoms, breadth 600 yards, current $1\frac{1}{2}$ knots, and sufficiently strong to drive us well into the edge of the vegetation. I noticed that the embouchures of some small streams flowing into the river were unmistakably turned from the lake, and that the weed set in the same direction. Wild date-palms grew thickly down the river."

In opposition to this statement of Cameron's was the evidence taken by me at Ujiji.

Para, his guide, said that the white man could not have seen the river flowing towards Rua, because it did not.

Ruango, the veteran guide, declared that he had crossed it five times, that it was a small river flowing into the Tanganika, and that if I found it to flow in a contrary direction, he would return me all his hire.

* My five trustworthy men arrived at Unyanyembé within fifteen days, but from some cause they never returned to the Expedition. We halted at Ujiji for seventy days after their departure, and when we turned our faces towards Nyangwé, we had given up all hopes of hearing from civilisation.

Natives from the Lukuga banks whom we found in Ujiji asserted positively that there were two Lukugas, one flowing into Lake Tanganika, the other into Rua.

Muini Kheri, governor of Ujiji, Mohammed bin Gharib, Muini Hassan, Bana Makombé, and Wadi Safeni, all of whom had travelled across this Lukuga river, also declared, in the most positive manner, that during the many times they had crossed the "Lukuga," they either passed over it on dry land or were ferried in canoes across the entrance, which appeared to them only an arm of the lake; that until the white man had come to Ujiji, they had never heard of an outflowing river, nor did they believe there was one.

The positiveness of their manner and their testimony, so utterly at variance with what Commander Cameron had stated, inspired me with the resolution to explore the phenomenon thoroughly, and to examine the entire coast minutely. At the same time, a suspicion that there was no present outlet to the Tanganika had crept into my mind, when I observed that three palm-trees, which had stood in the market-place of Ujiji in November 1871, were now about 100 feet in the lake, and that the sand beach over which Livingstone and I took our morning walks was over 200 feet in the lake.

I asked of Muini Kheri and Sheikh Mohammed if my impressions were not correct about the palm-trees, and they both replied readily in the affirmative. Muini Kheri said also, as corroborative of the increase of the Tanganika, that thirty years ago the Arabs were able to ford the channel between Bangwé Island and the mainland; that they then cultivated rice-fields three miles farther west than the present beach; that every year the Tanganika encroaches upon their shores and fields; and that they are compelled to move every five years farther inland. In my photograph of Ujiji, an inlet may be seen on a site which was dry land, occupied by fishing-nets and pasture ground, in 1871.

I proceeded to Bangwé Island, before setting out on my voyage, and sounded the channel separating it from the mainland. Between a pebble-covered point of Bangwé and the nearest tongue on the mainland, I dropped my lead thirteen times. In mid-channel I found 18, 21, 23, 24, 25, 22, 23, 20, 19, and 17 feet.

The Wajiji lake-traders and fishermen have two interesting legends respecting the origin of the Tanganika. Ruango, the veteran guide, who showed Livingstone and myself the

Rusizi river in 1871, and whose version is confirmed by Para, the other guide, related the first as follows:—

"Years and years ago, where you see this great lake, was a wide plain, inhabited by many tribes and nations, who owned large herds of cattle and flocks of goats, just as you see Uhha to-day.

"On this plain there was a very large town, fenced round with poles strong and high. As was the custom in those days, the people of the town surrounded their houses with tall hedges of cane, enclosing courts, where their cattle and goats were herded at night from the wild beasts and from thieves. In one of these enclosures lived a man and his wife, who possessed a deep well, from which water bubbled up and supplied a beautiful little stream, at which the cattle of their neighbours slaked their thirst.

"Strange to say, this well contained countless fish, which supplied both the man and his wife with an abundant supply for their wants; but as their possession of these treasures depended upon the secrecy which they preserved respecting them, no one outside their family circle knew anything of them. A tradition was handed down for ages, through the family, from father to son, that on the day they showed the well to strangers, they would be ruined and destroyed.

"It happened, however, that the wife, unknown to her husband, loved another man in the town, and by-and-by, her passion increasing, she conveyed to him by stealth some of the delicious fish from the wonderful well. The meat was so good, and had such a novel flavour, that the lover urged her to inform him whence and by what means she obtained it; but the fear of dreadful consequences, should she betray the secret of the well, constrained her to evade for a long time his eager inquiries. But she could not retain the secret long, and so, in spite of all her awe for the Muzimu of the well, and her dread of her husband's wrath, she at last promised to disclose the mystery.

"Now one day the husband had to undertake a journey to Uvinza, but before departure he strictly enjoined his wife to look after his house and effects, and to remember to be silent about the fountain, and by no means to admit strangers, or to go a-gadding with her neighbours, while he was absent. The wife of course promised to obey, but her husband had been gone only a few hours when she went to her lover and said, 'My husband is gone away to Uvinza, and will not be back for many days. You have often asked me whence I obtained that delicious meat we ate together. Come with me, and I will show you.'

"Her lover gladly accompanied her, and they went into the house, and the wife feasted him with Zogga (palm wine) and Maramba (plantain wine), Ugali porridge made of Indian corn, and palm-oil, seasoned with pepper—and an abundance of fish meat.

"Then when they had eaten the man said, 'We have eaten and drunk, and we are now full. Now pray show me whence you obtain this wondrous white meat that I have eaten, and which is far sweeter than the flesh of kid or lamb or fowl.'

"'I will,' said she, 'because I have promised to you to do so, and I love you dearly; but it is a great secret, and my husband has strictly warned me not to show it to any human being not related to the family. Therefore you, my love, must not divulge the secret, or betray me, lest some great evil happen to me and to us all.'

"'Nay, have no fear of me; my mouth shall be closed, and my tongue tied, lest danger should happen to the mistress of my heart.'

"So they arose, and she took him to the enclosure, jealously surrounded by a tall thick fence of mateté cane, and taking hold of his hand she led the impatient lover within, and showed him what appeared to be a circular pool of deep clear water, which bubbled upward from the depths, and she said—

"'Behold! This is our wondrous fountain—is it not beautiful?—and in this fountain are the fish.'

"The man had never seen such things in his life, for there were no rivers in the neighbourhood except that which was made by this fountain. His delight was very great, and he sat for some time watching the fish leaping and chasing each other, showing their white bellies and beautiful bright sides, and coming up to the surface and diving swiftly down to the bottom. He had never enjoyed such pleasure; but when one of the boldest of the fish came near to where he was sitting he suddenly put forth his hand to catch it. Ah, that was the end of all!—for the Muzimu, the spirit, was angry. And the world cracked asunder, the plain sank down, and down and down—the bottom cannot now be reached by our longest lines—and the fountain overflowed and filled the great gap that was made by the earthquake, and now what do you see? The Tanganika! All the people of that great plain perished, and all the houses and fields and gardens, the herds of cattle and flocks of goats and sheep, were swallowed in the waters.

"That is what our oldest men have told us about the Tanganika. Whether it is true or not I cannot say."

"And what became of the husband?" I asked.

"Oh, after he had finished his business in Uvinza, he began his return journey, and suddenly he came to some mountains he had never seen before, and from the top of the mountains he looked down upon a great lake! So then he knew that his wife had disclosed the secret fountain, and that all had perished because of her sin."

The other tradition imparted to me by the ancients of Ujiji relates that many years ago—how long no one can tell —the Luwegeri, a river flowing from the east to the lake near Urimba, was met by the Lukuga flowing from the westward, and the united waters filled the deep valley now occupied by the Tanganika. Hence the Luwegeri is termed "The mother of the Lukuga."

Still another tradition relates that the Luwegeri flowed through the plain by Uguha, and into the great river of Rua, but that when the plain sank the Luwegeri flowed into the profound gulf caused by the sudden subsidence of what had once been a plain.

The Waguha have also their legend, which differs slightly from that of the Wajiji. They say that at a very remote period there was a small hill near Urungu, hollow within, and very deep and full of water. This hill one day burst, and the water spread over a great depression that was made, and became the lake we now see.

I made many attempts to discover whether the Wajiji knew why the lake was called Tanganika. They all replied they did not know, unless it was because it was large, and canoes could make long voyages on it. They did not call small lakes Tanganika, but they call them Kitanga. The lake of Usukuma would be called Tanganika, but the little lakes in Uhha (Musunya) would be called Kitanga. Nika is a word they could not explain the derivation of, but they suggested that it might perhaps come from Nika, an electric fish which was sometimes caught in the lake.

A rational definition of Nika I could not obtain until one

day, while translating into their language English words, I came to the word "plain," for which I obtained *nika* as being the term in Kijiji. As Africans are accustomed to describe large bodies of water as being like plains, "it spreads out like a plain," I think that a satisfactory signification of the term has finally been obtained in, "the plain-like lake."

The people of Marungu call the lake Kimana, those of Urungu call it lemba, the Wakawendi call it Msaga, or, "the tempestuous lake."

Westward from Ujiji the lake spreads to a distance of about thirty-five miles, where it is bounded by the lofty mountain range of Goma, and it is when looking north-west that one comprehends, as one follows that vague and indistinct mountain line, ever paling as it recedes, the full magnificence of this inland sea. The low island of Bangwé on the eastern side terminates the bay of Ujiji, which rounds with a crescent curve from the market-place towards it.

On very clear days the eyes may trace the eastern shore to the south beyond the mouth of the Liuché, curving to the Ulambola hills, and then rounding slightly eastward, reappearing in the imposing mountain heights of Cape Kabogo.

Very pleasant are the idle hours of evening at Ujiji, watching the clouds of sunset banking themselves above dark Goma, and observing the lurid effects of the brilliant red on their gloomy masses and on the ever ruffled waves, tinging with strange shades the gorgeous verdure of the eastern shore, and the lofty mountain ridges which enfold the deep-lying lake. To the ears are borne the sonorous moan and plaint of the heavy waves, which, advancing from the south-west in serried foam-capped lines, roll unceasingly upon the resounding shore.

At this hour, too, the fuel-laden canoes from Ulambola are hurrying homeward, with oar and sail. The cattle, lowing to expectant calves, and the goats bleating for their kids, are hurrying from the pastures in advance of the tiny herd-boys, the asses' feet clatter as they go, bearing their masters home from Kigoma or Kasimbu, the loud hailing of native friends announces the evening meal ready, and the spiral columns of blue smoke ascend from many wood-fires, as we sit here to observe the advance of the evening shades, and to take a last look at the daylight, as it wanes and fades over the shores of the Tanganika.

CHAPTER II.

The *Lady Alice* afloat again—Her mate and crew—Anxiety on her behalf—On hallowed ground—Unwelcome visitors: in the haunts of the Ruga-Ruga—The aborigines' last retreat—A scene of blood—The robbers of the Lake, and their tutelary spirits—A geological problem: were there once two lakes?—Rising waters—The abode of the genii—A storm—Forest fires—At the mouth of Cameron's "outlet"—The Lukuga creek.

June 11.—THE saucy English-built boat which had made the acquaintance of all the bays and inlets of the Victoria Nyanza, which had been borne on the shoulders of sturdy men across the plains and through the ravines of Unyoro, had halted on the verge of the cliff rising above Beatrice Gulf, had thrust her bows among the papyrus of the Alexandra Nile, ridden gaily over the dark lakes of Karagwé, and crossed the inundated plains of Usagusi, and the crocodile-haunted river of Uvinza, is at last afloat upon the deep-blue waters of the Tanganika.

She is about to explore the mountain barriers which enfold the lake, for the discovery of some gap which lets out, or is supposed to let out, the surplus water of rivers which, from a dim and remote period, have been pouring into it from all sides.

She has a consort now, a lumbering, heavy, but staunch mate, a canoe cut out from an enormous teak-tree which once grew in some wooded gorge in the Goma mountains. The canoe is called the *Meofu*, and is the property of Muini Kheri, governor of Ujiji, who has kindly lent it to me. As he is my friend, he says he will not charge me anything for the loan. But the governor and I know each other pretty well, and I know that when I return from the voyage, I shall have to make him a present. In Oriental and African lands, remuneration, hire, compensation, guerdon, and present are terms nearly related to one another.

The boat and her consort are ready on the 11th of June, 1876. The boat's crew have been most carefully selected. They are all young, agile, faithful creatures. Their names and ages are as follows: Uledi, the coxswain, 25 years; Saywa, his cousin, 17; Shumari, his brother, 18; Murabo, 20; Mpwapwa, 22; Marzouk, 23; Akida, 20; Mambu, 20; Wadi Baraka, 24; Zaidi Rufiji, 27; Matiko, 19. Two supernumeraries are the boy gun-bearers, Billali and Mabruki, 17 and 15 years respectively. After eighteen months' experience with them it has been decided by all that these are the elect of the Expedition for boat-work, though they are by no means the champions of the march. But as they have only light loads, there has never been reason to complain of them.

There is much handshaking, many cries of "Take care of yourselves," and then both boat and canoe hoist sail, turning their heads along the coast to the south.

Kasimbu, two miles from Ugoy to Ujiji, sends forth her Arab and slave inhabitants to cry out their farewells, and half an hour afterwards we are at the mouth of the Liuché river.

The reason why Arabs, Wajiji, and Wangwana have been more than usually demonstrative is that they will not believe that such a frail structure as our boat will be able to endure the heavy waves of the Tanganika. They declared we should all be drowned, but our Wangwana have ridiculed their fears, and quoted her brilliant exploit round a lake twice the size of the Tanganika, and so at last they had come to be satisfied with a dismal "Well, you shall see!"

June 12.—During nearly the whole of the next day our voyage to the south is along the forest-clad slopes of Ulambola and the tawny plains of Ukaranga, until we arrive at the mouth of the Malagarazi River. At 3 P.M. we rowed up river, which at the mouth is about 600 yards wide, and sends a turbid brown stream into the lake. When a continuous south-west wind blows, its waters are known to tinge the lake with its colour as far as Ujiji. The river soon narrows to 200 yards, and about five miles up to 150 yards. I sounded twice, and obtained over 50 feet each time. The southern bank is very mountainous, but on the opposite side stretches a plain until the detached ranges of Ukaranga become massed, about five miles from the lake, and, running easterly, form the northern bank of the river.

June 13.—On the 13th our voyage was along the bold mountain spurs of Kawendi, forming a steep, rock-bound coast, indented at frequent intervals with calm, pool-like bays, and their heights clothed with solemn woods.

At noon we were off Kabogo's lofty headland, and remembering that Dr. Livingstone had said that he could find no bottom at 300 fathoms, I sounded a mile off shore, and found 109 fathoms. At two miles off I found no depth with 140 fathoms. I then fastened sixty fathoms more, but at 1200 feet obtained no bottom.

About four miles south of dreaded Kabogo, on a narrow strip of sand, we beached our boat and canoe far out of the heavy surf, and then climbed the 2000 feet-high slopes in search of game; but the grass was high, the jungle dense, the slope steep and fatiguing, and we had to return without sighting a single head.

June 14.—Next day we coasted along land familiar to me from my journey with Livingstone to Unyanyembé, and at 7 P.M. encamped at Urimba, about a mile south-west of the river Luwajeri or Luwegeri.

June 15.—Having been so successful in January 1872, I sallied out the next day over ground which I looked upon with reverence. The exact place covered by our little tent, only six feet square of land, was hallowed by associations of an intercourse which will never, never be repeated. I recognised the tree above which we hoisted our mighty crimson and white banner to attract the lagging land caravan, the plain where I had dropped the zebra, the exact spot where I shot a fine fat goose for breakfast, the aspiring peak of Kivanga, the weird looking mountains of Tongwé. I knew my road here, and dwelt upon all its features, until the old life seemed renewed, and all things seemed as before.

But I resumed my search. In an hour I am two miles from camp, and in view of a herd of zebra. Billali becomes feverish lest I should miss the game, and, like an honest, faithful servant taking enormous interest in his master's success, lies down to hug the ground in piteous stillness. I advance a few paces cautiously behind a scraggy acacia, and in a few seconds two of the noble creatures are dead, and the others are sweeping round a clump of hills, whimpering for their lost companions. As we have now enough meat to last us several days, I give them their liberty.

June 16.—The day is devoted to cutting the meat into long strips and drying it over wooden grates, while each of the forty men composing the lake exploring band seems profoundly impressed with the necessity of forestalling future demands on his digestive organs by consuming injudicious quantities there and then.

In the midst of this most innocent recreation there stepped forth to our view some sinister objects—Ruga-Ruga! As undesirable as wolves in a stern Siberian winter to an unarmed party in a solitary sledge are the Ruga-Ruga to peaceful travellers in an African forest or wilderness. Whatever the accident that brought them, their very presence suggested the possibility and probability of a bloody struggle. They are bandits, wretches devoted to plunder and murder, men whose hands are at all times ready to be imbrued in blood.

They are representatives of that tribe which has desolated and depopulated beautiful Kawendi from the Malagarazi river down to the Rungwa. All alike—whether Arabs, Wajiji, Wangwana, Wanyamwezi, or the aborigines of the land—owe them an unpaid debt of vengeance for the blood they have shed. It was not our special task, however, to undertake the repayment, therefore neither by word nor look did we betray any antipathy.

We gave them gifts of meat at their own request. The tobacco gourd passed round in their polluted, crimeful hands, and we grasped their hands in token of amity—and parted.

June 17.—On the 17th of June we continued our voyage from Urimba towards Kungwé cape, one of the projecting spurs from the Kungwé mountains, and in the evening camped on Bongo Island, a few miles south-west from Nderch, the robbers' village. We were visited in the night by about sixty of them armed with muskets. Though it was an unusual hour, and an unseasonable one for receiving visitors, we avoided trouble, and by parting with cloth and exhausting the powers of suavity, we happily avoided a rupture with the wild and bloody men of Nderch, and before dawn stole away unperceived on our journey.

June 18.—The peaks of Kungwé are probably from 2500 to 3000 feet above the lake. They are not only interesting from their singular appearance, but also as being a refuge for the last remaining families of the aborigines of Kawendi. On the topmost and most inaccessible heights dwells the remnant of the once powerful nation which in old times—so tradition relates—overran Uhha and Uvinza, and were a terror to the Wakalaganza. They cultivate the slopes of their strongholds, which amply repay them for their labour. Fuel is found in the gorges between the peaks, and means of defence are at hand in the huge rocks which they have piled up ready to repel the daring intruder. Their elders retain the traditions of the race whence they sprang; and in their charge are the Lares and Penates of old Kawendi—the Muzimu. In the home of the eagles they find a precarious existence, as a seed to reproduce another nation, or as a short respite before complete extermination.

KUNGWÉ PEAKS.

(From a sketch near the entrance to the Luwulungu torrent bed.)

The best view of this interesting clump of mountain heights is to be had off the mouth of the torrent Luwulungu.

From Cape Kungwé south, the coast as far as Ulambula consists of a lofty mountain front, pierced by several deep and most picturesque inlets, gorges, ravines, and rifts. Into these pours the Luwulungu, rushing along a steep, stony bed, from the chasms and defiles overshadowed by the tall peaks of Kungwé—and the Lubugwé, emptying its waters into a pretty cove penetrating to the very heart of the mountain wall. At an angle of 45° this mountain wall rises up to the height of 2000 feet, clothed from base to summit with the verdure of cane, wild grasses, and tall straight trees with silvery stems. Then next comes the Kasuma inlet, and here, straight before our eyes, is seen a river dropping, in a succession of falls, from the lofty summit, into shadowy depths of branching tamarinds, acacias, and teak. All is silent in the deep-bosomed cove except the rhythmic waterfall, and the trees stand still, as though fascinated by the music, and the grim heights frown a silent approval; the pale blue arm of the lake rests expectant for the moment when it shall receive the impetuous child of the mountains which it sees leaping down to it from above, and flashing so brightly at every great leap. Along the glorious, green, steep headlands we wind in and out, cast a glance in at Numbi's pretty cove, and encamp for the night near the bold cape of Ulambula.

June 19.—We resumed the voyage on the 19th, and, shortly after leaving our camp in the neighbourhood of the cape, saw a point of land connected by a narrow neck with the mainland, under which were two natural arches, spanning two channels. From the cape the mountain range gradually recedes from the lake, until, near the Rugufu river, it again approaches and finally forms the headlands of Buyramembé.

A little south of the cape the crest of a small and lately submerged island was also seen. At noon I took observations for latitude, at the north end of Kabogo, an island lying parallel to the mainland at a distance of from 300 to 500 yards. On the shores, both of mainland and island, flourishes the borassus palm. Kabogo was once densely peopled, but the bandits of Ndereh, the scourge of Kawendi, have caused them to emigrate to other districts to crave protection from chiefs more powerful than their own.

About 2 P.M. we came in view of Kiwesa, which appeared from the lake to be a very large village. But as we approached its shores under sail, we were struck with the silence which reigned around, and the sight of a large herd of buffalo grazing near the village still more astonished us.

The guides declared that only five weeks before they had stopped in it and traded with Ponda, the chief, and they could give no reason why—as two boats under sail would most likely attract the attention of the natives—the people of Ponda did not appear on the shore.

We resolved to venture in to discover the cause. There was a deathly silence around. Numbers of earthenware pots, whole, and apparently but little used, were strewn about the beach and among the reeds flanking the path which led to the village, besides stools, staffs, hand-brooms, gourds, etc., etc. This was ominous. There was probably a trap or a snare of some kind laid for us. We retreated therefore hastily to the boat and canoe, and thirty men were armed. Thus, better prepared against the wiles of savage men, we advanced again cautiously towards the village.

As we were surmounting the high ground on which the village was built, we saw a sight which froze the blood—the body of a poor old man, in a decomposed state, with a broad spear-wound in the back, and near it much dried blood. He had probably been dead five or six days.

A few yards farther, we saw the decapitated corpse of another man, and 10 feet from it, in a furrow or water channel, the bodies of three men and a woman, one of them dislimbed.

We arrived before the village. The defences were broken down and burnt. About fifty huts still stood unharmed by fire, but all the others were consumed. A few scorched banana stalks stood as a witness of the fury of the conflagration. But despite the black ruin and the charred embers which so plentifully strewed the ground, evidences were clear that flight had been hasty and compulsory, for all the articles that constitute the furniture of African families lay scattered in such numbers around us that an African museum might have been completely stocked. Stools, mats, spears, drinking-vessels, cooking-pots of all sizes, walking-staffs, war-clubs, baskets, trenchers, wooden basins, scoops, etc. There were also abundant proofs that this ruin was recent; a few wood-rails still smoked, the hearths were still warm, the dead were not putrefied. A coal-black cat made a dash from one of the houses yet standing, and the sudden motion startled us all in this place of death and vengeance.

Ponda, the chief of this village, had no doubt given some provocation to this unknown enemy. Para thought the enemy must have been the robbers of Ndereh, for the condition of the village bore signs of superior energy in the attack. And yet it had been constructed with a view to secure immunity from the fate which generally overtakes weak communities in Africa in the neighbourhood of ferocious and war-loving tribes. A wide ditch—in some parts 10 feet deep—and a strong palisade, with an earthwork, surrounded the settlement. The lake was close by to supply water, the country near it was open, and the sharpshooters' nest-like towers commanded a wide view. From some thirty bleached skulls arranged before Ponda's own house we argued that he did not himself fail to proceed to the same extremes which his enemies had now adopted to his utter ruin. It is the same story throughout Africa.

We resumed our voyage for the mouth of the Rugufu river. The shore between Kiwesa and the river is comparatively low. The waves have so beaten and shaken the low red bluffs and soft ferruginous clay that numerous landslips are constantly occurring. The débris are then vigorously pounded and crushed by the surf, and at length they are spread out into a narrow line of beach at their base, over which the spluttering waves surge up continuously.

The impression received at Ujiji, that the Tanganika is rising, was confirmed whenever we neared low shores. Especially was it the case at the Rugufu river, and Para the guide, as we entered it, stood up and exclaimed :—

"Oh, mother, mother, mother, see ye now! When I was with that other white man here, we camped on a strip of land which is now buried in the water! The Tanganika is indeed eating the land!"

The Rugufu oozes out from the midst of a broad bed of papyrus and reeds between precipitous banks.

On leaving the river we coasted along the bluff, steeply rising slopes of a mountain range which trends south-south-east as far as the settlements of Ruhinga, Kafisya, Katavi, and Kantamba.

Between the Rugufu and Buyramembé Point a stratum of a very dark hornblende slate is visible, resting upon gneiss in undulating, vertical, or diagonal lines; farther on we come to a stratified quartzose and greenstone rock. On the crest of this part of the range and its projecting spur is a thin forest of poor trees. The soil too is poor, and much mixed with shaly débris.

The mouth of the Gezeh river is a frequent haunt of herds of buffaloes, and also, being a fine haven, of trading canoes. Among the stories related of this place is one of a wonderful escape of a party of Wajiji traders from the bandits of Ndereh. The robbers stole into the camp while the Wajiji were all asleep, but some of the canoemen, awaking, punted their boats out of reach, and shouted to their comrades, who sprang into the water to avoid the fate that would otherwise have certainly overtaken them all.

The settlements of Kafisya, and the others just mentioned, have such an ill repute that I cannot imagine any necessity inducing a traveller to cultivate the acquaintance of the evil-conditioned people, unless, of course, he is so rich in cloth and followers that waste of them is of little consequence to him.

It is said that when they see the Wajiji trading canoes pass by them, the robbers pray to the Muzimu of Katavi to induce the Msaga—the tempestuous sea—to drive them ashore. The Muzimu of Katavi is one of the most powerful spirits along the shores of the Tanganika, according to legendary lore. Though he is capable of much mischief, he takes freaks of charity into his whimsical head, such as gratuitously killing buffaloes and then informing the inhabitants where the meat may be found; he is also said to have a relentless animosity towards the bandits of Ndereh, and frequently entraps them to their destruction. A conical knoll is called, after this spirit, Katavi's Hill.

Before the mouth of the Mkombé river there lies a low submerged island, just west of south from Katavi. Only a few shrubs and the heads of some tall cane were visible above the surface of the water.

June 20.—From Gezeh to Igangwé Cove was a good day's journey against the south-easter which blew strongly against us. Igangwé Cove penetrates about a mile deep into the mountain folds. Though it was the season when the grasses are becoming sere, and some of the trees lose that vivid greenness of foliage which is their glory during the rainy season, the aspect of the slopes had still a freshness and beauty which, with the placid mirror-like cove, made a picture worth preserving.

June 21.—A day's journey south by east took us to the village of Karema—the chief being Massi-Kamba, a sub-chief of Kapufi, king of Fipa. It is situated in the angle of a bay which begins at Igangwé Point and terminates in the weird rock-piles of Mpimbwé Cape.

All that mass of looming upland from Igangwé to within a few miles of Karema is included in the country of Kawendi or, as it is sometimes called, Tongwé. South of that line begins Fipa.

Arabs are beginning to establish themselves at Karema

for trade, the Wa-fipa being more amenable to reason than the "scattered and peeled" tribes of Tongwé.

Between Karema and Mpimbwé Cape lies a fine country studded with coves and hills, square-topped and round. Game is abundant and easy of approach. A buffalo and a small red antelope were obtained by me here, the two shots supplying the crews with abundance of meat.

Proceeding some eight miles south-west towards Mpimbwé, we come to a narrow ridge rising about 600 feet above the lake. Its shore is deeply indented, and the wash of waves has bared enormous masses of granite.

At the south-western corner of this bay there is a neck of low land which all but connects Mpimbwé ridge with the mainland; only half a mile's breadth of low land prevents Mpimbwé being an island. Near Kipendi Point, which is halfway between Mpimbwé ridge and Karema, there is a tree in the lake which was pointed out to me as being not many years ago on dry land. There is now 9 feet of water around it!

Mpimbwé Cape offers a view similar to the rocks of Wezi, only of a still more gigantic size and a ruder grandeur.

Their appearance betrays the effects of great waves which have at one time swept over them, pouring their waters into their recesses, cleansing by force every cranny and flaw of their vegetable mould, and washing out of them every particle of soil, until, one day, by some sudden convulsion of nature, the lake subsided, leaving, a hundred feet above its surface, these grey and naked masses of granite.

Any one who has seen on a rock-bound coast the war of sea-wave against granite, basalt, and sandstone, will at once recognize the effects visible at Mpimbwé. There lie piled up rocks, hundreds of tons in weight, some of them appearing to rest in such precarious positions that it seems as if the finger of an infant would suffice to push them into the deep blue lake. These, however, are not scored and grooved as are those exposed to the eroding influences of ceaseless ocean waves: they are cleanly fractured, with their external angles only exhibiting a rough polish or roundness which I take to be clear signs that at some remote time they were exposed to waves of great power. Besides, the condition of the rocks at the water-line confirms this theory.

Still, it is strange that the lake should have been rising steadily ever since living men can remember, and that those rocks of Mpimbwé should bear witness to the lake's subsidence.

June 25.—On the 25th of June, after coasting the western side of this extraordinary range and proceeding south some fifteen or sixteen miles, we arrived at Mkerengi Island, in the bay of Kirando; the large island of Makokomo lying to west of us a mile off. The natives of these parts are very amiable, though extremely superstitious. At the north-west end of Makokomo there is another lately submerged island. Close to the south-west end is a group of inhabited islands, Kankamba and Funch being the largest and most fertile.

Kirando is situated among other large villages in what appears to be a plain, hemmed in on the east by the continuation of the mountain ridges which we lost sight of when we left Karema Bay. The truncated cone of Chakavola terminates the ridge of Mpimbwé, and lies north-east from Mkerengi.

Continuing our voyage southerly along the coast between the isles of Kankamba and its brothers and the shore of the mainland, and passing a couple of creeks running deep inshore, we came to Cape Muntuwa. From this cape to Msamba Island, where we encamped, the lake is edged by one successive series of gigantic blocks and crags of granite. Rock rises above rock, and fragment above fragment. Here towers a colossal mass the size of a two-storied house, bearing upon it a similar mass perhaps entire, but more probably split with a singularly clean and fresh fracture, and there springs up from the surrounding chaos a columnar block like a closed hand with outstretched fore-finger—but everywhere there is the same huge disarray, ruin, and confusion.

We had need to be cautious in sailing along the coast, because for several hundred yards into the lake the rocky masses, which the uneasy billows only exposed in glimpses, rose nearly to the surface.

A suspicion flashed into my mind as these new features revealed themselves that in remote times this part of the lake—from Mpimbwé south—was a separate lake, and that Npimbwé ridge was connected with some portion of the western coast—probably the southern portion of Goma—for while coasting from the extreme north end of lake Tanganika down to Mpimbwé, I saw nothing resembling in character this portion of the coast. In no part of all the eastern coast down to Mpimbwé is there anything to lead me to suppose that the lake was ever higher than at present; but from Mpimbwé to Msamba I see numerous traces that the lake has been many yards higher than it is at present. All this dreary ruin of wave-dismantled and polished rock was at one time covered with water.

June 26.—On the 26th we camped at Mtosi, where Livingstone, who calls it Motoshi, camped on the 23rd of October, 1872. The chief's name is Kokira. A beautiful little bay leads from the lake to the miserable village where he lives.

June 27.—We rested on Msamba Island for the evening of the 27th. The islanders told us that there was a cave about 60 yards in length on the mainland opposite, where they sometimes hid in time of danger. For a small island Msamba is densely populated, and every inch seems cultivated. The islanders are clever manufacturers of a strong, coarse, cotton cloth: cotton being abundant in Fipa. The Rukugu river empties into Msamba Bay.

The irregular ridge which follows the coast between Msamba Island and Wanpembé, our next journey, is remarkable for a solitary columnar rock rising from 50 to 80 feet high and about half a mile from Column Point. Rounding Kantentich Point, we have a view of three columnar rocks, the central one being singularly like a mutilated Memnonium. These columns are visible from a considerable distance north or south.

Before reaching Wanpembé, Para, the guide, gathered a peculiar kind of berry called *owindi*, from a low scrubby tree, whose appearance was anything but promising for such a fragrant production as he now showed to us. The odour was not unlike that of lavender, and its strength was such that all in the boat near him were benefited by its exquisite perfume.

In the little cove close to Wanpembé, on the north side of the point on which it is situate, the boat floated over the submerged fence of a village, and her keel was 3 feet above it.

We obtained abundance of provisions at this large village, but as there were some Watuta strangers within the palisades, our visit was not an agreeable one. However, despite their insolence, the peace was not broken.

Minza, a neighbouring village, is also very large, and

possesses a strong stockade, the base of it being embanked with the earth excavated from the ditch.

There appears to be no diminution in the altitude of the mountain ranges which lie along the entire east coast of the Tanganika, or on the western side, as we have had the west mountains plainly in view since leaving Mpimbwé. Now and then we saw small streams issue into the lake, but met no river of any importance, until we came to the Zinga, or Mui-Zinga, as the Wajiji call it, which separates Fipa from Urungu.

June 30.—On the 30th we were coasting along the base of the mountain ranges of Urungu, and passing by Kalavera Point came to a bay before which were two small grass-covered islets. On a point of the mainland, nearly opposite these, stands Kakungu village. This point is formed of a grey shaly rock supporting a white clay, out of which the Wajiji on their return homeward paint the bows of their canoes. The scenery just beyond is bold and imposing.

Kirungwé Point consists of perpendicular walls—from 50 to 200 feet high above the lake—of a fine reddish sandstone with horizontal strata. Their peculiar appearance may be imagined when the boat's crew cried out:

"Oh, mother, this is a fort! See, there are the windows, and here is one of the gates."

Kirungwé Point appears to be a lofty swelling ridge, cut straight through to an unknown depth. There seems ground for believing that this ridge was once a prolongation of the plateau of Marungu, as the rocks are of the same material, and both sides of the lake show similar results of a sudden subsidence without disturbance of the strata.

South of Kirungwé, or Castle Point, there lies what we may almost call an island, which the guides said a few years ago was connected with the mainland. It is almost entirely separated now. A village which once nestled comfortably in the hollow between the rising ridges is now half buried in water. The huts appeared ready to collapse, for the water had already flooded them. This village was called Ma-Zombé.

In the evening, as we prepared to encamp, four canoes, of Ujiji, loaded with women and children, to the number of sixty-four—slaves from the Rufuvu river and from Muriro's—passed by our camp.

The bay of Kawa, which we passed through next day,

is very picturesque; woods clothe the slopes and heights, and huts for the accommodation of the Muzimus, or spirits, have been erected in several of the bends. Kawa river empties into this bay.

July 2, 3.—During the 2nd and 3rd of July we rowed close to the uninhabited shore, and at noon of the 3rd arrived at the extreme south end of the lake—which we ascertained to be 8° 47′ south latitude—in the district of Ukituta. The little stream Kapata issues into the lake at this end through a dense and dark grove, the dead trees

THE EXTREME SOUTHERN REACH OF LAKE TANGANIKA.

standing in front of the grove bearing witness to the destructive action of the rising waters.

I scoured the country in search of game, but, though tracks of buffalo were numerous, I failed to obtain a glimpse of a single head. Safeni, who was the coxswain of the *Meofu* canoe, accompanied me, and pointed out various points of interest in connection with Livingstone, as we followed the road which he had travelled over in his last fatal journey to Lake Bemba. The myombo and borassus palm flourished on the higher terraces.

July 4.—On the 4th, after rounding a point of a ridge—three miles from the Kapata—which lay north, we turned westward between Ntondwé Island and the mainland, and then passing by Murikwa Island, we reached, in two hours, the southern termination of the western shore of the Tanganika, whence may be seen the Wezi river tumbling down from the plateau of Urungu.

The village of Mwangala, where we camped, was at first hidden from our view by a dense line of water-cane, which sheltered its small fishing-canoes from the storms of the lake. One glance at the village fence informed us that here also was evidence that the lake was rising. We asked the natives if they did not think the water was gaining on them.

"Can you not see?" said they. "Another rain and we shall have to break away from here, and build anew."

"Where does the water of the lake go to?"

"It goes north, then it seems to come back upon us stronger than ever."

"But is there no river about here that goes towards the west?"

"We never heard of any."

That part of the western coast which extends from Mbeté or Mombeté to the south, as far as the Rufuvu river, is sacred ground in the lore of the ancients of Urungu. Each crag and grove, each awful mountain brow and echoing gorge, has its solemn associations of spirits. Vague and indescribable beings, engendered by fear and intense superstition, govern the scene. Any accident that may befall, any untoward event or tragedy that may occur, before the sanctuaries of these unreal powers, is carefully treasured in the memories of the people with increased awe and dread of the Spirits of the Rocks.

Such associations cling to the strange tabular mounts or natural towers, called Mtombwa. The height of these is about 1200 feet above the lake. They once formed parts of the plateau of Urungu, though now separated from it by the same agency which created the fathomless gulf of the Tanganika.

Within a distance of two miles are three separate mounts, which bear a resemblance to one another. The first is called Mtombwa, the next Kateye, the third Kapembwa. Their three spirits are also closely akin to one another, for they all rule the wave and the wind, and dwell on summits. Kateye is, I believe, the son of Kapembwa, the Jupiter, and Mtombwa, the Juno, of Tanganika tradition.

As we row past close to their base, we look up to admire

THE "HIGH PLACES" OF THE SPIRIT MTOMBWA: VIEW OF MTOMBWA UKUNGU.

[*To face page* 28.

the cliffy heights rising in terraces one above another; each terrace-ledge is marked by a thin line of scrubby bush. Beyond Kateye, the grey front of the paternal Kapembwa looms up with an extraordinary height and massive grandeur.

From Kapembwa to Polombwé Cape the plateau merges in a cliff-crowned wall 1500 feet above the lake. The cliff itself is probably 200 feet high, rising above a slope bristling with great rocks half hidden by the verdure of trees, bush, and grass. Yet the natives cultivate some part, and their fields were seen far up the steep ascending slopes.

KAPEMBWA.

July 6.—On the 6th we left the neighbourhood of Polombwé, at a place called Umisepa, and rowed round into the Rufuvu river.

This river is about 400 yards wide, and retains that width for about three miles—flowing with a current of a knot an hour, and between lofty wood-clothed mountains—and then broadens out into a lake-like expanse nearly a mile wide. From the right or south bank of the river, a plain slopes gradually to the grand cliffy walls of Kapembwa. From here to Liendé village, where we camped, our course lay east-south-east.

Here, as elsewhere, the water has encroached upon the

soil, and has flooded a large portion of land formerly devoted to tillage. It is a populous spot, indeed the most populous we had seen since leaving Ujiji. Our reception by the people was most cordial, and I was not sorry to become acquainted with such gentle creatures. Not one angry word or insolent look was exchanged, but they visited us with the greatest confidence, and a lively interest for barter. We obtained such abundance of provisions here that we might have cruised for a month without having to call at any native port.

The chief, Kiumeh, or Chiuma-Nanga, who lives at Mkigusa village, was visited with all due ceremony, and proved a most kindly old man. I gladly rewarded him for his small presents of food, and separated from him with feelings of attachment.

Livingstone, who was here in May 1867, writes of this plain and river as follows:—

"We came to a village about 2′ west of the confluence. The village has a meadow about four miles wide, in which buffaloes disport themselves, but they are very wild, and hide in the gigantic grasses. The Lofu—or Lofubu (Rufuvu)—is a quarter of a mile wide, but higher up 300 yards."

Between the 6th of July, 1876, and May 1867, that is, in nine years' time, the river Rufuvu has encroached upon the "meadow" which Livingstone saw by over a thousand yards!

It is true the plain or meadow is very low, and that 2 feet or more of a rise would extend the river over half a mile more of ground, but the proofs are gathering that the lake has been steadily rising. What was meadow land in the days when Livingstone made the acquaintance of the people of Liendé is now clear water half covered with growths of pale-blue lotus. The depth of the river in mid-channel is 21 feet.

I should estimate the population of the plain from Polombwé westward to where the river narrows between the hills, a district of about eight square miles, as about 2000 souls. We heard of Wangwana and some Arabs camping at a village called Kungwé higher up the river on the left bank, but as we had no occasion for their acquaintance we did not deem it necessary to go through the form of visiting them.

July 7.—On the 7th, soon after quitting the Rufuvu river, we had a rough experience of the worst Ma'anda—

"south-wester" Para or Ruango, our guides, had ever been in. The *Meofu* was soon disabled, for its rudder was swept away, but being towed behind by a rope, it was fortunately not lost, while our boat flew with double-reefed lug over the wild waves like a seagull. The tempest sang in our ears, and the waters hissed as they flew by us with great high curling crests. But Kasawa Cape was still before us, and no shelter could be obtained until we had rounded it. We shook a reef out, lest we might be swamped, and the increased force swept us over the topmost crests at such a speed as made Para and Ruango set their teeth. The canoe was out of sight; along the rock-bound shore thundered the surf; the wind was rising into a hurricane, but Kasawa was getting nearer to view, and we held on with all sail. In fifteen minutes we were safe behind the grey bluffs of the headland, in a little creek amid a heap of driftwood, and the haunt of hippopotamus and crocodile. I sent a land party back to hunt up news of the missing canoe, and by night received the glad news that soon after they were disabled they had managed to beach their boat without injury.

Between Kasawa and Kipimpi capes there are deep bays, which I have taken the liberty of calling the Cameron Bays.* A sterile and bleached country stretches on every hand around these bays, and the general appearance of their sterility is somewhat increased by the chalky character of some of the low cliffs.

North of the river Rufuvu extends Uemba. Ruemba—the country of the lake L'iemba—in the language of the great Bisa tribe, which all speak, with slight differences of dialect, in this region, signifies "lake." Mapota River separates Uemba from Marungu.

Between Kipimpi Cape and Kalambwé Cape, King Muriro, or "Fire," an immigrant from Unyamwezi, has, with the aid of a colony of restless spirits, established a formidable village called Akalunga, close to the lake. It is a resort for slavers, for Muriro has numbers of slaves on hand to exchange for powder and guns, and his people are always roving about on the look-out for more.

From Kalambwé Cape northward the mountains loom higher and steeper, the shore is indented with many narrow inlets, vertical strata of greenstone being thus exposed, with

* So called after Verney Lovett Cameron, Commander R.N., the first to navigate the southern half of Lake Tanganika.

thin forests crowning the loose soil which covers them. The depressions between the hilltops are numerous and shallow, consequently the drainage is quickly carried away in small rills.

Beyond the Mapota the scenery becomes still bolder, and the more imposing woods impart with their varied hues of foliage and waving crowns a picturesqueness that since leaving Fipa has been wanting in the landscape of the stupendous and upspringing, terraced plateau wall of Western Urungu, or in the uniform contours of Eastern Urungu.

July 11.—At a camp near an inlet north of Kalambwé Cape we set fire to some grass to have a more open view of our surroundings. In an hour it had ascended the steep slope, and was raging triumphantly on the summit. Three nights after we saw it still burning about fifteen miles north of the locality whence it had first started, like a crown of glory on a mountain-top.

Observation of this fire, and many others, explains why, in the midst of African uplands nourishing a dense forest, we suddenly come across narrow, far-penetrating plains covered with grass. They are, no doubt, so many tongue-like extensions from some broader, grass-covered expanses caused by fierce fires. Wherever the ground retains an excessive quantity of moisture, grasses, with stalks as thick as cane, spring up during three months' rain to a height of eight to ten, sometimes fifteen, feet. In May these grasses become sere, and by June are as dry as tinder. The smallest spark suffices to set them in a flame, and the noise of two brigades of infantry fighting would hardly exceed the terrible rack, crackle, and explosions made by the onrush of the wind-swept element. It devours everything that stands before it, and roasts the surface of the ground, leaving it parched, blackened, and fissured.

Though the mountains of Marungu are steep, rugged, and craggy, the district is surprisingly populous. Through the chasms and great cañons with which the mountains are sometimes cleft, we saw the summits of other high mountains, fully 2500 feet above the lake, occupied by villages, the inhabitants of which, from the inaccessibility of the position they had selected, were evidently harassed by some more powerful tribes to the westward.

The neighbourhood of Zongweh Cape is specially distinguished for its lofty cones and great mountain masses. Mount Murumbi, 2000 feet above the lake, near Muri-Kiassi Cape, is a striking feature of the coast of Marungu.

The wooded slopes and dense forest growths which fill the gorges are haunts of what the Wangwana call "Soko," a distinctive title they have given either to gorillas or chimpanzees. I heard the voices of several at Lunangwa river, but as they were at a considerable distance from me, I could not distinguish any great difference between the noise they created and that which a number of villagers might make while quarrelling.

The Rubuko, or Lofuko, a considerable river, divides Marungu from Tembwé. On the south side of the river is Mompara, or, for short, Para, remarkable as being the place whereat Livingstone embarked in canoes, February 1869, to proceed to Ujiji for the first time ('Last Journals,' vol. ii.):—

"*14th February*, 1869.—Arrived at Tanganika. Parra is the name of the land at the confluence of the river Lofuko."

The chief of the Para village is patronised by Jumah Merikani, who, while he is absent in Rua collecting slaves and ivory, entrusts his canoes to the chief's charge, from which it appears that the latter is a trustworthy man. Formerly Sheikh Sayid bin Habib honoured him with the same confidence.

Four hours' sail brought us to the wooded headlands of Tembwé, the most projecting of which is about twenty-five miles from Makokomo Island, in the Bay of Kirando, on the east coast of the lake.

Near this point is seen a lofty range, rising a few miles from the lake in an irregular line of peaks, which, as it is depressed towards the north, presents a more arid appearance, and presently forms a range of a much lower altitude than the mountains of Tongwé, Fipa, Urungu, or Marungu. This continues—with gaps here and there for rivers to escape through to the lake—until a little north of Kasengé Island, where it rises again into the mountains of Goma, the highest of all round Lake Tanganika.

At Kankindwa, which is in a little cove near Tembwé Cape, a native told us that the Lukuga flowed *out* of the lake to Rua; another denied that flatly, and a third said that the Lukuga flowed out of the lake towards Rua, but that, meeting another river descending towards the Tanganika, it was stopped, and the two rivers formed a lake.

July 14.—As we sailed north from Tembwé and observed the comparatively low altitude of the Uguha range, I began to feel that it was, of all the countries we had seen, the most likely to have a gap for the escape of the waters. It reminded me of some parts of Usukuma, on Lake Victoria. We explored the mouths of the Ruanda, Kasenga, Ruwye-ya,

MOUNT MURUMBI.

Rutuku, and Kahanda rivers, and then from Mirembwé Cape sailed for the Lukuga—the river that formed now the most interesting object of our exploration.

July 15.—On the evening of the 15th of July we made the acquaintance of Kawe-Niangeh, the chief of the district on the south bank of the Lukuga Creek near the mouth. He remembered Cameron distinctly, described his person and dress, and informed me that he had accompanied him to the reeds which he said blocked the head of the creek. At the time of his visit, he said—pointing at the same time to a long line of breakers which marked three-fourths of the broad entrance from the lake to the creek—there were two spits of sand running from either side of the mouth, and there was a small fishing settlement on the one which projected from our side. As they were now covered up, he entertained a suspicion that Cameron had dropped some powerful medicine, which had brought on this destruction! If one white man had brought so much mischief, what might not two white men do? "Why," said he, "the whole country will be inundated, and nothing will be left except the tops of the great mountains!"

We laughed at this, and, eventually joking him out of these ideas, succeeded in obtaining his guidance to explore the creek, and in eliciting the following items, which I jotted down in my journal the same evening:—

"*July* 15.—Opinion at the mouth of the Lukuga is much divided respecting this river, or creek, or inlet, or whatever it may be. The information, when compared with Cameron's statement, is altogether incomprehensible. The old men and chiefs say that formerly the Luwegeri met the Lukuga, and that the meeting of the waters formed the lake. The result of this marriage of the Lukuga from the west, and the Luwegeri from the east, is the Tanganika, and a cordial understanding between the waters has been kept up until lately, when it appears that the Lukuga has begun to be restive and wayward, for it sometimes flows west, and sometimes east; or, in other words, the Lukuga during the rainy season flows into the Tanganika, bearing with it an immense amount of water, grass, wood, and other matter, but during the dry season, when the south-east monsoon prevails, the Lukuga is borne west, lifting its head clear of the dry ground and mud-banks, and flows down to the Kamalondo, near Kalumbi's country, under the name of Ruindi or Luindi. Until this rainy season, or say March of this year, 1876, there stood a low bank of earth or mud, several hundred yards long, between the Luindi and Lukuga, but this year's rainfall has united the two rivers, the Lukuga flowing over this by Miketo's country into Rua. Kamalondo is a river, and not a lake, being another name for the Lualaba.

"When Cameron was here in 1874, there was a spit of dry sand lined with grass or cane, projecting from the south side, and a similar one from the north side, the two being separated by a narrow channel, but to-day both spits are covered with a line of wild breakers. The spot where Cameron camped is no longer tenable, but is exposed to the billows of the Tanganika, which at this season are driven in by the south-east monsoon.

"Take it any way you please, such conflict of opinions among people who ought to know what an outlet or an outflowing river is—many of them having seen the Luapula flow out from Bemba lake, others having seen the Lualaba plunge down from Mweru lake—makes it clear that there is either a crisis approaching in nature or that it has lately taken place, or is occurring—one cannot say which until the Lukuga is explored, and this work I propose to begin to-morrow."

Cameron says, on p. 304, in vol. i. of his 'Across Africa':—

"Its entrance was more than a mile across, but closed by a *grass-grown sandbank* with the exception of a channel 300 or 400 yards wide, and *across the channel there is a sill* where the surf breaks heavily at times, although there is more than a fathom of water at its most shallow part."

An inflowing river meeting the billows of the Tanganika might be supposed to form a "surf," or a sandy sill, it being only natural that there should be a conflict between the opposing forces. To this struggle then must be attributed the formation of the "sill of sand" which Cameron said ran across the channel.

July 16.—On the 16th we sailed up the creek.

The mouth of the Lukuga, which was about 2500 yards wide, narrowed after a mile to 800 yards, and after another mile to 400 or 500 yards. Upon rounding the point of land on which Mkampemba stands, and where there is a considerable tract under tillage, I observed that the water changed its colour to a reddish brown, owing to the ferruginous conglomerate of which the low bluffs on either side are composed. This was also a proof to me that there was no outflowing river here. Clear water outflowing from the Tanganika, only two miles from the lake, ought never to be so deeply discoloured.

As we proceeded on, the chief told us to stop, and threw a stick into the water, asking us to note how, despite the ripple and wind from lakeward, the stick and the water-bubbles persisted in struggling against them towards the lake. His face was triumphant as he thought he had completely proved one part of his statement, that water came into the lake. It only remained now, as he thought, to prove that water flowed out towards the west.

Wherever there were indentations in the bluffs that banked it in, or a dip in the low grass-covered débris beneath, a growth of Mateté or water-cane and papyrus filled up these bits of still water, but mid-channel was clear and maintained a breadth of open white water ranging from 90 to 450 yards.

Within an hour we arrived at the extremity of the open water, which had gradually been narrowed in width, by the increasing abundance of papyrus, from 250 yards to 40 yards. We ceased rowing, and gently glided up to the barrier of papyrus, which had now completely closed up the creek from bank to bank, like a luxuriant field of tall Indian corn. We sounded at the base of these reeds along a breadth of 40 yards, and obtained from 7 to 11 feet of water! With a portable level I attempted to ascertain a current; the level indicated none! Into a little pool, completely sheltered by the broadside of the boat, we threw a chip or two, and some sticks. In five minutes the chips had moved towards the reeds about a foot! We then crushed our way through about twenty yards of the papyrus, and came to impassable mud-banks, black as pitch, and seething with animal life. Returning to the boat, I asked four men to stand close together, and, mounting their shoulders with an oar for support, I endeavoured with a glass to obtain a general view. I saw a broad belt some 250 or 300 yards wide of a papyrus-grown depression, lying east and west between gently sloping banks, thinly covered with scrubby acacia. Here and there were pools of open water, and beyond were a few trees growing, as it seemed to me, right in the bed. I caused some of my men to attempt to cross from one bank to the other, but the muddy ooze was not sufficiently firm to bear the weight of a man.

I then cut a disc of wood a foot in diameter, drove a nail in, and folded cotton under its head. I then rove a cord 5 feet in length through this, suspending to one end an earthenware pot, with which I tried an experiment. Along the hedge of papyrus I measured 1000 feet with a tape line, both ends of the track marked by a broad riband of sheeting tied to a papyrus reed. Then, proceeding to the eastern or lake end of the track, I dropped the earthenware pot, which, after filling, sank and drew the wooden disc level with the water. I noted the chronometer instantly, while the boat was rowed away from the scene. The wind from the lake blew strong at the time.

The board floated from lakeward towards the papyrus 822 feet in one hour and forty seconds.

In the afternoon, wind calm and water tranquil, the disc floated in the opposite direction, or towards the lake, 159 feet in nineteen minutes and thirty seconds, which is at the rate of about 600 feet in the hour.

This was of itself conclusive proof that there was *no* current at this date (July 16, 1876). Still I was curious to see the river flowing out. The next day, therefore, accompanied by the chief and fifteen men of the Expedition, we started overland along the banks of this rush- and mud-choked depression for three or four miles. The trend of the several streams we passed was from north-west to south-east—that is, towards the lake. At Elwani village we came to the road from Monyi's, which is used by people proceeding to Uguvwa, Luwelezi, or Marungu on the other side of the Lukuga. Two men from the village accompanied us to the Lukuga ford. When we reached the foot of the hill, we first came to the dry bed of the Kibamba. In the rainy season this stream drains the eastern slopes of the Ki-yanja ridge with a south-east trend. The grass-stalks, still lying down from the force of the water, lay with their tops pointing lakeward.

From the dry mud-bed of the Kibamba to the cane-grass-choked bed of Lukuga was but a step. During the wet season the Kibamba evidently overflowed broadly, and made its way among the mateté of the Lukuga.

We tramped on along a path leading over prostrate reeds and cane, and came at length to where the ground began to be moist. The reeds on either side of it rose to the height of 10 or 12 feet, their tops interlacing, and the stalks, therefore, forming the sides of a narrow tunnel. The path sank here and there into ditch-like hollows filled with cool water from 9 inches to 3 feet deep, with transverse dykes of mud raised above it at intervals.

Finally, after proceeding some two hundred yards, we came to the centre of this reed-covered depression—called by the natives "Mitwanzi"—and here the chief, trampling a wider space among the reeds, pointed out in triumph water indisputably flowing westward!

The water felt cold, but it was only 68° Fahr., or 7° cooler than the Lukuga. I crossed over to the opposite or southern bank, on the shoulders of two of my men. The bed was uneven; sometimes the men rose until the water was barely over their ankles, then again they sank to their hips. The trees I had noticed from the open creek stood on a point projecting from the southern bank across the Mitwanzi, but they were now dead, as the former dry tract had become quaggy. The name Lukuga clings to the bed until a few miles west of Miketo's, when it becomes known as the Luindi, Ruindi, or Luimbi.

The Mitwanzi is still daily traversed without trouble by men, women, and children.

We travelled another three miles along the Mitwanzi, until we came to the southern end of the Ki-yanja ridge, for it is through the gap between this and the Kibunga ridge, which terminates on the south bank, that the Lukuga flows toward the west. Even here it was but a trivial stream, oozing and trickling through a cane-grass grove.

The most interesting object here was the rounded end of the Ki-yanja ridge, sloping at an angle of 30°. As the highest point is probably between 600 and 1000 feet, there has been some agency at work to wear down this gap through the ferruginous conglomerate and soft sandstone—and some agency stronger than this trivial stream smothered in reeds, for it has no force or power.

We got back to Lumba Creek, where we had left our boat and canoe, late at night. The next day was devoted to sounding the creek from the Mitwanzi to the outer bar.

July 17.—The next morning I took a trip to the top of the conical hill behind Mkampemba, a village of Kawe-Niangeh, to lay out and take bearings.

I am of the opinion, after taking all things into consideration, that Kahangwa Cape was, at a remote period, connected with Kungwé Cape on the east coast—that the Lukuga was the effluent of the lake as it stood then, that the lake was at that period at a much higher altitude than it is at present, that the northern half of the lake is of a later formation, and that, owing to the subsidence of that portion, and the collapsing of the barrier or the Kahangwa Cape and Kungwé Cape ridge, the waters south emptied into that of the deep gulf north, and left the channel of the Lukuga to be employed as the bed of the affluents Kibamba and Lumba, or the eastern slope of the Ki-yanja ridge, to feed the lake. But now that the extension of the profound bed—created by some great earthquake, which fractured and disparted the plateau of Uhha, Urundi, Ubembé, Goma, &c.—is on the eve of being filled up, the ancient affluent is about to resume its old duties of conveying the surplus waters of the Tanganika down into the valley of the Livingstone, and thence, along its majestic winding course, to the Atlantic Ocean.

I say this after having circumnavigated the lake and examined it most thoroughly. Underground caverns are myths, the fables of Wangwana and superstitious natives. The great deep lengthy cañon occupied by the fathomless lake is not closed in by rocks of such a nature as to admit of the theory of underground passages. It is rimmed by mountains and hills—the least altitude is 600 feet, the highest 4000 feet, above the lake. But to those seeking an elucidation of the fact that an enormous fresh-water lake is without an out-flowing river, are presented as rational solutions the stream-worn gap in the conglomerate of the ridges Kihunga and Liyanja, the wave-washed rocks and boulders of Mpembwé and all along the eastern coast down to Urungu, the bare headlands of Tembwé, and the naked steeps and cliffs of Kungwé and Karinzi. It is an undeniable fact that if the evaporation from a body of water be greater than the supply, that water must necessarily become saline from the particles washed into it from salt-beds and *salinas*.

It is also as undeniable that, if the supply to a body of water be greater than its evaporation, the quantity of the water must be increased until the receptacle—whether pool, pond, or lake—overflows and obtains an outlet.

In the instance of the Tanganika we have a fresh-water lake, which—according to the evidence of native Arabs and the observation of several travellers—is steadily rising. We

UBUJWÉ AND UGUHA HEAD-DRESS.

UGUHA HEAD-DRESS.

have also seen in the Lukuga the first symptoms of that overflowing which must come. At present there are only a few inches of mud-banks and a frail barrier of papyrus and reeds to interpose between the waters of the lake and its destiny, which it is now, year by year, steadily approaching. When the Tanganika has risen 3 feet higher, there will be no surf at the mouth of the Lukuga, no sill of sand, no oozing mud-banks, no rush-covered old river course, but the accumulated waters of over a hundred rivers will sweep through the ancient gap with the force of a cataclysm, bearing away on its flood all the deposits of organic débris at present in the Lukuga Creek, down the steep incline to swell the tribute due to the mighty Livingstone.

July 21.—On the 21st of July we sailed from the mouth of the future outlet Lukuga by Cape Kahangwa, to the Arab crossing-place near Kasengé Island.

The Waguha, along whose country we had voyaged south since leaving Tembwé, are an unusually ceremonious people. They are the first specimens of those nations among whom we are destined to travel in our exploration of the western regions.

A WOMAN OF UGUHA.

The art of the coiffeur is better known here than in any portion of Africa east of Lake Tanganika. The "waterfall" and "back-hair" styles are superb, and the constructions are fastened with carved wooden or iron pins. Full dress includes a semicircle of finely plaited hair over the forehead painted red, ears well ochred, the rest of the hair drawn up taut at the back of the head, overlaid and secured by a cross-shaped flat board, or with a skeleton crown of iron; the head is then covered with a neatly tasselled and plaited grass cloth, like a lady's breakfast-cap, to protect it from dust. In order to protect such an elaborate construction from being disordered, they carry a small head-rest of wood stuck in the girdle.

UHYEYA HEAD-DRESS.

Their mode of salutation is as follows :—

A man appears before a party seated: he bends, takes up a handful of earth or sand with his right hand, and throws a little into his left- the left hand rubs the sand or earth over the right elbow and the right side of the stomach, while the right hand performs the same operation for the left parts of the body, the mouth meanwhile uttering rapidly words of salutation. To his inferiors, however, the new-comer slaps his hand several times, and after each slap lightly taps the region of his heart.

Kasengé Island is a small island with a grassy cone rising from its centre. It is well-cultivated, and grows papaws, pomegranates, lemons, and sweet limes, having been favoured for a long period by Arabs, when their intercourse with the western regions was but beginning.

Between the lately severed promontory of Katenga, in Goma, which is now a large island, and Mtowa, the southern end of the bay, there is quite a cluster of islets, of which the largest are Kirindi, Kivizi, and Kavala.

When we have passed the northern point of Katenga Island we behold the Goma mountains in an apparently unbroken range of vast height and excessive steepness, and lengths of steep and cliffy slope. But as we sail on to the northward, we observe that from Katenga we saw only the profile or the shoulders of great lofty spurs. Behind almost all of these are beautiful secluded inlets and bays, overshadowed by black-bearded mountains, which give birth to myriads of clear crystal streams. Deep chasms in their huge fronts are filled with forests of enormous trees, out of which the famous Goma canoes are cut. Through every gap in the range roars and tumbles a clear cold stream, and piled up behind are the loftiest alps of Goma. The eye cannot fail to be struck with the contrast between the serene blue of the sky, the gloom of the chasm, and the dark tops of the tree-crested ranges. The margins of these calm havens are lined with green water-cane and eschinomenæ, to which hundreds of yellow-breasted birds have suspended their nests, where the industrious little creatures may be seen in flocks together, clinging belly upward, or flying up and down, ever chirping their wheedling, persuasive song. On a firm bough extended over the wave sits the glossy and sleek diver, contented, sated with his finny prey; or, perched upon the tall branch of some towering sycamore or teak, may be seen the white-collared fish-eagle, uttering at intervals his weird shrill call to his mate—a despairing, wailing cry. Presently, from some distant tree, at a commanding height, is heard the response, in the same doleful strain.

But from Katenga, as far as the Bald Mount, near Mugolwé, the crests of the ridges are tawny and treeless. From Tanga to Mdanga Cape, gaps and chasms, inlets and bays, like those above described are numerous, and between

Kabogo River and Missossi Mount there is a bay with five separate streams, descending from heights of 2000 feet in long silvery threads to the lake. The mountains seem to be dissolving in tears, for through every ravine or cleft or gap, chasm or rift, streams roll with impetuous course to the lake. Wherever foothold is obtained on a square-browed hill, terrace, or slope, cultivated fields and villages are seen, while on either side of them the cliffs drop sheer to profound depths.

The topmost height of Mount Missossi is about 3000 feet above the lake. As the lake is very wide between Goma and Ujiji—about forty miles—the waves rise very suddenly and drive in long billowy ridges against the massive and firm base of the mount, and when the south-easters prevail, the gale has command of sixty miles of clear water from Kabogo Cape. Navigation in canoes, while the wind is rising, is very dangerous.

We left Kabogo River's safe haven about 7 P.M., and at nine were pulling by Missossi Mount, exposed to a rising gale of great power about half a mile off a lee shore. To avoid being swept on the rocks, which were all afoam, we had to row direct eastward, and to handle both boat and canoe very delicately to avoid foundering. For two hours we laboured hard to get a mile to windward, and then, hoisting sail, we flew northward, just grazing the dreadful rocks of Mdanga Cape.

Nature, as already seen, has been in most frantic moods along the western coast of the Tanganika, but in Goma, where she has been most wanton, she has veiled herself with a graceful luxuriance of vegetation. Where the mountains are steepest and highest, and where their springs have channelled deepest, there the pillared mvulé and mcofu flourish most and attain their greatest height, and in loving fellowship they spread themselves up opposing slopes and follow the course of the stream in broad belts one either side down to the edge of the lake. Underneath their umbrageous foliage grows a tropical density of bush and plant, meshed and tangled, and of such variety that to class or specify them would require the labour and lifetime of an accomplished botanist.

As we look towards the lofty heights of Northern Goma we observe that they have a grassy pastoral aspect. We turn our eyes south to catch a farewell glimpse of those refreshing views which we had admired, and we see that distance has already transformed them into a long blue hazy outline.

We sailed all day within a stone's-throw of the shore of Goma, and in the evening put in at Kaganza, just north of Kiringi Point.

July 25.—On the 25th, on leaving Kaganza, we bade farewell to Goma, whose bare majestic front, as we continued north, was terminated by the low rounded hills of Kavunweh, and then, steering north-east, we skirted a low grassy land whose highest ridge was only 200 feet above the lake. This is the isthmus which connects the promontory of Ubwari and Karamba with the mainland. It is seven miles across to the gulf which separates Ubwari promontory from Ubembé and Usansi.

Burton describes Ubwari thus:—

"It is the only island near the centre of the Tanganika, a long narrow lump of rock, twenty to twenty-five geographical miles long, by four or five of extreme breadth."

Livingstone calls it in his 'Last Journals' the islet Mozima, and in 'How I Found Livingstone' I called it the island Muzimu.

The end of the isthmus is distinguished by two or three palms, which served us as a landmark when we had voyaged round into the gulf of the western side. It is also indented with two or three deep bays.

Near Karamba Cape, south latitude 4° 29′, the land again rises into a ridge about 1500 feet above the lake, and runs north from the southern cape to Panza Point, a distance of twenty-seven miles. Some very fine mountain scenes are presented here also, but after stupendous Goma they appear almost tame and commonplace.

Near the little round island of Muzimu, or the Spirit, we made a very comfortable camp near a fine gravel beach. The photograph of the Spirit Island given opposite suffices for description.

The Wabwari are by no means a handsome race: nor indeed are the Wavira, Wagoma, or Wabembé (cannibals); but they are all industrious tribes, and the Wabwari, though somewhat ready to take offence, are very much liked by all. They cultivate an enormous quantity of cassava, or manioc, and at this season the flat rocks were strewn with the sliced root. Dried whitebait is another article of commerce, and bags of millet are exchanged with the Warundi on the other side for palm-oil and butter, and with the Wajiji for cloth and beads.

July 27.—On the 27th we rounded Panza Point, and skirted the much-indented western side of Ubwari, until we reached the extreme southern reach of Burton Gulf.* At evening we camped in a tiny creek, near a grassy ridge, undisturbed. In the morning I ascended the ridge, and took bearings of Missossi Mount, Kiringi Cape, Karamba Cape, and by aid of the palms on the isthmus was able to identify the position. We rested until noon, and obtained south latitude 4° 22′. As Panza Point, the north end of

THE SPIRIT ISLAND.

Ubwari, is in south latitude 4° 2′, the length of Burton Gulf is twenty miles, by from five to seven miles in width.

Then coasting along the south end of Burton Gulf, we came to Masansi, which begins on the west side, and near each large village lowered our sail and inquired the names of the various rivers, villages, points, and countries. On coming near a village on the west bank of the Kasansagara river, we were forewarned of a rude reception. Approaching nearer, we were warned away by the Wabembé, who are most inimical to strangers. Wishing to test how far this hostile spirit would proceed, we continued to advance upon

* So named after Captain Richard Francis Burton, the commander of the Burton and Speke Expedition, which first discovered Lake Tanganika.

the shore. From wild gesture, such as striking the ground with their spears, beating the water, and frantic hopping up and down, they took to throwing stones of such large size as might well be termed dangerous missiles. Motioning a halt, we calmly surveyed the natives, watched the rocks fly through the air, and making deep pits in the water, as though we were simply looking on at an entertainment specially got up for our amusement. Not a word, gesture, or movement on our part indicated either resentment or pleasure, until the natives ceased their furious demonstrations. Para was then told to inform them that we would have nothing to say to such wild people, who at sight of strangers showed such foolish fury.

We turned away without another word, resumed our journey, and in an hour were abreast of Kiunyu, the village of the chief Mahonga. We spoke to them: they mocked us. We asked them if they would sell us some grain, but they replied that they were not our slaves, and that they had not sowed the land with grain to sell it to us. We pulled away from them without another word. The silly people cried out that we were running away, and at once launched about a dozen canoes and followed us. Encouraged by the infuriates and mockers on the shore, as also by our pacific behaviour, they became excited to a dangerous state, and gesticulated with their arrows and spears. Owing to the ferocious spirit of the people, we had to seek a camp among the reeds and papyrus in the delta of the Mtambara river, where, though troubled with mosquitoes, we slept undisturbed by the insensate ferocity of the Wabembé cannibals.

July 28.—On the 28th we skirted the low land which lies at the foot of the western mountains, and by noon had arrived at the little cove in Masansi, near the Rubumba or the Luvumba river, at which Livingstone and I terminated our exploration of the northern shores of Lake Tanganika in 1871. I had thus circumnavigated Lake Tanganika from Ujiji up the eastern coast, along the northern head, and down the western coast as far as Rubumba river in 1871, and in June–July 1876 had sailed south from Ujiji along the eastern coast to the extreme south end of the lake, round each inlet of the south, and up the western coast to Panza Point, in Ubwari, round the shores of Burton Gulf, and to Rubumba river. The north end of the lake was located by Livingstone in south latitude 3° 18′; the extreme south end I discovered to be in south latitude 8° 47′, which gives it a length of 329 geographical miles. Its breadth varies from ten to forty-five miles, averaging about twenty-eight miles, and its superficial area covers a space of 9240 square miles.

July 29.—On the 29th we crossed over from our haven near Muzimu Island, on the east side of Ubwari, to Kioga, in Urundi, where we were welcomed by our old friend Kinoza, the chief.

In mid-lake, I sounded, using a 3½-lb. sounding-lead with 1280 feet of cord, and found no bottom. I devoted an hour to this work, and tried a second time a mile nearer the Urundi coast, with the same results—no bottom. The strain at such a great depth on the whip-cord was enormous, but we met with no accident.

July 31.—On the 31st we arrived at Ujiji, after an absence of fifty-one days, during which time we had sailed without disaster or illness a distance of over 810 miles. The entire coast line of the Tanganika is about 930 miles.

CHAPTER III.

Back in camp—An epidemic of small-pox—Panic of desertion—Kalulu's disloyalty—Livingstone's lenience—Imaginary terrors—Hair dressing *ad absurdum*—Ruanga's opinion of white men—A village sketch—The villagers of Uhombo—*In puris naturalibus*—A touch of human nature—On Livingstone's traces—What is there in feathers?—The Manyema: their life and manners—Our ass astonishes the natives—Bloodless wars—Nicknames—A tribe with beards but no wives—The confluence of the Luama and the Livingstone.

Aug. 31.—The sky was of a stainless blue, and the slumbering lake faithfully reflected its exquisite tint, for not a breath of wind was astir to vex its surface. With groves of palms and the evergreen fig-trees on either hand, and before us a fringe of tall cane-grass along the shores all juicy with verdure, the square tembés of Ugoy, and the conical cotes of Kawelé, embowered by banana and plantain, we emerged into the bay of Ujiji from the channel of Bangwé.

The cheery view of the port lent strength to our arms. An animating boat-song was struck up, the sounds of which, carried far on the shore, announced that a proud, joyous crew was returning homeward.

Long-horned cattle are being driven to the water to drink; asses are galloping about, braying furiously; goats and sheep and dogs are wandering in the market-place—many familiar scenes recur to us as we press forward to the shore.

Our Wangwana hurry to the beach to welcome us. The usual congratulations follow—hand-shakings, smiles, and glad expressions. Frank, however, is pale and sickly; a muffler is round his neck, and he wears a greatcoat. He looks very different from the strong, hearty man to whom I gave the charge of the camp during my absence. In a few words he informs me of his sufferings from the fever of Ujiji.

"I am so glad you have come, sir. I was beginning to feel very depressed. I have been down several times with severe attacks of the horrible fever. Yesterday is the first

IN COUNCIL: THE COURTYARD OF OUR TEMBÉ AT UJIJI. [To face page 49

(From a photograph by the Author.)

time I got up after seven days' weary illness, and people are dying round me so fast that I was beginning to think I must soon die too. Now I am all right, and shall soon get strong again."

The news, when told to me in detail, was grievous. Five of our Wangwana were dead from small-pox; six others were seriously ill from the same cause. Among the Arab slaves, neither inoculated nor vaccinated, the mortality had been excessive from this fearful pest.

At Rosako, the second camp from Bagamoyo, I had foreseen some such event as this, and had vaccinated, as I had thought, all hands; but it transpired, on inquiry now, that there were several who had not responded to the call, through some silly prejudice against it. Five of those unvaccinated were dead, and five were ill, as also was one who had received the vaccine. When I examined the medicine-chest, I found the tubes broken and the lymph dried up.

The Arabs were dismayed at the pest and its dreadful havoc among their families and slaves. Every house was full of mourning and woe. There were no more agreeable visits and social converse; each kept himself in strict seclusion, fearful of being stricken with it. Khamis the Baluch was dead, his house was closed, and his friends were sorrowing. Mohammed bin Gharib had lost two children; Muini Kheri was lamenting the deaths of three children. The mortality was increasing: it was now from fifty to seventy-five daily among a population of about three thousand. Bitter were the complainings against the hot season and close atmosphere, and fervent the prayers for rain!

Frank had been assiduous in his assistance to our friends. He had elevated himself in their opinion by his devotion and sympathy, until sickness had laid its heavy hand on him. The Wangwana were now his sincere admirers, and the chiefs were his friends. Formerly, while ignorant of the language, he and they were, perhaps of necessity, mutually distant; they now fraternised warmly.

Our messengers had not returned with our letters from Unyanyembé, but, to escape the effects of the epidemic, it was necessary to move and resume our journey westward. The Wangwana were therefore ordered to prepare, and my last letters were written; but, though I hoped to be ready on the 17th to strike camp, I was attacked by a serious fever. This delayed me until the evening of the 25th.

When, on the morning of the 25th of August, the drum and bugle announced that our travels were to be resumed, I had cause to congratulate myself that I had foreseen that many desertions would take place, and that I was prepared in a measure for it by having discarded many superfluities. But I was not prepared to hear that thirty-eight men had deserted. Thirty-eight out of 170 was a serious reduction of strength. I was also told by the chiefs of the Expedition, who were almost beside themselves with fear, that this wholesale desertion threatened an entire and complete dissolution of our force, that many more would desert *en route* to

M'SEHAZY HAVEN AND CAMP, AT THE MOUTH OF M'SEHAZY RIVER.

Kabogo, as the people were demoralized by the prospect of being eaten by Manyema cannibals. As neither Frank nor I relished the idea of being compelled to return to Zanzibar before we had obtained a view of the Lualaba, I mustered as many as would answer to their names; and out of these, selecting such as appeared unstable and flighty, I secured thirty-two, and surrounded our house with guards.

After repairing the canoes and getting the boat ready, those who did not bear a good character for firmness and fidelity were conducted under guard to the transport canoes; the firm and faithful, and those believed to be so, were permitted to march on land with myself towards Kabogo

Cape, or M'sehazy Creek, whence the crossing of the Tanganika was to be effected. Out of the 132 men, of whom the Expedition now consisted, only thirty were entrusted with guns, as my faith in the stability of the Wangwana was utterly destroyed, despite their protestations to the contrary. I could afford to lose weak, fearful, and unworthy men; but I could not afford to lose one gun. Though we had such a show of strength left, I was only too conscious that there were barely forty reliable and effective in a crisis, or in the presence of danger; the rest were merely useful as bearers of burdens, or porters.

When we resumed our journey the second day from Ukaranga, three more were missing, which swelled the number of desertions to forty-one, and reduced our force to 129. After we had crossed the Tanganika and arrived in Uguha, two more disappeared, one of whom was young Kalulu, whom I had taken to England and the United States, and whom I had placed in an English school for eighteen months.

Induced to do so by the hope that I should secure their attachment to the cause of the Expedition, I had purchased from Sultan bin Kassim six bales of cloth at an enormous price, £350, and had distributed them all among the people gratuitously. This wholesale desertion at the very period when their services were about to be most needed was my reward! The desertion and faithless conduct of Kalulu did not, as may be imagined, augment my hopes, or increase my faith in the fidelity of my people. But it determined me to recover some of the deserters. Francis Pocock and the detective of the Expedition, the ever-faithful and gallant Kachéché, were therefore sent back with a squad to Ujiji, with instructions how to act; and one night Kachéché pounced upon six fellows, who, after a hard and tough resistance, were secured; and after his return to Uguha with these he successfully recovered the runaway Kalulu on Kasengé Island. These seven, along with a few others arrested in the act of desertion, received merited punishments, which put an end to misconduct and faithlessness, and prevented the wreck of the Expedition.

It must not be supposed that I was more unfortunate than other travellers; for to the faithlessness of his people may be attributed principally the long wanderings of poor Livingstone. Cameron also lost a great number at Unyanyembé, as well as at Ujiji. Experience had taught me on my first journey to Central Africa that Wangwana would desert at every opportunity, especially in the vicinity of the Arab depots. It was to lessen these opportunities for desertion that I had left the Unyanyembé road, and struck through Ituru and Iramba; and though my losses in men were great from famine, the ferocity of the natives, and sickness, they did not amount to half of what they certainly would have been had I touched at Unyanyembé. By adopting this route, despite the calamities that we were subjected to for a short season, I had gained time, and opened new countries, hitherto unexplored.

Sept.—Desertion had also been checked by voyaging Lake Victoria, instead of pursuing our journey by land, and troubles with Rwoma and the king of Usui had also been avoided. But when we received a check at the Muta Nzigé, it became necessary to visit Ujiji, and the long-sought-for opportunity to desert was thus presented to the disaffected, and those who had enlisted only for the sake of the advance-money given to them at Zanzibar. Among these cunning ones was Msenna, the terror of Zanzibar and the coast. He was renowned as a murderer, robber, and ruffian when he took service with me. This man was among the deserters at Ujiji.

Unless the traveller in Africa exerts himself to keep his force intact, he cannot hope to perform satisfactory service. If he relaxes his watchfulness, it is instantly taken advantage of by the weak-minded and the indolent. Livingstone lost at least six years of time, and finally his life, by permitting his people to desert. If a follower left his service, he even permitted him to remain in the same village with him, without attempting to reclaim him, or to compel that service which he had bound himself to render at Zanzibar. The consequence of this excessive mildness was that he was left at last with only seven men, out of nearly seventy. His noble character has won from us a tribute of affection and esteem, but it has had no lasting good effect on the African. At the same time over-severity is as bad as over-gentleness in dealing with these men. What is required is pure, simple justice between man and man.

The general infidelity and instability of the Wangwana arises, in great part, from their weak minds becoming a prey to terror of imaginary dangers. Thus, the Johanna men deserted Livingstone because they heard the terrible

Mafitté were in the way; my runaways of Ujiji fled from the danger of being eaten by the Manyema.

The slaves of Sungoro, the coast trader at Kagehyi, Usukuma, informed my people that Lake Victoria spread as far as the Salt Sea, that it had no end, and that the people on its shores loved the flesh of man better than that of goats. This foolish report made it a most difficult matter to man the exploring boat, and over a hundred swore by Allah that they knew nothing of rowing.

A similar scene took place when about to circumnavigate the Tanganika, for the Arab slaves had spread such reports of Muzimus, hobgoblins, fiery meteors, terrible spirits, such as Kabogo, Katavi, Kateyé, and Wanpembé, that the teeth of Wanyamwezi and Wangwana chattered with fright. But no reports exercised such a terrible effect on their weak minds as the report of the Manyema cannibals, none were so greedily listened to, none more readily believed.

The path which traders and their caravans follow to Manyema begins at Mtowa, in Uguha, and, continuing south a few miles over a series of hills, descends into the plain of the Rugumba river about halfway between the Lukuga river and the traders' crossing-place.

The conduct of the first natives to whom we were introduced pleased us all. They showed themselves in a very amiable light, sold their corn cheaply and without fuss, behaved themselves decently and with propriety, though their principal men, entertaining very strange ideas of the white men, carefully concealed themselves from view, and refused to be tempted to expose themselves within view or hearing of us.

Their doubts of our character were reported to us by a friendly young Arab as follows: "Kassanga, chief of Ruanda, says, 'How can the white men be good when they come for no trade, whose feet one never sees, who always go covered from head to foot with clothes? Do not tell me they are good and friendly. There is something very mysterious about them; perhaps wicked. Probably they are magicians; at any rate, it is better to leave them alone and to keep close until they are gone.'"

From Ruanda, where we halted only for a day, we began in earnest the journey to Manyema, thankful that the Tanganika was safely crossed, and that the Expedition had lost no more of its strength.

On the third day, after gradually ascending to a height of 800 feet above the lake, across a series of low hilly ridges and scantily wooded valleys, which abound with buffalo, we reached the crest of a range which divides the tributaries of the Lualaba from those of Lake Tanganika. This range also serves as a boundary between Uguha and Ubujwé, a country adjoining the former north-westerly. The western portion of Uguha, and south-eastern Ubujwé, is remarkable for its forests of fruit-trees, of which there are several varieties, called the Masuku, Mbembu (or wood-apple), Singwé (wild African damson), the Matonga (or nux-vomica), custard-apple, &c. A large quantity of honey was also obtained. Indeed, an army might subsist for many weeks in this forest on the various luscious fruits it contains. Our people feasted on them, as also on the honey and buffalo meat, which I was fortunate in obtaining.

NATIVES OF UBUJWÉ.

Our acquaintance with the Wabujwé commenced at Lambo, or Mulolwa's, situated at the confluence of the Rugumba with the Rubumba. In these people we first saw the mild, amiable, unsophisticated innocence of this part of Central Africa, and their behaviour was exactly the reverse of the wild, ferocious, cannibalistic races the Arabs had described to us.

From our experience of them, the natives of Rua, Uguha, and Ubujwé appear to be the *élite* of the hair-dressed fashionables of Africa. Hair-dressing is indeed carried to an absurd perfection throughout all this region, and among the various styles I have seen, some are surpassing in taste and neatness, and almost pathetic from the carefulness with which poor wild nature has done its best to decorate itself.

The Waguha and Wabujwé, among other characteristics, are very partial to the arts of sculpture and turning. They carve statues in wood, which they set up in their villages. Their house doors often exhibit carvings resembling the human face; and the trees in the forest between the two countries frequently present specimens of their ingenuity in this art. Some have also been seen to wear wooden medals, whereon a rough caricature of a man's features was represented. At every village in Ubujwé excellent wooden bowls and basins of a very light wood (Rubiaceæ), painted red, are offered for sale.

Between Kwaniwa's village, Lambo, and Kundi, we came to a hot stream issuing from a spring, buried amid a mass of spear-grass and dwarf papyrus. At the crossing the temperature was 106° Fahr., about twenty yards above it was 115° Fahr. Those at Bath, in England, are from 117° to 120° Fahr.; at Ursprung, Baden, 153½° Fahr. These hot springs at Kwaniwa's contain considerable iron in solution, judging from the ferruginous slime below and the ochreous tint which rests on the plants and grass.

Beyond Kundi our journey lay across chains of hills, of a conical or rounded form, which enclosed many basins or valleys. While the Rugumba, or Rubumba, flows northwesterly to the east of Kundi, as far as Kizambala on the Luama river, we were daily, sometimes hourly, fording or crossing the tributaries of the Luama.

Adjoining Ubujwé is Uhyeya, inhabited by a tribe who are decidedly a scale lower in humanity than their ingenious neighbours. What little merit they possess seems to have been derived from commerce with the Wabujwé. The Wahyeya are also partial to ochre, black paints, and a composition of black mud, which they mould into the form of a plate, and attach to the back part of the head. Their upper teeth are filed, "out of regard to custom," they say, and not from any taste for human flesh.

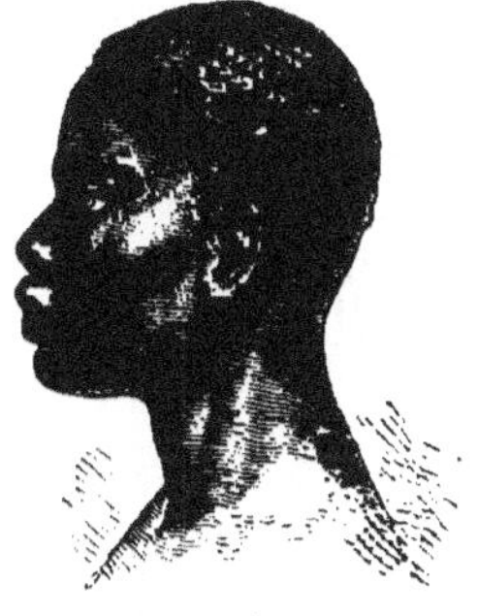
A NATIVE OF UHYEYA.

When questioned as to whether it was their custom to eat of the flesh of people slain in battle, they were positive in their denial, and protested great repugnance to such a diet, though they eat the flesh of all animals except that of dogs.

Simple and dirt-loving as these poor people were, they were admirable for the readiness with which they supplied all our wants, voluntarily offering themselves, moreover, as guides to lead us to Uvinza, the next country we had to traverse.

Uvinza now seems to be nothing more than a name of a small district which occupies a small basin of some few miles square. At a former period it was very populous, as the many ruined villages we passed through proved. The slave traders, when not manfully resisted, leave broad traces wherever they go.

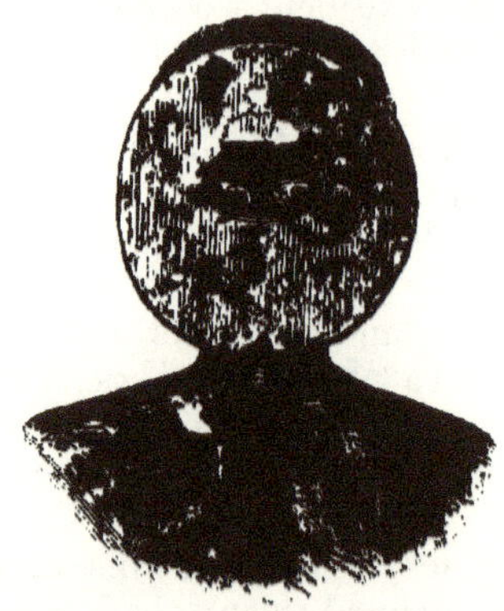

ONE OF THE WAHYEYA OF UHOMBO (BACK VIEW).

Oct.—A very long march from Kagongwé in Uvinza brought us to the pleasant basin of Uhombo, remarkable for its fertility, its groves of Guinea-palms, and its beauty. This basin is about six miles square, but within this space there is scarcely a two-acre plot of level ground to be seen. The whole forms a picture of hill-tops, slopes, valleys, hollows, and intersecting ridges in happy diversity. Myriads of cool, clear streams course through, in time united by the Lubangi into a pretty little river, flowing westerly to the Luama. It was the most delightful spot that we had seen. As the people were amiable, and disposed to trade, we had soon an abundance of palm-butter for cooking, sugar-cane, fine goats and fat chickens, sweet potatoes, beans, peas, nuts, and manioc, millet and other grain for flour, ripe bananas for dessert, plantain and palm wines for cheer, and an abundance of soft, cool, clear water to drink!

Subsequently we had many such pleasant experiences; but as it was the first, it deserves a more detailed description.

Travellers from Africa have often written about African villages, yet I am sure few of those at home have ever comprehended the reality. I now propose to lay it before them in this sketch of a village in the district of Uhombo. The village consists of a number of low, conical grass huts, ranged round a circular common, in the centre of which are three or four fig-trees kept for the double purpose of supplying shade to the community, and bark-cloth to the chief. The doorways to the huts are very low, scarcely 30 inches high. The common fenced round by the grass huts shows plainly the ochreous colour of the soil, and it is so well trodden that not a grass blade thrives upon it.

On presenting myself in the common, I attracted out of doors the owners and ordinary inhabitants of each hut, until I found myself the centre of quite a promiscuous population of naked men, women, children, and infants. Though I had appeared here for the purpose of studying the people of Uhombo, and making a treaty of friendship with the chief, the villagers seemed to think I had come merely to make a free exhibition of myself as some natural monstrosity.

I saw before me over a hundred beings of the most degraded, unpresentable type it is possible to conceive, and though I knew quite well that some thousands of years ago the beginning of this wretched humanity and myself were one and the same, a sneaking disinclination to believe it possessed me strongly, and I would even now willingly subscribe some small amount of silver money for him who could but assist me to controvert the discreditable fact.

But common-sense tells me not to take into undue consideration their squalor, their ugliness, or nakedness, but to gauge their true position among the human race by taking a view of the cultivated fields and gardens of Uhombo, and I am compelled to admit that these debased specimens of humanity only plant and sow such vegetables and grain as I myself should cultivate were I compelled to provide for my own sustenance. I see, too, that their huts, though of grass, are almost as well made as the materials will permit, and indeed I have often slept in worse. Speak with them in their own dialect of the law of *meum* and *tuum*, and it will soon appear that they are intelligent enough upon that point. Moreover, the muscles, tissues, and fibres of their bodies, and all the organs of sight, hearing, smell, or motion, are as well developed as in us. Only in taste and judgment, based upon larger experience, in the power of expression, in morals and intellectual culture, are we superior.

I strive, therefore, to interest myself in my gross and rudely-shaped brothers and sisters. Almost bursting into a laugh at the absurdity, I turn towards an individual whose age marks him out as one to whom respect is due, and say to him after the common manner of greeting:

"My brother, sit you down by me on this mat, and let

us be friendly and sociable"; and as I say it I thrust into his wide open hand twenty cowries, the currency of the land. One look at his hand as he extended it made me think I could carve a better-looking hand out of a piece of rhinoceros hide.

While speaking I look at his face, which is like an ugly and extravagant mask, clumsily manufactured from some strange, dark brown coarse material. The lips proved the thickness of skin which nature had endowed him with, and by the obstinacy with which they refused to meet each other the form of the mouth was but ill-defined, though capacious and garnished with its full complement of well-preserved teeth.

His nose was so flat that I inquired in a perfectly innocent manner as to the reason for such a feature.

"Ah," said he, with a sly laugh, "it is the fault of my mother, who, when I was young, bound me too tight to her back."

His hair had been compelled to obey the capricious fashion of his country, and was therefore worked up into furrows and ridges and central cones, bearing a curious resemblance to the formation of the land around Uhombo. I wonder if the art grew by perceiving nature's fashion and mould of his country?

Descending from the face, which, crude, large-featured, rough-hewn as it was, bore witness to the possession of much sly humour and a kindly disposition, my eyes fastened on his naked body. Through the ochreous daubs I detected strange freaks of pricking on it, circles and squares and crosses, and traced with wonder the many hard lines and puckers created by age, weather, ill-usage, and rude keeping.

His feet were monstrous abortions, with soles as hard as hoofs, and his legs as high up as the knees were plastered with successive strata of dirt; his loin-cover or the queer "girding tackle" need not be described. They were absolutely appalling to good taste, and the most ragged British beggar or Neapolitan lazzarone is sumptuously, nay, regally, clothed in comparison to this "king" in Uhombo.

If the old chief appeared so unprepossessing, how can I paint without offence my humbler brothers and sisters who stood round us? As I looked at the array of faces,

I could only comment to myself—ugly—uglier—ugliest. As I looked at their nude and filthy bodies, and the enormous dugs which hung down the bosoms of the women, and the general indecency of their nakedness, I ejaculated "Fearful!" as the sum total of what I might with propriety say, and what indeed is sufficiently descriptive.

And what shall I say of the hideous and queer appendages that they wear about their waists; the tags of monkey-skin and bits of gorilla bone, goat horn, shells, strange tags to stranger tackle? and of the things around their necks—brain of mice, skin of viper, "adder's fork, and blind worm's sting"? And how strangely they smell, all these queer man-like creatures who stand regarding me! Not silently: on the contrary, there is a loud interchange of comments upon the white's appearance, a manifestation of broad interest to know whence I come, whither I am going, and what is my business. And no sooner are the questions asked than they are replied to by such as pretend to know. The replies were followed by long-drawn ejaculations of "Wa-a-a-antu!" ("Men!") "Eha-a, and these are men!"

Now imagine this! While we whites are loftily disputing among ourselves as to whether the beings before us are human, here were these creatures actually expressing strong doubts as to whether we whites are men!

A dead silence prevailed for a short time, during which all the females dropped their lower jaws far down, and then cried out again "Wa-a-a-a-a-antu!" ("Men!") The lower jaws indeed dropped so low that, when, in a posture of reflection, they put their hands up to their chins, it really looked as if they had done so to lift the jaws up to their proper place and to sustain them there. And in that position they pondered upon the fact that there were men "white all over" in this queer, queer world!

The open mouths gave one a chance to note the healthy state and ruby colour of the tongues, palates, and gums, and, above all, the admirable order and brilliant whiteness of each set of teeth.

"Great events from trivial causes spring"—and while I was trying to calculate how many Kubaba (measure of 2 lbs.) of millet-seed would be requisite to fill all these Dutch-oven mouths, and how many cowries would be required to pay for such a large quantity of millet, and wondering at the antics of the juveniles of the population, whose uncontainable, irrepressible wonder seemed to find its natural expression in hopping on one leg, thrusting their right thumbs into their mouths to repress the rising scream, and slapping the hinder side of the thighs to express or give emphasis to what was speechless—while thus engaged, and just thinking it was time to depart, it happened that one of the youthful innocents already described, more restless than his brothers, stumbled across a long heavy pole which was leaning insecurely against one of the trees. The pole fell, striking one of my men severely on the head. And all at once there went up from the women a genuine and unaffected cry of pity, and their faces expressed so lively a sense of tender sympathy with the wounded man, that my heart, keener than my eyes, saw through the disguise of filth, nakedness, and ochre, the human heart beating for another's suffering, and I then recognised and hailed them as indeed my own poor and degraded sisters.

Under the new light which had dawned on me, I reflected that I had done some wrong to my dusky relatives, and that they might have been described less harshly, and introduced to the world with less disdain.

Before I quitted the village, they made me still more regret my former haughty feelings, for the chief and his subjects loaded my men with bounties of bananas, chickens, Indian corn, and malafu (palm-wine), and escorted me respectfully far beyond the precincts of the village and their fields, parting from me at last with the assurance that, should I ever happen to return by their country, they would endeavour to make my second visit to Uhombo much more agreeable than my first had been.

Oct. 5.—On the 5th of October our march from Uhombo brought us to the frontier village of Manyema, which is called Riba-Riba. It is noteworthy as the starting-point of another order of African architecture. The conical style of hut is exchanged for the square hut with more gradually sloping roof, wattled, and sometimes neatly plastered with mud, especially those in Manyema. Here, too, the thin-bodied and long-limbed goat, to which we had been accustomed, gave place to the short-legged, large-bodied, and capacious-uddered variety of Manyema. The grey parrots with crimson tails here also first began to abound, and the hoarse growl of the fierce and shy "soko" (gorilla ?) was first heard.

From the day we cross the watershed that divides the affluent of the Tanganika from the head waters of the Luama, there is observed a gradual increase in the splendour of nature. By slow degrees she exhibits to us, as we journey westward, her rarest beauties, her wealth and all the profligacy of her vegetation. In the forests of Miketo and on the western slopes of the Goma mountains she scatters with liberal hand her luxuries of fruits, and along the banks of streams we see revealed the wild profusion of her bounties.

As we increase the distance from the Tanganika, we find the land disposed in graceful lines and curves: ridges heave up, separating valley from valley, hills lift their heads in the midst of the basins, and mountain-ranges, at greater distances apart, bound wide prospects, wherein the lesser hill-chains, albeit of dignified proportions, appear but as agreeable diversities of scenery.

Over the whole, Nature has flung a robe of verdure of the most fervid tints. She has bidden the mountains loose their streamlets, has commanded the hills and ridges to bloom, filled the valleys with vegetation breathing perfume, for the rocks she has woven garlands of creepers, and the stems of trees she has draped with moss; and sterility she has banished from her domain.

Yet Nature has not produced a soft, velvety, smiling England in the midst of Africa. Far from it. She is here too robust and prolific. Her grasses are coarse, and wound like knives and needles; her reeds are tough and tall as bamboos; her creepers and convolvuli are of cable thickness and length; her thorns are hooks of steel; her trees shoot up to a height of a hundred feet. We find no pleasure in straying in search of wild flowers, and game is left undisturbed, because of the difficulty of moving about, for once the main path is left we find ourselves over head amongst thick, tough, unyielding, lacerating grass.

At Manyema, the beauty of Nature becomes terrible, and in the expression of her powers she is awful. The language of Swahili has words to paint her in every mood. English, rich as it is, is found insufficient. In the former we have the word Pori for a forest, an ordinary thickly wooded tract, but for the forests of Manyema it has four special words,

Mohuro, Mwitu, Mtambani, and Msitu. For Mohuro we might employ the words jungly forest; for Mwitu, dense woods; but for Msitu and Mtambani we have no single equivalent, nor could we express their full meaning without a series of epithets ending with "tangled jungle" or "impervious underwood in the midst of a dense forest"—for such is in reality the nature of a Manyema Msitu.

I am of opinion that Manyema owes its fertility to the mountains west of the Tanganika, which by their altitude suddenly cool and liquefy the vapours driven over their tops by the south-east monsoon, for while Uguha west was robed in green, its lake front was black with the ashes of burnt grass.

We left Riba-Riba's old chief, and his numerous progeny of boys and girls, and his wonderful subjects, encamped on their mountain-top, and journeyed on with rapid pace through tall forests, and along the crests of wooded ridges, down into the depths of gloomy dingles, and up again to daylight into view of sweeping circles of bearded ridges and solemn woods, to Ka-Bambarré.

Even though this place had no other associations, it would be attractive and alluring for its innocent wildness; but associated as it is with Livingstone's sufferings, and that self-sacrificing life he led here, I needed only to hear from Mwana Ngoy, son of Mwana Kusu,* "Yes, this is the place where the old white man stopped for many moons," to make up my mind to halt.

"Ah! he lived here, did he?"

"Yes."

By this time the population of Ka-Bambarré, seeing their chief in conversation with a white stranger, had drawn round us under a palm-tree, and mats were spread for us to seat ourselves.

"Did you know the old white man? Was he your father?"

"He was not my father; but I knew him well."

"Eh, do you hear that?" he asked his people. "He says he knew him. Was he not a good man?"

"Yes; very good."

"You say well. He was good to me, and he saved me from the Arabs many a time. The Arabs are hard men, and often he would step between them and me when they were

* Mwana, *lord*; Kusu, *parrot*.

hard on me. He was a good man, and my children were fond of him. I hear he is dead?"

"Yes, he is dead."

"Where has he gone to?"

"Above, my friend," said I, pointing to the sky.

"Ah," said he breathlessly, and looking up, "did he come from above?"

"No, but good men like him go above when they die."

We had many conversations about him. The sons showed me the house he had lived in for a long time when prevented from further wandering by the ulcers in his feet. In the village his memory is cherished, and will be cherished for ever.

It was strange what a sudden improvement in the physiognomy of the native had occurred. In the district of Uhombo we had seen a truly debased negro type. Here we saw people of the Ethiopic negro type, worthy to rank next the more refined Waganda. Mwana Ngoy himself was nothing very remarkable. Age had deprived him of his good looks; but there were about him some exceedingly pretty women, with winsome ways about them that were quite charming.

Mwana Ngoy, I suppose, is one of the vainest of vain men. I fancy I can see him now strutting about his village with his sceptral staff, an amplitude of grass cloth about him, which when measured gives exactly twenty-four square yards, drawn in double folds about his waist, all tags, tassels, and fringes, and painted in various colours, bronze and black and white and yellow, and on his head a plumy head-dress.

What charms lurk in feathers! From the grand British dowager down to Mwana-Ngoy of Ka-Bambarré, all admit the fascination of feathers, whether plucked from ostriches or barn-door fowl.

Mwana Ngoy's plumes were the tribute of the village chanticleers, and his vanity was so excited at the rustle of his feathered crest that he protruded his stomach to such a distance that his head was many degrees from the perpendicular.

Oct. 10.—On the 10th of October we arrived at Kizambala, presided over by another chief, called Mwana Ngoy, a relative to him of Ka-Bambarré.

Up to this date we had seen some twenty villages, and

probably 4000 natives, of Manyema, and may therefore be permitted some generalizations.

The Manyema, then, have several noteworthy peculiarities.

A YOUTH OF EAST MANYEMA.

A MANYEMA ADULT.

Their arms are a short sword scabbarded with wood, to which are hung small brass and iron bells, a light, beautifully balanced spear—probably, next to the spear of Uganda, the most perfect in the world. Their shields were veritable wooden doors. Their dress consisted of a narrow apron of antelope skin or finely made grass cloth. They wore knobs, cones, and patches of mud attached to their beards, back hair, and behind the ears. Old Mwana Ngoy had rolled his beard in a ball of dark mud: his children wore their hair in braids with mud fringes. His drummer had a great crescent-shaped patch of mud at the back of the head. At Kizambala, the natives had horns and cones of mud on the tops of their heads. Others, more ambitious, covered the entire head with a crown of mud.

A YOUNG WOMAN OF EAST MANYEMA.

The women, blessed with an abundance of hair, manufactured it with a stiffening of light cane into a bonnet-shaped head-dress, allowing the back hair to flow down to the waist in masses of ringlets. They seemed to do all the work of life, for at all hours they might be seen, with their large wicker baskets behind them, setting out for

A VILLAGE IN SOUTH-EAST MANYEMA.

[To face page 61.

the rivers or creeks to catch fish, or returning with their fuel baskets strapped on across their foreheads.

Their villages consist of one or more streets from 100 to 150 feet wide, flanked by low square huts arranged in tolerably straight lines, and generally situated on swells of land, to secure rapid drainage. At the end of one of these streets is the council and gossip house, overlooking the length of the avenue. In the centre is a platform of tamped clay, with a heavy tree trunk sunk into it, and in the wood have been scooped out a number of troughs, so that several women may pound grain at once. It is a substitute for the village mill.

The houses are separated into two or more apartments, and on account of the compact nature of the clay and tamped floor are easily kept clean. The roofs are slimy with the reek of smoke, as though they had been painted with coal-tar. The household chattels or furniture are limited to food baskets, earthenware pots, an assortment of wickerwork dishes, the family shields, spears, knives, swords, and tools, and the fish-baskets lying outside.

They are tolerably hospitable, and permit strangers the free use of their dwellings. The bananas and plantains are very luxuriant, while the Guinea palms supply the people with oil and wine; the forests give them fuel, the rivers fish, and the gardens cassava, ground-nuts, and Indian corn.

The chiefs enact strict laws, and, though possessed of but little actual power either of wealth or retinue, exact the utmost deference, and are exceedingly ceremonious, being always followed by a drummer, who taps his drum with masterly skill born of long and continued practice.

Oct. 11.—On the 11th we crossed the Luama river—a stream 200 yards wide and 8 feet deep in the centre at the ferry—called the Rugumba in Ubujwé. After uniting with the Rubumba, it flows northward, and takes a wide sweep round to clear the northern spurs of the Ka-Bambarré group of mountains, and thence, meeting another stream from the north-west near Uvira, flows west, bisecting the country of Manyema. Below the ford, as far as the Lualaba, its current is from three to six knots an hour, and about 5 feet deep, flowing over a shaly bed.

On the western side of the Luama the women at once fled upon the approach of our caravan—a certain sign that there had been trouble between them and Arabs.

Oct. 12.—On the 12th, following the Luama river, we reached Wusumbiri. My predecessors, Livingstone and Cameron, had, after crossing the stream, proceeded west, but I preferred to follow the Luama to its junction with the Lualaba, and thence to Nyangwé.

The Luama valley is about twenty miles wide, furrowed with many watercourses; the soil is poor, abounding with yellow quartz, but resting upon soft shale. The ridges are formed of dykes of granite, which peep out frequently in large masses from amongst the foliage of trees.

The people appeared to be very timid, but behaved amiably. Over fifty followed us, and carried loads most willingly. Three volunteered to follow us wherever we should go, but we declined their offer.

Our riding-asses were the first ever seen in Manyema, and effected a striking demonstration in our favour. They obtained more admiration than even we Europeans. Hundreds of natives ran up to us at each village in the greatest excitement to behold the strange long-eared animals, and followed us long distances from their homes to observe the asses' motions.

One ass, known by the name of Muscati, a high-spirited animal from Arabia, possessed braying powers which almost equalled the roar of a lion in volume, and really appeared to enjoy immensely the admiration he excited. His asinine soul took great delight in braying at the unsophisticated Africans of the trans-Luama, for his bray sent them flying in all directions. Scores of times during a day's march we were asked the name of the beast, and, having learnt it they were never tired of talking about the "Mpunda."

One must not rashly impute all the blame to the Arabs and Wa-Swahili of the Zanzibar coast for their excesses in Manyema, for the natives are also in a way to blame. Just as the Saxon and Dane and Jute, invited by the Britons, became their masters, so the Arabs, invited by the Manyema to assist them against one another, have become their tyrants.

Bribes were offered to us three times by Manyema chiefs to assist them in destroying their neighbours, to whom they are of near kin, and with whom they have almost daily intimate relations. Our refusal of ivory and slaves appeared to surprise the chiefs, and they expressed the opinion that we white men were not as good as the Arabs, for—though it was true we did not rob them of their wives, ravish and steal their daughters, enslave their sons, or despoil them of a single article—the Arabs would have assisted them.

One of my men, who knew Manyema of old, said, "I told you, master, what kind of people these were: they have always got a little war on hand, and they only wait the arrival of the Arabs to begin it. The quarrel is always with their nearest relatives and friends, whom, however, for the sake of the family alliances between them, they always take care to warn. I was once with Mohammed bin Gharib (Livingstone's friend) when he undertook to fight a tribe for Mwana Ngoy of Kizambala on the Luama. We were ten hours firing away as fast as we could, but not a single soul was wounded of either party!

"Mwana Ngoy, you must know, had told his friend the hour Mohammed would begin, and his friend obligingly left the field clear. Some of the boldest had amused themselves by showing their heads, just to let us know that they were there, but I assure you no one was hurt in the least.

"Of late years it has not been so bloodless, because the Arabs have learned their tricks. When they set out now, they never tell their native confederate when they intend to begin, because they don't like to throw away their powder for nothing. In this manner large numbers of slaves have been captured and many men killed. After such an event, both sides, those who have suffered and those who were the cause and who bribed the Arabs to the war, fall to weeping and abusing the Arabs violently, and with pathetic cries bewail the murdered, but never think of accusing themselves."

The above is the story of Wadi Safeni, the coxswain of the boat on Lake Victoria.

One really does not know whether to pity or to despise the natives of Manyema. Many are amiable enough to deserve good and kind treatment, but others are hardly human. They fly to the woods upon the approach of strangers, leaving their granaries* of Indian corn, erected like screens across the streets, or just outside the villages, in

* These granaries consist of tall poles—like telegraph poles—planted at a distance of about 10 feet from each other, to which are attached about a dozen lines of lliane, or creepers, at intervals, from top to bottom. On these several lines are suspended the maize, point downwards, by the shucks of the cob. Their appearance suggests lofty screens built up of corn.

tempting view of hungry people. If the strangers follow them into the woods to persuade them to return and sell food, the purpose of the visit is mistaken, and they are assailed from behind depths of bush and tall trees. They are humble and liberal to the strong-armed Arab, savage and murderous and cannibalistic to small bands, and every slain man provides a banquet of meat for the forest-natives of Manyema. Livingstone's uniform gentle treatment of all classes deserved a better return than to have his life attempted four times. His patience finally exhausted, and his life in danger, he gave the order to his men, "Fire upon them; these men are wicked."

Nevertheless, the best-natured Arabs confess that the present state of things is to some extent the result of the excesses and high-handed conduct of Muini Dugumbi, who, animated by greed for ivory and slaves, signalled his advent in the country by shooting men as soon as seen in their villages. Aware of the bad repute which Arabs had in Manyema, I refused to be accompanied by any trader from Ujiji, though some half-dozen earnestly entreated me to wait for them. As far as Nyangwé all the members of our Expedition had reason to rejoice in this decision, for we were neither threatened nor molested in the least.

An internecine "war" in Manyema is exceedingly comical. Old Riba-Riba, a patriarch of eighty or thereabouts, who with his few villages guards the frontier on the range separating Uhombo from Manyema, told me he was at "war" with Mwana Buttu of Nyembu. The cause was the murder of a young man of Riba-Riba's by Mwana Buttu's people.

When the shocking affair became known there was great excitement, much manifestation of anger, loud talk, sharpening of broad-bladed spears, and industrious preparation of stacks of fire-hardened wooden assegais and other deadly war *matériel.* All things being ready, Riba-Riba's people reluctantly set off to fight Mwana Buttu's villagers, not, however, without first communicating their intentions and publishing by criers a formal and fierce declaration of war.

But Mwana Buttu is of a sterner nature than is common in Manyema; consequently, to Riba-Riba's surprise, he did not abscond for fear of the invading host, but calmly arrayed his warriors in order of battle on the opposite side of a stream, that he might take advantage of the enemy's confusion while crossing.

Riba-Riba's warriors, on emerging from the depth of the forest, perceived the foe palisaded behind their tall, door-like shields, and immediately formed themselves in like order on their own side of the stream. From this position they opened on the enemy volleys of tongue abuse, which lasted for hours; until at last both sides, fatigued with the wordy encounter and hoarse with the prolonged vituperative exercise, mutually consented to defer the battle until next day.

The morrow dawned, and both sides, vigilantly active after their night's rest, reformed themselves in the same positions which they had occupied on the previous day, and resumed the wordy war with all its fierce gesture, and a great clangour of wooden shields, until sunset, when both parties retired from the field with no decisive advantage to either side.

On the third day the wordy war was resumed, until both tribes, exhausted from the bloodless conflict, mutually agreed that they would postpone the war with spears to an indefinite period. Meanwhile they have left off visiting. The affair will only be settled by the arrival of some Arab mercenary, who, for a consideration of five or six tusks of ivory, will undertake, with a few explosions of that mischievous compound called gunpowder, to send Mwana Buttu flying and to "beat his back with his own shield," thus avenging Riba-Riba.

Oct. 13.—On the 13th, after a march of thirteen miles in a west-south-west direction, along a very crooked path, we arrived at Kabungwé.

At this settlement we observed for the first time spears all of wood, having their points sharp and hardened in fire, and shafts 8 to 10 feet long. As each warrior possesses a sheaf of these weapons, besides a vast wooden shield, he is sufficiently armed against a native enemy, and might, by a little boldness, become a dangerous foe to an Arab.

The currency throughout Manyema consists of cowries. Six cowries formed the ration money of the Wangwana, three cowries purchased a chicken, two procured ten maize ears, one cowrie obtained the service of a native to grind the grain, two cowries were a day's hire for a porter; so that the Wangwana and Wanyamwezi were enjoying both abundance and relief from labour while we were travelling through Manyema.

At Kabungwé I was alarmed at an insufferable odour that pervaded the air we breathed, for, whether in the house or without, the atmosphere seemed loaded with an intolerable stench. On enquiring of the natives whether there was any dead animal putrefying in the neighbourhood, they pointed to the firewood that was burning, and to a tree—a species of laurel—as that which emitted the smell. Upon examination I found it was indeed due to this strange wood, which, however, only becomes offensive under the action of fire.

Between Kabungwé and Mtuyu, our next camp, the country is extremely populous. Were all the villages we passed inhabited by brave men, a brigade of European troops could not move without precaution. The people, however, did not attempt to molest us, though an enormous number came out to stare at us and our asses.

The natives are quick to adopt nicknames. In some places the Arabs were known by the name of Mwana Ngombé, "lords of cows"; in others, Wasambyé, or the "uncircumcised," because of their Wanyamwezi followers, which last name has penetrated over an immense region.

Majwara, Frank Pocock's servant, upon receiving the present of a bride from Mtesa because he was the son of Namujurilwa, the champion of Uganda, gave her the name of Tuma-leo, or "sent-to-day."

The Sarmeen of my first expedition received from his comrades, for his detective qualities, the name of Kachéché, or the "weasel."

Lukoma, who accompanied us to Muta Nzigé, called himself Mkanga, or "the one who looks behind."

Sambuzi received the title of Mta-uza, or the "spoiler"; and one of his subordinates was called Kiswaga, or "fleet-foot."

Kalulu's name was formerly Ndugu Mali, "brother of money."

Wadi Safeni had a young relative in the Expedition entitled Akili Mali, or "one who is wise with his money."

Mgongo-Tembo, or "elephant's back"; Mambu, or "noise"; Khamis, or "Thursday"; Juma, or "Friday"; Muini Kheri, or "lord of fortune"; Muini Pembé, or "lord of ivory"; and scores of others I might mention.

In the same manner countries receive appellations distinctive of peculiarities, such as—

Unya-Nyembé, land of hoes.
U-Yofu, land of elephants.
Unya-Mbewa, land of goats.
Unya-Nkondo, land of sheep.
Unya-Ngoma, land of drums.
U-Konongo, land of travellers.
Unya-Nguruwé, land of hogs.
U-Nguru, land of mountains.
U-Kusu, land of parrots.
U-Ganda, land of drums.
U-Lungu or U-Rungu, plain land.
Ma-Rungu, plateau land.
U-Kutu, land of ears (long ears?).
U-Karanga, land of ground-nuts.
U-Lua or U-Rua, land of lakes.
U-Emba, lake land.
U-Bwari, land of food.

Lakes also have names significative of native ideas, such as the Tanganika, "the great lake spreading out like a plain," or "plain-like lake"; Niyanja Muta Nzigé, or "the lake of dead locusts," from, no doubt, the swarms of locusts on the plains of Ankori, Unyoro, and Western Uganda, and the salinas of Usongora, being swept into it by strong winds; Niyanja, or Nianja Ukerewé, "the great lake around Ukerewé."

KITETÉ
THE CHIEF OF MPUNGU.

Mtuyu is the easternmost settlement of the country of Uzura. On arrival we perceived that all their women were absent, and naturally enquired what had become of them They replied, in pathetic strains, "Oh, they are all dead, all cut off, every one. It was the small-pox!"

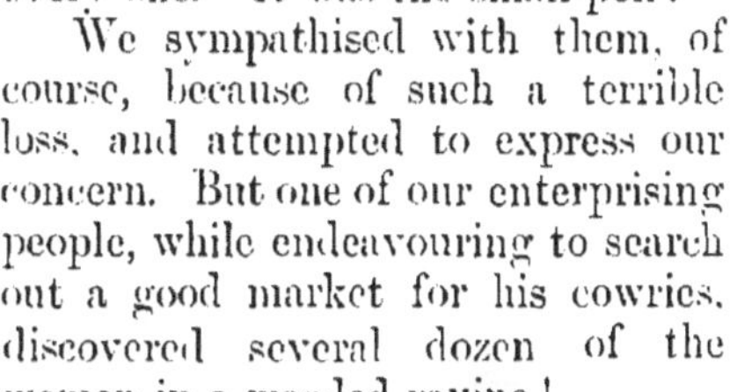

We sympathised with them, of course, because of such a terrible loss, and attempted to express our concern. But one of our enterprising people, while endeavouring to search out a good market for his cowries, discovered several dozen of the women in a wooded ravine!

Skirting the range of hills which bounds the Luama valley on the north, we marched to Mpungu, which is fifteen miles west of Mtuyu. Kiteté, its chief, is remarkable for a plaited beard twenty inches long, decorated at the tips with a number of blue glass beads. His hair was also trussed up on the crown of his head in a shapely mass. His brother possessed a beard six inches long; there were half-a-dozen others with beards of three or four inches long. Kiteté's symbol of royalty was a huge truncheon, or Hercules club, blackened and hardened by fire. His village was neat, and the architecture of the huts peculiar, as the picture at foot shows.

The Luama valley at Uzura at this season presents a waving extent of grass-grown downs, and while crossing over the higher swells of land, we enjoyed uninterrupted views of thirty or forty miles to the west and south.

From Mpungu we travelled through an interesting country (a distance of four miles), and suddenly from the crest of a low ridge saw the confluence of the Luama with the majestic Lualaba. The former appeared to have a breadth of 400 yards at the mouth; the latter was about 1400 yards wide, a broad river of a pale grey colour, winding slowly from south and by east.

We hailed its appearance with shouts of joy, and rested on the spot to enjoy the view. Across the river, beyond a tawny, grassy stretch towards the south-south-west, is Mount Kijima; about 1000 feet above the valley, to the south-south-east, across the Luama, runs the Luhye-ya ridge; from its base the plain slopes to the swift Luama. In the bed of the great river are two or three small islands, green with the verdure of trees and sedge. I likened it even here to the Mississippi, as it appears before the impetuous, full-volumed Missouri pours its rusty-brown water into it.

A secret rapture filled my soul as I gazed upon the majestic stream. The great mystery that for all these centuries Nature had kept hidden away from the world of science was waiting to be solved. For two hundred and twenty miles I had followed one of the sources of the Livingstone to the confluence, and now before me lay the superb river itself! My task was to follow it to the Ocean.

NATIVE HOUSES AT MTUYU.

CHAPTER IV.

At a swinging pace—Tippu-Tib, the Arab trader—News of Cameron and his difficulties—The river that flows north for ever—In Dwarf-land, fighting the dwarfs—Tippu-Tib's conditions—Friends in council—Heads or tails—Kalulu's accident at Nyangwé—Its residents and market—A muster of the Expedition.

Oct.—We resumed our journey. The men, women, and children joined in a grand chorus, while a stentor from Unyamwezi attempted, in a loud and graphic strain, a description of the joy he felt.

How quickly we marched! What a stride and what *verve* there was in our movements! Faster, my friends, faster! that you may boast to the Arabs at Nyangwé what veterans you are!

There was no word uttered enjoining quicker speed, but my people seemed intuitively to know my wish; even the youthful gun-bearers vied with each other in an exhibition of pedestrianism.

Over hill and dale we paced through Uzura, and about noon entered the village of Mkwanga, eight miles north-north-west of the confluence of the Luama and the Lualaba.

At Mkwanga we met two Wangwana, who informed us that the Arabs at Mwana Mamba's had just returned from an expedition into the forest of Manyema, to avenge the murder of an Arab called Mohammed bin Soud, and his caravan of ten men, by Mwana Ntpunda and his people.

The next day we crossed the Lulindi—a small river thirty-five yards wide, and fordable—and made a brilliant march of eighteen miles north-west, across a broad and uninhabited plain which separates Uzura from Mwana Mamba's district, Tubanda, where, having come by a "back door," and having travelled so quickly, we burst upon the astonished Arabs before they were aware of our approach. Contrary, moreover, to the custom of Arabs and Wangwana, I had strictly prohibited the firing of musketry to announce our arrival; considering the drum and trumpet sufficient, and less alarming.

Soon, however, the Arabs advanced—Sayid Mezrui, Mohammed bin Sayid, Muini Hassan, and others, who conducted us to the broad verandah of Mezrui's tembé until quarters could be prepared for us.

Last came the famous Hamed bin Mohammed, alias Tippu-Tib, or, as it is variously pronounced by the natives, Tipo-Tib, or Tibbu-Tib. He was a tall black-bearded man, of negroid complexion, in the prime of life, straight, and quick in his movements, a picture of energy and strength. He had a fine intelligent face, with a nervous twitching of the eyes, and gleaming white and perfectly-formed teeth. He was attended by a large retinue of young Arabs, who looked up to him as chief, and a score of Wangwana and Wanyamwezi followers whom he had led over thousands of miles through Africa.

With the air of a well-bred Arab, and almost courtier-like in his manner, he welcomed me to Mwana Mamba's village, and his slaves being ready at hand with mat and bolster, he reclined vis-à-vis, while a buzz of admiration of his style was perceptible from the on-lookers. After regarding him for a few minutes, I came to the conclusion that this Arab was a remarkable man—the most remarkable man I had met among Arabs, Wa-Swahili, and half-castes in Africa. He was neat in his person, his clothes were of a spotless white, his fez-cap brand new, his waist was encircled by a rich dowlé, his dagger was splendid with silver filigree, and his *tout ensemble* was that of an Arab gentleman in very comfortable circumstances.

The person above described was the Arab who had escorted Cameron across the Lualaba as far as Utotera, south latitude 5°, and east longitude 25° 54′. Naturally, therefore, there was no person at Nyangwé whose evidence was more valuable than Tippu-Tib's as to the direction that my predecessor at Nyangwé had taken. The information he gave me was sufficiently clear—and was, moreover, confirmed by Sayid Mezrui and other Arabs—that the greatest problem of African geography was left untouched at the exact spot where Dr. Livingstone had felt himself unable to prosecute his travels, and whence he had retraced his steps to Ujiji never to return to Nyangwé.

This was momentous and all-important news to the Expedition. We had arrived at the critical point in our travels: our destinies now awaited my final decision.

But first I was anxious to know why Cameron had declined the journey. Sayid Mezrui said it was because he could not obtain canoes, and because the natives in the Mitamba or forest were exceedingly averse to strangers. Tippu-Tib averred also that Cameron's men decidedly opposed following the river, as no one knew whither it went.

"In the same way I am told the old man Daoud Liviston" —David Livingstone—" was prevented from going. The old man tried hard to persuade the Arabs to lend him canoes, but Muini Dugumbi refused, upon the ground that he would be rushing to his death. Cameron also asked for canoes, and offered high prices for them, but Dugumbi would not be persuaded, as he declined to be held responsible by the British Consul at Zanzibar for any accident that might happen to him. Bombay, I believe, wished to go, but Bilal was resolute in his objections to the river, and each night intrigued with the Arabs to prevent his master. When Cameron reached Imbarri at Kasongo's, I offered to take him for a sum of money as far as the Sankuru river, provided he would give me a paper stating that I took him at his own request, and releasing me from all responsibility in the event of a conflict with the natives. He declined to go. I therefore, at his own request, supplied him with guides to take him to Juma Merikani, at Kasongo's, in Rua, where he would meet Portuguese traders. I have received word from Juma Merikani that Cameron, after many months' stay with him, went on his way, escorted by a large number of Portuguese traders, towards the western sea. That is all I know about it."

Out of this frank explanation, I had, therefore, elicited the information that "want of canoes and hostility of the savages," reluctance of the Arabs to permit him to proceed by the river from an officious regard for his safety, and the "cowardice of his followers," were the main causes that prevented the gallant officer from following the river.

These were difficulties for me also to surmount in some manner not yet intelligible. How was I to instil courage into my followers, or sustain it, to obtain the assistance of the Arabs to enable me to make a fair beginning, and afterwards to purchase or make canoes?

"I suppose, Tippu-Tib," I said, "having offered the other

white man your assistance, you would have no objections to offer it to me for the same sum?"

"I don't know about that," he replied, with a smile. "I have not many people with me now. Many are at Imbarri, others are trading in Manyema."

"How many men have you with you?"

"Perhaps three hundred—or say two hundred and fifty."

"That number would be a grand escort, amply sufficient, if well managed, to ensure perfect protection."

"Yes, united with your party, it would be a very strong force, but how would it be when I returned alone? The natives would say, seeing only my own little force, 'These people have been fighting—half of them are killed, because they have no ivory with them; let us finish them!' I know, my friend, these savages very well, and I tell you that that would be their way of thinking."

"But, my friend," said I, "think how it would be with me, with all the continent before me, and only protected by my little band!"

"Ah, yes! if you Wasungu" (white men) "are desirous of throwing away your lives, it is no reason we Arabs should. We travel little by little to get ivory and slaves, and are years about it—it is now nine years since I left Zanzibar—but you white men only look for rivers and lakes and mountains, and you spend your lives for no reason, and to no purpose. Look at that old man who died in Bisa! What did he seek year after year, until he became so old that he could not travel? He had no money, for he never gave any of us anything, he bought no ivory or slaves, yet he travelled farther than any of us, and for what?"

"I know I have no right to expect you to risk your life for me. I only wish you to accompany me sixty days' journey, then leave me to myself. If sixty days' journey is too far, half that distance will do; all I am anxious for is my people. You know the Wangwana are easily swayed by fear, but if they hear that Tippu-Tib has joined me, and is about to accompany me, every man will have a lion's courage."

"Well, I will think of it to-night, and hold a shauri with my relatives and principal people, and to-morrow night we will have another talk."

The next evening, at about eight o'clock, Hamed bin Mohammed, or Tippu-Tib, appeared with his cousin,

Mohammed bin Sayid, and others, to confer upon the important business broached the evening before, and, after the usual courteous and ceremonious greetings, I was requested to state my intentions.

"I would like to go down the river in canoes until I reach the place where the river turns for good either to the west or east."

"How many days' journey on land would that be?" asked Tippu-Tib.

"I don't know. Do you?"

"No; indeed, I was never in that direction; but I have a man here who has reached farthest of all."

"Where is he?"

"Speak, Abed, son of Jumah, what you know of this river," said Tippu-Tib.

The son of Jumah, thus urged by his superior, spoke and said, "Yes, I know all about the river, El hamd ul illah!" ("the thanks be to God").

"In which direction does it flow, my friend?"

"It flows north."

"And then?"

"It flows north."

"And then?"

"Still north!"

"Come, my friend, speak; whither does it flow after reaching the north?"

"Why, master," replied he, with a bland smile of wonder at my apparent lack of ready comprehension, "don't I tell you it flows north, and north, and north, and there is no end to it? I think it reaches the salt sea, at least some of my friends say so."

"Well, in which direction is this salt sea?"

"Allah yallim!" ("God knows!")

"I thought you said you knew all about the river?"

"I know it goes north!" said he decisively, and sharply.

"How do you know?"

"Because I followed Mtagamoyo to Usongora Meno, and, crossing the Ugarowa,* near the Urindi, went with him to the Lumami and to the dwarf country."

"How many days is it from here to the dwarf country?"

* The Ugarowa river is the Arab corruption of the word Lu-alowa, which Livingstone called Lualaba.

"About nine months."

"And is the dwarf country near the Ugarowa?"

"It is not far from it."

"Could you point with your hand the direction of the Ugarowa—near the dwarf country?"

"Yes, it is there," pointing north by west, magnetic.

"What are the dwarfs like?—but tell us the story of your journey with Mtagamoyo."

After clearing his throat and arranging his cleanly white dress, he gave me the account of his wanderings to the unknown lands north, as follows:—

"Mtagamoyo is a man who knows not what fear is—Wallahi! He is as bold as a lion. When he gave out to the Arabs and Wangwana of Nyangwé that he was about to proceed as far as possible to hunt up ivory, of course we all felt that if any man could guide us to new ivory fields it was Mtagamoyo. Many of the youngest Arabs prepared themselves to follow him, and all of us mustering our armed slaves, followed in his track.

"We first reached Uregga, a forest land, where there is nothing but woods, and woods, and woods, for days, and weeks, and months. There was no end to the woods. The people lived surrounded by woods. Strangers were few before they saw us, and we had shauri after shauri with them. We passed along easily for a few days, and then came trouble; we struck for the Ugarowa, and in about a month we reached Usongora Meno, where we fought day after day. They are fearful fellows and desperate. We lost men every day. Every man of ours that was killed was eaten. They were hiding behind such thick bushes that we could not see them, and their arrows were poisoned.

"Then the Arabs held another shauri. Some were for returning, for they had lost many men, but Mtagamoyo would not listen. He said that the pagans should not drive him away.

"Well, the end of the shauri was that we crossed the Ugarowa, and went to Ukusu. Wallahi! the Wakusu were worse than those of Usongora Meno, but Mtagamoyo heard of a country called Unkengeri, where the natives were said to be better. We pushed on, and arrived at Kima-Kima's. When we reached Kima-Kima's, we possessed 290 guns; we had lost twenty guns and any number of slaves on the road.

"Kima-Kima, who is on the Lumami, told us about the land of the little men, where the ivory was so abundant that we might get a tusk for a single cowrie. You know, master, that when we Arabs hear of ivory being abundant there is no holding us back. Oh! we started instantly, crossed the Lumami, and came to the land of the Wakuna. Among the Wakuna, who are big men themselves, we saw some six or seven of the dwarfs; the queerest-looking creatures alive, just a yard high, with long beards and large heads.

"The dwarfs asked us a lot of questions, where we came from, where we were going, and what we wanted. They seemed to be plucky little devils, though we laughed to see them. They told us that in their country was so much ivory that we had not enough men to carry it, but they were very curious to know what we wanted with it. Did we eat it? 'No.' 'What then?' 'We sell it to other men who make charms of it.' 'Oh! What will you give us if we show the ivory to you?' 'We will give you cowries and beads.' 'Good, come along.'

"We travelled six days, and then we came to the border village of their country. They would not allow us to penetrate farther until they had seen their king and obtained his consent. In the meantime they said we might trade round about. We did trade. We purchased in two days more ivory than the other countries could have supplied us with in two weeks.

"On the third day the little people came back and told us we might go and live in the king's village. It was a mere long street, you know, with houses, extending a long distance on either side. They gave us a portion of the village to live in. The king was kind, at least he appeared so the first day; the next day he was not so kind, but he sold us ivory in plenty. There was no lack of that. The dwarfs came from all parts. Oh! it is a big country! and everybody brought ivory, until we had about four hundred tusks, big and little, as much as we could carry. We had bought it with copper, beads, and cowries. No cloths, for the dwarfs were all naked, king and all.

"They told us that eleven days' journey south-west was another country, where there was even more ivory than they had, and four days beyond that again was a great lake, where there were ships. The lake was near the country of a king whom they called Ngombé.

"We did not starve in the dwarf land the first ten days. Bananas as long as my arm, and plantains as long as the dwarfs were tall. One plantain was sufficient for a man for one day.

"We thought, seeing that we had obtained as much ivory as we were able to carry, that we had better return. We told the king that we wanted to depart. To our surprise, the king—he was no longer than my leg—said that we should not be allowed to go. 'Why?' we asked. 'Because this is my country, and you are not to go away until I say.' 'But we have finished our business, and we have had trade sufficient; we don't wish to buy any more.' 'You must buy all I have got; I want more cowries;' and he ground his teeth, and he looked just like a wild monkey.

"Mtagamoyo laughed at him, for he was very funny, and then told him that we would have to go away, because we had many friends waiting for us. He said, 'You shall not go from my country.'

"We held another shauri, when it was agreed that if we stayed longer we might get into trouble and lose our ivory, and that it was better to leave within two days. But we did not have to wait two days for the trouble! It came even before we had finished our shauri. We heard a woman scream loud. We rushed out, and met some Wangwana running towards us, and among them a woman with a dwarf's arrow in her breast.

"'What's this, what's this?' we asked, and they cried out, 'The dwarfs shot this woman while she was drawing water, and they are coming in immense numbers towards us from all the other villages. It's a war, prepare yourselves!'

"We were not a bit too soon: we had scarcely put on our belts and seized our guns before the vicious wretches were upon us, and shooting their reed arrows in clouds. They screamed and yelled just like monkeys. Many of our people fell dead instantly from the poison before we could get together and fire on them. Mtagamoyo! he was everywhere brandishing his two-handed sword, and cleaving them as you would cleave a banana. The arrows passed through his shirt in many places. There were many good fellows like Mtagamoyo there, and they fought well; but it was of no use. The dwarfs were firing from the top of the trees; they crept through the tall grass close up to us, and shot their arrows in our faces. Then Mtagamoyo, seeing it was getting hot work, shouted 'Boma! Boma! Boma!' (palisade), and some hundreds of us cut down banana-trees, tore doors out, and houses down, and formed a boma at each end of the street, and then we were a little better off, for it was not such rapid, random shooting; we fired more deliberately, and after several hours drove them off.

"Do you think they gave us peace? Not a bit; a fresh party came up and continued the fight. They were such small things, we could not see them very well; had they been tall men like us, we might have picked off hundreds of them. We could not fight all the time, for some of us had to sleep, so Mtagamoyo divided us into two parties, one party to go to sleep, the other to watch the boma. All night we heard the reed arrows flying past, or pattering on the roofs or the boma fence; all night we heard their yells. Once or twice they tried to storm the boma, but we had twenty muskets at each end.

"Well, the fight lasted all that night, and all the next day, and throughout the next night. And we could get no water, until Mtagamoyo called out a hundred fellows, fifty with muskets and fifty with big water-pots, to follow him. Mtagamoyo was a lion; he held up a shield before him, and looking around he just ran straight where the crowd was thickest; and he seized two of the dwarfs, and we who followed him caught several more, for they would not run away until they saw what our design was, and then they left the water clear. We filled our pots, and carried the little Shaitans (devils) into the boma; and there we found we had caught the king!

"We all argued that we should kill him, but Mtagamoyo would not consent. 'Kill the others,' he said, and we cut all their heads off instantly and tossed them outside. But the king was not touched.

"Then the dwarfs stopped fighting; they came to us, and cried 'Sennené! Sennené!' ('Peace, peace'). We made peace with them; and they said that if we gave them their king we might go away unmolested. After a long shauri we gave him up. But the war was worse than ever. Thousands came towards us, and every man was as busy as he could be shooting them. We fought all that day and night, and then we saw that the powder would not last; we had only two kegs left.

"So our chiefs then mustered us all together, and told us

all that the only way was to rush out of the boma again and catch them and kill them with our swords in the way that Mtagamoyo had fought.

"After making everything ready we rushed out, and every man, bending his head, made straight for them. It was a race! When they saw us coming out with our broad long swords, bright as glass, they ran away; but we followed them like wolves for a couple of hours. Ah, we killed many, very many, for they could not run as fast as we could.

"We then returned, packed up quickly, took up one half of our ivory, and started for the forest. We travelled until night, and then, quite tired out, we slept. Master, in the middle of the night they were again on us! Arrows sounded 'twit,' 'twit' in all directions; some one was falling down every minute. Our powder was fast going. At last we ran away, throwing down everything except our guns and swords. Now and then we could hear Mtagamoyo's horn, and we followed it. But nearly all were so weakened by hunger and want of water that they burst their hearts running, and died. Others lying down to rest found the little devils close to them when too late, and were killed. Master, out of that great number of people that left Nyangwé, Arabs, Wangwana, and our slaves, only thirty returned alive, and I am one of them."

"What is your name, my friend?" I demanded.

"Bwana Abedi," he replied.

"And you follow Tippu-Tib now, do you, or Mtagamoyo?"

"I follow Tippu-Tib," he answered.

"Ah! good. Did you see anything else very wonderful on your journey?"

"Oh yes! There are monstrous large boa-constrictors in the forest of Uregga, suspended by their tails to the branches, waiting for the passer-by or a stray antelope. The ants in that forest are not to be despised. You cannot travel without your body being covered with them, when they sting you like wasps. The leopards are so numerous that you cannot go very far without seeing one. Almost every native wears a leopard-skin cap. The Sokos (gorillas) are in the woods, and woe befall the man or woman met alone by them; for they run up to you and seize your hands, and bite the fingers off one by one, and as fast as they bite one off, they spit it out. The Wasongora Meno and Waregga are cannibals, and unless the force is very strong, they never let strangers pass. It is nothing but constant fighting. Only two years ago a party armed with three hundred guns started north of Usongora Meno; they only brought sixty guns back, and no ivory. If one tries to go by the river, there are falls after falls, which carry the people over and drown them. A party of thirty men, in three canoes, went down the river half a day's journey from Nyangwé, when the old white man was living there. They were all drowned, and that was the reason he did not go on. Had he done so, he would have been eaten, for what could he have done? Ah, no. Master, the country is bad, and the Arabs have given it up beyond Uregga. They will not try the journey into that country again, after trying it three times and losing nearly five hundred men altogether."

"Your story is very interesting, Abedi," said I; "some of it, I think, is true, for the old white man said the same thing to me when I was at Ujiji some four years ago. However, I want to hear Tippu-Tib speak."

During all the time that Abedi had related his wonderful experiences, the other Arabs had been listening, profoundly interested; but when I turned inquiringly to Tippu-Tib, he motioned all to leave the room, except his cousin Mohammed bin Sayid.

When we were alone, Tippu-Tib informed me that he had been consulting with his friends and relatives, and that they were opposed to his adventuring upon such a terrible journey; but that, as he did not wish to see me disappointed in my prospects, he had resolved to accompany me a distance of sixty camps, each camp to be four hours' march from the other, for the sum of 5000 dollars, on the following conditions:—

1. That the journey should commence from Nyangwé in any direction I choose, and on any day I mentioned.

2. That the journey should not occupy more time than three months from the first day it was commenced.

3. That the rate of travel should be two marches to one halt.

4. That if he accompanied me sixty marches—each march of four hours' duration—I should at the end of that distance return with him back again to Nyangwé, for mutual protection and support, unless we met traders from the west coast, whom I might accompany to the western sea, provided I

permitted two-thirds of my force to return with him to Nyangwé.

5. That, exclusive of the 5000 dollars, I should provision 140 men during their absence from Mwana Mamba—going and returning.

6. That if, after experience of the countries and the natives, I found it was impracticable to continue the journey, and decided upon returning before the sixty marches were completed, I should not hold him responsible, but pay him the sum of 5000 dollars without any deduction.

These terms I thought reasonable—all except article 4; but though I endeavoured to modify the article, in order to ensure full liberty to continue the journey alone if I thought fit, Tippu-Tib said he would not undertake the journey alone, from a distance of sixty camps to Mwana Mamba, even though 50,000 dollars were promised him, because he was assured he would never return to enjoy the money. He would much prefer continuing with me down to the sea, for a couple of thousand dollars more, to returning alone with his 140 men for 50,000 dollars. He agreed, however, after a little remonstrance, to permit the addition of article 7, which was to the effect that if he, Tippu-Tib, abandoned the journey through faint-heartedness, before the full complement of the marches had been completed, he was to forfeit the whole sum of 5000 dollars, and the return escort.

"There is no hurry about it," said I. "You may change your mind, and I may change mine. We will both take twenty-four hours to consider it. To-morrow night the agreement shall be drawn up ready for our seals, or else you will be told that I am unable to agree to your conditions."

The truth was that I had opened negotiations without having consulted my people; and as our conversation had been private, it remained for me to ascertain the opinion of Frank, before my next encounter with Tippu-Tib.

At 6 P.M., a couple of saucers, filled with palm-oil and fixed with cotton-wick, were lit. It was my after-dinner hour, the time for pipes and coffee, which Frank was always invited to share.

When he came in, the coffee-pot was boiling, and little Mabruki was in waiting to pour out. The tobacco-pouch, filled with the choicest production of Africa, that of Masansi near Uvira, was ready. Mabruki poured out the coffee, and retired, leaving us together.

"Now Frank, my son," I said, "sit down. I am about to have a long and serious chat with you. Life and death—yours as well as mine, and those of all the Expedition--hang on the decision I make to-night."

And then I reminded him of his friends at home, and also of the dangers before him; of the sorrow his death would cause, and also of the honours that would greet his success; of the facility of returning to Zanzibar, and also of the perilous obstacles in the way of advance—thus carefully alternating the *pro* with the *con.*, so as not to betray my own inclinations. I reminded him of the hideous scenes we had already been compelled to witness and to act in, pointing out that other wicked tribes, no doubt, lay before us; but also recalling to his memory how treachery, cunning, and savage courage had been baulked by patience and promptitude; and how we still possessed the power to punish those who threatened us or murdered our friends. And I ended with words something like these:—

"There is no doubt some truth in what the Arabs say about the ferocity of these natives before us. Livingstone, after fifteen thousand miles of travel, and a lifetime of experience among Africans, would not have yielded the brave struggle without strong reasons; Cameron, with his forty-five Snider rifles, would never have turned away from such a brilliant field if he had not sincerely thought that they were insufficient to resist the persistent attacks of countless thousands of wild men. But while we grant that there may be a modicum of truth in what the Arabs say, it is in their ignorant superstitious nature to exaggerate what they have seen. A score of times have we proved them wrong. Yet their reports have already made a strong impression on the minds of the Wangwana and Wanyamwezi. They are already trembling with fear, because they suspect that I am about to attempt the cannibal lands beyond Nyangwé. On the day that we propose to begin our journey, we shall have no Expedition.

"On the other hand, I am confident that, if I am able to leave Nyangwé with the Expedition intact, and to place a breadth of wild country between our party and the Arab depot, I shall be able to make men of them. There are good stuff, heroic qualities, in them; but we must get free from the Arabs, or they will be very soon demoralized. It is for this purpose I am negotiating with Tippu-Tib. If I can arrange with him and leave Nyangwé without the dreadful loss we experienced at Ujiji, I feel sure that I can inspire my men to dare anything with me.

"The difficulty of transport, again, is enormous. We cannot obtain canoes at Nyangwé. Livingstone could not. Cameron failed. No doubt I shall fail. I shall not try to obtain any. But we might buy up all the axes that we can see between here and Nyangwé, and travelling overland on this side the Lualaba, we might, before Tippu-Tib's contract is at an end, come across a tribe which would sell their canoes. We have sufficient stores to last a long time, and I shall purchase more at Nyangwé. If the natives will not sell, we can make our own canoes, if we possess a sufficient number of axes to set all hands at work.

"Now, what I wish you to tell me, Frank, is your opinion as to what we ought to do."

Frank's answer was ready.

"I say, 'Go on, sir.'"

"Think well, my dear fellow; don't be hasty, life and death hang on our decision. Don't you think we could explore to the east of Cameron's road?"

"But there is nothing like this great river, sir."

"What do you say to Lake Lincoln, Lake Kamolondo, Lake Bemba, and all that part, down to the Zambezi?"

"Ah! that is a fine field, sir, and perhaps the natives would not be so ferocious. Would they?"

"Yet, as you said just now, it would be nothing to the great river, which for all these thousands of years has been flowing steadily to the north through hundreds, perhaps thousands, of miles, of which no one has ever heard a word!"

"Let us follow the river, sir."

"Yet, my friend, think yet again. Look at all these faithful fellows whose lives depend on our word; think of our own, for we are yet young, and strong, and active. Why should we throw them away for a barren honour, or if we succeed, have every word we said doubted, and carped at, and our motives misconstrued by malicious minds, who distort everything to our injury?"

"Ah, true, sir. I was one of those who doubted that you had ever found Livingstone. I don't mind telling you now. Until I came to Zanzibar, and saw your people, I did not believe it, and there are hundreds in Rochester who shared my opinion."

"And do you believe, Frank, that you are in Manyema now?"

"I am obliged to, sir."

"Are you not afraid, should you return to England, that when men say you have never been to Africa, as no doubt they will, you will come to disbelieve it yourself?"

"Ah no, sir," he replied. "I can never forget Ituru; the death of my brother in that wild land; the deaths of so many Wangwana there; the great Lake; Uganda; our march to Muta Nzigé; Rumanika; my life in Ujiji; the Tanganika; and our march here."

"But what do you think, Frank? Had we not better explore north-east of here, until we reach Muta Nzigé, circumnavigate that lake, and strike across to Uganda again, and return to Zanzibar by way of Kagehyi?"

"That would be a fine job, sir, if we could do it."

"Yet, if you think of it, Frank, this great river which Livingstone first saw, and which broke his heart almost to turn away from and leave a mystery, is a noble field too. Fancy, by-and-by, after buying or building canoes, our floating down the river day by day, either to the Nile or to some vast lake in the far north, or to the Congo and the Atlantic Ocean! Think what a benefit our journey will be to Africa. Steamers from the mouth of the Congo to Lake Bemba, and to all the great rivers which run into it!"

"I say, sir, let us toss up; best two out of three to decide it."

"Toss away. Here is a rupee."

"Heads for the north and the Lualaba; tails for the south and Katanga."

Frank stood up, his face beaming. He tossed the rupee high up. The coin dropped.

"What is it?" I asked.

"Tails, sir!" said Frank, with a face expressive of strong disapproval.

"Toss again."

He tossed again, and "tails" was again announced—and six times running "tails" won.

We then tried straws—the short straws for the south, the long straws for the river Lualaba—and again we were disappointed, for Frank persisted in drawing out the short straws, and in leaving the long straws in my hands.

"It is of no use, Frank. We'll face our destiny, despite

the rupee and straws. With your help, my dear fellow, I will follow the river."

"Mr. Stanley, have no fear of me. I shall stand by you. The last words of my dear old father were, 'Stick by your master.' And there is my hand, sir, you shall never have cause to doubt me."

"Good, I shall go on then. I will finish this contract with Tippu-Tib, for the Wangwana, on seeing him accompany us, will perhaps be willing to follow me. We may also recruit others at Nyangwé. And then, if the natives will

"HEADS FOR THE NORTH AND THE LUALABA; TAILS FOR THE SOUTH AND KATANGA."

allow peaceful passage through their countries, so much the better. If not, our duty says, 'Go on.'"

The next night Tippu-Tib and his friends visited me again. The contract was written, and signed by the respective parties and their witnesses. The Wangwana chiefs were then called, and it was announced to them that Tippu-Tib, with 140 guns and seventy Wanyamwezi spearmen, would escort us a distance of sixty camps, when, if we found the countries hostile to us, and no hopes of meeting other traders, we should return with him to Nyangwé. If we met Portuguese or Turkish traders, a portion of us would continue the journey with them, and the remainder would return with

Tippu-Tib to Nyangwé. This announcement was received with satisfaction, and the chiefs said that, owing to Tippu-Tib's presence, no Arab at Nyangwé would dare to harbour a runaway from the Expedition.

Cowries and beads were then counted out and given that evening to Tippu-Tib, as ration money for ten days from the day of his departure from Mwana Mamba.

Oct. 24.—The next morning, being the 24th of October, the Expedition left Mwana Mamba in high spirits. The good effect of the contract with Tippu-Tib had already brought us recruits, for on the road I observed several strange faces of men who, on our arrival at the first camp, Marimbu, eleven miles north-west from Mwana Mamba, appeared before my tent, and craved to be permitted to follow us. They received an advance in cloth, and their names were entered on the muster-list of the Expedition at the same rate of pay as the other Wanyamwezi and Wangwana.

Oct. 25.—Through a fine rolling country, but depopulated, with every mile marked by ruined villages, we marched in a north-westerly direction, thirteen miles to Benangongo, from Marimbu, and, on the 25th, arrived at Kankumba, after a journey of twelve miles, crossing the Mshama stream by the way.

From our camp at Kankumba we were pointed out Nyangwé, and, as it was only five miles distant, some of the people pretended to be able to see it. About one mile from us was the marshy valley of the Kunda river, another tributary of the Lualaba, which rises in Uzimba; to the east-north-east of us, about eight miles off, rose some hilly cones, spurs of the Manyema hills; on the west stretched a rolling grassy land extending to the Lualaba.

The grass (genus *Panicum*) of Manyema is like other things in this prolific land, of gigantic proportions, and denser than the richest field of corn. The stalks are an inch in diameter, and about 8 feet high. In fact, what I have called "grassy land" is more like a waving country planted with young bamboo.

Young Kalulu, who, since his recapture at the Uguha port on Lake Tanganika, had been well behaved, and was in high favour again, met with a serious and very remarkable accident at Kankumba. A chief, called Mabruki the elder, had retained a cartridge in his Snider, contrary to orders.

and, leaving it carelessly on the stacked goods, a hurrying Mgwana kicked it down with his foot, which caused it to explode. Kalulu, who was reclining on his mat near a fire, was wounded in no fewer than *eight* places, the bullet passing through the outer part of his lower leg, the upper part of his thigh, and, glancing over his right ribs, through the muscles of his left arm. Though the accident had caused severe wounds, there was no danger; and, by applying a little arnica, lint, and bandages, we soon restored him to a hopeful view of his case.

Oct. 27.—On the morning of the 27th we descended from our camp at Kankumba to the banks of the Kunda, a river about 40 yards wide, and 10 feet deep at the ferry. The canoe-men were Wagenya or Wenya fishermen under the protection of Sheikh Abed bin Salim, alias "Tanganika."

A rapid march of four miles brought us to the outskirts of Nyangwé, where we were met by Abed bin Salim, an old

A CANOE OF THE WENYA OR WAGENYA FISHERMEN.

man of sixty-five years of age, Mohammed bin Sayid, a young Arab with a remarkably long nose and small eyes, Sheikh Abed's fundis or elephant hunters, and several Wangwana, all dressed in spotless white shirts, crimson fezzes, and sandals.

Sheikh Abed was pleased to monopolize me, by offering me a house in his neighbourhood.

The manner that we entered Nyangwé appeared, from subsequent conversation, to have struck Sheikh Abed, who, from his long residence there, had witnessed the arrival and departure of very many caravans. There was none of the usual firing of guns and wild shouting and frenzied action; and the order and steadiness of veterans, the close files of a column which tolerably well understood by this time the difference between discipline and lawlessness with its stragglers and slovenly laggards, made a marked impression upon the old Arab. Ever since the murder of Kaif Halleck in Ituru, our sick had never been permitted to crawl to camp unaided and unprotected. The asses, four in number, and supernumeraries were always at hand to convey those unable to travel, while those only slightly indisposed were formed into a separate company under Frank and six chiefs.

Another thing that surprised the Arab was the rapidity of the journey from the Tanganika—338 miles in forty-three days, inclusive of all halts. He said that the usual period occupied by Arabs was between three and four months. Yet the members of the Expedition were in admirable condition. They had never enjoyed better health, and we had not one sick person; the only one incapacitated from work was Kalulu, and he had been accidentally wounded only the very night before. Between the Tanganika and the Arab depot of Nyangwé neither Frank nor I had suffered the slightest indisposition.

Nyangwé is the extreme westernmost locality inhabited by the Arab traders from Zanzibar. It stands in east longitude 26° 16′, south latitude 4° 15′, on the right or eastern side of the Lualaba, on the verge of a high and reddish bank rising some forty feet above the river, with clear open country north along the river for a distance of three miles, east some ten miles, south over seventy miles, or as far as the confluence of the Luama with the Lualaba. The town called Nyangwé is divided into two sections. The northern section has for its centre the quarters of Muini Dugumbi, the first Arab arrival here (in 1868); and around his house are the commodious quarters of his friends, their families and slaves—in all, perhaps, 300 houses. The southern section is separated from its neighbour by a broad hollow, cultivated and sown with rice for the Arabs. When the Lualaba rises to its full amplitude, this hollow is flooded. The chief house of the southern half of Nyangwé is the large and well-built clay *banda* of Sheikh Abed bin Salim. In close neighbourhood to this are the houses and huts of those Arab Wagwana who prefer the company of Abed bin Salim to Muini Dugumbi. Abed showed me his spacious court-yard, wherein he jealously guards his harem of thirty fine, comely, large-eyed women. He possesses two English hens which came from India, and several chickens of mixed breed, two dozen tame pigeons, and some guinea-fowls: in his store-room were about sixty or seventy tusks, large and small.

Between the two foreign chiefs of Nyangwé there is

great jealousy. Each endeavours to be recognized by the natives as being the most powerful. Dugumbi is an east coast trader of Sa'adani, a half-caste, a vulgar, coarse-minded old man of probably seventy years of age, with a negroid nose and a negroid mind. Sheikh Abed is a tall, thin old man, white-bearded, patriarchal in aspect, narrow-minded, rather peevish and quick to take offence, a thorough believer in witchcraft, and a fervid Muslim.

Close to Abed's elbows of late years has been the long-nosed young Arab Mohammed bin Sayid: superstitious beyond measure, of enormous cunning and subtlety, a pertinacious beggar, of keen trading instincts, but in all matters outside trade as simple as a child. He offered, for a consideration and on condition that I would read the Arabic Koran, to take me up and convey me to any part of Africa within a day. By such unblushing falsehoods he has acquired considerable influence over the mind of Sheik Abed. The latter told me that he was half afraid of him, and that he believed Mohammed was an extraordinary man. I asked the silly old Sheik if he had lent him any ivory. No; but he was constantly being asked for the loan of ten Frasilah (350 lbs.) of ivory, for which he was promised fifteen Frasilah, or 525 lbs., within six months.

Mohammed, during the very first day of my arrival, sent one of his favourite slaves to ask first for a little writing-paper, then for needles and thread, and, a couple of hours afterwards, for white pepper and a bar of soap; in the evening, for a pound or two of sugar and a little tea, and, if I could spare it, he would be much obliged for some coffee. The next day petitions, each very prettily worded—for Mohammed is an accomplished reader of the Koran—came, first for medicine, then for a couple of yards of red cloth, then for a few yards of fine white sheeting, &c. I became quite interested in him—for was he not a lovable, genial character, as he sate there chewing betel-nut and tobacco to excess, twinkling his little eyes with such malicious humour in them that, while talking with him, I could not withdraw mine from watching their quick flashes of cunning, and surveying the long, thin nose with its impenetrable mystery and classic lines? I fear Mohammed did not love me, but my admiration was excessive for Mohammed.

"La il Allah—il Allah!" he was heard to say to Sheik Abed, "that old white man Daoud never gave much to any man; this white man gives *nothing*." Certainly not, Mohammed. My admiration is great for thee, my friend; but thou liest so that I am disgusted with thee, and thou hast such a sweet, plausible, villainous look in thy face, I could punch thee heartily.

Oct. 28.—The next morning Muini (Lord) Dugumbi and following came—a gang of veritable freebooters, chiefest of whom was the famous Mtagamoyo—the butcher of women and fusillader of children. Tippu-Tib, when I asked him a few weeks after what he thought of Mtagamoyo, turned up his nose and said, "He is brave, no doubt, but he is a man whose heart is as big as the end of my little finger. He has no feeling, he kills a native as though he were a serpent—it matters not of what sex."

This man is about forty-four years of age, of middle stature and swarthy complexion, with a broad face, black beard just greying, and thin-lipped. He spoke but little, and that little courteously. He did not appear very formidable, but he might be deadly nevertheless. The Arabs of Nyangwé regard him as their best fighter.

Dugumbi the patriarch, or, as he is called by the natives, Molemba-Lemba, had the rollicking look of a prosperous and coarse-minded old man, who was perfectly satisfied with the material aspect of his condition. He deals in humour of the coarsest kind—a vain, frivolous old fellow, ignorant of everything but the art of collecting ivory; who has contrived to attach to himself a host of nameless half-castes of inordinate pride, savage spirit, and immeasurable greed.

The Arabs of Nyangwé, when they first heard of the arrival of Tippu-Tib at Imbarri from the south, were anxious to count him as their fellow-settler; but Tippu-Tib had no ambition to become the chief citizen of a place which could boast of no better settlers than vain old Dugumbi, the butcher Mtagamoyo, and silly Sheik Abed; he therefore proceeded to Mwana Mamba's, where he found better society with Mohammed bin Sayid, Sayid bin Sultan, Msé Ani, and Sayid bin Mohammed el Mezrui. Sayid bin Sultan, in features, is a rough copy of Abdul Aziz, late Sultan of Turkey.

One of the principal institutions at Nyangwé is the Kituka, or the market, with the first of which I made acquaintance in 1871, in Ujiji and Urundi. One day it is held in the open plaza in front of Sheik Abed's house; on the next day in Dugumbi's section, half a mile from the other; and on the third at the confluence of the Kunda and the Lualaba; and so on in turn.

In this market everything becomes vendible and purchasable, from an ordinary earthenware pot to a fine handsome girl from Samba, Marera, or Ukusu. From one thousand to three thousand natives of both sexes and of all ages gather here from across the Lualaba and from the Kunda banks, from the islands up the river and from the villages of the Mitamba or forest. Nearly all are clad in the fabrics of Manyema, fine grass cloths, which are beautifully coloured and very durable. The articles sold here for cowries, beads, copper and iron wire, and lambas, or squares of palm cloth,* represent the productions of Manyema. I went round the market and made out the following list:—

Sweet potatoes.
Yams.
Maize.
Sesamum.
Millet.
Beans.
Cucumbers.
Melons.
Cassava.
Ground-nuts.
Bananas.
Sugar-cane.
Pepper (in berries).
Vegetables for broths.
Wild fruit.
Palm-butter.
Oil-palm nuts.
Pine-apples.
Honey.
Eggs.
Fowls.
Black pigs.
Goats.
Sheep.
Parrots.
Palm-wine (Malofu).
Pombé (beer).
Mussels and oysters from the river.
Fresh fish.
Dried fish.
Whitebait.
Snails (dried).
Salt.
White ants.
Grasshoppers.
Tobacco (dried leaf).
Pipes.
Fishing-nets.
Basket-work.
Cassava bread.
Cassava flour.
Copper bracelets.
Iron wire.
Iron knobs.
Hoes.
Spears.
Bows and arrows.
Hatchets.
Rattan-cane staves.
Stools.
Crockery.
Powdered camwood.
Grass cloths.
Grass mats.
Fuel.
Ivory.
Slaves.

From this it will be perceived that the wants of Nyangwé are very tolerably supplied. And how like any other market-place it was! with its noise and murmur of human voices. The same rivalry in extolling their wares, the eager quick action, the emphatic gesture, the inquisitive look, the facial expressions of scorn and triumph, anxiety, joy, plausibility, were all there. I discovered, too, the surprising fact that the aborigines of Manyema possess just the same inordinate

* Made from the fibre of the *Raphia vinifera* palm.

ideas in respect to their wares as London, Paris, and New York shopkeepers. Perhaps the Manyema people are not so voluble, but they compensate for lack of language by gesture and action, which are unspeakably eloquent.

During this month of the year the Lualaba reached its lowest level. Our boat, the *Lady Alice*, after almost being re-built, was launched in the river, and with sounding-line and sextant on board, my crew and I, eager to test the boat on the grey-brown waters of the Great River, pushed off at 11 A.M. and rowed for an island opposite, 800 yards distant, taking soundings as we went.

The following are the figures, noted down after each trial with the lead, beginning thirty yards from shore, and ending at the low brush-covered island opposite Nyangwé :—

18	23	24	15
19	24	24½	15
18	25	22	15½
18½	24½	23	14
20	25	22	13
20½	26	21	12
19	27	19	9
21	27½	17	9½
		16	8

—the total of which gives a mean of 18 feet 9 inches.

The easternmost island in mid-river is about 100 yards across at its widest part, and between it and another island is a distance of from 250 to 300 yards. From the second island to the low shore opposite Nyangwé is about 250 yards, and these channels have a slightly swifter flow than the main river. The mean depth of the central channel was 12½ feet, the westernmost 11 feet, and the entire width of clear water flow was about 1300 yards. During the months of April, May, and June, and the early part of July, the Lualaba is full, and overspreads the low lands westward for nearly a mile and a half. The Lualaba then may be said to be from four thousand to five thousand yards wide opposite Nyangwé.

The Arabs, wherever they settle throughout Africa, endeavour to introduce the seeds of the vegetables and fruit-trees which grow in their beloved island of Zanzibar. At Unyanyembé, therefore, they have planted papaws, sweet limes, mangoes, lemons, custard-apples, pomegranates, and have sown wheat and rice in abundance. At Ujiji also they have papaws, sweet limes, pomegranates, lemons, wheat, rice, and onions. At Nyangwé, their fruit consists of pine-apples, papaws, and pomegranates. They have succeeded admirably in their rice, both at Nyangwé, Kasongo's, and Mwana Mamba's. Onions are a failure, the Arabs say, because of a species of worm which destroys them. The banana (*Musa paradisaica*) and plantain (*Musa sapientum*) are indigenous.

The Wagenya, as the Arabs call them, or Wenya—pronounced Wainya—as they style themselves, are a remarkable tribe of fishers, who inhabit both banks of the Lualaba, from the confluence of the Kamalondo on the left bank down to the sixth cataract of the Stanley Falls, and on the right bank from the confluence of the Luama down to Ubwiré or Usongora Meno.

The Wenya were the aborigines of Nyangwé, when the advanced party of Muini Dugumbi appeared on the scene, precursors of ruin, terror, and depopulation to the inhabitants of 700 square miles of Manyema. Considering that the fertile open tract of country between the Luama and Nyangwé was exceedingly populous, as the ruins of scores of villages testify, sixty inhabitants to the square mile would not be too great a proportion. The river border, then, of Manyema, from the Luama to Nyangwé, may be said to have had a population of 42,000 souls, of which there remain probably only 20,000. The others have been deported, or massacred, or have fled to the islands or emigrated down the river.

The Arabs and Wangwana have murdered also the word Lualaba, or Lualowa. They have given us instead Ugalowa, Ugarowa, which must be rejected, as I never heard a single native west of the Tanganika use the term. It originated, no doubt, from some slave of Uhiyau, or Nyassa, Bisa, Unyamwezi, or other parts. Had an intelligent Arab heard the name first, we should most probably have received something nearer the correct word.

Manyema is variously pronounced as Mani-yema, Manuema, Mani-wema, but the first is the most popular.

For the spelling of the name Tanga-nika, I still maintain that that is the most correct, and that it is purer African than Tanga-ny-ika. Neither Arab, Mgwana, nor aborigine of the interior ever approached such a sound. It is pronounced the same as Amerika, Afrika, Angel-ica, Freder-ica. I have only heard one name throughout Africa resembling that which I reject, and that was Ny-ika, king of Gambaragara, pronounced Nye-ika.

Nov. 2.—Tippu-Tib arrived at Nyangwé on the 2nd of November, with a much larger force than I anticipated, for he had nearly 700 people with him. However, he explained that he was about to send some 300 of them to a country called Tata, which lies to the east of Usongora Meno.

Nov. 4.—On the 4th of November the members of the Expedition were mustered, and we ascertained that they numbered 146,* and that we possessed the following arms—Sniders, 29; percussion-lock muskets, 32; Winchesters, 2; double-barrelled guns, 2; revolvers, 10; axes, 68. Out of this number of sixty-four guns, only forty were borne by trustworthy men; the others were mere pagazis, who would prefer becoming slaves to fighting for their freedom and lives. At the same time they were valuable as porters, and faithful to their allotted duties and their contract when not enticed away by outside influences or fear. The enormous force that Tippu-Tib brought to Nyangwé quite encouraged them, and when I asked them if they were ready to make good their promise to me at Zanzibar and Muta Nzigé lake, they replied unanimously in the affirmative.

"Then to-night, my friends," said I, "you will pack up your goods, and to-morrow morning at the first hour let me see you in line before my house ready to start."

* This number was finally increased by the addition of six stout young fellows from Nyangwé, which made our total number of men, women, and children (sons of the Wangwana, from Zanzibar), 154.

CHAPTER V.

Tippu-Tib's henchmen—In the primeval forest, a wilderness of trees—Primitive furniture—Our sufferings in the pagans' forest—Tippu-Tib breaks down—A village blacksmith—Soko skulls; the missing link—Professor Huxley's opinion thereon—THE LIVINGSTONE—A day dream—The road to the ocean—Timid counsels—"The Wasambye!"—"Ooh-hu! ooh-hu!"—Successful diplomacy.

Nov. 5.—When, on the 5th of November, 1876, we had left Nyangwé behind us, and had ascended an elevated grassy ridge, we saw before us a black curving wall of forest, which, beginning from the river bank, extended south-east, until hills and distance made it indistinct.

I turned round to look at Nyangwé, which we were leaving. How loveable and cheerful it appeared as it crowned the shoulder of one of those lengthy grassy undulations overlooking the grey-brown Livingstone! How bright and warm appeared the plain-border of the river as the sun shone over its wind-fanned waves of grass! Even the hill-cones of Uzura and Western Manyema ranked in line between the forest and the grassy plain, which were now purpling and becoming like cloud-forms, seemed to me to have a more friendly and brighter appearance than the cold blackness of the dense forest which rose before us to the north!

What a forbidding aspect had the Dark Unknown which confronted us! I could not comprehend in the least what lay before us. Even the few names which I had heard from the Arabs conveyed no definite impression to my understanding. What were Tata, Meginna, Uregga, Usongora Meno and such uncouth names to me? They conveyed no idea, and signified no object; they were barren names of either countries, villages, or peoples, involved in darkness, savagery, ignorance, and fable.

Yet it is our destiny to move on, whatever direction it may be that that narrow winding path, running among tall grasses, and down into gullies and across small streams, takes us, until we penetrate that cold, dark, still horizon before us, and emerge whithersoever the narrow path will permit us—a distance of 240 hours' travel.

The object of the desperate journey is to flash a torch of light across the western half of the Dark Continent. For from Nyangwé east, along the fourth parallel of south latitude, are some 830 geographical miles, discovered, explored, and surveyed, but westward to the Atlantic Ocean along the same latitude are 956 miles—over 900 geographical miles of which are absolutely unknown. Instead, however, of striking direct west, we are about to travel north on the eastern side of the river, to prevent it bending easterly to Muta Nzigé, or Nilewards, unknown to us, and to ascertain, if the river really runs westward, what affluents flow to it from the east; and to deduce from their size and volume some idea of the extent of country which they drain, and the locality of their sources.

A thousand things may transpire to prevent the accomplishment of our purpose: hunger, disease, and savage hostility may crush us; perhaps, after all, the difficulties may daunt us, but our hopes run high, and our purpose is lofty; then in the name of God let us set on, and as He pleases, so let Him rule our destinies!

After journeying a distance of nine miles and a half north-east, over a rolling plain covered with grass, we arrived at the villages of Nakasimbi; Tippu-Tib, with 700 people, men, women, and children, occupying two villages, while our Expedition occupied another overlooking a depression drained by a sluggish affluent of the Kunda river.

Tippu-Tib is accompanied by about a dozen Arabs, young or middle-aged, who have followed him in the hope of being rewarded by him or myself at the end of a prosperous journey.

Sheikh Hamed bin Mohammed, alias Tippu-Tib, alias Mtipula, we know already. To-day he is bland and courteous, enthusiastic, and sanguine that we shall succeed without trouble. The next in importance to him is an Arab—full-bearded, fine-featured, of a dark complexion, called Sheikh Abdallah, alias Muini Kibwana—a name adopted solely for Manyema. He is very ignorant, can neither read nor write, but has a vast regard for those who have mastered the secrets of literature, like Tippu-Tib. He is armed with a flintlock Brummagem musket, for which he has considerable affection, because—according to him—it has saved his life many a time. "It never lies."

The next is Muini Ibrahim, a Mrima (coast) man, of Arab descent, though ruder and unpolished. Americans would have nothing much to do with him, because the negroid evidences are so great that he would be classed as a full-blooded negro. Yet he speaks Arabic well, and is a fervid Muslim, but withal as superstitious as any primitive African. He affects to be religious, and consequently is not bloodthirsty, having some regard for the lives of human beings, and for this receiving due praise from me. He is also armed with a flintlock musket. Sheikh Abdallah and he are bosom friends, and possess five or six female slaves each, and from thirty to forty male slaves, likewise armed with flintlocks.

Tippu-Tip's Arab dependants, who dip their hands in the same porridge and meat-dish with the independent Sheikh Abdallah and Muini Ibrahim, consist of Muini Jumah (Master Friday), a nervous, tall young man; Chéché (Weasel) a short, light-complexioned young man of twenty-five years of age; Bwana Abed bin Jumah, the author of the dwarf story, who has consented to act as our guide; Muini Hamadi, a half-caste man of sturdy form and resolute appearance; and six or seven others of no special individuality or importance, except as so many dependants of Tippu-Tib.

The 700 followers who follow our Expedition at present consist of two parties; one party, composed of 300 men, women, and children, and commanded by Bwana Shokka (master of the axe), the confidential man of Tippu-Tib's staff, of great strength, tall and gaunt of person, and a renowned traveller; a man of great tact, and worth a fortune to his master, as he is exceedingly cool, speaks slowly, and by some rare gift conciliates the savages (when not actually attacked on the road), and makes them friends. In a few days he is to part from us, striking north-easterly for some dozen marches, the utmost reach of Arab intercourse.

The 400 who are to accompany us for a distance of sixty camps consist of about 250 men—Arabs, half-castes, Wangwana, 100 Wanyamwezi, Ruga-Ruga—mostly armed with spears and bows and arrows; others possess flintlocks. One hundred men consist of Barua, Manyema, Bakusu, Ba-Samba, and Utotera slaves; most of these slaves are armed with flintlocks, the others with formidable spears and shields

There are also about fifty youths, ranging from ten to eighteen years of age, being trained by Tippu-Tib as gun-bearers, house servants, scouts, cooks, carpenters, house-builders, blacksmiths, and leaders of trading parties. Meanwhile such young fellows are useful to him; they are more trustworthy than adults, because they look up to him as their father; and know that if they left him they would inevitably be captured by a less humane man. The remainder of this motley force consists of women, twenty of whom belong to the household of Tippu-Tib, all purchased with ivory, guns, cloth, or beads. Thirty women are the properties of the Arab dependants, chiefly half-castes and Wangwana, following Tippu-Tib.

Two hundred and ten out of the 400 I have pledged to support until they shall return to Nyangwé, at the same rate of ration currency that may be distributed to the members of our Expedition.

Nov. 6.—On the 6th of November we drew nearer to the dreaded black and chill forest called Mitamba, and at last, bidding farewell to sunshine and brightness, entered it.

We had made one mistake—we had not been up early enough. Tippu-Tib's heterogeneous column of all ages were ahead of us, and its want of order and compactness became a source of trouble to us in the rear.

We, accustomed to rapid marching, had to stand in our places minutes at a time, waiting patiently for an advance of a few yards, after which would come another halt, and another short advance to be again halted. And all this time the trees kept shedding their dew upon us like rain in great round drops. Every leaf seemed weeping. Down the boles and branches, creepers and vegetable cords, the moisture trickled and fell on us. Overhead the wide-spreading branches, in many interlaced strata, each branch heavy with broad thick leaves, absolutely shut out the daylight. We knew not whether it was a sunshiny day or a dull, foggy, gloomy day; for we marched in a feeble solemn twilight, such as you may experience in temperate climates an hour after sunset. The path soon became a stiff clayey paste, and at every step we splashed water over the legs of those in front, and on either side of us.

To our right and left, to the height of about twenty feet, towered the undergrowth, the lower world of vegetation. The soil on which this thrives is a dark-brown vegetable humus, the débris of ages of rotting leaves and fallen branches, a very forcing-bed of vegetable life, which, constantly fed with moisture, illustrates in an astonishing degree the prolific power of the warm moist shades of the tropics.

The stiff clay lying under this mould, being impervious, retains the moisture which constantly supplies the millions of tiny roots of herb, plant and bush. The innumerable varieties of plants which spring up with such marvellous rapidity, if exposed to the gale, would soon be laid prostrate. But what rude blast can visit these imprisoned shades? The tempest might roar without the leafy world, but in its deep bosom there is absolute stillness. One has but to tug at a sapling to know that the loose mould has no retentive power, and that the sapling's roots have not penetrated the clays. Even the giants of the forest have not penetrated very deeply, as one may see by the half-exposed roots; they appear to retain their upright positions more by breadth of base than by their grasp of earth.

Every few minutes we found ourselves descending into ditches, with streams trending towards the Kunda river, discharged out of leafy depths of date-palms, Amoma, Carpodinæ, and Phrynia. Climbing out from these streams, up their steep banks our faces were brushed by the broad leaves of the Amomum, or the wild banana, ficus of various kinds, and climbing, crawling, obstructing lengths of wild vines.

Naturally our temper was not improved by this new travelling. The dew dropped and pattered on us incessantly until about 10 A.M. Our clothes were heavily saturated with it. My white sun-helmet and puggaree appeared to be weighted with lead. Being too heavy, and having no use for it in the cool dank shades, I handed it to my gun-bearer, for my clothes, gaiters, and boots, which creaked loudly with the water that had penetrated them, were sufficient weight for me to move with. Added to this vexation was the perspiration which exuded from every pore, for the atmosphere was stifling. The steam from the hot earth could be seen ascending upward and settling like a grey cloud above our heads. In the early morning it had been so dense that we could scarcely distinguish the various trees by their leafage.

At 3 P.M. we had reached Mpotira, in the district of Uzimba, Manyema, twenty-one miles and a half from the Arab depot on the Lualaba.

The poor boatmen did not arrive until evening, for the boat sections—dreadful burdens—had to be driven like blunted ploughs through the depths of foliage. The men complained bitterly of fatigue, and for their sake we rested at Mpotira.

The nature of the next two days' experiences through the forest may be gathered by reading the following portions of entries in my journal:—

"*November* 8.—N. ½ W., nine miles to district of Karindi, or Kiouga, Uregga.

"We have had a fearful time of it to-day in these woods, and Bwana Shokka, who has visited this region before, declares with superior pride that what we have experienced as yet is only a poor beginning to the weeks upon weeks which we shall have to endure. Such crawling, scrambling, tearing through the damp, dank jungles, and such height and depth of woods! . . . Once we obtained a side-long view from a tree on the crown of a hill, over the wild woods on our left, which swept in irregular waves of branch and leaf down to the valley of the Lualaba. Across the Lualaba, on the western bank, we looked with wistful eyes on what appeared to be green grassy plains. Ah, what a contrast to that which we had to endure! It was a wild weird scene, this outlook we obtained of the top of the leafy world! . . . It was so dark sometimes in the woods that I could not see the words, recording notes of the track, which I pencilled in my note-book. At 3.30 P.M. we arrived in camp, quite worn out with the struggle through the intermeshed bush, and almost suffocated with the heavy atmosphere. Oh, for a breath of mountain air!"

"*November* 9, 1876.—N. ½ W., ten and a half miles' march to Kiussi, Uregga.

"Another difficult day's work in the forest and jungle. Our Expedition is no longer the compact column which was my pride. It is utterly demoralized. Every man scrambles as he best may through the woods: the path, being over a clayey soil, is so slippery that every muscle is employed to assist our progress. The toes grasp the path, the head bears the load, the hand clears the obstructing bush, the elbow puts aside the sapling. Yesterday the boatmen complained so much that I organized all the chiefs into a pioneer party, with axes to clear the path. Of course we could not make a wide road. There were many prostrate giants fallen across the path, each with a mountain of twigs and branches, compelling us to cut roads through the bush a long distance to get round them. My boat-bearers are utterly wearied out."

Nov. 10.—On the 10th we halted for a well-deserved rest. We were now in Uregga—the forest country. Fenced round by their seldom penetrated woods, the Waregga have hitherto led lives as secluded as the troops of chimpanzees in their forest. Their villages consist of long rows of houses, all

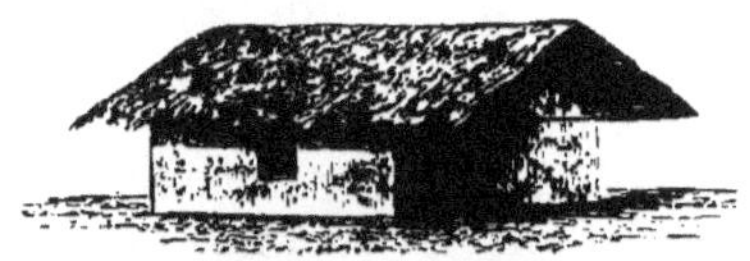

UREGGA HOUSE.

connected together in one block from 50 yards to 300 yards in length. The doorways are square apertures in the walls, only 2 feet square, and cut at about 18 inches above the ground. Within, the long block is divided into several apartments for the respective families. Like the Manyema houses, the roofs glisten as though smeared with coal-tar. There are shelves for fuel, and netting for swinging their crockery; into the roof are thrust the various small knick-knacks which such families need—the pipe, and bunch of tobacco-leaves, the stick of dried snails, various mysterious compounds wrapped in leaves of plants, pounded herbs, and what not. Besides these we noted, as household treasures, the skins of goats, mongoose or civet, weasel, wild cat, monkey, and leopard, shells of land snails, very large and prettily marked, and necklaces of the *Achatina monetaria.* There is also quite a store of powdered camwood, besides

STOOL OF UREGGA.

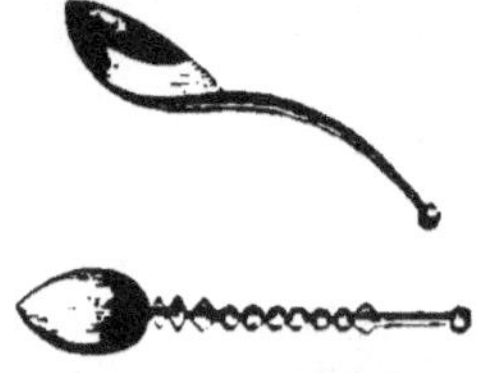

SPOONS OF UREGGA.

curiously carved bits of wood, supposed to be talismans against harm, and handsome spoons, while over the door are also horns of goats and small forest deer, and, occupying conspicuous places, the gaudy war head-dress of feathers of the grey-bodied and crimson-tailed parrots, the drum, and some heavy broad-bladed spears with ironwood staffs.

UREGGA SPEAR.

In the "arts and sciences" of savage life, these exceedingly primitive Africans, buried though they have been from all intercourse with others, are superior in some points to many tribes more favourably situated. For instance, until the day I arrived at Kiussi village, I had not observed a settee. Yet in the depths of this forest of Uregga every family possessed a neatly made water-cane settee, which would seat comfortably three persons.

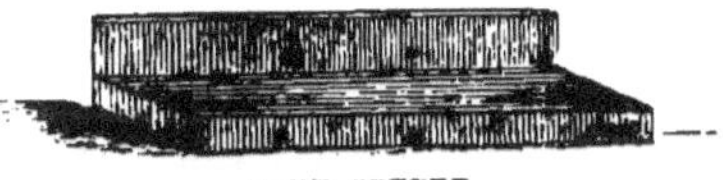

CANE SETTEE.

Another very useful article of furniture was the bench 4 or 5 feet long, cut out of a single log of the white soft wood of one of the Rubiaceæ, and significant as showing a more sociable spirit than that which seems to govern Eastern Africans, among whom the rule is, "Every man to his own stool."

BENCH.

Another noteworthy piece of furniture is the fork of a tree, cut off where the branches begin to ramify. This, when trimmed and peeled, is placed in an inverted position. The branches, sometimes three or even four, serve as legs of a singular back-rest.

The southern Waregga who border upon Uzimba and Manyema say they came from the north some five or six generations ago; that they found the forest in possession of the Wavinza and Wazimba, and dispossessed them of the land. They retain the names of their forefathers from six to ten generations back. Sheikh Abdallah questioned the chief of Kiussi in my presence of his forefathers, and he gave in succession ten different names in answer to questions such as these: "What is your name?" "Who was your father?" and "Whose son was he?" "Then who was his father?"

All the adult males wear skull-caps of goat or monkey-skin, except the chief and elders, whose heads were covered with the aristocratic leopard-skin, with the tail of the leopard hanging down the back like a tassel.

AN AFRICAN FEZ OF LEOPARD-SKIN.

The women were weighted with massive and bright iron rings. One of them, who was probably a lady of importance, carried at least 12 lbs. of iron and 5 lbs. of copper rings on her arms and legs, besides a dozen necklaces of the indigenous *Achatina monetaria.*

From Kinssi, through the same dense jungle and forest, with its oppressive atmosphere and its soul-wearying impediments, we made a journey of fourteen miles to Mirimo. Four streams were crossed, all trending westward to the Lualaba, the two principal being the Rugunsi and Rumuna rivers. Mirimo is a populous settlement, and its people are good natured.

The boatmen did not arrive at all on this day, the obstacles having been too great, but on the 12th, about noon, they appeared, utterly disheartened at the delays which had deprived them of their food and rest.

Nov. 13.—On the 13th we moved to Wanekamankua, crossing *en route* the Kariba river and two small streams.

Nov. 14.—Our next march was to Wane-Mbeza, in Uregga, eight miles in a north-westerly direction. We crossed the Kipembwé, a river 40 yards wide, deep and swift, which flows westward.

Uregga, it appears, occupies a broad belt of country lying north-east and south-west. Its people know nothing of the immediate settlements contiguous to them, and though within twenty miles of the Lualaba, many adult males at Wane-Mbeza had never seen it. They have been imprisoned now for some five or six generations within their almost impenetrable forest fastnesses, and the difficulty of travelling, and the danger that would be incurred unless they united in strong bands, are the causes of their knowing nothing of the world outside, and the outside world knowing nothing of them.

The Wangwana began at this place to murmur loudly, while the boatmen, though assisted by a dozen supernumeraries, and preceded by a gang of pioneers, were becoming perfectly savage; but the poor fellows had certainly cause for discontent. I pitied them from my soul, yet I dared not show too great a solicitude, lest they should have presumed upon it, and requested me either to return to Nyangwé or to burn my boat.

Even Tippu-Tib, whom I anxiously watched, as on him I staked all my hopes and prospects, murmured. Sheikh Abdallah was heard to growl ominously, and Bwana Ibrahim was particularly severe in his remarks upon "the pagans' forest." The evil atmosphere created sickness in the Arab escort, but all my people maintained their health, if not their temper.

At this camp we parted from Bwana Shokka and his 300, who were about to penetrate some eight or ten marches more to the north-east to Tata country. I have a suspicion that "Tata" is not a proper name, but that it simply signifies "farther in."

Nov. 15.—On the 15th we marched six miles and a half to Wane-Kirumbu. From this village, which, like all the villages that we had passed, crowned a hill, we obtained the most extended view we had enjoyed since entering the forest. Towards the north and north-east the outlook was over a jumble of forest-clad hills separating narrow and deep valleys. The view was indeed most depressing and portentous.

Our march, short as it was, was full of incidents. The constant slush and reek which the heavy dews caused in the forest through which we had travelled the last ten days had worn my shoes out, and half of the march I travelled with naked feet. I had then to draw out of my store my last pair of shoes. Frank was already using his last pair. Yet we were still in the very centre of the continent. What should we do when all were gone? was a question which we asked of each other often.

The faces of the people, Arabs, Wangwana, Wanyamwezi, and the escort, were quite a study at this camp. All their courage was oozing out, as day by day we plodded through the doleful, dreary forest. We saw a python 10 feet long, a green viper, and a monstrous puff-adder on this march, besides scores of monkeys, of the white-necked or glossy black species, as also the small grey, and the large howling baboons. We heard also the "soko" or chimpanzee, and saw one "nest" belonging to it in the fork of a tall bombax. A lemur was also observed; its loud harsh cries made each night hideous.

The path presented myriapedes, black and brown, 6 inches in length, while beetles were innumerable, and armies of the deep brown "hot-water" ants compelled us to be cautious how we stepped.

The difficulties of such travel as we had now commenced may be imagined when a short march of six miles and a half occupied the twenty-four men who were carrying the boat sections an entire day, and so fatigued them that we had to halt another day at Wane-Kirumbu, to recruit their exhausted strength.

The terrible undergrowth that here engrossed all the space under the shade of the pillared bombax and mast-like mvulé was a miracle of vegetation. It consisted of ferns, spear-grass, water-cane, and orchidaceous plants mixed with wild vines, cable thicknesses of the *Ficus elastica*, and a sprinkling of mimosas, acacias, tamarinds; llianes, palms of various species, wild date, *Raphia vinifera*, the elais, the fan, rattans, and a hundred other varieties, all struggling for every inch of space, and swarming upward with a luxuriance and density that only this extraordinary hothouse atmosphere could nourish. We had certainly seen forests before, but this scene was an epoch in our lives ever to be remembered for its bitterness; the gloom enhanced the dismal misery of our life; the slopping moisture, the unhealthy reeking atmosphere, and the monotony of the scenes; nothing but the eternal interlaced branches, the tall aspiring stems, rising from a tangle through which we had to burrow and crawl like wild animals, on hands and feet.

Nov. 16.—About 9 A.M. Tippu-Tib and the Arabs came to my hut at Wane-Kirumbu. After a long preamble, wherein he described the hardships of the march, Tippu-Tib concluded by saying that he had come to announce his wish that our contract should be dissolved!

In a moment it flashed on my mind that a crisis had arrived. Was the Expedition to end here? I urged with all my powers the necessity for keeping engagements so deliberately entered into.

"It is of no use," Tippu-Tib replied, "to have two tongues. Look at it how you may, those sixty camps will occupy us at the rate we are travelling over a year, and it will take as much time to return. I never was in this forest before, and I had no idea there was such a place in the world; but the air is killing my people, it is insufferable. You will kill your own people if you go on. They are grumbling every day more and more. This country was not made for travel; it was made for vile pagans, monkeys, and wild beasts. I cannot go farther."

"Will Tippu-Tib then return to Nyangwé, and break his word and bond? What will all the Arabs at Nyangwé, Mwana Mamba, and Kasongo's say when they hear that Tippu-Tib, who was the first Arab to penetrate Rua, proceeded only a few days with his friend, and then returned?"

"Show me a man's work, and I will do it."

"Well, look here, Tippu-Tib. The land on the west bank of the Lualaba is more open than this, and the road that Mtagamoyo took to go to the Lumami is on that side. Though the land is more open, I hear that the people are worse there than on this side. However, we are not Mtagamoyo, and they may behave better with us. Let us try the other side.

"Now, I will give you choice of two contracts. Accompany me to the river, and wait while I transport my people across, and I will give you 500 dollars; or accompany me twenty marches farther along the west bank, and I will give you 2600 dollars. At the end of that time, if you see your way clear, I will engage you for another journey, until I am quite satisfied that I can go no farther. Provisions will be given your people until we part, and from that point back to Nyangwé."

For two hours I plied him with arguments, and at last, when I was nearly exhausted, Tippu-Tib consented to accompany me twenty marches farther, beginning from the camp we were in. It was a fortunate thing indeed for me that he agreed to this, as his return so close to Nyangwé in the present dispirited condition of my people's minds would have undoubtedly ensured the destruction of all my hopes.

The natives of Uregga are not liberally disposed. Wane-Kirumbu's chief was the first who consented to exchange gifts with me. He presented me with a chicken and some bananas, and I reciprocated the gift with five cowries, which he accepted without a murmur. On witnessing this pleasing and most uncommon trait of moderation, I presented him with ten more, which appeared to him so bounteous that he left my presence quite affected, indeed almost overcome by his emotions of gratitude.

The men of these forest communities of Uregga, upon the decease of their wives, put on symbols of mourning, namely, a thick daub of charcoal paste over the face, which they retain for five "years"—two and a half European years. Widows also mourn for their husbands a like period, with the same disfigurement of features, but with the addition of bands of sere leaf of the banana round the forehead. In Uzimba and Manyema, of North Luama districts, the mourning only lasts two native years, or one European year.

At Wane-Kirumbu we found a large native forge and smithy, where there were about a dozen smiths busily at

A FORGE AND SMITHY AT WANE-KIRUMBU, UREGGA.

work. The iron ore is very pure. Here were the broad-bladed spears of Southern Uregga, and equally broad knives of all sizes, from the small waist knife, an inch and a half in length, to the heavy Roman sword-like cleaver. The bellows for the smelting furnace are four in number, double-handled, and manned by four men, who, by a quick up and down motion, supply a powerful blast, the noise of which is heard nearly half a mile from the scene. The furnace consists of tamped clay, raised into a mound about 4 feet high. A hollow is then excavated in it, 2 feet in diameter and 2 feet deep. From the middle of the slope four apertures are excavated into the base of the furnace, into which are fitted funnel-shaped earthenware pipes to convey the blasts to the fire. At the base of the mound a wide aperture for the hearth is excavated, penetrating below the furnace. The hearth receives the dross and slag.

Close by stood piled up mat-sacks of charcoal, with a couple of boys ready to supply the fuel, and about two yards off was a smaller smithy, where the iron was shaped into hammers, axes, war-hatchets, spears, knives, swords, wire, iron balls with spikes, leglets, armlets, and iron beads, &c. The art of the blacksmith is of a high standard in these forests, considering the loneliness of the inhabitants. The people have much traditional lore, and it appears from the immunity which they have enjoyed in these dismal retreats that from one generation to another, something has been communicated and learned, showing that even the jungle man is a progressive and an improvable animal.

Nov. 17.—On the 17th of November we crossed several lofty hilly ridges, separated by appallingly gloomy ravines, through which several clear streams flowed westward, and after a march of eleven miles north-westerly through the dank, dripping forests, arrived at Kampunzu, in the district of Uvinza, where dwell the true aborigines of the forest country.

Kampunzu village is about five hundred yards in length, formed of one street thirty feet wide, flanked on each side by a straight, symmetrical, and low block of houses, gable-roofed. Several small villages in the neighbourhood are of the same pattern.

The most singular feature of Kampunzu village were two rows of skulls, ten feet apart, running along the entire length of the village, imbedded about two inches deep in the ground, the "cerebral hemispheres" uppermost, bleached, and glistening white from weather. The skulls were 186 in number in this one village. To me they appeared to be human, though many had an extraordinary projection of the posterior lobes, others of the parietal bones, and the frontal bones were unusually low and retreating; yet the sutures and the general aspect of the greatest number of them were so similar to what I believed to be human, that it was with almost an indifferent air that I asked my chiefs and Arabs what these skulls were. They replied, "sokos"—chimpanzees (?).

"Sokos from the forest?"

"Certainly," they all replied.

"Bring the chief of Kampunzu to me immediately," I said, much interested now because of the wonderful reports of them that Livingstone had given me, as also the natives of Manyema.

The chief of Kampunzu—a tall, strongly-built man of about thirty-five years of age—appeared, and I asked,

"My friend, what are those things with which you adorn the street of your village?"

He replied, "Nyama" (meat).

"Nyama! Nyama of what?"

"Nyama of the forest."

"Of the forest! What kind of thing is this Nyama of the forest?"

"It is about the size of this boy," pointing to Mabruki, my gun-bearer, who was 4 feet 10 inches in height. "He walks like a man, and goes about with a stick, with which he beats the trees in the forest, and makes hideous noises. The Nyama eat our bananas, and we hunt them, kill them, and eat them."

"Are they good eating?" I asked.

He laughed, and replied that they were very good.

"Would you eat one if you had one now?"

"Indeed I would. Shall a man refuse meat?"

"Well, look here. I have one hundred cowries here. Take your men, and fetch one, and bring him to me alive or dead. I only want his skin and head. You may have the meat."

Kampunzu's chief, before he set out with his men, brought me a portion of the skin of one, which probably covered the back. The fur was dark grey, an inch long, with the points inclined to white; a line of darker hair marked the spine. This, he assured me, was a portion of the skin of a "soko." He also showed me a cap made out of it, which I purchased.

The chief returned about evening unsuccessful from the search. He wished us to remain two or three days that he might set traps for the "sokos," as they would be sure to visit the bananas at night. Not being able to wait so many days, I obtained for a few cowries the skull of a male and another of a female.*

* These two skulls were safely brought to England, and shown to Professor Huxley, who has passed judgment upon them as follows:—

"Of the two skulls submitted to me for examination, the one is that of a

In this village were also observed those carved benches cut out of the Rubiaceæ already mentioned, backgammon trays, and stools carved in the most admirable manner, all being decorated around the edges of the seats with brass tacks and "soko teeth."

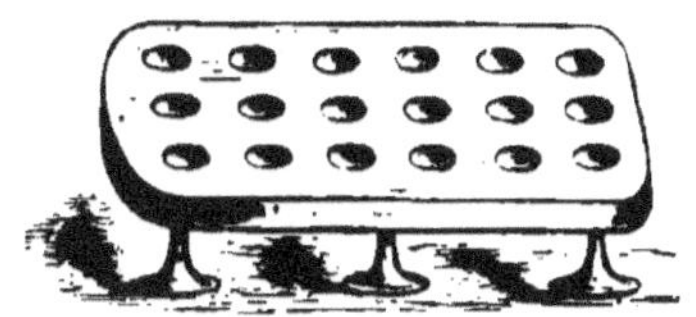

BACKGAMMON TRAY.

Copper appeared to be abundant with the Wavinza. It was wound around their spear-staffs, and encircled the lower limbs and arms, the handles of their knives, walking-staffs, and hung from their necks in beads, and small shot-like balls of it were fastened to their hair.

In addition to their short broad-bladed spears, the Wavinza were armed with small but strong bows, the strings of which were formed of strips of the rattan cane. The arrows are about a foot in length, made of reeds, pointed, and smeared with vegetable poison. The Wavinza do not employ iron heads. It requires a peculiar skill for these weapons. The Wanyamwezi bowmen were unable to shoot the arrows farther than from fifty to seventy yards. An aboriginal, smiling at their awkwardness, shot an arrow a distance of 200 yards. The natives boast that the slightest scratch is sufficient to doom even an elephant, for it is by this means they have been able to obtain ivory for Molembalemba (Dugumbi of Nyangwé).

Blood-brotherhood being considered as a pledge of good-will and peace Frank Pocock and the chief went through the ordeal, and we interchanged presents.

From this village a path leads to Meginna and Miango,

man probably somewhat under thirty years of age, and the other that of a woman over fifty.

"The man's skull exhibits all the characteristic peculiarities of the negro type, including a well-marked, but not unusual, degree of prognathism. In the female skull the only point worth notice is a somewhat unusual breadth of the anterior nasal aperture in proportion to its height, indicating that the nostrils may have been slightly farther apart, and the extremity of the nose a little flatter than usual.

"In both skulls the cephalic index is 75. Nothing in these skulls justifies the supposition that their original possessors differed in any sensible degree from the ordinary African negro."

Professor Huxley, by the above, startles me with the proof that Kampunzu's people were cannibals, for at least one half of the number of skulls seen by me bore the mark of a hatchet, which had been driven into the head while the victims were alive.

near the Urindi river, on the south side of which the Arabs say there is abundance of coal, "very black and shining." A path also leads north-east to Kirari, four hours', and Makongo, seven hours' distance from Kampunzu. They also say that a two months' journey east-north-east (magnetic) would bring us to open country, where there is abundance of cattle.

The women of Uregga wear only aprons 4 inches square, of bark or grass cloth, fastened by cords of palm fibre. The men wear skins of civet, or monkey, in front and rear, the tails downwards. It may have been from a hasty glance of a rapidly disappearing form of one of these people in the wild woods that native travellers in the lake regions felt persuaded that they had seen "men with tails."

The ficus trees, which supply Uganda, Unyamwezi, Ukonongo, Goma, and Uregga with bark cloth, register the age of the respective settlements where they are found, and may be said to be historical monuments of the people which planted them. In Uddu-Uganda, especially in Southern Uddu, I saw patriarchs which must have been four or five hundred years old. If a cloth-producing ficus is 2 feet in diameter, it may be regarded as a monument of antiquity; one ten inches in diameter as over a hundred years old; one six inches in diameter as over forty years. The oldest tree of this species in Southern Uregga that I saw could not have exceeded eighty years.

Nov. 19.—On the 19th a march of five miles through the forest west from Kampunzu brought us to the Lualaba, in south latitude 3° 35′, just forty-one geographical miles north of the Arab depot Nyangwé. An afternoon observation for longitude showed east longitude 25° 49′. The name Lualaba terminates here. I mean to speak of it henceforth as THE LIVINGSTONE.

We found, when twenty miles from the river, that many of the Waregga had never seen it, though they had heard of it as the Lu-al-ow-wa. Had not Livingstone spoken of the river at Nyangwé as the Lualaba, I should not have mentioned the word except as a corruption by the Waguha of the Wenya term Lu-al-ow-wa, but as the river changes its name each time after receiving an affluent, it would be useless to endeavour to retain so many names in the memory.

The Livingstone was 1200 yards wide from bank to bank opposite the landing-place of Kampunzu. As there were no people dwelling within a mile of the right bank, we prepared to encamp. My tent was pitched about thirty feet from the river, on a grassy spot; Tippu-Tib and his Arabs were in the bushes; while the 550 people of whom the Expedition consisted began to prepare a site for their huts, by enlarging the open space around the landing-place.

While my breakfast (for noon) was cooking, and my tent was being drawn taut and made trim, a mat was spread on a bit of short grass, soft as an English lawn, a few yards from the water. Some sedgy reeds obstructed my view, and as I wished while resting to watch the river gliding by, I had them all cropped off short.

Frank and the Wangwana chiefs were putting the boat sections together in the rear of the camp; I was busy thinking, planning a score of things—what time it would be best to cross the river, how we should commence our acquaintance with the warlike tribes on the left bank, what our future would be, how I should succeed in conveying our large force across, and, in the event of a determined resistance, what we should do, &c.

Gentle as a summer's dream, the brown wave of the great Livingstone flowed by; broad and deep. On the opposite bank loomed darkly against the sky another forest, similar to the one which had harrowed our souls. I obtained from my seat a magnificent view of the river, flanked by black forests, gliding along, with a serene grandeur and an unspeakable majesty of silence about it that caused my heart to yearn towards it.

"Downward it flows to the unknown! to night-black clouds of mystery and fable, mayhap past the lands of the anthropoids, the pigmies, and the blanket-eared men of whom the gentle pagan king of Karagwé spoke, by leagues upon leagues of unexplored lands, populous with scores of tribes, of whom not a whisper has reached the people of other continents; perhaps that fabulous being the dread Macoco, of whom Bartolomeo Diaz, Cada Mosto, and Dapper have written, is still represented by one who inherits his ancient kingdom and power, and surrounded by barbarous pomp. Something strange must surely lie in the vast space occupied by total blankness on our maps, between Nyangwé and 'Tuckey's Farthest!'"

"I seek a road to connect these two points. We have laboured through the terrible forest, and manfully struggled through the gloom. My people's hearts have become faint.

I seek a road. Why, here lies a broad watery avenue cleaving the Unknown to some sea, like a path of light! Here are woods all around, sufficient for a thousand fleets of canoes. Why not build them?"

I sprang up; told the drummer to call to muster. The people responded wearily to the call. Frank and the chiefs appeared. The Arabs and their escort came also, until a dense mass of expectant faces surrounded me. I turned to them and said:—

"Arabs! sons of Unyamwezi! children of Zanzibar! listen to words. We have seen the Mitamba of Uregga. We have tasted its bitterness, and have groaned in spirit. We seek a road. We seek something by which we may travel. I seek a path that shall take me to the sea. I have found it."

"Ah! ah—h!" and murmurs and inquiring looks at one another.

"Yes! El hamd ul Illah. I have found it. Regard this mighty river. From the beginning it has flowed on thus, as you see it flow to-day. It has flowed on in silence and darkness. Whither? To the Salt Sea, as all rivers go! By that Salt Sea, on which the great ships come and go live my friends and your friends. Do they not?"

Cries of "Yes! yes!"

"Yet, my people, though this river is so great, so wide and deep, no man has ever penetrated the distance lying between this spot on which we stand and our white friends who live by the Salt Sea. Why? Because it was left for us to do."

"Ah, no! no! no!" and desponding shakes of the head.

"Yes," I continued, raising my voice; "I tell you, my friends, it has been left from the beginning of time until to-day for us to do. It is our work, and no other. It is the voice of Fate! The ONE GOD has written that this year the river shall be known throughout its length! We will have no more Mitambas; we will have no more panting and groaning by the wayside; we will have no more hideous darkness; we will take to the river, and keep to the river. To-day I shall launch my boat on that stream, and it shall never leave it until I finish my work. I swear it.

"Now, you Wangwana! You, who have followed me through Turu, and sailed around the great lakes with me; you, who have followed me, like children following their father, through Unyoro, and down to Ujiji, and as far as this wild, wild land, will you leave me here? Shall I and my white brother go alone! Will you go back and tell my friends that you left me in this wild spot, and cast me adrift to die? Or will you, to whom I have been so kind, whom I love as I would love my children, will you bind me, and take me back by force? Speak, Arabs? Where are my young men, with hearts of lions? Speak, Wangwana, and show me those who dare follow me?"

Uledi, the coxswain, leaped upward, and then sprang towards me, and kneeling grasped my knees, and said, "Look on me, my master! I am one! I will follow you to death!" "And I," Kachéché cried; "and I, and I, and I," shouted the boat's crew.

"It is well. I knew I had friends. You then who have cast your lot with me stand on one side, and let me count you."

There were thirty-eight! Ninety-five stood still and said nothing.

"I have enough. Even with you, my friends, I shall reach the sea. But there is plenty of time. We have not yet made our canoes. We have not yet parted with the Arabs. We have yet a long distance to travel with Tippu-Tib. We may meet with good people from whom we may buy canoes. And by the time we part I am sure that the ninety-five men now fearing to go with us will not leave their brothers, and their master and his white brother, to go down the river without them. Meantime I give you many thanks, and shall not forget your names.

The assembly broke up, and each man proceeded about his special duties. Tippu-Tib, Sheikh Abdallah, and Muini Ibrahim sat on the mat, and commenced to try to persuade me not to be so rash, and to abandon all idea of descending the river. In my turn I requested them not to speak like children, and, however they might think, not to disclose their fears to the Wangwana; but rather to encourage them to do their duty, and share the dangers with me, because the responsibility was all my own, and the greatest share of danger would be mine; and that I would be in front to direct and guide and save, and for my own sake as well as for their sake would be prudent.

In reply, they spoke of cataracts and cannibals, and war-like tribes. They depreciated the spirit of the Wangwana, and declaimed against men who were once slaves; refused to concede one virtue to them, either of fidelity, courage, or gratitude, and predicted that the end would be death to all.

"Speak no more, Tippu-Tib. You who have travelled all your life among slaves have not yet learned that there lies something good in the heart of every man that God made. Men were not made all bad, as you say. For God is good, and He made all men. I have studied my people: I know them and their ways. It will be my task to draw the good out of them while they are with me; and the only way to do it is to be good to them, for good produces good. As you value my friendship, and hope to receive money from me, be silent. Speak not a word of fear to my people, and when we part, I shall make known my name to you. To you, and to all who are my friends, I shall be 'the white man with the open hand.' But if not, then I shall be 'Kiparamoto.'"

While I had been speaking, a small canoe with two men was seen advancing from the opposite bank. One of the interpreters was called, and told to speak to them quietly, and to ask them to bring canoes to take us across.

"Ndugu, O ndugu" ("Brother, O brother"), the interpreter hailed them, "we are friends; we wish to cross the river. Bring your canoes and take us to the other side, and we will give you plenty of shells and beads."

"Who are you?"

"We are Warungwana" (Wangwana).

"Where from?"

"From Nyangwé."

"Ah! you are Wasambye!" (the uncircumcised).

"No; we have a white man with us as chief, and he is kind."

"If he fills my canoe with shells, I will go and tell the Wenya that you want to cross the river."

"We cannot give so much as that, but we will give ten shells for each man."

"We want a thousand shells for each man, or you shall never cross the river."

"Ah, but, Ndugu, that is too much; come, we will give you twenty shells for each."

"Not for ten thousand, brother. We do not want you to cross the river. Go back, Wasambye; you are bad!

Wasambye are bad, bad, bad! The river is deep, Wasambye! Go back, Wasambye; you are bad, bad! The river is deep, Wasambye! You have not wings, Wasambye! Go back, Wasambye!"

After saying which they sang the wildest, weirdest note I ever heard, and sent it pealing across the river. "Ooh-hu, ooh-hu-hu-hu!" In response we heard hundreds of voices sing out a similar note—"Ooh-hu, ooh-hu-hu-hu!"

"That is a war-cry, master," said the interpreter.

"Nonsense, don't be foolish. What cause is there for war?"

"These wild people do not need cause; they are simply wild beasts."

"I will prove to you before two hours you are wrong," I said.

By the time I had finished my breakfast the *Lady Alice* was in the river, and a loud shout of applause greeted her appearance on her natural element.

The boat's crew, with Uledi as coxswain, and Tippu-Tib, Sheikh Abdallah, Muini Ibrahim, Bwana Abed (the guide), Muini Jumah, and two interpreters and myself as passengers, entered the boat. We were rowed up the river for half an hour, and then struck across to a small island in mid-stream. With the aid of a glass I examined the shores, which from our camp appeared to be dense forest. We saw that there were about thirty canoes tied to the bank, and amongst the trees I detected several houses. The bank was crowded with human beings, who were observing our movements.

We re-entered our boat, and pulled straight across to the left bank, then floated down slowly with the current, meantime instructing the interpreters as to what they should say to the Wenya.

When we came opposite, an interpreter requested them to take a look at the white man who had come to visit their country, who wished to make friends with them, who would give them abundance of shells, and allow none of his men to appropriate a single banana, or do violence to a single soul; not a leaf would be taken, nor a twig burned, without being paid for.

The natives, gazing curiously at me, promised after a consultation, that if we made blood-brotherhood with them there should be no trouble, and that for this purpose the white chief, accompanied by ten men, should proceed early next morning to the island, where he would be met by the chief of the Wenya and his ten men, and that after the ceremony, all the canoes should cross and assist to carry our people to their country.

Nov. 20.—After thanking them, we returned to camp, highly elated with our success. At 4 A.M., however, the boat secretly conveyed twenty men with Kachéché, who had orders to hide in the brushwood, and, returning to camp at 7 A.M., conveyed Frank and ten men, who were to perform the ceremony of brotherhood, to the island. On its return, I entered the boat, and was rowed a short way up-stream along the right bank, so that, in case of treachery, I might be able to reach the island within four minutes to lend assistance.

About 9 A.M. six canoes full of men were seen to paddle to the island. We saw them arrive before it, and finally to draw near. Earnestly and anxiously I gazed through my glass at every movement. Other canoes were seen advancing to the island. It was well, I thought, that Frank had his reserve hidden so close at hand. A few seconds after the latest arrivals had appeared on the scene, I saw great animation, and almost at once those curious cries came pealing up the river. There were animated shouts, and a swaying of bodies, and, unable to wait longer, we dashed towards the island, and the natives on seeing us approach paddled quickly to their landing-place.

"Well, Frank. What was the matter?" I asked.

"I never saw such wretches in my life, sir. When that last batch of canoes came, their behaviour, which was decent before, changed. They surrounded us. Half of them remained in the canoes; those on land began to abuse us violently, handling their spears, and acting so furiously that if we had not risen with our guns ready they would have speared us as we were sitting down waiting to begin the ceremony. But Kachéché, seeing their wild behaviour and menacing gestures, advanced quietly from the brushwood with his men, on seeing which they ran to their canoes, where they held their spears ready to launch when you came."

"Well, no harm has been done yet," I replied; "so rest where you are, while I take Kachéché and his men across to their side, where a camp will be formed; because, if we delay to-day crossing, we shall have half of the people starving by to-morrow morning."

After embarking Kachéché, we steered for a point in the woods above the native village, and, landing thirty men with axes, proceeded to form a small camp, which might serve as a nucleus until we should be enabled to transport the Expedition. We then floated down river opposite the village, and, with the aid of an interpreter, explained to them that as we had already landed thirty men in their country, it would be far better that they should assist us in the ferriage, for which they might feel assured they would be well paid. At the same time I tossed a small bag of beads to them. In a few minutes they consented, and six canoes, with two men in each, accompanied us to camp. The six canoes and the boat conveyed eighty people safely to the left bank; and then other canoes, animated by the good understanding that seemed to prevail between us, advanced to assist, and by night every soul associated with our Expedition was rejoicing by genial camp-fires in the villages of the Wenya.

CHAPTER VI.

"Mama, the Wasambye!"—The fight in the Ruiki—The lost found—Dangerous disobedience—In the nick of time—A savage captive—Music hath charms—In the haunts of Nature—A town of one street Deserted village—Organising a hospital—An island wasted by lightning—"The people of the filed teeth"—Primitive salt-making—Hostages captured—At close quarters—Raining arrows—"Bo-bo, bo-bo, bo-bo-o-o-oh!"—A desperate affair and opportune reinforcements—Cutting the canoes adrift—Tippu-Tib deserts me—My appeal to the "sea-children"—Christmas Day among the cannibals—"Victory or death!"

Nov. 21.—We had hoped to pass our first day in the Wenya land in kindly interchange of gifts, and engaging the wild hearts of the natives by ostentatious liberality. But lo! when we searched in the morning for the aborigines they were gone!

Many a village stood in the neighbourhood of the main landing, embowered in the thick shade of tamarind and bombax, teak, iron-wood, and elais palm, but the inhabitants were fled! Each village street had its two rows of bleached trophies of eaten humanity, with an attempt at a ghastly decoration similar to "rockery." The canoes were all left at the landing-place; the fruit of the banana and the plantain hung on the stalks, and the crimson palm-nuts swayed in clusters above our heads, but word was given to our people that nothing should be touched on penalty of fearful punishment.

It was absolutely necessary that our introduction to the Wenya tribe should be heralded by peaceful intercourse. We therefore rested, and sent people round about with shells to purchase food for their respective messes. Only Kachéché and Murabo, one of the boat-boys, succeeded in reaching an inhabited village, but no sooner were they seen than they had to run for their lives back to camp.

Leaving everything untouched, we departed from this first village of the Wenya. My boat floated down river with thirty-six people on board according to agreement, with Frank, Tippu-Tib, and the land party following the riverbank, until we should arrive at a village where we might purchase food.

From the villages below, at least from many, long before we had floated abreast of them, rang out the strange war-cries, "Ooh-hu-hu! Ooh-hu-hu!" and the natives decamped into the bush, leaving everything they possessed *in situ*. This was only to lure us to our destruction, for had we been tempted to capture their goats and black pigs, they would no doubt have rushed from the bushes on the unwary. We, however, were not to be thus tempted to felony and our destruction, and quietly floated down past them.

We then came abreast of a forest, uninhabited, and about three miles in length, and after that sighted a plantation of bananas. We could see the tops of the low gable-roofed houses, but none of the natives descried us until we were within a hundred yards of a large and wealthy village. Then a little child, coming down the high banks to fetch water, suddenly lifting her head, saw us close to the landing, and screamed out, "Mama, the Wasambye! the Wasambye are coming!"

At the name, which seemed to be a dreaded one—no doubt because of Mtagamoyo and his uncircumcised Wanyamwezi—the people, who, it seemed, were holding a market, scattered immediately, the women screaming, "Wasambye! Wasambye!" and the banana stalk and bushes shaking violently, as everybody in a panic flew into the jungle, like a herd of buffaloes stung to frenzy by a fly pest. By the time we had glided down a few paces beyond the landing there was a deathly silence.

We passed by three or four other villages, but the inhabitants simply responded to our attempts at intercourse by protruding their heads from the bushes and shouting "Ooh-hu-hu! Ooh-hu-hu! Ooh-hu-hu!"

At 3 P.M. we came to the Ruiki river, which at the mouth was about 100 yards wide, a black and sluggish stream, with an average depth of about twelve feet. As the land division would be unable to cross this stream without the aid of a boat, we camped at a point between the right bank and the left bank of the Livingstone, in east longitude 25° 33′ and south latitude 3° 26′.

Nov. 23.—We halted on the 23rd of November, awaiting the arrival of the land division, and meanwhile built a strong camp. We saw several forms on the opposite side of the

Ruiki, in the village of chief Kasongo, but they would not deign to answer us, though our interpreter made frequent attempts to induce them to converse. Our party was only thirty-six in number, including myself, and we had but a few bananas, which had been obtained at Kampunzu. Before we could hope to purchase anything from the natives an intercourse of some kind had to be opened. But the aborigines, for some reason, persisted in their distrustful reserve. However, we waited patiently for the land force until sunset, and all night maintained a strict watch lest our boat should be stolen.

Nov. 24th.—Early on the 24th, no news having as yet arrived of our friends, I manned the boat and rowed some ten miles up the Ruiki river, hoping to find them encamped on the bank waiting for us. The general course of the river, though very winding, was from south-west to north-east. A few miles above its mouth it is filled with snags, and becomes narrow, crooked, and swift, and of an inky colour, from a particular tree, whose branches drop in dense masses into the stream.

About 2 P.M. we began to return, and, after rowing hard for about an hour and a half, were approaching our lonely camp when we heard guns being fired rapidly. Unless as a measure of defence there could be no earthly reason why the men in the camp should fire their guns. We therefore urged the crew to full speed, and in a short time were astonished to see the mouth of the Ruiki blocked with canoes filled with savages, launching spears and shooting arrows.

With a loud shout we dashed down the last straight reach of the Ruiki, which attracted the attention of the savages, who immediately turned and fled down stream, uttering in harmonious but weird concord their strange war-cries.

After first learning that no one was wounded, though there were several sheaves of iron-headed and wooden spears, besides reed arrows, in the camp, we inquired the cause of the attack, and heard with astonishment that the people of Kasongo's had signalled to all the neighbouring villages that the "Nwema" (white chief) was gone away, and had invited them to arm and man their canoes to get meat before he should return. About thirty canoes, manned by a great number of savages, had entered the Ruiki, and, without listening to warning, had persisted in advancing on the camp, until fired upon. They had been engaged only a few minutes before I appeared.

Billali, the youth in charge of the heavy rifle, and my factotum on hunting excursions, had shot a man, who lay dead in the stream. When asked how he dared to use my guns to shoot people, he replied with alarm, "I could not help it, sir, indeed I could not. If I had waited but a little minute, he would have killed me, for he was aiming with his spear only a few feet off!"

Night came, but with it no tidings of the land party. We listened all through the dark hours for the sound of signal gun-shots, but none cheered us. In the early morning I despatched Uledi, the coxswain, and five of the younger boatmen, through the jungles, with a caution to observe the

WAR HATCHET OF UKUSU.

STOOL OF UKUSU.

villages, and by no means to risk an unequal contest with people who would dog them through the bushes like leopards. Uledi, with a calm smile, bade me rest assured: he was confident he would soon find them. They set out, leaving us alone to indulge in gloomy thoughts.

At 4 P.M. we heard the roar of a musket-shot through the forest, and soon Uledi emerged from the jungle behind us, his face all aglow with triumph, "They are coming, master, close by," he said.

True enough, the advance-guard appeared in a few seconds, and presently the column, weary, haggard, sick and low spirited. The people had been wandering. Having found a road, they followed it, till they came upon a tribe, who attacked them with arrows, and killed three of them. They retaliated, and the advance-guard captured one of the assailants, and asked what tribe he belonged to. "The

Bakusu," he had said, "and the great river is a long way east of you."

They compelled him to show the way, and after some fifteen hours' marching from the place of the fight, they had met with gallant Uledi and his scouting party, and had hurried after him.

Within four hours the boat had transported the entire party to the left bank of the Ruiki. I was here compelled to relax the rigour of the command that no one should appropriate food without payment, for the suffering of the people was excessive.

Nov. 26.—On the 26th, we floated down river to Nakan-

VIEW BETWEEN THE RUIKI AND NAKANPEMBA.

pemba, the land division on this day keeping close to the river, and though it was buried frequently in profound depths of jungle, we were able to communicate with it occasionally by means of drum-taps.

The river had widened gradually to 1700 yards, and was studded with large tree-clad islands, both banks presenting dense masses of tall woods and undergrowth.

Not a soul had been seen in any of the villages passed through; now and then we heard screams of "Wasambye! Wasambye!" and sometimes we heard voices crying out something about Bwana Muhala, or Mtagamoyo, the notorious land-pirate and kidnapper. Nakanpemba possessed also its dreadful relics, arranged in ghastly lines along the streets—

relics of many a feast, as Professor Huxley has now taught us, on dead humanity.

The march through the jungles and forests, the scant fare, fatigue, and consequent suffering, resulted in sickness. Small-pox and dysentery attacked the land division. Thorns had also penetrated the feet and wounded the legs of many of the people, until dreadful ulcers had been formed, disabling them from travel. In the course of two days' journey we found six abandoned canoes, which, though unsound, we appropriated and repaired, and, lashing them together, formed a floating hospital.

Four miles below Nakanpemba, as we were gliding down at the rate of 1½ knot per hour, we heard the dull murmur of rapids, and from the opposite bank eight canoes were seen to dash swiftly down river, disappearing most mysteriously from view. There being no necessity for us to seek acquaintance with people who appeared to think it undesirable, we did not attempt to disturb them, but, clinging to the left bank, cautiously approached the rapids of Ukassa. These were caused by a ledge of greenish shale, mixed with iron-stone and pudding rock, projecting from the Ukassa hills on the right bank.

The hospital was warned in-shore, while I dropped down as near as possible to the rapids and there landed.

The land division was requested to encamp for the day abreast the rapids while, selecting ten stout young fellows, in addition to the boat's crew, I proceeded to explore along the river; but before departing, I gave the strictest orders to Frank and Manwa Sera that upon no account should any one be permitted to move from camp until I returned.

The rapids were parted by a couple of long rocky islets running parallel and separated from each other and the left bank by two narrow streams, which descended into a quiet, creek-like portion of the river after a fall of 10 feet within half a mile, but on the eastern side the river was of a breadth of 800 yards, and descended with a furious whirl for the distance of a mile and a half, where it was joined by the quiet flowing creek on the left or western side.

We continued our inspection of the shore and river for about two miles, where we very nearly fell into an ambuscade. In a little creek, hidden by high overhanging banks, densely clothed, were some forty or fifty small canoes, the crews all seated, silent, and watching the river. We instantly retreated without disturbing their watchful attitude, and hurried to camp.

On arriving at the boat I was alarmed at hearing that Frank had permitted Manwa Sera, the chief, and five others, to detach two of the hospital canoes, and to descend the great rapids. As this was a suicidal act, I felt my blood run cold, and then recollecting the ambuscade in the creek, I lost no time in selecting fifty men and retracing our steps.

When we reached the creek, we ascertained it to be empty. I then offered high rewards to the first scout who sighted the Wangwana, Uledi and Shumari, his brother, gave wild yells, and dashed forward like antelopes through the jungle, Saywa (their cousin) and Murabo hard after them. With startling echoes some gun-shots soon rang through the forest. Away we tore through the jungle in the direction of the sounds. We came in sight of the river, and heard the rifles close to us. In mid-stream were the five Wangwana riding on the keels of the upset canoes, attacked by half-a-dozen native canoes. Uledi and his comrades had without hesitation opened fire upon them, and thus saved the doomed men. We soon had the gratification of receiving them on shore, but four Snider rifles were lost. The party, it appeared, had been swept into a whirlpool, drawn down, and ejected out of it several feet below the dreadful whirl. This disobedience to orders, which had entailed on me such a loss of valuable rifles, when I was already so weakly armed, on themselves such a narrow escape, besides bringing us into collison with the natives, was punished by well-merited reproaches—so keenly felt moreover that Manwa Sera proceeded to Tippu-Tib's camp, and sent word to me that he would not serve me any longer, I laughed, and returned word to him that I was sure he would. To Frank I solemnly protested against such breach of duty, as life or death now depended on the faithful execution of instructions.

Tippu-Tib and the Arabs advanced to me for a shauri. They wished to know whether I would not now abandon the project of continuing down the river—now that things appeared so gloomy, with rapids before us, natives hostile, cannibalism rampant, small-pox raging, people dispirited, and Manwa Sera sulky. "What prospects?" they asked, "lie before us but terrors, and fatal collapse and ruin? Better turn back in time." I told them to be resigned until the morning. They returned to their camp, which was about half a mile from the vicinity of the rapids.

Nov. 27.—Early next day the Wangwana were mustered. They lifted the boat out of the water above their heads, and cautiously conveyed her in about an hour below the rapids, and launched her on the quiet waters of the creek. Then a messenger was despatched to order Safeni to push the four remaining canoes into the rapids. Within an hour the rapids of Ukassa had been passed.

As there was abundance of time yet, it being only three in the afternoon, and I burned to know whether any more falls were below the rocky islets, I started down river with twenty men in the four canoes to explore. In about an hour we came to exceedingly swift rough water, much whirling and eddying, but no rapids; then, satisfied that there was no immediate prospect of meeting impediments to navigation, we started on our return, and arrived at camp at sunset, after an exceedingly eventful day.

Nov. 29.—On the 29th we moved down river four miles to Mburri, on the left bank, which is opposite Vinarunga, which is a large settlement of Wenya villages on the right bank. From our camp compass bearings showed Ukassa or Ussi Hills on right bank to be south-south-west (magnetic).

Just as we were retiring for the night, a canoe came down river, and cautiously made its way towards the boat. Shumari, the young brother of Uledi, who was on guard, waited until it was well within shore, and then suddenly seized the canoe-man, calling for assistance on the ever-ready boat's crew. The native was secured, and carried in before me; and when lights were brought we saw he was an old man bent almost double with age. His face was one of the most vicious my memory can recall. I presented him with about a dozen cowries, which he snatched from me as a surly dog might bite at a piece of meat from a stranger's hand. He was a true savage, hardened by wildness, and too old to learn. We put him back into his canoe, and set him adrift to find his way home.

An hour later, another stranger was found in the camp. He was also caught and brought to me. He was a lad of sixteen or seventeen years of age, a facsimile in miniature of the older savage. I smiled kindly, and conversed softly. I presented him with a string of bright red beads, and filled one of his hands with shells, and then I had him asked some questions. He replied to five, when he said he was tired, and would answer no more. We set a guard over him for the night, and in the morning permitted him to depart. I confessed my impotence to charm the savage soul.

As we were about to leave camp, three canoes advanced towards us from the Ukassa side of the river. Through our interpreters we spoke to them mildly, requested to know what offence we had committed, or whom we had harmed, to inspire them with such mortal hatred of strangers. Would they not make a bond of friendship with us? We had beads, cloth, brass, copper, iron, with which to buy food, goats, bananas, corn.

They listened attentively, and nodded their heads in approval. They asked if we would beat our drum for their amusement. Kadu, one of Mtesa's pages, who was an expert at the art, was called and commanded to entertain them after the best Kiganda fashion. Kadu seized his drum-sticks and drum, and after a few preliminary taps dashed out a volume of sound that must have been listened to with unbounded admiration by many hundreds of savages crouching in the woods.

"Ah," said the poor naked, mop-headed wretches, "it is delightful!" and they clapped their hands gleefully—and paddled away rapidly down river, steering for the right bank.

Nov. 30.—On the 30th the journey was resumed. The river ran with sharp bends, with many dangerous whirls, and broad patches of foam on its face, and was narrow, not above eight hundred yards in width, for a distance of three miles and a half, when it suddenly widened to 1700 yards. Two fine wooded islands stood in mid-stream. On the northern side of a little tributary we camped at the market-place of Usako Ngongo, Ukassa Hills bearing south-south-west. The southern end of the largest of the two islands, Nionga, bore east by north from camp.

These market-places on the banks of the Livingstone, at intervals of three or four miles, are central resorts of the aborigines from either bank, and considered as neutral ground, which no chief may claim, nor any individual assert claims or tribute for its use. Many of them are wide grassy spaces under the shade of mighty spreading trees, affording admirable river scenes for an artist. In the background is the deeply black forest, apparently impenetrable in its density; here and there a taller giant, having released itself from acquaintance and familiarity, overlooks its neighbours. Its branches are favoured by the white-collared eagle and the screaming ibis. Here and there rise the feathery and graceful fronds of the elais palm. In the foreground flows the broad brown river.

In the morning, on market days, the grassy plots are thronged. From the depths of the forest, and from isolated clearings, from lonely islands, and from the open country of the Bakusu, come together the aborigines with their baskets of cassava, their mats of palm-fibre and sedge, their gourds of palm-wine, their beans and maize, millet and sugar-cane, crockery and the handiwork of their artisans in copper and iron and wood, the vermilion camwood, their vegetables, and fruit of banana and plantain, their tobacco and pipes and bangles, their fish-nets and baskets, fish, and a multitude of things which their wants and tastes have taught them to produce. All is animation and eager chatter, until noon, when the place becomes silent again and untenanted, a prey to gloom and shade, where the hawk and the eagle, the ibis, the grey parrot, and the monkey, may fly and scream and howl, undisturbed.

STEW-POT OF THE WAHIKA.

Dec. 1.—On the 1st of December we floated down to the market-place of Ukongeh, opposite Mitandeh Island, in south latitude 3° 6′.

On this day we found ourselves in the vicinity of a place, of which a whisper had reached Livingstone on the 10th of March, 1871, who, while at Nyangwé, busied himself in noting down the reports of Wangwana and natives. Ukongeh market-place is the resort of the Wahika, whose chief, Luapanya, was killed by Mohammed bin Gharib's men. Behind the Wahika villages, about ten miles, lies the territory of the belligerent and cannibalistic Bakusu, an open and palm-growing country. The Arabs, each time they have attempted to penetrate Ukusu, have been repulsed with slaughter. On the right bank, opposite Mitandeh Island, is the territory of the Waziri.

By several islands of great beauty, and well-wooded with all varieties of tropical trees, we floated down to the market-place of Mivari, opposite the northern end of the island of

Mitangi. Uvitera village is a mile south, and opposite it is the settlement of Chabogwé.

The river here ran in two broad streams, each 1000 yards wide, on either side of a series of islands remarkable for their fertility. Where the islands are large, the mainland is but thinly populated, though a dense population occupies the country about two miles back from the river. On these neutral market-places, the islander and the backwoods people meet on equal terms for the purpose of bartering their various productions.

Dec. 4.—On the 4th of December we halted, because of a rain-storm, and also to forage for food, in which we were only partially successful. No conflicts resulted, fortunately.

Dec. 5.—The next day, the river flowing a little east of north, we came to Muriwa Creek, on the northern bank of which was a remarkably long village, or rather a series of villages, from fifty to a hundred yards apart, and a broad, uniform street, thirty feet wide, and two miles in length! Behind the village were the banana and the palm groves, which supplied the inhabitants with fruit, wine, and oil.

This remarkable town was called Ikondu, and was situated in south latitude 2° 53′. The huts were mere double cages, made very elegantly of the Panicum grass cane, 7 feet long by 5 feet wide and 6 feet high, separated, as regards the main building, but connected by the roof, so that the central apartments were common to both cages, and in these the families meet and perform their household duties, or receive their friends for social chat. Between each village was the burial-place or vault of their preceding kings, roofed over with the leaves of the *Phrynium ramosissimum*, which appears to be as useful a plant for many reasons as the banana to the Waganda. These cane cages are as cosy, comfortable, and dry as ships' cabins, as we found in the tempests of rain that every alternate day now visited us.

The town of Ikondu was quite deserted, but food was abundant; the wine-pots were attached to the palm-trees, bananas were hanging in clusters, in the gardens were fine large melons, luxuriant plantations of cassava, extensive plots of ground-nuts, and great tracts of waving sugar-cane.

We were very much dispirited, however. This desertion of their villages, without an attempt on the part of the natives to make terms, or the least chance of communicating with them, showed a stern contempt for the things of this life that approached the sublime. Whither had such a large population fled? For assuredly the population must have exceeded two thousand.

We were dispirited for other reasons. The small-pox was raging, dysentery had many victims, over fifty were infected with the itch, some twenty suffered from ulcers, many complained of chest-diseases, pneumonic fever, and pleurisis; there was a case or two of typhoid fever, and others suffered from prolapsus ani and umbilical pains; in short, there was work enough in the stricken Expedition for a dozen physicians. Every day we tossed two or three bodies into the deep

A HOUSE OF IKONDU.

waters of the Livingstone. Frank and I endeavoured our utmost to alleviate the misery, but when the long caravan was entering camp I had many times to turn my face away lest the tears should rise at sight of the miserable victims of disease who reeled and staggered through the streets. Poor creatures, what a life! wandering, ever wandering, in search of graves.

At Ikondu, left high and dry by some mighty flood years ago, there was a large condemned canoe with great holes in its keel, and the traces of decay both at bow and stern, yet it was capacious enough to carry sixty sick people, and by fastening cables to it the boat might easily take it in tow. I therefore called my carpenters, Uledi the coxswain, Saywa, his cousin, and Salaam Allah, and offered twelve yards of cloth to each if they would repair it within two days. They required twelve men and axes. The men were detailed, and day and night the axes and hatchets were at work trimming poles into narrow planking. The carpenters fitted the boards, and secured them with wooden pins, and with the bruised pulp of banana and bark cloth they caulked it. Then the Wangwana were called to launch the monster, and we presently had the satisfaction of seeing it float. It leaked a good deal, but some of the sick were not so ailing but that they might bale it sufficiently to keep themselves afloat.

The success of the repairs which we had made in this ancient craft proved to me that we possessed the means to construct a flotilla of canoes of sufficient capacity to float the entire Expedition. I resolved, therefore, should Tippu-Tib still persist in his refusal to proceed with us, to bribe him to stay with us until we should have constructed at least a means of escape.

Dec. 6.—About noon of the next day, while we were busy repairing the canoe, a native was found in the bushes close to the town with a small bow and a quiver of miniature arrows in his hand, and, it being a suspicious circumstance, he was secured and brought to me. He was a most remarkable specimen for a warrior, I thought, as I looked at the trembling diminutive figure. He stood, when measured, 4 feet $6\frac{1}{2}$ inches, round the chest 30 inches, and at the waist 24 inches. His head was large, his face decked with a scraggy fringe of whiskers, and his complexion light chocolate. As he was exceedingly bow-legged and thin-shanked, I at first supposed him to be a miserable abortion cast out by some tribe, and driven to wander through the forest, until he mentioned the word "Watwa." Recollecting that the Watwa were well known to be dwarfs, I asked Bwana Abed, the guide, if this man resembled those Watwa dwarfs Muhala's people had fought with. He replied that the Watwa he had met were at least a head shorter, though the man might be a member of some tribe related to those he had seen! His complexion was similar, but the dwarfs west of Ukuna, in the West Lumami country, had very long beards, and bushy whiskers. His weapons were also the same—the short bow, and tiny reed arrows, a foot long, with points smeared over with a dark substance, with an odour resembling that of cantharides. Everybody seemed to be particularly careful, as they examined the arrows, not to touch the points, and, as many of them were folded in leaves, it appeared to me that the native had some reason for this precaution. In order to verify this opinion, I uncovered one of the leaf-guarded points, and, taking hold of one of his arms, I gravely pretended to be about to inoculate the muscle with the dark substance on the arrow. His loud screams, visible terror, and cries of "Mabi! Mabi!" ("Bad, Bad,") with a persuasive eloquence of gesture, left no doubt in my mind that the arrows were poisoned.

But the native possessed the talent of pronunciation in an eminent degree. For the first time I heard the native name of the Livingstone, as known to the Manyema and Wenya, pronounced as distinctly and deliberately as though Haji Abdallah himself was endeavouring to convey to my interested ears the true word RU-A'R-OW-A, emphasizing the ante-penultimate syllable. I requested several Wangwana, Wanyamwezi, and Arabs to pronounce the word after him. Only the principal Arabs were able to articulate distinctly "Rua'rowa"; the black people transformed the word instantly into "Lualawa."

The ugly, prognathous-jawed creature, among other information he gave us, related that just below Ikondu there was an island called Maturu, whose people the "Kirembo-rembo" (lightning) had completely destroyed.

"Who sent the Kirembo-rembo, my friend?" I asked.

"Ah, who knows? Perhaps 'Firi Niambi'"—the deity.

"Were they all killed?"

"All—men, women, children, goats, bananas, everything."

He also told us that the chief of Ikondu, with all his people, was on the opposite side; that from the wooded bluffs fronting the Urindi river extended the powerful tribe of the Wabwiré, or Wasongora Meno ("the people of the filed teeth").

Dec. 8.—On the 8th of December we moved down river to Unya-N'singé, another large town, a mile in length, on the north side of a creek, about thirty yards wide. On the south side, on the summit of bluffs 125 feet high, was a similar town called Kisui-cha-Uriko.

About four miles up the river from Unya-N'singé, the Lira river entered the Livingstone. At the mouth it was

300 yards wide and 30 feet deep, but two miles above it narrowed to 250 yards of deep and tolerably clear water. A hostile movement on the part of the natives, accompanied by fierce demonstrations on shore, compelled us, however, to relinquish the design of penetrating farther up, and to hurry back to camp at Unya-N'singé.

We had not been long there before we heard the war-horns sounding on the right bank, and about 4 P.M. we saw eight large canoes coming up river along the islands in mid-stream, and six along the left bank. On approaching the camp they formed in line of battle near a small grassy island about four hundred yards from us, and shouted to us to come and meet them in mid-river. Our interpreters were told to tell them that we had but one boat, and five canoes loaded with sick people; and that as we had not come for the purpose of fighting, we would not fight.

A jeering laugh greeted the announcement, and the next minute the fourteen canoes dashed towards us with wild yells. I disposed my people along the banks, and waited. When they came within thirty yards, half of the men in each canoe began to shoot their poisoned arrows, while the other half continued to paddle in-shore. Just as they were about to land, the command to fire was given to about thirty muskets, and the savages fell back, retiring to the distance of about a hundred and fifty yards, whence they maintained the fight. Directing the people on shore to keep firing, I chose the boat's crew, including Tippu-Tib and Bwana Abdallah, and dashed out into mid-stream. The savages appeared to be delighted, for they yelled triumphantly as they came towards us; only for a short time, however, for we were now only some fifty yards from them and our guns were doing terrible execution. In about a minute the fight was over, and our wild foes were paddling down river; and we returned to our camp, glad that this first affair with the Wasongora Meno had terminated so quickly. Three of our people had been struck by arrows, but a timely application of caustic neutralized the poison, and, excepting swellings, nothing serious occurred.

Unya-N'singé is in south latitude 2° 49'. Nearly opposite it is Urangi, another series of small villages; while on the north bank of the Lira River, at the confluence, is the village of Uranja, and opposite to it is Kisui Kachamba. The town of Meginna is said to be about twenty miles south-east (magnetic) from Unya-N'singé. All this portion is reported to have been the scene of Muini Muhala's exploits.

Dec. 9, 10, 11.—On the 9th and the 10th we halted, waiting for the land division under Frank. On the morning of the 11th, as our friends had not arrived, I set out in my boat up river, and four miles above Unya-N'singé entered a creek, about forty yards wide, where I discovered them endeavouring to cross the stream. The boat was heartily welcomed, and in a few hours all were safely across.

They had, it appeared, again gone astray, and had entered Ukusu, where they were again obliged to fight. Four had received grievous wounds, and one had been killed. Three Wanyamwezi, moreover, had died of small-pox *en route* from Ikondu.

This creek, like all the rest in the neighbourhood, was half-choked with the *Pistia stratiotes*, which the aborigines had enclosed with logs of wood, as a considerable quantity of salt is obtained from these asparagus-like plants. When the log-enclosed spaces are full, the plants are taken out, exposed to the sun until they are withered, dried, and then burnt. The ashes are collected in pots with punctured bottoms, and the pots filled with water which is left to drip through into shallow basins. After the evaporation by fire of this liquid, a dark grey sediment of a nitrous flavour is left, which, re-cleansed, produces salt.

At the head of this creek the land division reported a hot-water spring, but I did not see it. On the bluffs, overhanging the creek, the Rubiaceæ, bombax, red-wood, iron-wood, and stink-wood, with various palms, flourished.

The bed of the river consists of shale. Twenty yards from the bank the river was about 12 feet deep; at 100 yards I obtained 23 feet soundings. The bluffs exhibit at the water-line horizontal strata of greenish shale; above, near the summit, the rock is grey with age and weather.

Here we dismissed our dwarf to his home, with a handful of shells and four necklaces of beads for his very intelligent geographical knowledge and his civilized pronunciation. He could not comprehend why we did not eat him; and though we shook hands with him and smiled, and patted him on the shoulder, I doubt whether he felt himself perfectly safe until he had plunged out of sight into his native woods once more.

Tibbu-Tib determined to journey on land, and Frank and

Sheikh Abdallah were invited to the boat. Eight more victims to small-pox were admitted into the hospital canoes, among them being three young girls, the favourites of Tippu-Tib's harem. For the accommodation of the raving and delirious sick, we constructed a shed over the hospital-canoe. Before we moved from Unya-N'singé, we had thrown eight corpses into the Livingstone.

Dec. 14.—On the 14th, gliding down river without an effort on our part, we reached Kisui-Kachiambi, another large town about a mile in length, and consisting of about three hundred long houses—situated on the left bank, in south latitude 2° 35′. Opposite Mutako the natives made a brilliant and well-planned attack on us, by suddenly dashing upon us from a creek; and had not the ferocious nature of the people whom we daily encountered taught us to be prepared at all times against assault, we might have suffered considerable injury. Fortunately, only one man was slightly punctured with a poisoned arrow, and an immediate and plentiful application of nitrate of silver nullified all evil effects.

During our halt at Kisui-Kachiambi, two of the favourite women of Tippu-Tib died of small-pox, and three youths also fell victims; of the land division only one perished.

Dec. 18.—On the 18th, after floating down a few miles, we came to a broad channel which ran between the populous island of Mpika and the left bank, and arriving at a market-green, under the shade of fine old trees, halted for breakfast. The aborigines of Mpika at once gathered opposite, blew war-horns, and mustered a large party, preparing to attack us with canoes. To prevent surprise from the forest while the porridge for the sick was being cooked, I had placed scouts on either side of each of the roads that penetrated inland from the market green, at about a couple of hundred yards' distance from the camp. It happened that, while drums were beating and horns were blowing on the island, and everybody seemed mustering for a grand attack on us, a party of ten people (among whom were three very fine-looking women), who had been on a trading excursion to a village inland, and were returning to their island home, had been waiting to be ferried across from the market-place when we occupied it. The scouts surrounded them, and, seeing there was no escape, they came into the market-place. The interpreters were called to calm their fears, and to tell them that we were simply travellers going down river, with no intention of hurting anybody.

By means of these people we succeeded in checking the warlike demonstrations of the islanders, and in finally persuading them to make blood-brotherhood, after which we invited canoes to come and receive their friends. As they hesitated to do so, we embarked them in our own boat, and conveyed them across to the island.

The news then spread quickly along the whole length of the island that we were friends, and as we resumed our journey, crowds from the shore cried out to us, "Mwendé Kivuké-vuké." ("Go in peace!")

The crest of the island was about eighty feet above the river, and was a marvel of vegetation, chiefly of plantain and banana plantations. On our left rose the other bank, with similar wooded heights, dipping occasionally into small creeks and again rising into ridges, with slopes, though steep, clothed with a perfect tangle of shrubs and plants.

After a descent of ten miles by this channel, we found the river increased in width to 2000 yards. While rowing down, close to the left bank, we were suddenly surprised by hearing a cry from one of the guards of the hospital canoes, and, turning round, saw an arrow fixed in his chest. The next instant, looking towards the bank, we saw the forms of many men in the jungle, and several arrows flew past my head in extremely unpleasant proximity.

We sheered off instantly, and, pulling hard down stream, came near the landing-place of an untenanted market-green. Here we drew in-shore, and, sending out ten scouts to lie in wait in the jungle, I mustered all the healthy men, about thirty in number, and proceeded to construct a fence of brushwood, inspired to unwonted activity by a knowledge of our lonely, defenceless state.

Presently a shriek of agony from another of my men rang out through the jungle, followed immediately by the sharp crack of the scouts' Sniders, which again was responded to by an infernal din of war-horns and yells, while arrows flew past us from all directions. Twenty more men were at once sent into the jungle to assist the scouts, while, with might and main, we laboured to surround our intended camp with tall and dense hedges of brushwood, with sheltered nooks for riflemen.

After an hour's labour the camp was deemed sufficiently

tenable, and the recall was sounded. The scouts retreated on the run, shouting as they approached, "Prepare! prepare! they are coming!"

About fifty yards of ground outside our camp had been cleared, which, upon the retreat of the scouts who had been keeping them in check, was soon filled by hundreds of savages, who pressed upon us from all sides but the river, in the full expectation that we were flying in fear. But they were mistaken, for we were at bay, and desperate in our resolve not to die without fighting. Accordingly, at such close quarters the contest soon became terrific. Again and again the savages hurled themselves upon our stockade, launching spear after spear with deadly force into the camp, to be each time repulsed. Sometimes the muzzles of our guns almost touched their breasts. The shrieks, cries, shouts of encouragement, the rattling volleys of musketry, the booming war-horns, the yells and defiance of the combatants, the groans and screams of the women and children in the hospital camp, made together such a medley of hideous noises as can never be effaced from my memory. For two hours this desperate conflict lasted. More than once, some of the Wangwana were about to abandon the struggle and run to the canoes, but Uledi, the coxswain, and Frank threatened them with clubbed muskets, and with the muzzles of their rifles drove them back to the stockade. At dusk the enemy retreated from the vicinity of the clearing; but the hideous alarums produced from their ivory horns, and increased by the echoes of the close forest, still continued; and now and again a vengeful poison-laden arrow flew by with an ominous whizz to quiver in the earth at our feet, or fall harmlessly into the river behind us.

Sleep, under such circumstances, was out of the question; yet there were many weak, despairing souls whom even the fear of being eaten could not rouse to a sense of manliness and the necessity for resistance. Aware of this, I entrusted the task of keeping the people awake to Frank Pocock, Sheikh Abdallah, and Wadi Rehani, the "treasurer" of the Expedition, who were ordered to pour kettles of cold water over their heads upon the least disposition to go to sleep.

About 11 P.M. a dark form was seen creeping from the bush on all fours towards our stockade. I moved quietly to where vigilant Uledi was maintaining watch and ward, and whispered to him to take two men and endeavour to catch him. Uledi willingly consented, and burrowed out through a slight opening in the fence. The eyes of those in the secret became fastened upon the dim shadows of the hostile forms, so similar, it seemed to me, in their motions to a crocodile which I had seen on a rock near Kisorya in Ukerewé, as it endeavoured to deceive a large diver into the belief that it was asleep while actually meditating its murder.

Soon we saw Uledi's form leap upon that of the prostrate savage and heard him call out for help, which was at once given him by his two assistants; but an ominous rustling in the bushes behind announced that the cunning enemy were also on the alert, and as they rushed to the rescue, Uledi snatched his captive's spears, and with his two friends retreated into the camp, while our guns again awoke the echoes of the forest and the drowsy men in the camp to a midnight action as brisk as it was short.

Twit, twit, fell the arrows once more in showers, piercing the brush fence, perforating the foliage, or smartly tapping the trunks and branches, while we, crouching down on the ground, under the thick shadows of the brushwood, replied with shot, slugs, and bullets, that swept the base of the jungle.

Silence was soon again restored and the strict watch renewed. From a distance the poisoned reeds still pattered about us, but, protected by our snug stockade and lying low in our covert, they were harmless, though they kept us awake listening to the low whizz and reminding one another that the foe was still near.

Dec. 19.—Morning dawned upon the strange scene. The cooks proceeded to make fires, to cook some food, under the shelter of the high banks, that we might break our long fasts. Frank and I made a sufficient meal out of six roasted bananas and a few cups of sugarless coffee.

After which, giving strict orders to Frank and Sheikh Abdallah to be vigilant in my absence, the boat was manned, and I was rowed to a distance of 500 yards from the camp towards the right bank. There stopping to examine the shores, I was surprised to see, only a quarter of a mile below our camp, a large town, consisting, like those above, of a series of villages, in a uniform line along the high bank, while a perfect wealth of palm-trees and banana plantations proved unquestionably the prosperity of the populous district.

I recollected then that the intelligent dwarf already mentioned had spoken of a powerful chief, whose district, called Vinya-Njara, possessed so many men that it would be utterly impossible to pass him.

My plans were soon made. It was necessary that we should occupy the southernmost village in order to house the sick, to obtain food for ourselves, and to keep up communication with the land division when it should announce its presence.

We rowed back to the camp, by this time the observed of a thousand heads which projected from the jungle between our camp and the first village. As nothing had been unpacked from the boat and the hospital-canoes, and only the defenders of the camp had disembarked, every soul was in a few seconds seated in his place, and pulling swiftly over that intervening quarter of a mile down to the landing of the first village—targets, it is true, for several arrows for a short time, but no one could stop to reply. Arriving at the landing, two men were detailed off to each canoe and the boat, and we rushed up the high and steep bank. The village was empty, and, by cutting some trees down to block up each end, became at once perfectly defensible.

We were not long left unmolested. The savages recovered their wits, and strove desperately to dislodge us, but at each end of the village, which was about three hundred yards long, our muskets blazed incessantly. I also caused three or four sharpshooters to ascend tall trees along the river banks, which permitted them, though unseen, to overlook the tall grasses and rear of the village, and to defend us from fire. Meanwhile, for the first time for twenty-four hours, the sick (seventy-two in number) were allotted one-fourth of the village for themselves, as over one-half of them were victims of the pest, of which three had died in the canoes during the fearful hours of the previous night.

The combat lasted until noon, when, mustering twenty-five men, we made a sally, and succeeded in clearing the skirts of the village for the day. Uledi caught one of the natives by the foot, and succeeded in conveying him within the village, where he was secured as a most welcome prize, through whom we might possibly, if opportunities offered, bring this determined people to reason.

Then while the scouts deployed in a crescent form from beyond the ends of the village into the forest, the rest of our force formed in line, and commenced to cut down all weeds and grass within a distance of a hundred yards. This work consumed three hours, after which the scouts were withdrawn, and we rested half an hour for another scant meal of bananas. Thus refreshed after our arduous toil, we set about building marksmen's nests at each end of the village 15 feet high, which, manned with ten men each, commanded all approaches. For our purpose there were a number of soft-wood logs, already prepared in the village, and bark rope and cane-fibre were abundant in every hut, for the inhabitants of Vinya-Njara devoted themselves, among other occupations, to fishing, and the manufacture of salt from the Pistia plants.

By evening our labours were nearly completed. During the night there was a slight alarm, and now and then the tapping on the roofs and the pattering among the leaves informed us that our enemies were still about, but we did not reply to them.

Dec. 20.—The next morning an assault was attempted, for the enemy emerged from the bush on the run into the clearing; but our arrangements seemed to surprise them, for they retreated again almost immediately into the gloomy obscurities of the jungle, where they maintained, with indomitable spirit, horn-blowing and a terrific "bo-bo-boing."

We had, it seems—though I have not had time to mention it before—passed the tribes which emitted cries of "Ooh-hu-hu, ooh-hu, ooh-hu-hu," for ever since our arrival at Vinya-Njara we had listened with varied feelings to the remarkable war-strains of "Bo-bo, bo-bo, bo-bo-o-o-oh," uttered in tones so singular as to impress even my African comrades with a sense of its eccentricity.

About noon a large flotilla of canoes was observed ascending the river close to the left bank, manned by such a dense mass of men that any number between five hundred and eight hundred would be within the mark. We watched them very carefully until they had ascended the river about half a mile above us, when, taking advantage of the current, they bore down towards us, blowing their war-horns, and drumming vigorously. At the same moment, as though this were a signal in concert with those on land, war-horns responded from the forest, and I had scarcely time to order every man to look out when the battle-tempest of arrows broke upon us from the woods. But the twenty men in the nests at the corners of the village proved sufficient to resist the attack from the forest side, Frank Pocock being in charge of one, and Sheikh Abdallah of the other, while I, with twenty men lining the bushes along the water line, defended the river side.

This was a period when every man felt that he must either fight or resign himself to the only other alternative, that of being heaved a headless corpse into the river. Our many successful struggles for a precarious existence had begun to animate even the most cowardly with that pride of life that superiority creates, and that feeling of invulnerability that frequent lucky escapes foster. I was conscious, as I cast my eyes about, that my followers were conspicuously distinguishing themselves, and were at last emerging from that low level of undeveloped manhood which is the general state of men untried and inexperienced. With a number of intelligent whites, that acquisition of courageous qualities would have been assisted by natural good sense, and a few months' hard service such as we had undergone would have sufficed to render them calm and steady in critical times; but with such people as I had, who had long shown—with the exception of a few—a wonderful inaptitude for steadiness, the lesson had taken two years. These last few days on the Livingstone river had been rapidly perfecting that compact band for the yet more dangerous times and periods to come.

Therefore, though the notes of the war-horns were dreadful, our foe numerous and pertinacious, and evidently accustomed to victory, I failed to observe one man amongst my people then fighting who did not seem desirous to excel even Uledi, the coxswain.

The battle had continued half an hour with a desperate energy, only qualified by our desperate state. Ammunition we possessed in abundance, and we made use of it with deadly effect, yet what might have become of us is doubtful, had not the advanced-guard of Tippu-Tib and our land division arrived at this critical juncture, causing dismay to the savages in the forest, who announced the reinforcement by war-horns to the savages in the canoes, many of whom were, at the moment, making most strenuous efforts to effect a landing. The river savages, upon hearing these signals, withdrew, but as they were paddling away they proclaimed their intention of preventing all escape, either up river or down river, and expressed their enormous contempt for us by throwing water towards us with their paddles. We saw all the canoes mysteriously disappear behind an island, situated about 1600 yards off, and opposite to our camp.

It was a great pleasure to greet all our people once more, though they were in a wretched plight. Bad food, and a scarcity of even that during three days in the jungle, constantly losing the road, wandering aimlessly about, searching for thinly grown spots through which they might creep more easily, had reduced their physical strength so much that it was clear at a glance that several days must elapse before they would be able to resume their journey.

When all had arrived, I called the forty defenders of the camp together, and distributing cloth to each of them, told them that as the enemy had taken their canoes behind the island opposite, they very probably intended to resume the fight; that it was, therefore, our duty to prevent that if possible, by making a night expedition, and cutting the canoes adrift, which would leave them under the necessity of abandoning the project of attacking us; "besides," said I, "if we can do the job in a complete way, the enormous loss of canoes will have such an effect on them that it will clear our progress down river."

Frank Pocock was requested to take his choice of crews and man the four little canoes, which would carry about twenty men, and, proceeding to the south end of the islet, to spread his canoes across the mouth of the channel, between the islet and the right bank, while I proceeded in the boat to the north end of the islet, and, bearing down the channel, sought out the enemy's canoes and cut them adrift, which floating down, were to be picked up by him.

It was a rainy, gusty night, and dark; but at 10 P.M., the hour of deepest sleep, we set out with muffled oars, Frank to his appointed position, and I up river, along the left bank, until, having ascended nearly opposite the lower end of Mpika Island, we cut rapidly across river to the right bank. Then, resting on our oars, we searched the bank narrowly, until seeing a fire on the bank we rowed cautiously in, and discovered eight large canoes, each tied by a short cable of rattan to a stake, driven deep into the clay. Uledi, Bwana Hamadi, and myself soon set these free, and giving each a push successively far into the stream, waited a short time, and then followed them in our boat. Four other canoes were cut adrift a few hundred yards below. On coming into the channel between the islet and the bank, numerous bright fires informed us that the largest number of the enemy was encamped on it, and that their canoes must be fastened below the several camps. We distinctly heard the murmur of voices, and the coughing of shivering people, or of those who indulged in the pernicious *bhang*; but gliding under the shadows of the tall banks and in the solemn blackness of the trees, we were unperceived, and canoe after canoe, each with its paddles and scoops within, was pushed into the swift stream, which conveyed it down river to where we felt assured Frank was ready with his sharp and quick-eyed assistants. In this manner thirty-six canoes, some of great size, were sent adrift; and not being able to discover more, we also followed them noiselessly down stream, until we came to Frank's canoes, which were being borne down stream by the weight of so many. However, casting the great stone anchor of the boat, canoe after canoe was attached to us, and leaving twenty-six in charge of Frank, we hoisted sail and rowed up stream, with twelve canoes in tow. Arriving at camp, the canoes were delivered in charge to the Wangwana, and then the boat hastily returned to lend assistance to Frank, who made his presence known to us by occasionally blowing the trumpet. After relieving him of eight more canoes, he was able almost to keep up with us to camp, where we all arrived at 5 A.M., after a most successful night expedition.

CANOE SCOOP.

SCOOPS.

Dec. 21.—At 9 A.M. the boat was manned again, and we rowed to the scene of our midnight labours. The island was all but abandoned! Only a few persons were left, and to them, with the aid of our interpreters, we communicated our terms, viz., that we would occupy Vinya-Njara, and retain all the canoes unless they made peace. We also informed them that we had one prisoner, who would be surrendered to them if they availed themselves of our offer of peace; that we had suffered heavily, and they had also suffered; that war was an evil which wise men avoided; that if they came with two canoes with their chiefs, two canoes with our chiefs should meet them in mid-stream, and make blood-brotherhood; and that on that condition some of their canoes should be restored, and we would purchase the rest.

They replied that what we had spoken was quite true, but as their chiefs were some distance away in the woods they must have time to communicate with them, but that they would announce their decision next day. We then left them, not, however, without throwing packets of shells towards them, as an earnest of our wish to be friends, and rowed to our camp at Vinya-Njara.

The forests for a distance of ten miles around Vinya-Njara were clear of enemies. The friendly natives of Mpika Island came down to our assistance in negotiating a peace between us and the surly chiefs, who had all withdrawn into the forests on the right bank.

Dec. 22.—On the 22nd of December, the ceremony of blood-brotherhood having been formally concluded, in mid-river, between Safeni and the chief of Vinya-Njara, our captive and fifteen canoes were returned, and twenty-three canoes were retained by us for a satisfactory equivalent, and thus our desperate struggle terminated. Our losses at Vinya-Njara were four killed and thirteen wounded.

In the afternoon, Tippu-Tib, Sheikh Abdallah, and Muini Ibrahim declared their intention of returning to Nyangwé by another route, and with such firmness of tone that I renounced the idea of attempting to persuade them to change their decision. Indeed, the awful condition of the sick, the high daily mortality, the constant attacks on us during each journey, and the last terrible struggle with Vinya-Njara, had produced such dismal impressions on the minds of the escort that no amount of money would have bribed the undisciplined people of Tippu-Tib to have entertained for a moment the idea of continuing the journey.

Though eight marches were still wanting to complete the twenty camps from Wané-Kirumbu, in Uregga, I felt that their courage was exhausted. I therefore consented to release Tippu-Tib from his engagement, on condition that he used his influence with the people of the Expedition to follow me. He consented to do so, and in consideration for his services thus far and the calamities that his people had undergone, I distributed the following gifts :—

To Tibbu-Tib, a draft for 2,600 dollars, 1 riding-ass, 1 trunk, 1 gold chain, 30 doti of fine cloth, 150 lbs. of beads, 16,300 shells, 1 revolver, 200 rounds of ammunition, 50 lbs. of brass wire.
" Sheikh Abdallah, 20 doti of cloth.
" Muini Ibrahim, 10 doti of cloth.
" Bwana Abed, the guide, 10 doti of cloth.

To Bwana Hamadi, 5 doti of cloth.
" " Cheché, 5 doti of cloth.
" " Khamis, 5 doti of cloth.
" 50 of his principal men, 2 doti of cloth.
" 90 of his escort, 1 doti of cloth.
" each of the Wangwana chiefs, 2½ doti of cloth.
" each of the Wanyamwezi and Wangwana of the Expedition, 1½ doti of cloth.
" each woman and boy, 1 doti of cloth.

It was then announced that—inasmuch as my duty compelled me to endeavour to do my utmost to trace the great river to the sea, and as the chiefs and the principal men of the Expedition were resolved to follow me wherever I should lead them—on the fifth day from then we should strike our camp, and form a new and separate camp, and that on the sixth day we should embark, and begin our journey down the river to the ocean—or to death.

Said I: "Into whichever sea this great river empties, there shall we follow it. You have seen that I have saved you a score of times, when everything looked black and dismal for us. That care of you to which you owe your safety hitherto, I shall maintain, until I have seen you safe and sound in your own homes, and under your own palm-trees. All I ask of you is, perfect trust in whatever I say. On your lives depends my own; if I risk yours, I risk mine. As a father looks after his children, I will look after you. It is true we are not so strong as when the Wanyaturu attacked us, or when we marched through Unyoro to Muta Nzigé, but we are of the same band of men, and we are still of the same spirit. Many of our party have already died, but death is the end of all; and if they died earlier than we, it was the will of God, and who shall rebel against His will? It may be we shall meet a hundred wild tribes yet, who, for the sake of eating us, will rush to meet and fight us. We have no wish to molest them. We have moneys with us, and are, therefore, not poor. If they fight us, we must accept it as an evil, like disease, which we cannot help. We shall continue to do our utmost to make friends, and the river is wide and deep. If we fight, we fight for our lives. It may be that we shall be distressed by famine and want. It may be that we shall meet with many more cataracts, or find ourselves before a great lake, whose wild waves we cannot cross with these canoes; but we are not children, we have heads, and arms, and are we not always under the eye of God, who will do with us as He sees fit? Therefore, my children, make up your minds as I have made up mine, that, as we are now in the very middle of this continent, and it would be just as bad to return as to go on, we shall continue our journey, that we shall toil on, and on, by this river and no other, to the salt sea." *

A loud shout of applause greeted me as I concluded, and Manwa Sera followed it up, and in a few spirited words said that they were bound to let the Wanyamwezi see of what stuff the sea children were made, and, turning to the Arabs, he asked them to look at the black men who were about to perform what they dreaded. Uledi, the coxswain, on behalf of the boat-boys, said that I was their father, and though every one else should refuse to move farther, Frank and I might step into the boat, and he and his friends would dare the long journey that very day!

There was ample work for us all before setting out on our adventurous journey. Food had to be procured and prepared for at least twenty days. Several of the canoes required to be repaired, and all to be lashed in couples, to prevent them from capsizing; and special arrangements required to be made for the transport of three riding-asses, which we had resolved upon taking with us, as a precaution in the event of our being compelled to abandon the canoes and to journey along the banks.

Dec. 25.—Christmas Day we passed most pleasantly and happily, like men determined to enjoy life while it lasted. In the morning we mustered all the men, and appointed

* A poetical friend on hearing this address brought to my notice a remarkable coincidence. In one of Tennyson's poems, Ulysses addresses his followers thus:—

"My mariners,
Souls that have toiled, and wrought, and thought with me,
That ever with a frolic welcome took
The thunder and the sunshine, and opposed
Free hearts, free foreheads: come, my friends,
'Tis not too late to seek a newer world.
Push off, and sitting well in order smite
The sounding furrows; for my purpose holds
To sail beyond the sunset until I die.
It may be that the gulfs will wash us down;
It may be we shall touch the happy isles
And see the great Achilles whom we knew.
Though much is taken, much abides; and tho'
We are not now that strength which in old days
Moved earth and heaven; that which we are, we are,
One equal temper of heroic hearts,
Made weak by time and fate, but strong in will
To strive, to seek, to find, and not to yield."

them to their respective canoes. Names taken from those British cruisers which had become familiar to the east coast people were also given to them by the Zanzibaris, amid loud laughter, except to half-a-dozen which Frank and I reserved to bear such names as we selected for them.

1. The exploring boat, Lady Alice.
2. Ocean, commanded by Frank.
3. Livingstone.
4. Stanley.
5. Telegraph.
6. Herald.
7. Jason.
8. Argo.
9. Penguin.
10. Wolverine.
11. Fawn.
12. Glasgow (flag-ship, commanded by Manwa Sera).
13. London Town.
14. America.
15. Hart.
16. Daphne.
17. Lynx.
18. Nymph.
19. Vulture.
20. Shark.
21. Arab.
22. Mirambo.
23. Mtesa.

Canoe races were afterwards instituted between the various vessels, and to the crews who excelled were awarded gifts of cloth. The afternoon was celebrated by foot-races, in which, for the sake of the prizes offered, the Arabs joined, occasioning much amusement to the people. The great event was the race between the famous Tippu-Tib and Francis Pocock. The Arab prepared himself with unusual determination to compete for the prize, a richly chased silver goblet and cup, one of the presents bestowed on me before leaving England. The course was 300 yards, from end to end of the village street. Though Frank exerted himself to the utmost. the sinews of the muscular Arab carried him to the front at the finish by 15 yards. Then the little boys of the Expedition competed with the little boys of the escort, and finally ten young women were induced to attempt to compete for a prize, and their presence on the racecourse convulsed the hundreds assembled to witness the unusual scene. Some were very ungainly and elephantine in their movements, especially Muscati, the wife of the chief Safeni, but others were most graceful of body and lithe of limb, and raced with the swiftness of Atalanta. But the girl Khamisi of Zanzibar was declared the winner.

A dance, by a hundred Wanyamwezi, adorned in all the feathered glory and terror of war, with sounding drums and melodious blasts from ivory horns, terminated the extraordinary festivities.

Dec. 26.—On the 26th Tippu-Tib gave a banquet of rice

and roasted sheep to the Expedition, and malofu, or palm-wine, from Mpika Island, assisted to maintain the high spirits and sanguine prospects of success with which these cheery proceedings, festivities, and sports inspired us.

The next day at dawn we embarked all the men, women, and children, 149 souls in all, and the riding-asses of the Expedition, and, telling Tippu-Tib we should on the morrow pull up stream and descend the river close to the village of Vinya-Njara for a last farewell, we pulled across to the islet near the right bank, where we constructed a rude camp for the only night we should remain.

When I ascertained, after arrival, that every soul connected with the Expedition was present, my heart was filled with a sense of confidence and trust such as I had not enjoyed since leaving Zanzibar.

In the evening, while sleep had fallen upon all save the watchful sentries in charge of the boat and canoes, Frank and I spent a serious time.

Frank was at heart as sanguine as I that we should finally emerge somewhere, but, on account of the persistent course of the great river towards the north, a little uneasiness was evident in his remarks.

"Before we finally depart, sir," said he, "do you really believe, in your inmost soul, that we shall succeed? I ask this because there are such odds against us—not that I for a moment think it would be best to return, having proceeded so far."

"Believe? Yes, I do believe that we shall all emerge into light again some time. It is true that our prospects are as dark as this night. Even the Mississippi presented no such obstacles to De Soto as this river will necessarily present to us. Possibly its islands and its forests possessed much of the same aspect, but here we are at an altitude of sixteen hundred and fifty feet above the sea. What conclusions can we arrive at? Either that this river penetrates a great distance north of the Equator, and, taking a mighty sweep round, descends into the Congo—this, by the way, would lessen the chances of there being many cataracts in the river;—or that we shall shortly see it in the neighbourhood of the Equator, take a direct cut towards the Congo, and precipitate itself, like our Colorado river, through a deep cañon, or down great cataracts; or that it is either the Niger or the Nile. I believe it will prove to be the Congo; if the Congo, then there must be many cataracts. Let us only hope that the cataracts are all in a lump, close together.

"Any way, whether the Congo, the Niger, or the Nile, I am prepared, otherwise I should not be so confident. Though I love life as much as you do, or any other man does, yet on the success of this effort I am about to stake my life, my all. To prevent its sacrifice foolishly I have devised numerous expedients with which to defy wild men, wild nature, and unknown terrors. There is an enormous risk, but you know the adage, 'Nothing risked, nothing won.'

* * * * * *

"Now look at this, the latest chart which Europeans have drawn of this region. It is a blank, perfectly white. We will draw two curves just to illustrate what I mean. One shows the river reaching the Equator and turning westward. Supposing there are no cataracts, we ought to reach 'Tuckey's Furthest' by the 15th of February; but if the river takes that wider sweep from 2° north of the Equator, we may hope to reach by the 15th of March, and, if we allow a month for cataracts or rapids, we have a right to think that we ought to see the ocean by either the middle or the end of April, 1877.

"I assure you, Frank, this enormous void is about to be filled up. Blank as it is, it has a singular fascination for me. Never has white paper possessed such a charm for me as this has, and I have already mentally peopled it, filled it with most wonderful pictures of towns, villages, rivers, countries, and tribes—all in the imagination—and I am burning to see whether I am correct or not. *Believe!* I see us gliding down by tower and town, and my mind will not permit a shadow of doubt. Good-night, my boy! Good-night! and may happy dreams of the sea, and ships, and pleasure, and comfort, and success attend you in your sleep! To-morrow, my lad, is the day we shall cry—'Victory or death!'"

"TOWARDS THE UNKNOWN."

CHAPTER VII.

Farewell to Tippu-Tib—Attacked from both banks—The fat savage takes a bad shot at me—In the home of the elephants—Insect life—Under covert—The Lowwa river—A storm on the river—New Year's Day—Bullets against spears—"Sennenneh!"—Tempting the female mind—The reward of a good deed—A river armada: crocodile boats—Betwixt cataracts and cannibals.

Dec. 28.—The crisis drew nigh when the 28th of December dawned. A grey mist hung over the river, so dense that we could not see even the palmy banks on which Vinya-Njara was situated. It would have been suicidal to begin our journey on such a gloomy morning. The people appeared as cheerless and dismal as the foggy day. We cooked our breakfasts in order to see if, by the time we had fortified the soul by satisfying the cravings of the stomach, the river and its shores might not have resumed their usual beautiful outlines, and their striking contrasts of light and shadow.

Slowly the breeze wafted the dull and heavy mists away until the sun appeared, and bit by bit the luxuriantly wooded banks rose up solemn and sad. Finally the grey river was seen, and at 9 A.M. its face gleamed with the brightness of a mirror.

"Embark, my friends! Let us at once away! and a happy voyage to us."

The drum and trumpet proclaimed to Tippu-Tib's expectant ears that we were ascending the river. In half an hour we were pulling across to the left bank, and when we reached it a mile above Vinya-Njara we rested on our oars. The strong brown current soon bore us down within hearing of a deep and melodious diapason of musical voices chanting the farewell song. How beautiful it sounded to us as we approached them! The dense jungle and forests seemed to be penetrated with the vocal notes, and the river to bear them tenderly towards us. Louder the sad notes swelled on our ears, full of a pathetic and mournful meaning. With bated breath we listened to the rich music which spoke to us unmistakably of parting, of sundered friendship, a long, perhaps eternal farewell. We came in view of them as, ranged along the bank in picturesque costume, the sons of Unyamwezi sang their last song. We waved our hands to them. Our hearts were so full of grief that we could not speak. Steadily the brown flood bore us by, and fainter and fainter came the notes down the water, till finally they died away, leaving us all alone in our loneliness.

But, looking up, I saw the gleaming portal to the Unknown: wide open to us and away down, for miles and miles, the river lay stretched with all the fascination of its mystery. I stood up and looked at the people. How few they appeared, to dare the region of fable and darkness! They were nearly all sobbing. They were leaning forward, bowed, as it seemed, with grief and heavy hearts.

"Sons of Zanzibar," I shouted, "the Arabs and the Wanyamwezi are looking at you. They are now telling one another what brave fellows you are. Lift up your heads and be men. What is there to fear? All the world is smiling with joy. Here we are altogether like one family, with hearts united, all strong with the purpose to reach our homes. See this river; it is the road to Zanzibar. When saw you a road so wide? When did you journey along a path like this? Strike your paddles deep, cry out Bismillah! and let us forward."

Poor fellows! with what wan smiles they responded to my words! How feebly they paddled! But the strong flood was itself bearing us along, and the Vinya-Njara villages were fast receding into distance.

Then I urged my boat's crew, knowing that thus we should tempt the canoes to quicker pace. Three or four times Uledi, the coxswain, gallantly attempted to sing, in order to invite a cheery chorus, but his voice soon died into such piteous hoarseness that the very ludicrousness of the tones caused his young friends to smile even in the midst of their grief.

We knew that the Vinya-Njara district was populous from the numbers of natives that fought with us by land and water, but we had no conception that it was so thickly populated as the long row of villages we now saw indicated. I counted fourteen separate villages, each with its respective growth of elais palm and banana, and each separated from the other by thick bush.

Every three or four miles after passing Vinja-Njara, there were small villages visible on either bank, but we met with no disturbance, fortunately. At 5 P.M. we made for a small village called Kali-Karero, and camped there, the natives having retired peacefully. In half an hour they returned, and the ceremony of brotherhood was entered upon, which insured a peaceful night. The inhabitants of Rukura, opposite us, also approached us with confidence, and an interchange of small gifts served us as a healthy augury for the future.

Dec. 29.—On the morning of the 29th, accompanied by a couple of natives in a small fishing-canoe, we descended the river along the left bank, and, after about four miles, arrived at the confluence of the Kasuku, a dark-water stream of a hundred yards' width at the mouth. Opposite the mouth, at the southern end of Kaimba—a long wooded island on the right bank, and a little above the confluence—stands the important village of Kisanga-Sanga.

Below Kaimba Island and its neighbour, the Livingstone assumes a breadth of 1800 yards. The banks are very populous: the villages of the left bank comprise the district of Luavala. We thought for some time we should be permitted to pass by quietly, but soon the great wooden drums, hollowed out of huge trees, thundered the signal along the river that there were strangers. In order to lessen all chances of a rupture between us, we sheered off to the middle of the river, and quietly lay on our paddles. But from both banks at once, in fierce concert, the natives, with their heads gaily feathered, and armed with broad black wooden shields and long spears, dashed out towards us.

Tippu-Tib before our departure had hired to me two young men of Ukusu—cannibals—as interpreters. These were now instructed to cry out the word "Sennenneh!" ("Peace!"), and to say that we were friends.

But they would not reply to our greeting, and in a bold peremptory manner told us to return.

"But we are doing no harm, friends. It is the river that takes us down, and the river will not stop, or go back."

"This is our river."

"Good. Tell it to take us back, and we will go."

"If you do not go back, we will fight you."

"No, don't; we are friends."

"We don't want you for our friends; we will eat you."

But we persisted in talking to them, and as their curiosity was so great they persisted in listening, and the consequence was that the current conveyed us near to the right bank;

WAR DRUMS OF THE TRIBES OF THE UPPER LIVINGSTONE.

and in such near neighbourhood to another district, that our discourteous escort had to think of themselves, and began to skurry hastily up river, leaving us unattacked.

The villages on the right bank also maintained a tremendous drumming and blowing of war-horns, and their wild men hurried up with menace towards us, urging their sharp-prowed canoes so swiftly that they seemed to skim over the water like flying-fish. Unlike the Luavala villagers, they did not wait to be addressed, but as soon as they came within fifty or sixty yards they shot out their spears, crying out, "Meat! meat! Ah! ha! We shall have plenty of meat! Bo-bo-bo-bo, Bo-bo-bo-bo-o o!"

Undoubtedly these must be relatives of the terrible "Bo-bo-bo's" above, we thought, as with one mind we rose to respond to this rabid man-eating tribe. Anger we had none for them. It seemed to me so absurd to be angry with people who looked upon one only as an epicure would regard a fat capon. Sometimes also a faint suspicion came to my mind that this was all but a part of a hideous dream. Why was it that I should be haunted with the idea that there were human beings who regarded me and my friends only in the light of meat? Meat! *We?* Heavens! what an atrocious idea!

"Meat! Ah! we shall have meat to day. Meat! meat! meat!"

There was a fat-bodied wretch in a canoe, whom I allowed to crawl within spear-throw of me; who, while he swayed the spear with a vigour far from assuring to one who stood within reach of it, leered with such a clever hideousness of feature that I felt, if only within arm's length of him, I could have bestowed upon him a hearty thump on the back, and cried out applaudingly, "Bravo, old boy! You do it capitally!"

Yet not being able to reach him, I was rapidly being fascinated by him. The rapid movements of the swaying spear, the steady wide-mouthed grin, the big square teeth, the head poised on one side with the confident pose of a practised spear-thrower, the short brow and square face, hair short and thick. Shall I ever forget him? It appeared to me as if the spear partook of the same cruel inexorable look as the grinning savage. Finally, I saw him draw his right arm back, and his body incline backwards, with still that same grin on his face, and I felt myself begin to count, one, two, three, four—and *whizz!* The spear flew over my back, and hissed as it pierced the water. The spell was broken.

It was only five minutes' work clearing the river. We picked up several shields, and I gave orders that all shields should be henceforth religiously preserved, for the idea had entered my head that they would answer capitally as bulwarks for our canoes. An hour after this we passed close to the confluence of the Urindi—a stream 400 yards in width at the mouth, and deep, with water of a light colour and tolerably clear.

We continued down river along the right bank, and at 4 P.M. camped in a dense low jungle, the haunt of the hippopotamus and elephant during the dry season. When the river is in flood, a much larger tract must be under water.

The left bank was between seventy and eighty feet high; and a point bearing from camp north-west was about one hundred and fifty feet high.

The traveller's first duty in lands infested by lions and leopards, is to build a safe corral, kraal, or boma, for himself, his oxen, horses, servants; and in lands infested like Usongora Meno and Kasera—wherein we now were—by human lions and leopards, the duty became still more imperative. We drew our canoes, therefore, half-way upon the banks, and our camp was in the midst of an impenetrable jungle.

On the high bluffs opposite was situated Vina-Kya. The inhabitants at once manned their drums and canoes, and advanced towards our camp. We could not help it. Here we were camped in a low jungle. How could the most captious, or the most cruel, of men find any cause or heart to blame us for resting on this utterly uninhabitable spot? Yet the savages of Vina-Kya did. Our interpreters were urged to be eloquent. And indeed they were, if I may judge by the gestures, which was the only language that was comprehensible to me. I was affected with a strange, envious admiration for those two young fellows, cannibals it is true, but endowed, none the less, with a talent for making even senseless limbs speak—and they appeared to have affected the savages of Vina-Kya also. At any rate, the wild natures relented for that day; but they promised to decapitate us early in the morning, for the sake of a horrid barbecue they intended to hold. We resolved not to wait for the entertainment.

Dec. 30.—At dawn we embarked, and descended about two miles, close to the right bank, when, lo! the broad mouth of the magnificent Lowwa, or Rowwa river burst upon the view. It was over a thousand yards wide, and its course by compass was from the south-east, or east-south-east true. A sudden rainstorm compelled us to camp on the north bank, and here we found ourselves under the shadows of the primeval forest.

Judging from the height and size of these trees, I doubt whether the right bank of the Livingstone at the mouth of the Lowwa river was ever at any time inhabited. An impenetrable undergrowth consisting of a heterogeneous variety of ferns, young palms, date, doum, *Raphia vinifera*, and the *Mucuna pruriens*—the dread of the naked native for the tenacity with which its stinging sharp-pointed bristles attach themselves to the skin—masses of the capsicum plant, a hundred species of clambering vines, caoutchouc creepers, llianes, and endless lengths of rattan-cane intermeshed and entangled, was jealously sheltered from sunlight by high, over-arching, and interlacing branches of fine grey-stemmed Rubiaceæ, camwood and bombax, teak, elais palms, ficus, with thick fleshy leaves, and tall gum-trees. Such is the home of the elephants which through this undergrowth have trodden the only paths available. In the forks of trees were seen large lumps, a spongy excrescence which fosters orchids and tender ferns, and from many of the branches depended the Usneæ moss in graceful and delicate fringes. Along the brown clayey shores, wherever there is the slightest indentation in the banks and still water, were to be found the Cyperaceæ sedge, and in deeper recesses and shallow water the papyrus.

In such cool, damp localities as the low banks near the confluence of these two important streams, entomologists might revel. The Myriapedes, with their lengthy sinuous bodies of bright shiny chocolate or deep black colour, are always one of the first species to attract one's attention. Next come the crowded lines of brown, black, or yellow ants, and the termites, which, with an insatiable appetite for destruction, are ever nibbling, gnawing, and prowling. If the mantis does not arrest the eye next, it most assuredly will be an unctuous earth caterpillar, with its polished and flexible armour, suggestive of slime and nausea. The mantis among insects is like the python among serpents. Its strange figure, trance-like attitudes, and mysterious ways have in all countries appealed to the imagination of the people. Though sometimes five inches in length, its waist is only about the thickness of its leg. Gaunt, weird, and mysterious in its action, it is as much a wonder among insects as a mastodon would be in a farmyard. The ladybird attracts the careless eye, as it slowly wanders about, by its brilliant red, spotted with black—but if I were to enter into details of the insect life I saw within the area of a square foot, an entire chapter might readily be filled. But to write upon the natural wonders of the tropics seems nowadays almost superfluous; it is so well understood that in these humid shades the earth seethes with life, that in these undrained recesses the primitive laboratory of nature is located, for disturbing which the unacclimatised will have to pay the bitter penalty of malarial fever.

One hears much about the "silence of the forest," but the tropical forest is not silent to the keen observer. The hum and murmur of hundreds of busy insect tribes make populous the twilight shadows that reign under the primeval growth. I hear the grinding of millions of mandibles, the furious hiss of a tribe just alarmed or about to rush to battle, millions of tiny wings rustling through the nether air, the march of an insect tribe under the leaves, the startling leap of an awakened mantis, the chirp of some eager and garrulous cricket, the buzz of an ant-lion, the roar of a bull-frog. Add to these the crackle of twigs, the fall of leaves, the dropping of nut and berry, the occasional crash of a branch, or the constant creaking and swaying of the forest tops as the strong wind brushes them or the gentle breezes awake them to whispers. Though one were blind and alone in the midst of a real tropical forest, one's sense of hearing would be painfully alive to the fact that an incredible number of minute industries, whose number one could never hope to estimate, were active in the shades. Silence is impossible in a tropical forest.

About ten o'clock, as we cowered in most miserable condition under the rude, leafy shelters we had hastily thrown up, the people of the wooded bluffs of Iryamba, opposite the Lowwa confluence, came over to see what strange beings were those who had preferred the secrecy of the uninhabited grove to their own loud roystering society. Stock still we sat cowering in our leafy coverts, but the mild reproachful voice of Katembo, our cannibal interpreter, was heard labouring in the interests of peace, brotherhood, and goodwill. The rain pattered so incessantly that I could from my position only faintly hear Katembo's voice pleading, earnestly yet mildly, with his unsophisticated brothers of Iryamba, but I felt convinced from the angelic tones that they would act as a sedative on any living creature except a rhinoceros or a crocodile. The long-drawn bleating sound of the word "Sen-nen-neh," which I heard frequently uttered by Katembo, I studied until I became quite as proficient in it as he himself.

Peace was finally made between Katembo on the one hand and the canoemen of Iryamba on the other, and they drew near to gaze at their leisure at one of the sallow white men, who with great hollow eyes peered, from under the vizor of his cap, on the well-fed bronze-skinned aborigines.

After selling us ten gigantic plantains, 13 inches long and 3 inches in diameter, they informed us that we had halted on the shore of Luru, or Lulu, in the uninhabited portion of the territory of Wanpuma, a tribe which lived inland; that the Lowwa came from the east, and was formed of two rivers, called the Lulu from the north-east, and the Lowwa from the south-east; that about a day's journey up the Lowwa river was a great cataract, which was "very loud."

The Livingstone, from the base of Iryamba bluffs on the left bank to our camp on the right bank, a mile below the confluence, was about two thousand yards in width. By dead reckoning we ascertained the latitude to be south 1° 28′, or 24 miles north of the Urindi affluent of the Livingstone, 95 miles north of the Lira, and 199 geographical miles north of the mouth of the Luama affluent.

The relative rank of these four great tributaries may be estimated by their width, at or near the confluence. The Luama was 400 yards wide; the Lira 300 yards, but deep; the Urindi, 500 yards; the Lowwa, 1000 yards. The parallel of latitude in which the Lowwa mouth is situated is fifty miles north of the extreme north end of Lake Tanganika. From all I could gather by a comparison of names and the relative authenticity of my informants, I am inclined to believe that the sources of this last great river may be placed near the south-west corner of Lake Muta-Nzigé; also, that the Urindi's head streams must approach the sources of the Luanda, which joins the Rusizi, and flows into Lake Tanganika, and that the Lira must drain the country west of Uvira.

The length of the Urindi river, which empties into the Livingstone only fifteen miles south of the Lowwa, may be estimated by a glance at the course of the Luama, which I followed from its source to its confluence with the Lualaba. In the same manner, the Lira's course and length may be judged.

The growing importance and volume of the tributaries as we proceed north also proves a northern prolongation of the mountain chain, which shuts in Tanganika on the west, and probably a slight deflection to the eastward. It will be observed also that while the Luama, the Lulindi, the Kunda, the Kariba, the Rumuna, the Kipembwé, the Lira, Urindi, and Lowwa rivers all issue from the country east, within a length of about two hundred miles of the Livingstone, we have only discovered two comparatively small rivers, the Ruiki and the Kasuku, issuing from the west side during the same course. The nature of the eastern country may be judged after a study of the chapter descriptive of our journey from Lake Tanganika to the mouth of the Luama.

At 2 P.M. we left our camp in the forest of Luru, and pulled across to the Iryamba side of the Livingstone. But as soon as the rain had ceased, a strong breeze had risen, which, when we were in mid-river, increased to a tempest from the north, and created great heavy waves, which caused the foundering of two of our canoes, the drowning of two of our men, Farjalla Baraka and Nasib, and the loss of four muskets and one sack of beads. Half-a-dozen other canoes were in great danger for a time, but no more fatal accidents occurred.

I feared lest this disaster might cause the people to rebel and compel me to return, for it had shocked them greatly; but I was cheered to hear them remark that the sudden loss of their comrades had been ordained by fate, and that no precautions would have availed to save them. But though omens and auguries were delivered by the pessimists among us, not one hazarded aloud the belief that we ought to relinquish our projects; yet they were all evidently cowed by our sudden misfortune.

Dec. 31.—On the 31st, the last day of the year 1876, we resumed our voyage. The morning was beautiful, the sky blue and clear, the tall forest still and dark, the river flowed without a ripple, like a solid mass of polished silver. Everything promised fair. But from the island below, the confluence of the Lowwa and the Livingstone, the warning drum sounded loudly over the river, and other drums soon echoed the dull boom.

"Keep together, my men," I cried, "there may be hot work for us below."

We resolved to keep in mid-stream, because both the island and the left bank appeared to be extremely populous, and to paddle slowly and steadily down river. The canoes of the natives darted from either shore, and there seemed to be every disposition made for a furious attack; but as we drew near, we shouted out to them, "Friends, Sennenneh!

Keep away from us. We shall not hurt you; but don't lift your spears, or we'll fight."

There was a moment's hesitation, wherein spears were clashed against shields, and some fierce words uttered, but finally the canoes drew back, and as we continued to paddle, the river with its stiff current soon bore us down rapidly past the populous district and island.

Before we finally passed by the latter, we came to another island which was uninhabited, and, after descending by a narrow channel, we crossed the mouth of a stream about twenty-five yards wide, flowing from the west side, in which were several small canoes and some dozen fishermen, lifting their nets from among the sedge.

At noon of this day we came to the southern end of an uninhabited low and sandy island, where I ascertained the latitude to be south 1° 20′ 30″. The altitude, above sea-level, of the river at this place is 1729 feet.

South of this position we struck across to the right bank again and discovered a small river 40 yards wide at the mouth, nearly opposite which, about mid-stream, are five low and bush-covered islets. After descending some five miles we formed our camp in the woods on the right bank.

Jan. 1.—The beginning of the new year, 1877, commenced, the first three hours after sunrise, with a delicious journey past an uninhabited tract, when my mind, wearied with daily solicitude, found repose in dwelling musingly upon the deep slumber of Nature. Outwardly the forest was all beauty, solemn peace, and soft dreamy rest, tempting one to sentiment and mild melancholy. Though it was vain to endeavour to penetrate with our eyes into the dense wall of forest—black and impervious to the sunlight which almost seemed to burn up the river—what could restrain the imagination? These were my calm hours, periods when my heart, oblivious of the dark and evil days we had passed, resolutely closed itself against all dismal forebodings, and revelled in the exquisite stillness of the uninhabited wilderness.

But soon after nine o'clock we discovered we were approaching settlements, both on islands and on the banks, and again the hoarse war-drums awaked the echoes of the forest, boomed along the river, and quickened our pulses.

We descend in close order as before, and steadily pursue our way. But, heading us off, about ten long canoes dart out from the shadow of palmy banks, and the wild crews begin to chant their war-songs, and now and then, in attitudes of bravado and defiance, raise spears and shields aloft and bring them downward with sounding clash.

As we approached them we shouted out "Sen-nen-neh" —our Sesame and Shibboleth, our watchword and countersign. But they would not respond.

Hitherto they had called us Wasambye; we were now called Wijiwa (people of the sun?); our guns were called Katadzi, while before they were styled Kibongeh, or lightning. Katembo was implored to be eloquent, mild of voice, pacific in gesture.

They replied, "We shall eat Wajiwa meat to-day, Oho, we shall eat Wajiwa meat!" and then an old chief gave some word of command, and at once 100 paddles beat the water into foam, and the canoes darted at us. But the contest was short, and we were permitted to pursue our voyage.

The river, beyond these islands, expanded to a breadth of 3000 yards: the left bank being high, and the right low. At noon we were in south latitude 1° 10′.

Five miles below, the river narrowed to about 2800 yards, and then we floated down past an uninhabited stretch, the interval affording us rest, until, reaching the southern end of a large island, we camped, lest we might be plunged into hostilities once more.

Jan. 2.—The second of January was a lively day. We first ran the gauntlet past Mirembuka, an exciting affair, and next we were challenged by Mwana-Mara's fierce sons, who were soon joined by Mwana Vibondo's people, and about 10.30 A.M. we had to repulse an attack made by the natives of Lombo a Kiriro. We had fought for three hours almost without a pause, for the Kewanjawa and Watomba tribe from the left bank had joined in the savage mêlée, and had assisted the tribes of the right bank. Then for an hour we had rest; but after that we came to islands, which we afterwards discovered were called Kibombo, and, finding the tribe of Amu Nyam preparing for battle with animation, we took advantage of one of the group to see if we could not negotiate a peaceful passage before risking another fight. The latitude of this island was south 0° 52′ 0″.

Katembo, our interpreter, and his friend, were despatched in a canoe manned by eight men, halfway to the shore, to speak fair and sweet words of peace to the Amu Nyam. No verbal answer was given to them, but they had to retreat in a desperate hurry before a rapidly advancing crowd of canoes. The Amu Nyams had evidently not had time to be undeceived by their friends above, for they came up with a dauntless bearing, as though accustomed to victory. Yet we held out copper armlets and long strings of shells to them, vociferously shouting out "Sen-nen-neh," with appropriate and plausible gestures. They laughed at us; and one fellow, who had a mighty door-like shield painted black with soot, using his long spear as an index finger, asked us—if Katembo spoke correctly—if we thought we could disappoint them of so much meat by the presents of a few shells and a little copper.

Our canoes were lying broadside along the reedy island, and as soon as the first spears were thrown, the Wangwana received orders to reply to them with brass slugs, which created such a panic that a couple of shots from each man sufficed to drive them back in confusion. After a while they recovered, and from a distance began to fly their poisoned arrows; but the Sniders responded to them so effectually that they finally desisted, and we were again free from our meat-loving antagonists.

About 2 P.M. we dropped down river again a few miles, and at 4.30 P.M. halted to camp at an old clearing on the right bank. Had we dared, we might have continued our journey by night, but prudence forbade the attempt, as cataracts might have been more disastrous than cannibals.

Near sunset we were once more alarmed by finding arrows dropping into the camp. Of course there was a general rush to the guns; but, upon noting the direction whence the arrows came, I ordered the people simply to go on about their duties as though nothing had occurred, while I sent twenty men in two canoes down the river with instructions to advance upon the enemy from behind, but by no means to fire unless they were overwhelmed in numbers.

Just at dark our canoes came back with three prisoners bound hand and foot. Except the poor dwarf at Ikondu up river, I had not seen any human creatures so unlovable to look at. There was no one feature about them that even extravagant charity could indicate as elevating them into the category of noble savages. I do not think I was prejudiced; I examined their faces with eyes that up to that time had gazed into the eyes of over five hundred thousand black men. They were intolerably ugly. I would not disturb them, however, that evening, but releasing their feet, and relaxing the bonds on their arms, appointed Katembo and his friend to keep them company and feed them, and Wadi Rehani to stimulate the keepers to be hospitable.

Jan. 3.—By the morning they were sociable, and replied readily to our questions. They were of the Wanongi—an inland tribe—but they had a small fishing village about an hour's journey below our camp called Katumbi. A powerful tribe called the Mwana Ntaba occupied a country below Katumbi, near some falls, which they warned us would be our destruction. On the left side of the river, opposite the Mwana Ntaba, were the Wavinza, south of a large river called the Rumami, or Lumami. The great river on which we had voyaged was known to them as the Lowwa.

As we stepped into our canoes we cut their bonds and permitted the unlovable and unsympathetic creatures to depart, a permission of which they availed themselves gladly.

The banks were from 10 to 30 feet high, of a grey-brown clay, and steep with old clearings, which were frequent at this part until below Katumbi. Half an hour afterwards we arrived at a channel which flowed in a sudden bend to the north-east, and, following it, we found ourselves abreast of a most populous shore, close to which we glided. Presently several large canoes appeared from behind an island to our right, and seemed to be hesitating as to whether they should retreat or advance.

The "Open Sesame"—"Sen-nen-neh!"—was loudly uttered by Katembo with his usual pathetic, bleating accent, and to our joy the word was repeated by over a hundred voices. "Sen-nen-neh! Sennenneh! Sennenneh!"—each voice apparently vying with the other in loudness. The river bore us down, and as they would not shorten the distance, we thought it better to keep this condition of things, lest the movement might be misconstrued, and we might be precipitated into hostilities.

For half an hour we glided down in this manner, keeping up a constant fire of smiling compliments and pathetic Sennennehs. Indeed, we were discovering that there was much virtue in a protracted and sentimental pronunciation of Sen-nen-neh! The men of the Expedition, who had previously ridiculed with mocking Ba-a-a-a-as, the absurd moan and plaintive accents of Sen-nen-neh, which Katembo had employed, now admired him for his tact. The good natives with whom we were now exchanging these suave, bleating courtesies proved to us that the true shibboleth of peace was to prolong each word with a quavering moan and melancholic plaint.

We came to a banana grove of a delicious and luxuriant greenness, which the shadowy black green of the antique forest behind it only made more agreeable and pleasant. Beyond this grove, the bank was lined by hundreds of men and women, standing or sitting down, their eyes directed towards our approaching flotilla.

"Sen-nen-neh!" was delivered with happy effect by one of the boat-boys. A chorus of Sen-nen-nehs, long-drawn, loud, and harmonious, quickly following the notes of the last syllable, burst from the large assembly, until both banks of the great river re-echoed it with all its indescribable and ludicrous pathos.

The accents were peaceful, the bearing of the people and the presence of the women were unmistakably pacific, so the word was given to drop anchor.

The natives in the canoes, who had hitherto preceded us, were invited to draw near, but they shrugged their shoulders, and declined the responsibility of beginning any intercourse with the strangers. We appealed to the concourse on the banks, for we were not a hundred feet from them. They burst out into a loud laughter, yet with nothing of scorn or contempt in it, for we had been so long accustomed to the subtle differences of passion that we were by this time adepts in discovering the nicest shades of feeling which wild humanity is capable of expressing. We held out our hands to them with palms upturned, heads sentimentally leaning on one side, and, with a captivating earnestness of manner, begged them to regard us as friends, strangers far from their homes, who had lost their way, but were endeavouring to find it by going down the river.

The effect is manifest. A kind of convulsion of tenderness appears to animate the entire host. Expressions of pity break from them, and there is a quick interchange of sympathetic opinions.

"Ah," thought I, "how delighted Livingstone would have been had he been here to regard this scene! Assuredly he would have been enraptured, and become more firmly impressed than ever with the innocence and guilelessness of true aborigines," and I am forced to admit it is exceedingly pleasant, but—I wait.

We hold up long necklaces of beads of various colours to view: blue, red, white, yellow, and black.

"Ah-h-h," sigh a great many, admiringly, and heads bend towards heads in praise and delight of them.

"Come, my friends, let us talk. Bring one canoe here. These to those who dare to approach us." There is a short moment of hesitation, and then some forms disappear, and presently come out again bearing gourds, chickens, bananas, and vegetables, &c., which they place carefully in a small canoe. Two women step in and boldly paddle towards us, while a deathly silence prevails among my people as well as among the aborigines on the bank.

I observed one or two coquettish airs on the part of the two women, but though my arm was getting tired with holding out so long in one position those necklaces of glorious beads, I dared not withdraw them, lest the fascination might be broken. I felt myself a martyr in the cause of public peace, and the sentiment made me bear up stoically.

"Boy," I muttered, in an undertone, to Mabruki, my gun-bearer, "when the canoe is alongside, seize it firmly and do not let it escape."

"Inshallah, my master."

Nearer the canoe came, and with its approach my blandness increased, and further I projected my arm with those beads of tempting colours.

At last the canoe was paddled alongside. Mabruki quietly grasped it. I then divided the beads into sets, talking the while to Katembo—who translated for me—of the happiness I felt at the sight of two such beautiful women coming out to see the white chief, who was so good, and who loved to talk to beautiful women. "There! these are for you—and these are for you," I said to the steerswoman and her mate.

They clapped their hands in glee, and each woman held out her presents in view of the shore people; and hearty hand-claps from all testified to their grateful feelings.

The women then presented me with the gourds of malofu—palm-wine—the chickens, bananas, potatoes, and cassava they had brought, which were received by the boat's crew and the interested members of the Expedition with such a hearty clapping of hands that it sent the shore people into convulsions of laughter. Mabruki was now told to withdraw his hand, as the women were clinging to the boats themselves, and peace was assured. Presently the great native canoes drew near and alongside the boat, forming dense walls of strange humanity on either side.

"Tell us, friends," we asked, "why it is you are so friendly, when those up the river are so wicked?"

Then a chief said, "Because yesterday some of our fishermen were up the river on some islets near Kibombo Island, opposite the Amu-Nyam villages; and when we heard the war-drums of the Amu-Nyam we looked up, and saw your canoes coming down. You stopped at Kibombo Island, and we heard you speak to them, saying you were friends. But the Amu-Nyam are bad; they eat people, we don't. They fight with us frequently, and whomsoever they catch they eat. They fought with you, and while you were fighting our fishermen came down and told us that the Wajiwa" (we) "were coming; but they said that they heard the Wajiwa say that they came as friends, and that they did not want to fight. To-day we sent a canoe, with a woman and a boy up the river, with plenty of provisions in it. If you had been bad people, you would have taken that canoe. We were behind the bushes of that island watching you; but you said 'Sen-nen-neh' to them, and passed into the channel between the island and our villages. Had you seized that canoe, our drums would have sounded for war, and you would have had to fight us, as you fought the Amu-Nyam. We have left our spears on one of those islands. See, we have nothing."

It was true, as I had already seen, to my wonder and admiration. Here, then, I had opportunities for noting what thin barriers separated ferocity from amiability. Only a couple of leagues above lived the cannibals of Amu-Nyam, who had advanced towards us with evil and nauseous intentions; but next to them was a tribe which detested the unnatural custom of eating their own species, with whom we had readily formed a pact of peace and goodwill!

They said their country was called Kankoré, the chief of which was Sangarika, and that the village opposite to us was Maringa; and that three miles below was Simba-Simba; that their country was small, and only reached to the end of the islands: that after we had passed the islands we should come to the territory of the Mwana Ntaba, with whom we should have to fight: that the Mwana Ntaba people occupied the country as far as the falls; that below the falls were several islands inhabited by the Baswa, who were friends of the Mwana Ntaba. It would be impossible, they said, to go over the falls, as the river swept against a hill, and rolled over it, and tumbled down, down, down, with whirl and uproar, and we should inevitably get lost. It would be far better, they said, for us to return.

The strange disposition to rechristen the great river with the name of its last great affluent, was here again exemplified, for the Kankoré tribe called the river at the falls the Rumami, or Lumami, and it became known no more as the Lowwa.

Other information we received was that the Watwa and Waringa tribes lived on the other side of the Lumami. The dwarfs, called Wakwanga, were said to be in a south-west direction. The Wavinza occupied the tract between the Lumami and the Lowwa opposite to us. The Bakutzi, or Wakuti, live west across the Lumami, which agrees with Abed the guide's story. On the right bank are situate Kankura, Mpassi, and Mburri; the chief of the last-mentioned country being Mungamba. There is also a tribe called the Ba-ama, whose chief, Subiri, trades in dogs and shells. Dogs are considered by the Ba-ama as greater delicacies than sheep and goats. But we were specially instructed to beware of the Bakumu, a powerful tribe of light-complexioned cannibals, who came originally from the north-east, and who, armed with bows and arrows, had conquered a considerable section of Uregga, and had even crossed the great river. They would undoubtedly, we were told, seek us out and massacre us all.

The Kankoré men were similar in dress and tattooing to the Waregga, through whose forests we had passed. The women wore bits of carved wood and necklaces of the Achatina fossil shell around their necks, while iron rings, brightly polished, were worn as armlets and leg ornaments.

Jan. 4.—Having obtained so much information from the amiable Kankoré, we lifted our stone anchors and moved gently down stream. Before each village we passed groups of men and women seated on the banks, who gave a genial response to our peaceful greeting.

We were soon below the islands on our left, and from a course north by west the river gradually swerved to north by east, and the high banks on our right, which rose from 80 to 150 feet, towered above us, with grassy breaks here and there agreeably relieving the sombre foliage of groves.

About 2 P.M., as we were proceeding quietly and listening with all our ears for the terrible falls of which we had been warned, our vessels being only about thirty yards from the right bank, eight men with shields darted into view from behind a bush-clump, and shouting their war-cries, launched their wooden spears. Some of them struck and dinted the boat deeply, others flew over it. We shoved off instantly, and getting into mid-stream found that we had heedlessly exposed ourselves to the watchful tribe of Mwana Ntaba, who immediately sounded their great drums, and prepared their numerous canoes for battle.

Up to this time we had met with no canoes over fifty feet

MWANA NTABA CANOE (THE "CROCODILE").

long, except that antique century-old vessel which we had repaired as a hospital for our small-pox patients; but those which now issued from the banks and the shelter of bends in the banks were monstrous. The natives were in full war-paint, one half of their bodies being daubed white, the other half red, with broad black bars, the *tout ensemble* being unique and diabolical. There was a crocodilian aspect about these lengthy vessels which was far from assuring, while the fighting men, standing up alternately with the paddlers, appeared to be animated with a most ferocious cat-o'-mountain spirit. Horn-blasts which reverberated from bank to bank, sonorous drums, and a chorus of loud yells, lent a fierce éclat to the fight in which we were now about to be engaged.

We formed line, and having arranged all our shields as bulwarks for the non-combatants, awaited the first onset with apparent calmness. One of the largest canoes, which we afterwards found to be 85 feet 3 inches in length, rashly made the mistake of singling out the boat for its victim; but we reserved our fire until it was within fifty feet of us, and after pouring a volley into the crew, charged the canoe with the boat, and the crew, unable to turn her round sufficiently soon to escape, precipitated themselves into the river and swam to their friends, while we made ourselves masters of the *Great Eastern* of the Livingstone. We soon exchanged two of our smaller canoes and manned the monster with thirty men, and resumed our journey in line, the boat in front acting as a guide. This early disaster to the Mwana Ntaba caused them to hurry down river, blowing their horns, and alarming with their drums both shores of the river, until about forty canoes were seen furiously dashing down stream, no doubt bent on mischief.

At 4 P.M. we came opposite a river about 200 yards wide, which I have called the Leopold River, in honour of his Majesty Leopold II., King of the Belgians, and which the natives called either the Kankora, Mikonju, or Munduku. Perhaps the natives were misleading me, or perhaps they really possessed a superfluity of names, but I think that whatever name they give it should be mentioned in connection with each stream.

Soon after passing by the confluence, the Livingstone, which above had been 2500 yards wide, perceptibly contracted, and turned sharply to the east-north-east, because of a hill which rose on the left bank about 300 feet above the river. Close to the elbow of the bend on the right bank we passed by some white granite rocks, from one to six feet above the water, and just below these we heard the roar of the First Cataract of the Stanley Falls series.

But louder than the noise of the falls rose the piercing yells of the savage Mwana Ntaba from both sides of the great river. We now found ourselves confronted by the inevitable necessity of putting into practice the resolution which we had formed before setting out on the wild voyage—to conquer or die. What should we do? Shall we turn and face the fierce cannibals, who with hideous noise drown the solemn roar of the cataract, or shall we cry out "Mambu Kwa Mungu"—"Our fate is in the hands of God"—and risk the cataract with its terrors!

Meanwhile, we are sliding smoothly to our destruction, and a decision must therefore be arrived at instantly. God knows, I and my fellows would rather have it not to do, because possibly it is only a choice of deaths, by cruel knives or drowning. If we do not choose the knives, which are already sharpened for our throats, death by drowning is certain. So finding ourselves face to face with the inevitable, we turn to the right bank upon the savages, who are in the woods and on the water. We drop our anchors and begin the fight, but after fifteen minutes of it find that we cannot force them away. We then pull up anchors and ascend stream again, until, arriving at the elbow above mentioned, we strike across the river and divide our forces. Manwa Sera is to take four canoes and to continue up stream a little distance, and, while we occupy the attention of the savages in front, is to lead his men through the woods and set upon them in rear. At 5.30 P.M. we make the attempt, and keep them in play for a few minutes, and on hearing a shot in the woods dash at the shore, and under a shower of spears and arrows effect a landing. From tree to tree the fight is continued until sunset, when, having finally driven the enemy off, we have earned peace for the night.

Until about 10 P.M. we are busy constructing an impenetrable stockade or boma of brushwood, and then at length, we lay our sorely fatigued bodies down to rest, without comforts of any kind and without fires, but (I speak for myself only) with a feeling of gratitude to Him who had watched over us in our trouble, and a humble prayer that His protection may be extended to us, for the terrible days that may yet be to come.

CHAPTER VIII.

Fighting betimes—Blazing a path—We take an island by storm—A desperate dilemma—Road-making under fire—A miraculous escape—A terrible march—Peace by stratagem—Below the Fifth Cataract—Our cannibal captives—Fighting the Wana-Rukura—The Wana-Rukura islanders—Approaching the Seventh Cataract—A deserted island—The Seventh Cataract of the Stanley Falls—The first of the cataracts—Clear of the Stanley Falls.

Jan. 5.—At 4 A.M. of the 5th of January we were awake, cooking betimes the food that was to strengthen us for the task that lay before us, while the screaming lemur and the soko still alarmed the dark forest with their weird cries.

We were left undisturbed until 8 A.M. when the canoes of the Mwana Ntaba were observed to cross over to the left bank, and in response to their signals the forest behind our camp was soon alive with wild men.. Frank distributed thirty rounds to each of the forty-three guns which now remained to us. Including my own guns, we possessed only forty-eight altogether, as Manwa Sera had lost four Sniders in the Ukassa Rapid, and by the capsizing of the two canoes in the tempest, which struck us as we crossed the Livingstone below its confluence with the Lowwa, we had lost four muskets. But more terrible for our enemies than Sniders or muskets was the courage of despair that now nerved every heart and kept cool and resolute every head.

By river the cannibals had but little chance of success, and this the Mwana Ntaba after a very few rounds from our guns discovered; they therefore allied themselves with the Baswa tribe, which during the night had crossed over from its islands, below the first falls. Until 10 A.M. we held our own safely in the camp; but then breaking out of it, we charged on the foe, and until 3 P.M. were incessantly at work. Ten of our men received wounds, and two were killed. To prevent them becoming food for the cannibals, we consigned them to the swift brown flood of the Livingstone.

The Mwana Ntaba and the Baswas at length retired, and though we momentarily expected a visit from them each day, for the next two or three days we were unmolested.

Jan. 6.—Early on the morning of the 6th I began to explore the First Cataract of the Stanley Falls. I found a small stream about two hundred yards wide, separated by a lateral dyke of igneous rocks from the main stream, which took the boat safely down for a couple of miles. Then presently other dykes appeared, some mere low narrow ridges of rock and others, much larger and producing tall trees, inhabited by the Baswa tribe. Among these islets the left stream rushed down in cascades or foamy sheets, over low terraces, with a fall of from one foot to ten feet. The Baswas, no doubt, have recently fled to these islets to seek refuge from some powerful tribe situated inland west of the river.

The main stream, 900 yards wide, rushed towards the east-north-east, and, after a mile of rapids, tilted itself against a hilly ridge that lay north and south, the crest of which was probably 300 feet above the river. With my glass, from the fork of a tree twenty feet above the ground, I saw at once that a descent by the right side was an impossibility, as the waves were enormous, and the slope so great that the river's face was all a foam; and that at the base of the hilly ridge which obstructed its course the river seemed piling itself into a watery bank, whence it escaped into a scene of indescribable confusion down to the horror of whirling pools, and a mad confluence of tumbling rushing waters. It was now quite easy to understand why our friends the Kankoré people, in attempting to illustrate the scene at the First Cataract, placed one hand overlapping the other—they meant to say that the water, driven with impetuosity against the hill, rose up and overlapped the constant flow from the steep slope.

I decided, therefore, to go down along the left stream, overland, and to ascertain the best route, I took eight men with me, leaving five men to guard the boat. Within two hours we had explored the jungle, and "blazed" a path below the falls—a distance of two miles.

Then returning to camp I sent Frank off with a detachment of fifty men with axes, to clear the path, and a musket-armed guard of fifteen men, to be stationed in the woods parallel with the projected land route, and, leaving a guard of twenty men to protect the camp, I myself rowed up river along the left bank, a distance of three miles. Within a bend, a mile above our camp, I discovered a small black-water river, about forty yards wide, issuing from the south-west, which I named Black River, from the colour of its water. Two miles above this, the affluent Lumami, which Livingstone calls "Young's River," entered the great stream, by a mouth 600 yards wide, between low banks densely covered with trees. At noon I took an observation of the sun—the declination of which being south gave me a clear water horizon—and ascertained it to be south latitude 0° 32′ 0″.

Jan. 7.—By noon of the 7th, having descended with the canoes as near as prudence would permit to the first fall of the left stream, we were ready for hauling the canoes over-land. A road, fifteen feet in width, had been cut through the tangle of rattan, palms, vines, creepers and brushwood, tolerably straight except where great forest monarchs stood untouched, and whatever brushwood had been cut from the jungle had been laid across the road in thick piles. A rude camp had also been constructed half-way on the river side of the road, into which everything was conveyed. By 8 A.M. we had hauled the canoes over one mile of ground.

Jan. 8.—The next day, while the people were still fresh, we buckled on to the canoes and by 3 P.M. of the 8th had passed the falls and rapids of the First Cataract, and were afloat in a calm creek between Baswa Island and the left bank!

Not wishing to stay in such a dangerous locality longer than was absolutely necessary, we re-embarked, and descending cautiously down the creek, came in a short time to the great river, with every prospect of a good stretch of serene water. But soon we heard the roar of another cataract, and had to hug the left bank closely. Then we entered other creeks, which wound lazily by jungle-covered islets, and after two miles of meanderings among most dismal islands and banks, emerged in view of the great river, with the cataract's roar sounding solemnly and terribly near. As it was near evening, and our position was extremely unpleasant, we resolved to encamp for the night at an island which lay in mid-stream. Meanwhile, we heard drums and war-horns sounding on the left bank, and though the islanders also responded to them, of the two evils it was preferable to risk an encounter with the people of the island rather than with those of the main, until we could discover our whereabouts. We had no time for consultation, or even thought—the current was swift, and the hoarse roar of the Second Cataract was more sonorous than that of the first, thundering into our affrighted ears that, if we were swept over, destruction, sudden and utter, awaited us.

The islanders were hostilely alert and ready, but, spurred on by our terror of the falls, we drove our vessels straight on to the bank, about 500 feet above the falling water. In fifteen minutes we had formed a rude camp, and enclosed it by a slight brushwood fence, while the islanders, deserting the island, crossed over to their howling, yelling friends on the left bank. In a small village close to our camp we found an old lady, of perhaps sixty-five years of age, who was troubled with a large ulcer in her foot, and had therefore been unable to escape. She was a very decent creature, and we carried her to our camp, where, by dressing her foot and paying her kind attentions, we succeeded in making her very communicative. But Katembo could understand only very few words of her speech, which proved to me that we were rapidly approaching lands where no dialect that we knew would be available.

We managed to learn, however, that the name of the island was Cheandoah, or Kewandoah, of the Baswa tribe; that the howling savages on the left bank were the renowned Bukumu—cannibals, and most warlike; that the Bakumu used bows and arrows, and were the tribe that had driven the Baswa long ago to seek refuge on these islands. When we asked her the name of the river she said Lumami was the name of the left branch, and the Lowwa of the right branch. She gave the word Kukeya as indicating the left bank, and Ngyeyeh for the right bank. Waki-biano, she said, was the name of the large island which we had passed when we saw the villages of the Baswa below the first cataract. The words Ubi, or Eybiteri, we understood her to employ for the Falls as being utterly impassable.

Jan. 9.—During the morning of the 9th we explored the island of Cheandoah, which was much longer than we at first supposed. It was extremely populous, and contained five villages. We discovered an abundance of spears here and ironware of all kinds used by the natives, such as knives, hammers, hatchets, tweezers, anvils of iron, or, in other words, inverted hammers, borers, hole-burners, fish-hooks, darts, iron rods; all the spears possessed broad points, and were the first of this style I had seen. Almost all the knives, large and small, were encased in sheaths of wood covered with goat-skin, and ornamented with polished iron bands. They varied in size, from a butcher's cleaver to a lady's dirk, and belts of undressed goatskin, of red buffalo or antelope hide, were attached to them for suspension from the shoulders. There were also seen here iron bells, like our cow and goat bells, curiously carved whistles, fetishes or idols of wood, uncouth and rudely cut figures of human beings, brightly painted in vermilion, alternating with black; baskets made of palm fibre, large wooden and dark clay pipes, iron rings for arms and legs, numerous treasures of necklaces of the *Achatina monetaria*, the black seeds of a species of plantain, and the crimson berries of the *Abrus precatorius*; copper, iron, and wooden pellets. The houses were all of the gable-roofed pattern which we had first noticed on the summit of the hills on which Riba-Riba, Manyema, is situate; the shields of the Baswa were also after the same type.

A BASWA KNIFE.

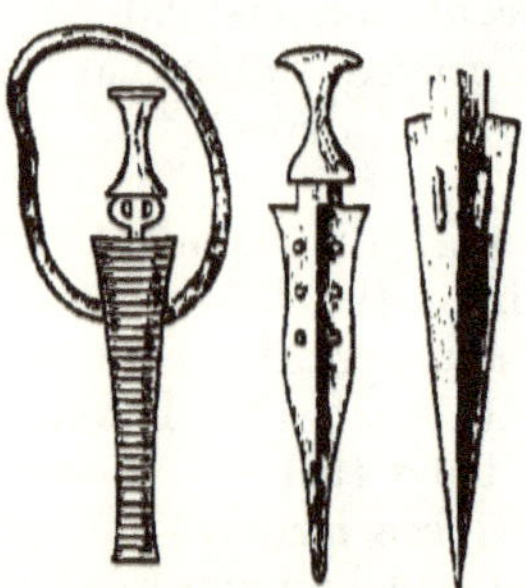

STYLE OF KNIVES.

The vegetation of the island consisted of almost every variety of plant and tree found in this region, and the banana, plantain, castor-oil, sugar-cane, cassava, and maize flourished; nor must the oil-palm be forgotten, for there were great jars of its dark-red butter in many houses.

BASWA BASKET AND COVER.

The grand problem now before me was how to steer clear of the Bukumu savages of the left bank, whose shouts and fierce yells came pealing to our ears, and were heard even above the roar and tremendous crash of the cataract. As I travelled round the island, many desperate ideas suggested themselves to me, and if I had been followed by a hundred practised and daring men it might

THE DESPERATE SITUATION OF ZAIDI, AND HIS RESCUE BY ULEDI, THE COXSWAIN OF THE BOAT.

[To face page 178.

have been possible to have dragged the canoes the length of the island past the first terrace of the cataract, and, after dashing across to Ntunduru Island, to have dragged them through its jungle and risked the falls by Asama Island; but there were not thirty men in the entire Expedition capable of listening to orders and implicitly obeying instructions.

To the east of Cheandoah the right branch was again forked by another island, and the whole face of the river was wild beyond description, and the din of its furious waves stunning; while the western branch, such was its force, went rushing down a terrace, and then swept round in an extensive whirlpool with a central depression quite eighteen inches below the outer rim. We pushed a rotten and condemned canoe above the fall, watched it shoot down like an arrow, and circle round that terrible whirling pool, and the next instant saw it drawn in by that dreadful suction, and presently ejected stern foremost 30 yards below. Close to the bank were nooks and basin-like formations in the trap rocks, in which every now and again the water became strongly agitated, and receding about twelve inches, would heave upwards with a rushing and gurgling that was awful.

Jan. 10.—There was only one way to resolve the problem, and that was to meet the Bakumu and dare their worst, and then to drag the canoes through the dense forest on the left bank. Accordingly, we prepared for what we felt assured would be a stubborn contest. At early dawn of the 10th of January, with quick throbbing pulses, we stole up river for about a mile, and then with desperate haste dashed across to the shore, where we became immediately engaged. We floated down to the bend just above the cataract, and there secured our boats and canoes out of the influence of the stream. Leaving Frank with eight musketeers and sixty axes to form a stockade, I led thirty-six men in a line through the bushes, and drove the united Baswa and Bakumu backward to their villages, the first of which were situated a mile from the river. Here a most determined stand was made by them, for they had piled up heaps of brushwood, and cut down great trees to form defences, leaving only a few men in front. We crept through the jungle on the south side and succeeded in forcing an entrance, and driving them out. We had thus won peace for this day, and retreated to our camp. We then divided the Expedition into two parties, or relays, one to work by night, the other by day, after which I took a picked body of pioneers with axes and guns and cut a narrow path three miles in length, which brought us opposite Ntunduru Island, blazing the trees as a guide, and forming rude camps at intervals of half a mile. Material—dried palm branches and bundles of cane smeared over with gum frankincense—was also brought from the village to form lights for the working parties at night: these were to be fastened at elevated positions on trees to illuminate the jungle.

Jan. 11.—We were not further disturbed during this day. In the evening Frank began his work with fifty axe-men, and ten men as scouts deployed in the bushes in front of the working parties. Before dawn we were all awakened, and, making a rush with the canoes, succeeded in safely reaching our first camp by 9 A.M. with all canoes and baggage. During the passage of the rear-guard the Bakumu made their presence known to us by a startling and sudden outburst of cries; but the scouts immediately replied to them with their rifles, and maintained their position until they were supported by the other armed men, who were now led forward as on the day before. We chased the savages two miles inland, to other villages which we had not hitherto seen, and these also we compelled them to abandon.

Jan. 12.—In the evening, Frank, who had enjoyed but a short rest during the day, manfully set to work again, and by dawn had prepared another three-quarters of a mile of road. At 10 A.M. of the 12th, by another rush forward, we were in our second camp. During this day also there was a slight interchange of hostilities, but, being soon released from the savages, the day party was able to prepare half a mile of good road, which Frank during the night was able to extend to a mile and a quarter. By 5 P.M. of the 13th therefore we were safe in our third camp. Excepting Kachéché and a few men detailed as sentries, we all rested for this night, but in the morning, refreshed from our labours, made the fourth and final rush, and thus, after seventy-eight hours' terrific exertion, succeeded in reaching the welcome river and launching our canoes.

The Bakumu, utterly disheartened by their successive punishments and bad success, left us alone to try our hands at the river, which, though dangerous, promised greater progress than on land. The following two days' accounts of our journey are extracted from my journal:—

"*January* 14.—As soon as we reached the river we began to float the canoes down a two-mile stretch of rapids to a camp opposite the south end of Ntunduru Island. Six canoes were taken safely down by the gallant boat's crew. The seventh canoe was manned by Muscati, Uledi Muscati, and Zaidi, a chief. Muscati, the steersman, lost his presence of mind, and soon upset his canoe in a piece of bad water. Muscati and his friend Uledi swam down the furious stream to Ntunduru Island, whence they were saved by the eighth canoe, manned by stout-hearted Manwa Sera, and Uledi, the coxswain of the Lady Alice; but poor Zaidi, the chief, paralysed by the roar of the stream, unfortunately thought his safety was assured by clinging to his canoe, which was soon swept past our new camp, in full view of those who had been deputed with Frank to form it, to what seemed inevitable death. But a kindly Providence (which he has since, himself gratefully acknowledged) saved him even on the brink of eternity. The great fall at the north end of Ntunduru Island happens to be disparted by a single pointed rock, and on this the canoe was driven, and, borne down by the weight of the waters, was soon split in two, one side of which got jammed below, and the other was tilted upward. To this the almost drowned man clung, while perched on the rocky point, with his ankles washed by the stream. To his left, as he faced up-stream, there was a stretch of 50 yards of falling water; to his right were nearly fifty yards of leaping brown waves, while close behind him the water fell down sheer six to eight feet, through a gap 10 yards wide, between the rocky point on which he was perched and a rocky islet 30 yards long.

"When called to the scene by his weeping friends, from my labours up-river, I could scarcely believe my eyes, or realise the strange chance which placed him there, and, certainly, a more critical position than the poor fellow was in cannot be imagined. The words 'there is only a step between me and the grave' would have been very appropriate coming from him. But the solitary man on that narrow-pointed rock, whose knees were sometimes washed by rising waves, was apparently calmer than any of us; though we could approach him within fifty yards he could not hear a word we said; he could see us, and feel assured that we sympathised with him in his terrible position.

"We then, after collecting our faculties, began to prepare means to save him. After sending men to collect rattans, we formed a cable, by which we attempted to lower a small canoe, but the instant it seemed to reach him the force of the current hurrying to the fall was so great that the cable snapped like pack-thread, and the canoe swept by him like an arrow, and was engulfed, shattered, split, and pounded into fragments. Then we endeavoured to toss towards him poles tied to creepers, but the vagaries of the current and its convulsive heaving made it impossible to reach him with them, while the man dared not move a hand, but sat silent, watching our futile efforts, while the conviction gradually settled on our minds that his doom, though protracted, was certain.

"Then, after anxious deliberation with myself, I called for another canoe, and lashed to the bow of it a cable consisting of three one-inch rattans twisted together and strengthened by all the tent ropes. A similar cable was lashed to the side, and a third was fastened to the stern, each of these cables being 90 yards in length. A shorter cable, 30 yards long, was lashed to the stern of the canoe, which was to be guided within reach of him by a man in the canoe.

"Two volunteers were called for. No one would step forward. I offered rewards. Still no one would respond. But when I began to speak to them, asking them how they would like to be in such a position without a single friend offering to assist in saving them, Uledi, the coxswain, came forward and said, 'Enough, master, I will go. Mambu Kwa Mungu'—'My fate is in the hands of God'—and immediately began preparing himself, by binding his loin-cloth firmly about his waist. Then Marzouk, a boat-boy, said, 'Since Uledi goes, I will go too.' Other boat-boys, young Shumari and Saywa, offered their services, but I checked them, and said, 'You surely are not tired of me, are you, that you all wish to die? If all my brave boat-boys are lost, what shall we do?'

"Uledi and his friend Marzouk stepped into the canoe with the air of gladiators, and we applauded them heartily, but enjoined on them to be careful. Then I turned to the crowd on the shore who were manning the cables, and bade them beware of the least carelessness, as the lives of the three young men depended on their attention to the orders that would be given.

"The two young volunteers were requested to paddle across river, so that the stern might be guided by those on shore. The bow and side cables were slackened until the canoe was within twenty yards of the roaring falls, and Uledi endeavoured to guide the cable to Zaidi, but the convulsive heaving of the river swept the canoe instantly to one side, where it hovered over the steep slope and brown waves of the left branch, from the swirl of which we were compelled to draw it. Five times the attempt was made, but at last, the sixth time, encouraged by the safety of the cables, we lowered the canoe until it was within ten yards of Zaidi, and Uledi lifted the short cable and threw it over to him and struck his arm. He had just time to grasp it before he was carried over into the chasm below. For thirty seconds we saw nothing of him, and thought him lost, when his head rose above the edge of the falling waters. Instantly the word was given to 'haul away,' but at the first pull the bow and side cables parted, and the canoe began to glide down the left branch with my two boat-boys on board! The stern cable next parted, and, horrified at the result, we stood muttering 'La il Allah, il Allah,' watching the canoe severed from us drifting to certain destruction, when we suddenly observed it halted. Zaidi in the chasm clinging to his cable was acting as a kedge-anchor, which swept the canoe, against the rocky islet. Uledi and Marzouk sprang out of the canoe, and leaning over assisted Zaidi out of the falls, and the three, working with desperate energy, succeeded in securing the canoe on the islet.

"But though we hurrahed and were exceedingly rejoiced, their position was still but a short reprieve from death. There were fifty yards of wild waves, and a resistless rush of water, between them and safety, and to the right of them was a fall 300 yards in width, and below was a mile of falls and rapids, and great whirlpools, and waves rising like little hills in the middle of the terrible stream, and below these were the fell cannibals of Wane-Mukwa and Asama.

"How to reach the islet was a question which now perplexed me. We tied a stone to about a hundred yards of whipcord, and after the twentieth attempt they managed to catch it. To the end of the whipcord they tied the tent rope which had parted before, and drawing it to our side we tied the stout rattan creeper, which they drew across taut, and fastened to a rock, by which we thought we had begun to bridge the stream. But night drawing nigh, we said to them that we would defer further experiment until morning.

"Meantime the ninth canoe, whose steersman was a supernumerary of the boat, had likewise got upset, and he out of six men was drowned, to our great regret, but the canoe was saved. All other vessels were brought down safely, but so long as my poor faithful Uledi and his friends are on the islet, and still in the arms of death, the night finds us gloomy, sorrowing and anxious.

"*January* 15.—My first duty this morning was to send greetings to the three brave lads on the islet, and to assure them that they should be saved before they were many hours older. Thirty men with guns were sent to protect thirty other men searching for rattans in the forest, and by nine o'clock we possessed over sixty strong canes, besides other long climbers, and as fast as we were able to twist them together they were drawn across by Uledi and his friends. Besides, we sent light cables to be lashed round the waist of each man, after which we felt trebly assured that all accidents were guarded against. Then hailing them I motioned to Uledi to begin, while ten men seized the cable, one end of which he had fastened round his waist. Uledi was seen to lift his hands up to heaven, and waving his hand to us he leapt into the wild flood, seizing the bridge cable as he fell into the depths. Soon he rose, hauling himself hand over hand, the waves brushing his face, and sometimes rising over his head, until it seemed as if he scarcely would be able to breathe, but by jerking his body occasionally upward with a desperate effort, he so managed to survive the waves and to approach us, where a dozen willing hands were stretched out to snatch the half-smothered man. Zaidi next followed, but after the tremendous proofs he had given of his courage and tenacious hold we did not much fear for his safety, and he also landed, to be warmly congratulated for his double escape from death. Marzouk, the youngest, was the last, and we held our breaths while the gallant boy was struggling out of the fierce grasp of death. While yet midway the pressure of water was so great that he lost his hold of two cables, at which the men screamed in terror lest he should relax his hold altogether from despair, but I shouted harshly to him, 'Pull away, you fool. Be a man,' at which with three hauls he approached within reach of our willing hands, to be embraced and applauded by all. The cheers we gave were so loud and hearty that the cannibal Wane-Mukwa must have known, despite the roar of the waters, that we had passed through a great and thrilling scene."

At the northern end of Ntunduru Island four separate branches rushing down from between Cheandoah and its neighbours unite, and their united waters tumble into one huge boiling, heaving cauldron, wherein mounds of water are sometimes lifted upward, and are hurled down several feet with tremendous uproar, along an island between Ntunduru and Asama. The distance is only about a mile and a half, and the breadth is but 500 yards, but it presents one of the wildest water scenes conceivable.

To avoid this terrific locality, it was now necessary to cut a road, nearly three miles in length, to the quiet creek flowing between Asama Island and the left bank. Spurs from inland like "hogs' backs," which projected into that boiling gulf, compelled us to make detours, which, though they lengthened our toil, rendered the transport of our vessels overland much easier. Minute red ants covered every leaf of the shrubby Asclepiadæ, and attacked the pioneers so furiously that their backs were soon blistered, while my scalp smarted as though wounded with a steel comb. A species of burr-bearing and tall spear-grass, which covered what formerly must have been inhabited ground, also tormented us. The men, however, on approaching this ground, armed themselves with heavy sticks, marched steadily in line, and beat down the growth before them, thus forming a road 30 feet in width. By night we were only a few hundred yards from the creek.

Jan. 16, 17.—In order to prevent the cannibals of Asama Island and the Wané-Mukwa from being aware of our purpose, we returned to our camp opposite Ntunduru Island, and during the 16th and 17th of January were employed in dragging our canoes to the end of the road, perfectly screened from observation by the tall wild grass and shrubs. Though fearfully tired after this steady strain on our energies, an hour before dawn we rose, and, arming ourselves with poles, crushed through the remaining 300 yards of grass by sunrise.

The people of Asama Island soon roused one another with most heroic and stunning crashes on their huge drums, and launched their war-canoes, of which they had a great number, excellently built; but as our existence depended upon our dash, twenty men only were reserved to guard the road, while Frank and Manwa Sera, with the assistance of every other healthy man, woman, and child, hauled the canoes to the landing-place. Though the Asamas made but little resistance to our embarking, they attacked us as soon as we began to move with a frenzy which, had it not been so perilous to our poor hunted selves, I might have heartily applauded. I had recourse to a little strategy. Manwa Sera was told to loiter behind with one-half of the canoes and land his party on the island above, while I made a bold push at the savages and landed below. We in the advance at once charged on the war-canoes, shouting and drumming, and making up in noise what we lacked in numbers, and having descended a mile, suddenly made for the island at a low landing-place, and while the savages were confused at this manœuvre I detached twenty men and sent them up to meet Manwa Sera and his party, and in a short time they had captured two villages, with all the non-combatant inhabitants, besides a large herd of goats and sheep. When these were brought to the landing-place where the war-canoes were still engaged with us, they were shown to the warriors, and out of sheer surprise hostilities ceased, and the war canoes retired to the left bank of the stream to consider what they should do. Meantime Katembo was industrious in making himself understood by the women, and we made great progress in calming their fears, but we did not quite succeed until I opened a bag of shells, and distributed a few to each person with appropriate soothing tones. The Asamas opposite, though still sullen in their canoes, were not disinterested spectators of what was transpiring, and they were soon communicating with their relatives and children, asking what we were doing. While my people were busy surrounding the landing-place with a brushwood fence, the negotiations for peace and goodwill proceeded. At noon a canoe with two men cautiously approached us, and while it was still hesitating to comply with our request to come alongside, one of my boat-boys dexterously grasped it and brought it near, while the word "Senneneh" was loudly repeated. Into this as a beginning we put six women, three children, and some goats, and shoved it off towards the cannibal warriors, who could scarcely believe their senses until the canoe was safe in their hands. Then it seemed as though their sullenness was conquered, for presently five men and a chief approached, who likewise, receiving presents of shells and a few pieces of cloth, entered zealously into the strangely formed compact of peace, and sealed it by permitting themselves to be inoculated with the blood of the Wangwana in small incisions made in the arms. Every captive, every goat and fowl was religiously surrendered, while shouts of applause from both parties rent the air.

It could not be expected, of course, that they should feel at once like old friends after the fury of the early morning, but sunset found some dozens of men in our camp without arms in their hands, responding as well as they were able to our numerous queries about the geography of the country. Our people also traversed the southern end of the island with perfect confidence, and neither side had cause to regret having become friends.

Human skulls ornamented the village streets of the island, while a great many thigh-bones and ribs and vertebræ lay piled at a garbage corner, bleached witnesses of their hideous carnivorous tastes. Like the Waregga, the Asama wore caps of lemur, monkey, otter, goat, red buffalo and antelope skin, with long strips of fur or the tails dropped behind. Palms, bananas, cassava, red pepper, maize, and sugar-cane flourished; their houses were large, though not so neat as those at Vinya-Njara. Fish-nets and baskets lay scattered around in abundance, while great bundles of iron and wooden spears proved that the Asamas were as warlike as they were industrious.

The islanders were not ungrateful, for they supplied us, by order of the chief, with sufficient bananas to settle our canoes deeply in the water, which proved that, provided one were well able to defend oneself, and were his superior in force, even a cannibal could show that he was possessed of human qualities.

Jan. 19.—On the 19th we resumed our voyage, gliding down the stream that flowed between Asama Island and the left bank. The river's course had continued a (magnetic) north-north-easterly course ever since we had left the confluence of the Leopold with the Livingstone, which caused serious doubts in my mind for a time as to whether my boiling-points might not be in error. It certainly caused me to believe that Livingstone's hypothesis is correct after all, though the great river itself, by its vast magnitude, breadth, and depth, was a decided protest against such a proposition.

At the foot of the Fifth Cataract, which fell at the south end of Asama Island, the altitude of the river was about 1630 feet above the ocean—after Kew corrections—and we were in about south latitude 0° 23′ 0″, just 270 geographical miles south of where the Nile was known to have an altitude of 1525 feet above the sea. The river, at a stage where I expected to see it at least incline to the west, ran due north-north-east.

Four soundings were obtained during the forenoon of the 19th: 33 feet, 40 feet, 47 feet, and 41 feet respectively, where the left branch flowed at the rate of about two knots an hour past Asama.

The left bank rose from the low swampy level to beautiful bluffs, 60, 80, and 100 feet high, garnished with a magnificent forest of tall trees, amid which were frequently seen the Elais, wild date, and Hyphene palms.

North of Asama the river widened to the stately breadth of 2000 yards. On the right were the Wané-Mpungu and the Wané-Kipanga tribes, but I was told by one of the Asama islanders that they were inland people of Uregga. I have been struck with the similarity of some of these names with those given me by Rumanika of Karagwé. For instance, one of the native names—Mikonju—of the Leopold River. Might not the man who gave us the information have intended it for a tribe called Wakonju—people of Ukonju—who, according to Rumanika, were cannibals, and occupied a country west of Muta-Nzigé? The "Wané-Mpungu" has a remarkable resemblance to the Mpundu, described by the same authority.

In about south latitude 14′ we discovered a small river 40 yards wide at the mouth entering the Livingstone from the left bank, nearly opposite Kyya Kamba Island.

In the afternoon we passed several old settlements, which were probably abandoned because of the Wakumu, who are the great dread of this section on both banks. One of these old settlements is called Kyyo Kaba. Just below on the right bank, opposite Kanjebé Islands, is Aruko country, a district of Uregga, and on the left is Wandeiwa, separated from Kyyo Kaba by a small sluggish creek 20 yards wide.

We camped on the night of the 19th on the right bank in what we believed to be a market-place. The green was inviting, the trees were patriarchal, the forest at the hour approaching sunset was lonely, and we flattered ourselves that before the next sun was sufficiently high to cause the natives to appear at the market-place, we should have departed. I also flattered myself that I was tolerably well acquainted with the arts of savages, but my astonishment was very great to find myself but a novice after all, for in the morning one of my people came to inform me, with a grave face, that we were netted!

"Netted," I said. "What do you mean?"

"True, master; there is a tall high net round the camp from above to below, and the net is made of cord."

"Ah, if there is a net, there must be men behind waiting to spear the game."

I called Manwa Sera, and gave him thirty men, ordering him to pull up river half a mile or so, and after penetrating into the woods behind our camp, to lie in wait near some path which led to the market-place on which we were encamped. After waiting an hour to give the men time, we blew a loud blast on the horn as a signal, and sent four men with shields to cut the net, while ten men with guns, and thirty men with spears, stood by ready to observe what happened. While the net was being cut, four or five heavy spears came hurtling from the bushes. We fired at random into the bushes, and made a rush forward, and saw several forms run swiftly away from the vicinity of the camp. Soon I heard a few of my men utter sharp screams, and saw them hop away, with blood streaming from their feet, while they cried, "Keep away from the path"; "Get away from the road."

Upon examining the paths we discovered that each bristled with sharp-pointed splinters of the Pennisetum reed-cane, which had pierced the men's feet to the bone. However, the ambuscade had been very successful, and had captured eight of the Wané-Mpungu without an accident or the firing of a shot. The savages were not unpleasant to look at, though the prejudices of our people made them declare that they smelled the flesh of dead men when they caught hold of their legs and upset them in the road! Each man's upper row of teeth was filed, and on their foreheads were two curved rows of tattoo-marks; the temples were also punctured.

Katembo questioned them, and they confessed that they lay in wait for man-meat. They informed us that the people inland were Waregga, but that the Wakumu, coming from the eastward, were constantly in the habit of fighting the Waregga; that the Waregga were black, like the Wané-Mpungu, but that the Bakumu were light-complexioned, like a light-coloured native of Zanzibar whom they pointed to. The captives also declared that their village was an hour's journey from the camp, that they ate old men and old women, as well as every stranger captured in the woods. Our three asses seemed to awe them greatly, and when one of them was led up to the asses he begged so imploringly that we would be merciful that we relented. We obtained considerable amusement from them; but at 9 A.M. we embarked them in our canoes to show us the falls, which they said we should meet after four hours' journey.

We struck across river to the left bank, which was high and steep. An hour afterwards we saw rounded hills on both banks approaching each other; but our guides said there was no danger at Kabombo, as they were called. Still hugging the left bank, we presently came to a curious cavern in a smooth water-worn porphyry rock, which penetrated about a hundred feet within. At first I thought it to be the work of human hands, but examination of it proved that in old times there had extended a ledge of this porphyry rock nearly across river, and that this cavern had been formed by whirling eddies. At the farther end there are three modes of exit to the high ground above. Some natives had scrawled fantastic designs, squares and cones, on the smooth face of the rock, and, following their example, I printed as high as I could reach the title of our Expedition and date of discovery, which will no doubt be religiously preserved by the natives as a memento of the white man and his people who escaped being eaten while passing through their country.

Two miles below we came to some rocky straits and the ten islets of Kabombo. The current ran through these at the rate of about five knots an hour, but, excepting a few eddies, there was nothing to render the passage difficult. Down to this point the course of the great river had been north-east, north-north-east, and east-north-east, but below it sheered to north. On our right now began the large country of Koruru, and on our left Yambarri.*

We descended rapidly for two miles down the river, here about two thousand yards wide, after which the hoarse murmur of falls was again heard. Our cannibal guides warned us not to venture near the left bank, and, relying on their information, we approached the Sixth Cataract along the right bank, and camped not four hundred yards from an

CAVERN, NEAR KABOMBO ISLANDS.

island densely inhabited by a tribe of the Waregga called Wana-Rukura.

We here released our cannibal guides, and surrendered their weapons to them. They availed themselves of their liberty by instantly running along the river bank up the river. We were not long left unmolested in our jungle camp, for while we were still engaged in constructing a stockade, war-cries, horns, and drums announced the approach of the ever-fierce aborigines; and in a short time we were hotly engaged. In an hour we had driven them away. Following them up rapidly a little distance we came to a

* Colonel Long, of the Egyptian army, on his way to the Nyam-Nyam country, in 1874, met with a tribe called the Yanbari, in about 5° north latitude.

large village, where we discovered three or four women well advanced in years, and, in order to obtain information of the country and its inhabitants, conveyed them to camp, where we began to practise such arts of conciliation and kindness as calm and soothe the fears of excited captives, and which had been so successful up river.

We had hardly returned to camp before a larger force —the inhabitants of the islands—appeared in head-dresses of parrot-feathers, and skull-caps of civet, squirrel, goat, and "soko," and with a bold confidence born of ignorance made a rush upon the stockade. The attack was promptly repelled, and in turn we attacked, driving the savages back step by step, and following them to a creek about fifty yards wide, into which they sprang to swim to their island. Two of the wounded warriors we caught and conveyed to our camp, where their wounds were dressed, and other attentions paid to them, which were much appreciated by them.

The pioneers were during the afternoon engaged in cutting a broad road to the creek past the first fall, and by sunset our canoes and boat were dragged out of the river into the stockade, ready for transport overland.

Jan. 20.—The morning of the 20th was occupied in hauling our vessels into the creek, which the flying Waregga islanders had first shown to us, and, by desperate labour, the whole Expedition was able to move from the right bank across the creek to the island.

During the night the Wana-Rukura had abandoned the large island at its northern end, and thus we were left happily undisturbed in our occupation of it to obtain a few hours' deserved rest.

Jan. 23.—The Sixth Cataract is caused by a broad dyke of greenish shale, projecting from the base of the tall bluffs on the left bank of the river. Being of many thin strata, the current has succeeded in quarrying frequent gaps through it, one of which on the left side, where the current is greatest, and the scene of raging waters wildest, is very deep and wide. Nearer the right bank the cataract has more the aspect of furious rapids; and a narrow branch has been formed between the numerous Wana-Rukura islets and the right bank, which drops over a dozen low terraces from 6 inches to 2 feet, and a series of shallow rapids for a distance of six miles, when it has reached the level of the main river below the Sixth Cataract. By noon of the 23rd we had succeeded in clearing this cataract without loss of life or serious accident.

We were very patient with our captives, and succeeded in inducing them to be communicative, but unhappily we understood but little of what they so volubly imparted to us. But what we did learn was interesting.

They had heard of Ruanda, and indicated for it an east-north-east direction; and also of the Wakombeh, or Wabembé, cannibals, who occupy the country between Goma and Uvira, and most certainly a large tract north-north-west from Tanganika. The Bakumu were the tribe that had first attacked us, of which the four middle-aged females from the village of Wati-Kytzya were representatives. They were much lighter-coloured than the Wana-Rukura islanders. I feel convinced that these Bakumu must be a branch of the Wanya-Ruanda, for they have a great many of those facial Ethiopic characteristics which elevate that great nation above the ordinary negroid type. Ukumu is said to extend very far to the east, and must therefore lie between Northern and Southern Uregga. The king is said to be called Sarindi, and his village was pointed out as being east. The negative "Nangu," which the women employed, is the same as that used by the natives of Ruanda, Unyoro, Usongora, Uzongora, Wanyambu, Watusi, and Wakerewé.

"Ubingi" signified rapid river with the Waregga, Bakumu, and Baswa tribes; and "Chare-reh" means the gentle flow of water. The word "Mavira" with the Waregga is used to denote rocks; while the Bakumu, Baswa, Southern Waregga, Wabwiré, and Wenya employ the word "Matari."

Two miles below the Sixth Cataract of the Stanley Falls we came to a bit of bad water; but, after successfully passing it, we halted an hour on the right bank to discharge the captives who belonged to the Wana-Rukura tribe and the Bakumu. The two wounded warriors had behaved very patiently during their four days' stay with us, and were progressing favourably. Meanwhile we had employed every leisure hour in endeavouring to master the rudiments of their language, and I had obtained a list of nearly two hundred words from them, with which, if the people below spoke it, we might be able to communicate a little with them.

At noon of January 20, we landed on the first island of

the Wana-Rukura, and found the south latitude, by solar observation, 0° 2′ 0″. Noon of the 23rd, having meanwhile passed the Sixth Cataract, we found ourselves four miles north of the Equator by observation.

Three miles below the rapids we passed a small river about thirty yards wide entering the Livingstone between high banks, and soon after the right and left bank, rising up to hills, approached each other within seven hundred yards, and there seemed to be every prospect of another cataract. As we rushed through the straits, I dropped the lead with twenty fathoms of line into the river, but found no bottom, but I could not repeat the experiment, as the rapidity of the current compelled me to be mindful of my course, and everybody in the canoes was trusting to my guidance.

At ten miles north of the Equator, below the straits, we crossed to the left bank, and occupied the village of Utikera, the sole inhabitant remaining being one very reserved old man. Utikera is situated opposite the three rocky islands of Mikuna. I suspect this settlement was abandoned because of some war that had taken place between them and some more powerful tribes down river, for according to all appearance the people must have left several days previously. Indeed the old man as much as indicated this, though we were not certain that we understood him. The village was large, and constructed after the pattern of those up-river already described.

Jan. 24.—On the 24th we halted to repair the boat and canoes, and the next day resumed our journey. The course of the Livingstone from the Sixth Cataract to the straits near Utikera had been north-north-west; it now ran north-west by west, with a breadth of 2000 yards. We preferred the right bank again, and soon entered a deep branch between a long and exceedingly picturesque island and a low shore, edged with mangrove brushwood. When about halfway, we heard the hoarse rumble of rapids on the left branch, but the right was undisturbed. The island we discovered to be about ten miles in length, and soon after passing three small islands the roar of the seventh and last cataract of the Stanley Falls burst upon our ears with a tremendous crash.

It was soon evident that the vicinity of the last fall was as thickly peopled as any of the Stanley series, for the sonorous boom of the great war-drums was soon heard mustering every stray and loitering fisherman from the creeks, and every hunter from the woods that clothed the bank, to the war. While I wondered at the senseless hate and ferocity which appeared to animate these primitive aborigines, we were compelled to adopt speedy measures for defence and security; for these people, if confident in numbers, do not require much time to snatch up their spears and shields and rush to the fight. Accordingly, dropping down as near to the first line of broken water as prudence would permit me, we seized upon a position in the dense forest, and, posting the riflemen in a crescent form in our front, busied ourselves as usual with axes in heaping up a high and dense wall of brushwood for our protection. By the time this had been completed, the Wenya were on us with a determined impetuosity that would have been fatal to us had we been taken unprepared. Again and again they tried to break through the concealed musketeers, but they were utterly unable to pierce within view of our camp. The loud notes of their war-horns, of which they seemed to possess an unusual number, rang through the forest with wailing notes, and the great drums at the numerous villages which commanded the narrows through which the great river precipitated itself, responded with energy to the signals transmitted to them.

At sunset they abandoned the unavailing assault, and, to guard against any nocturnal surprise, we piled up more brushwood, and drew the boat and canoes out of the water on land. I resolved to make a bold stroke early next morning, and by appearing in front of their villages before cockcrow, to occupy some place near the falls which would enable Frank and a few of the chiefs to begin transporting the vessels overland, and to continue the work even though we might be actively engaged by the Wenya.

Jan. 25.—At 5 A.M. I led thirty-five men from the camp, and after a desperate struggle through the tangled jungle emerged near the place where the right bank swept round to the straits, over and above which a large number of villages were situated. A shallow branch, 40 yards wide, supplied by thin streams of water that poured down a dyke of loose rocks 20 feet high from the great river, separated the right bank from the point occupied by the settlements. During the wet months it was evident that this dyke must be washed by a furious cataract, and that the right branch is then almost impassable, and it is for this reason probably that the locality was chosen by the Wenya. At this season, however, we crossed over to the inhabited island without trouble, and resolved to guard the approach to this branch. From our camp to this point there was not the slightest danger to fear from the river; and Uledi and his boat-mates were therefore signalled to bring the boat and canoes near to the dyke.

After waiting until 9 A.M. for the islanders to begin their

THE SEVENTH CATARACT, STANLEY FALLS.

attack, I sent a few scouts through the brushwood to ascertain what the Wenya were doing, and within an hour they returned to say that nothing could be heard of them. Moving forwards by the path, we discovered to our good fortune that the people had abandoned the island apparently. The extent of the villages proved them to be a populous community, and the manner in which they were arranged gave them an appearance resembling a town on the Upper Nile. Each village, however, was distinct from the next, though only short distances separated them, and each possessed four or five streets 30 feet wide, running in parallel lines, with cross alleys leading from one side of the village to the other. The entire population of this town or cluster of villages might be moderately estimated at 6000. On the opposite side was another large community, whose inhabitants manned every rock to gaze at us in perfect security, for, since they could not hurt us, we certainly entertained no designs against them.

The Livingstone from the right bank across the island to the left bank is about 1300 yards broad, of which width 40 yards is occupied by the right branch, 760 yards by the island of the Wenya, 500 yards by the great river. Contracted to this narrow space, between the rocky and perpendicular bluffs of the island and the steep banks opposite, the uproar, as may be imagined, is very great. As the calm river, which is 1300 yards wide one mile above the falls, becomes narrowed, the current quickens, and rushes with resistless speed for a few hundred yards, and then falls about 10 feet into a boiling and tumultuous gulf, wherein are lines of brown waves 6 feet high leaping with terrific bounds, and hurling themselves against each other in dreadful fury.

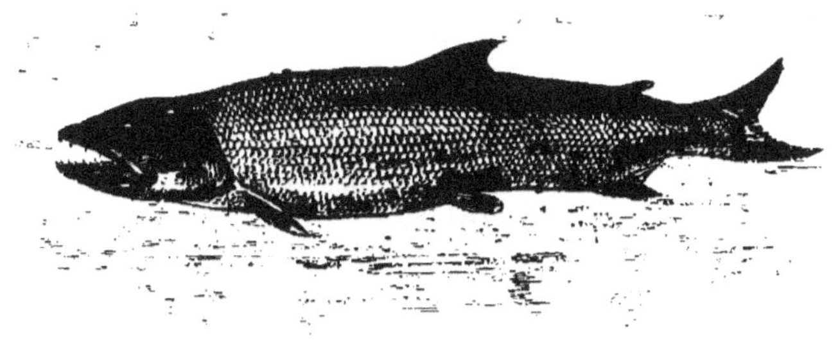

PIKE, STANLEY FALLS.

Until I realized the extent of the volume that was here precipitated, I could hardly believe that it was indeed a vast river that was passing before me through this narrowed channel. I have seen many waterfalls during my travels in various parts of the world, but here was a stupendous river flung in full volume over a waterfall only 500 yards across. The river at the last cataract of the Stanley Falls does not merely *fall*: it is precipitated downwards. The Ripon Falls at the Victoria Lake outlet, compared to this swift descent and furious on-rush, were languid. The Victoria Nile, as it swept down the steep declivity of its bed towards Unyoro, is very pretty, picturesque, even a sufficiently exciting scene; but the Livingstone, with over ten times the volume of the Victoria Nile, though only occupying the same breadth of bed, conveys to the sense the character of irresistible force, and unites great depth with a tumultuous rush.

A solar observation taken opposite the last of the Stanley Falls proved the latitude to be north 0° 15′ 0″, or seventeen miles north of the first broken water of the Sixth Cataract;

FISH, SEVENTH CATARACT, STANLEY FALLS.

28 inches long; 16 inches round body; round snout; no teeth; broad tail large scales; colour, pale brown.

and a few miles below the falls, on the 28th of January, we obtained north latitude 0° 20′ 0″. By boiling point I ascertained that the declination was nearly 120 feet in these twenty-two miles, the altitude above sea at the Seventh Cataract being 1511 feet. As there are only seven miles really occupied by the Sixth and Seventh Cataracts, the

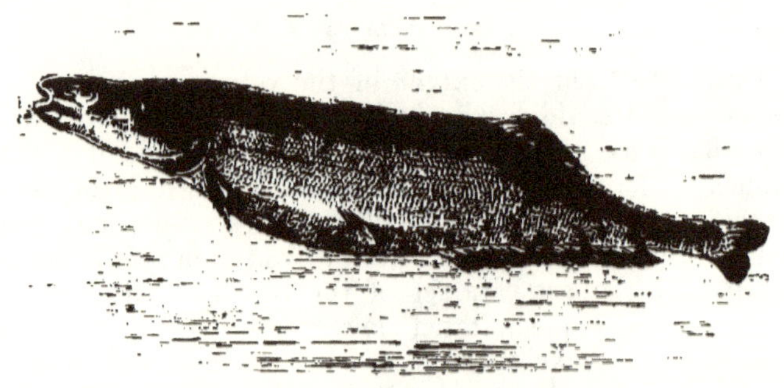

FISH, STANLEY FALLS.

Fine scales; weight, 23 lbs.; thick broad snout; 26 small teeth in upper jaw, 23 teeth in lower jaw; broad tongue; head, 11 inches long.

intermediate fifteen miles being calm flowing water, we may not be far wrong in giving the slope of the river at the two falls a declination of 17 feet to the mile.

The rocky point of the left bank was formerly connected with the rocky island of the Wenya by a ridge, which appears to have fallen southward, judging from the diagonal strata, but since that period the river has worn down this obstruction, and the cataract is now about three hundred yards south-east of the straits, pounding away at the ledge with the whole of its force.

A glance at the sketch of the Seventh Cataract of the Stanley Falls shows a line of tall poles planted below the falls, which assist us not only to form some estimate of the depth of the water, but also of the industry of the Wenya. A space of about 300 yards, in the middle of the falls, is unapproachable, but to a distance of 100 yards on each side, by taking advantage of the rocks, the natives have been enabled to fix upright heavy poles, 6 inches in diameter, to each of which they attach enormous fish-baskets by means of rattan-cane cables. There are probably sixty or seventy baskets laid in the river on each side, every day; and though some may be brought up empty, in general they seem to be tolerably successful, for out of half-a-dozen baskets that my boatmen brought up next day for examination twenty-eight large fish were collected, one of which—a pike—was 40 inches long, 24 inches round the body, and weighed 17 lbs.

Higher up the river we had also been accustomed to see piles of oysters and mussel-shells along the banks, especially while passing the lands of the Upper Wenya, between Rukombeh's landing near Ukusu and the First Cataract of Stanley Falls. These in some instances, might be taken as the only remaining traces of departed generations of Wenya, settled here when, through internecine troubles, they had been ejected from some more favoured locality.

The Wenya of the Seventh Cataract struck me as being not only more industrious than the aboriginal Baswas, but also more inventive than any we had yet seen, for in their villages we discovered square wooden chests, as large as an ordinary portmanteau, wherein their treasures of beads and berries, large oyster and mussel-shells, were preserved. The paddles were beautiful specimens, made out of wood very much resembling mahogany: a vast quantity of half-inch cord made out of Hyphene palm and banana-fibre was also discovered. In almost every house, also, there were one or more ten-gallon earthenware jars filled with palm butter, while ivory seemed to be a drug, for we found three large tusks entirely rotten and useless, besides numbers of ivory war-horns, and ivory pestles for pounding cassava into flour.

After building another camp above the creek-like branch near the right bank, we availed ourselves of some of the numerous piles of poles which the Wenya had cut for sinking in the river to lay a roadway over the rocks, from the level of the great river down to the lower level of the creek, and by night the boat and canoes were in the water and out of danger.

PALM-OIL JAR AND PALM-WINE COOLER.

Jan. 27.—The next day, while descending this creek, we were attacked both from front and rear, and almost the whole of the afternoon we were occupied in defending a rude camp we had hastily thrown up, while our non-combatants

MOUTH OF DRUM.

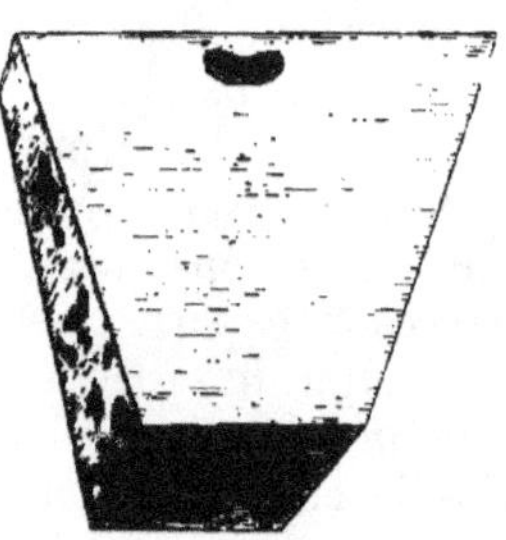

WOODEN SIGNAL DRUM OF THE WENYA OR WAGENYA AND THE TRIBES ON THE LIVINGSTONE.

DRUMSTICKS, KNOBS BEING OF INDIA-RUBBER.

lay sheltered by a high bank and our canoes. Towards sunset the savages retired.

Jan. 28.—On the morning of the 28th we resumed our labours with greater energy, and by 10 A.M. we were clear of the last of the Stanley Falls, thus closing a series of desperate labours, which had occupied us from the 6th of January, a period of twenty-two days, during the nights and days of which we had been beset by the perverse cannibals and insensate savages who have made the islands amid the cataracts their fastnesses, and now—

> "Our troubled thoughts to distant prospects leap,
> Desirous still what flies us to o'ertake;
> For hope is but the dream of those that wake.
> But looking back we see the dreadful train
> Of woes anew, which, were we to sustain,
> We should refuse to tread the path again."

CHAPTER IX.

Again in open water—Frank Pocock feels the position—The Mburra or Yaryembi—A running fight—"Ya-Mariwa! Ya-Mariwa!"—Our tactics of capture—Monster spears—Growing weary of fighting for life—The power of laughter—Fish creeks—A wasp swarm of canoes—Another invincible armada—A village of ivory—Relics of cannibal feasts—The Wellé of Schweinfurth—Hunted to despair—Their meat escapes the cannibals—Wild nature—Among friendly natives—The Congo!

Jan. 28.—We hastened away down river in a hurry, to escape the noise of the cataracts which, for many days and nights, had almost stunned us with their deafening sound.

The Livingstone now deflected to the west-north-west, between hilly banks—

"Where highest woods, impenetrable
To star, or sunlight, spread their umbrage broad
And brown as evening."

We are once again afloat upon a magnificent stream, whose broad and grey-brown waters woo us with its mystery. We are not a whit dejected after our terrible experiences; we find our reward in being alive to look upon wild nature, and a strange elasticity comes over us. The boat-boys amuse me by singing their most animating song, to which every member of our Expedition responds with enthusiasm. The men, women, and children are roused to maintain that reckless, exuberant spirit which assisted me to drive through the cannibal region of the Stanley Falls, for otherwise they might lose that dash and vigour on which depends our success. They are apt, if permitted thinking-time, to brood upon our situation, to become disquieted and melancholy, to reflect on the fate of those who have already been lost, and to anticipate a like dolorous ending to their own lives.

I thought even Frank was half affected by the sudden cessation of trouble, and the sight of the now broad tranquil river to which we had been a stranger for some time; for after the boat-boys had become hoarse from chanting, his voice was heard in a doleful and sad strain, of which the words were as follows:—

"The home land, the fair land,
Refuge for all distressed,
Where pain and sin ne'er enter in,
But all is peace and rest.

"The home land! I long to meet
Those who have gone before;
The weeping eyes and weary feet
Rest on that happy shore.

"The home land, the bright land!
My eyes are filled with tears,
Remembering all the happy band,
Passed from my sight for years.

"When will it dawn upon my soul?
When shall I meet that strand?
By night and day I watch and pray
For thee, dear, blest home land."

I thought the voice trembled as the strain ended; and, lest I should be affected also, by no means a desirable thing, I said cheerily, "Frank, my dear fellow, you will make everybody cry with such tunes as those; they are too lachrymose altogether for our present state. The men are so weak and excited that mournfulness will derange their nerves, and make us all utterly unfit for the work before us. Choose some heroic tune, whose notes will make us all feel afire, and drive our canoes down stream as though we were driven by steam."

"All right, sir," he replied with a bright, cheerful face, and sang the following:—

"Brightly gleams our banner,
Pointing to the sky,
Waving wanderers onward
To their home on high.

"Journeying o'er the desert
Gladly thus we pray,
And with hearts united
Take our heavenward way."

"Ah, Frank, it is not the heavenward way you mean, is it? I should think you would prefer the homeward way, for that is the way I pray to be permitted to lead you."

"How do you like this, sir?" he asked.

"My God, my Father, while I stray,
Far from my home, in life's rough way,
O teach me from my heart to say,
Thy will be done.

"Though dark my path, and sad my lot,
Let me be still and murmur not,
Or breathe the prayer divinely taught,
Thy will be done.

"What though in lonely grief I sigh
For friends beloved no longer nigh!
Submissive would I still reply,
Thy will be done."

"Frank, you are thinking too much of the poor fellows we have lately lost. It is of no use, my son; we have taken the bit in our teeth, and must drive on—drive right through to the sea. The time for regret and sorrow will come by and by, but just now we are in the centre of Africa; savages before you, savages behind you, savages on either side of you. Onward, I say; onward to death, if it is to be. I will not listen to regrets now. Sing, my dear Frank, your best song."

He responded by singing:—

"Onward, Christian soldiers,
Marching as to war,
With the cross of Jesus
Going on before!"

This was too much for me. I saw that he was in a serious and religious vein of mind, and refrained therefore from disturbing him further. The boat-boys now resumed their barbarous but exhilarating chorus, and again the woods on either side re-echoed with the stirring notes of our boat-song.

At 3 P.M. we arrived at a fine river, 300 yards wide at the mouth, which flowed from the east-south-east, with low wooded banks on either side. After proceeding a mile, we discovered another branch of the same river, about 300 yards wide, the two branches joining at about two miles above. Subsequently we received two names for it—the Mburra, and the Yaryembi—but I believe the Mburra is the correct title for the joint river.

The great stream a mile below the confluence opened out again into a breadth of 2000 yards, and was soon disparted by the broad and fertile island of Ukioba into two branches of equal breadth. We preferred the right branch, which had a course north-west by north for about two miles, when it again deflected to west-north-west. Much of the right bank showed a horizontal substructure of sandstone, with about 10 feet of alluvium above it, and ranged from 20 to 100 feet in height, wooded throughout, except at market-greens and old settlements.

We prepared to camp at one of these abandoned settlements, but a neighbouring community at Usimbi advanced to contest our right to remain on the soil of Koruru, and obliged us to continue our journey. We then chose the lower end of the Ukioba Island, nearly opposite Usimbi; but the stupid aborigines could not understand this forbearance, and, manning their canoes, called on the Wakioba to unite with them in expelling us. This compelled us to defend ourselves, which ended in the dispersion of the people of Koruru, and the capture of one of their war-vessels and five men.

Their canoes differed from those above the Stanley Falls, being capacious, flat-bottomed scows, dug out of a fragrant gum-tree (probably of the genus Boswellia), which grows to very large dimensions in the forests.

Jan. 29.—On the morning of the 29th we crossed the river, and finding Usimbi abandoned, entered it. The arrangement of the villages was the same as with the Wenya at the Stanley Falls, possessing lateral and transverse streets at right angles, and not consisting, as those on the Upper Livingstone, of one long street. Each house also possessed a court, neatly surrounded with a fence of upright logs. Behind, or on the inland side, the village was protected by two deep ditches, the earth from the excavations being thrown inwards. In the middle of what seemed to be a principal street was a rude wooden figure of a bearded man, under a small conical-shaped roof, which was supported by nine ivory tusks, raised upon a platform of tamped clay, and carefully swept, showing that great care was bestowed upon it. The people appear to have considerable faith in a whitewash of cassava meal, with which they had sprinkled the fences, posts, and lintels of doors, and the stems of the ficus, planted for shade here and there in small plazas. Great drums, 6 feet long, 3 feet deep, and 2 feet wide, resting on broad and solid legs, and carved out of a single log, also stood in the plazas.

We released our captives, and then crying out "Bismillah!" continued our voyage down river, which had a breadth of 2500 yards below Ukioba Island. Both banks were high, steep, and wooded. The right bank showed a reddish and rippled sandstone up to a foot above the waterline for a few miles below Usimbi. But the substructure afterwards changed to a greyish calcareous rock, with a perpendicular face varying from 20 to 50 feet high. Numerous creeks, 20 and 25 yards wide, emptied into the great river from the right bank.

At noon, when approaching a large village, we were again assaulted by the aborigines. We drove them back, and obtained a peaceful passage past them, until 1 P.M. During this interval I obtained an observation for latitude, and ascertained we had reached north latitude 0° 22′ 29″.

From 1 P.M. we were engaged with a new tribe, which possessed very large villages, and maintained a running fight with us until 4 P.M., when, observing the large village of Ituka below us, and several canoes cutting across river to head us off, we resolved to make our stand on the shore. Material for constructing a boma was soon discovered in the outlying houses of the village, and by five o'clock we were tolerably secure on the edge of the steep banks — all obstructions cleared away on the land side, and a perfect view of the river front and shore below us.

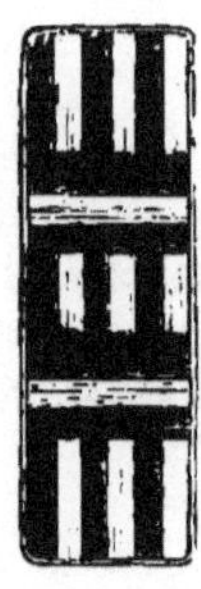

SHIELDS OF ITUKA PEOPLE.

The savages were hideously bepainted for war, one-half of their bodies being white, the other ochreous. Their shields were oblong squares, beautifully made of rattan-cane, light, tough, and to spears and knives impenetrable. A square slab of ebony wood with a cleat, and one long thin board placed lengthways, and another crossways, sufficed to stiffen them. Shouting their war-cries—"Ya-Mariwa! Ya-Mariwa!"—they rushed on our boma fences like a herd of buffaloes several times, in one of which charges Muftah Rufiji was killed, a broad spear-blade sharp as a razor ripping nearly eight inches of his abdomen open; another man received a wound from a spear, which had glanced along his back. As the heavy spears hurtled through the boma, or flew over it, very many of us had extremely narrow escapes. Frank, for instance, avoided one by giving his body a slight jerk on one side. We, of course, had the advantage, being protected by doors, roofs of houses, poles, brushwood, and our great Mwana-Ntaba shields, which had been of invaluable use to us, and had often in the heat of fights saved us and made us almost invulnerable.

From the Ruiki river up to this afternoon of January 29th we had fought twenty-four times, and out of these struggles we had obtained sixty-five door-like shields, which upon the commencement of a fight on the river at all times had been raised by the women, children, and non-combatants as bulwarks before the riflemen, from behind which, cool and confident, the forty-three guns were of more avail than though there were 150 riflemen unprotected. The steersmen, likewise protected, were enabled to steer their vessels with the current while we were engaged in these running fights. Against the spears and arrows the shields were impervious.

At sunset our antagonists retired, leaving us to dress our wounds and bury our dead, and to prepare for the morrow by distributing a new store of cartridges; and, after waiting until 9 A.M. next day unattacked, we sailed out and embarked once more.

Below Ituka the river was deflected to north-west by west by a long ridge called Tugarambusa, from 300 to 500 feet high, with perpendicular red cliffs for four miles, until terminated by a point 300 feet high, the summit of which was crowned with a fine forest. Beyond the point we were sheltered by a sandstone bluff, and steep slopes covered by beautiful ferns, and shrubby trees with blossoms like lilacs, which exhaled a delightful fragrance. On the lower portions of the banks, where landslips had occurred, we observed a reddish sandstone capped by yellow clay.

After six miles of these high banks the river flowed west by north half west, while the high banks already mentioned became a ridge, running north-west, leaving a lower level at its base extending to the river, which was highly populous and cultivated.

Jan. 30.—About ten o'clock of the 30th another conflict began, in the usual way, by a determined assault on us in canoes. By charging under cover of our shields we captured one canoe and eight men, and withdrew to a low grassy islet opposite Yangambi, a settlement consisting of five populous villages. We had discovered by this that nothing cowed the natives so much as a capture, and as it was the most bloodless mode of settling what might have been a protracted affair, I had adopted it. Through our captives we were enabled to negotiate for an unmolested passage, though it involved delay and an expenditure of lung force that was very trying; still, as it ended satisfactorily in many ways, it was preferable to continued fighting. It also increased our opportunities of knowing who our antagonists were, and to begin an acquaintance with these long-buried peoples.

We understood a captive to say that the river here was called Izangi, that the settlements on the right bank were in the country of Koruru, and that on the left bank still extended the country of Yambarri, or Vambari.

When the natives observed us preparing to halt on the grassy islet directly opposite their villages, with their unfortunate friends in our power, they withdrew to their village to consult. The distance between our grassy islet and the right bank was only 500 yards, and as it was the eastern bank the sun shone direct on them; enabling me, with the aid of a field-glass, to perceive even the differences of feature between one man and another.

Though hostilities had ceased, the drumming continued with unabated fury; bass and kettle-drums gave out a thunderous sound, which must have been heard to an immense distance. The high ridge, which was three miles behind Yangambi, exhibited cultivated slopes and many villages, which discharged their hundreds to the large council-circle sitting down in view of us. Many of the aborigines paraded up and down the banks for our benefit, holding up to our view bright spear-blades, 6 feet in length and 6 inches broad! the sight of which drew curious remarks from my hard-pressed followers.

One, named Mpwapwa, cried out, "Oh, mother, those fellows mean to split a man in two with such spears as those!" Another said, "No, man, those are the spears from their idol temples, for mere show; for were a man to be carved with such a big spear, there would be nothing left of him." But Baraka, the humourist, opined they were intended to spit children on. A chorus of war-cries sometimes broke out from the immense concourse of people, wherein we could distinguish very plainly the words "Ya, Mariwa!"

While all this was at its height, and as we were unable to comprehend anything that the natives bawled out to us, we placed our captives in their canoe, and, giving each a few shells, motioned them to depart. As the warriors on the bank saw their friends return, they all gathered round the landing-place, and, as they landed, asked scores of questions, the replies to which elicited loud grunts of approval and wonder. The drumming gradually ceased, the war-cries were heard no more, the people left their processions to crowd round their countrymen, and the enormous spear-blades no longer flashed their brightness on us. We waited about an hour, and, taking it for granted that after such a signal instance of magnanimity they would not resume their hostile demeanour, we quietly embarked, and glided down the river unopposed.

Not desirous of risking another encounter this day, we sought the shelter of a wooded island opposite an uninhabited forest, and arranged ourselves in the wild woods with due regard to safety. Yet we were not unobserved. Some stray fishermen gave notice to the populous settlements below, and a furious drumming at once began from each bank, which was maintained without intermission until morning.

The river was gradually increasing in breadth; from 3000 yards it grew to 4000 yards wide. Islands also were more numerous, with dense roofs of green foliage upheld by the trunks of the tall patriarchs. We were getting weary of fighting every day. The strain to which we were exposed had been too long, the incessant, long-lasting enmity shown to us was beginning to make us feel baited, harassed, and bitter. Dared we but dash down by night? Ah, but who could tell us what lay below! Whom could we ask, when everything in the shape of man raised his spear and screamed his rage at us as soon as we were observed!

So we emerged out of the covert and forest shades of the island with soured and embittered feelings. But we would cling to the islands, and close our ears against their infernal noise, and turn our eyes resolutely away from the advancing cannibals until they came within spear-throw of us, and then, why—we will fight again.

Jan. 31.—We did cling to the islands. An enormous breadth of river—on our right and on our left—separated us from either bank, but it was totally insufficient to win a free passage. We must either sacrifice a few men or women or children to their lust for human meat, or we must sacrifice a few cartridges. Fourteen canoes already lying in wait below Divari Island surprised us by their ferocious precipitancy, but we preferred to lose the cartridges, and after delivering over to them a sufficient number, we crossed the river again, lest there might be more canoes lying in wait, and followed the right bank, where we had a short tussle with a few more Wariwa canoes at Yavunga, which, fortunately for us, was the last trouble we experienced on the 31st. The people of Irendé and Uganja on the left bank had behaved as boisterously as those of Yavunga, and had offended our ears with bold demands for our flesh, and had even affected a chase; but the defeated heroes of Yavunga advised them not to be absurd.

About 10 A.M. we approached, after quite an interval of peace—two hours!—another settlement on the right bank. We sheered off again to the islands. The river was evidently getting wider, and with its increased width the banks became lower, and no longer showed those picturesque hills, tall, wooded ridges, brown, red, or grey bluffs capped with the forest marvels of the tropics, which had so often elicited our admiration. Grassy islets alternated with wooded ones, and these are the haunts of the salt-makers, who extract salt out of the lye. Opposite a large palisaded village called Mawembé, which was holding a market even then, we came to a grassy islet, where were two women in a canoe. We ceased paddling at once. Our blandishments were most effectual on them. They laughed so loud that it appeared as if the market people at Mawembé, 1500 yards from us, must have heard them. Out of real sympathy we too laughed—but whether they were victims of our blandishments or we of theirs, would be difficult to tell. I had heard of the power of negroes to laugh, but I had never realised their powers so thoroughly as when these two women lay back, opened their mouths, and gave forth those surprising volumes of laughter that so perfectly captivated us. They understood the value of beads, and we tossed ten necklaces to them; but all we could understand from them was that the great palisaded village was Mawembé and the country Koruru.

The current finally swept us out of sight of them, and three miles below we discovered another palisaded village, for which we could obtain no name. Grassy islets vomited smoke in dense clouds, but man was such an obnoxious animal in these regions that we dared not seek his acquaintance. At noon I obtained an altitude of the sun, and ascertained that we had reached north latitude 0° 35′ 50″.

The right bank here rose again, high and steep, shadowed

with a glorious forest, the islands were wooded to an intense blackness, and between them flowed the river in broad bands of silver. The left bank was so far off that we obtained no view of it! In a recess amid palms and vines and patriarchal trees, bound together by giant creepers of ficus and serpent-like lengths of *Calamus secundiflorus*, we sheltered our weary souls, and thought to do honour to the deity of those lonesome woods, who had reserved this loneliness to protect us in our outlawed state.

Feb. 1.—The sun came out above the forest, round and large and bright, shooting broad gleams of light into the island shades, and lighting up their gloom until they seemed most envied retreats. Not for us, however. Destiny urged us on. There were no retreats for us. Man refused us, and the forest rejected us, for it had nothing to support us.

Almost straight the river flows—north-west half west. The right bank, to which we again cling, is steep and high, and crowned with solemn woods. At the water line is yellow clay; above it, alluvium and vegetable mould, on which a hundred varieties of tropical plants flourish. Presently we are made aware that we are approaching settlements, by a number of ditches excavated in the lower banks, at an obtuse angle to the course of the river, which during the flooding season will become filled by the full river and the resort of numerous fish. We had observed this before. The larger islands and banks ever since leaving the Stanley Falls, exhibited proofs of that love of the natives for fish which has stimulated them to undertake these laborious excavations, often over a hundred yards in length, to plait huge basket-traps and reedy fences at the mouths of creeks, to manufacture coils of stout rope out of plantain and palm (Hyphene) fibre, large cord nets, to plant great poles in the middle of cataracts, and undeterred by its dangers, to risk their lives daily in fish-catching.

About 8 P.M. we came in view of a market-place, near which there were scores of small canoes. The men at once rushed into them, and advanced all round us. We refrained a long time, but finally, as they began to get brave by our quiescence, and to launch their wooden spears, which they proceeded to do unanimously as soon as somebody cried out "Mutti"—sticks—we were obliged to reply to them with a few shots, which compelled them to scamper away ahead of us. Drums then awakened the whole country, and horns blew deafening blasts. Some canoes pertinaciously followed us. We came about 10 A.M. to another market-green. Here, too, warriors were ready, and the little canoes, like wasps, hovered round us, and again we had recourse to our weapons. The little canoes with loud threats disappeared quickly down river: the land warriors rushed away into the woods. We did not wish to hurry, because the faster we proceeded the quicker we found we were involved in trouble. We therefore loitered languidly: rest was so rare that it became precious when we obtained it.

At noon I observed the sun, and found we were in north latitude 0°50′17″. We resumed our journey, rowing at a steady though not a fast pace. We had descended the river for about an hour when we came again in sight of those waspish little canoes, and from the left bank, 3000 yards off, canoes were seen heading across the river at a terrific pace, while horns blew and drums beat. We heard shouts of defiance, or threats, we knew not which—we had become indifferent to the incessant noise and continued fury.

In these wild regions our mere presence excited the most furious passions of hate and murder, just as in shallow waters a deep vessel stirs up muddy sediments. It appeared to be a necessity, then why should we regret it? Could a man contend with the inevitable?

At 2 P.M., heralded by savage shouts from the wasp swarm, which from some cause or other are unusually exultant, we emerge out of the shelter of the deeply wooded banks in presence of a vast affluent, nearly 2000 yards across at the mouth. As soon as we have fairly entered its waters, we see a great concourse of canoes hovering about some islets, which stud the middle of the stream. The canoe-men, standing up, give a loud shout as they discern us, and blow their horns louder than ever. We pull briskly on to gain the right bank, and come in view of the right branch of the affluent, when, looking up stream, we see a sight that sends the blood tingling through every nerve and fibre of the body, arouses not only our most lively interest, but also our most lively apprehensions—a flotilla of gigantic canoes bearing down upon us, which both in size and numbers utterly eclipse anything encountered hitherto! Instead of aiming for the right bank, we form in line, and keep straight down river, the boat taking position behind. Yet after a moment's reflection, as I note the numbers of the savages, and the daring manner of the pursuit, and the desire of our canoes to abandon the steady compact line, I give the order to drop anchor. Four of our canoes affect not to listen, until I chase them, and threaten them with my guns. This compelled them to return to the line, which is formed of eleven double canoes, anchored 10 yards apart. The boat moves up to the front, and takes position 50 yards above them. The shields are next lifted by the non-combatants, men, women, and children, in the bows, and along the outer lines, as well as astern, and from behind these, the muskets and rifles are aimed.

We have sufficient time to take a view of the mighty force bearing down on us, and to count the number of the war-vessels which have been collected from the Livingstone and its great affluent. There are fifty-four of them! A monster canoe leads the way, with two rows of upstanding paddles, forty men on a side, their bodies bending and swaying in unison as with a swelling barbarous chorus they drive her down towards us. In the bow, standing on what

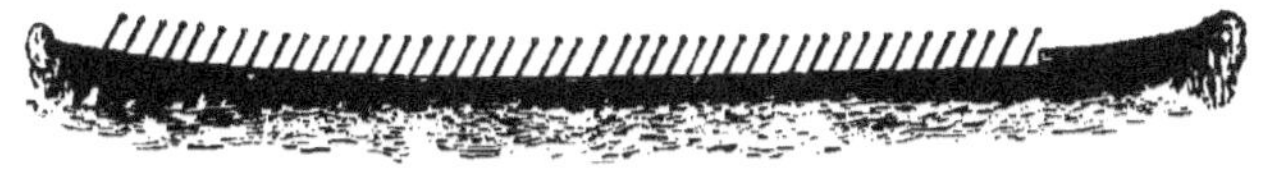

MONSTER CANOE.

appears to be a platform, are ten prime young warriors, their heads gay with feathers of the parrot, crimson and grey: at the stern, eight men, with long paddles, whose tops are decorated with ivory balls, guide the monster vessel; and dancing up and down from stem to stern are ten men, who appear to be chiefs. All the paddles are headed with ivory balls, every head bears a feather crown, every arm shows gleaming white ivory armlets. From the bow of the canoe streams a thick fringe of the long white fibre of the Hyphene palm. The crashing sound of large drums, a hundred blasts from ivory horns, and a thrilling chant from two thousand human throats, do not tend to soothe our nerves or to increase our confidence. However, it is "neck or nothing." We have no time to pray, or to take sentimental looks at the savage world, or even to breathe a sad farewell to it. So many other things have to be done speedily and well.

As the foremost canoe comes rushing down, and its consorts on either side beating the water into foam, and raising their jets of water with their sharp prows, I turn to take a last look at our people, and say to them :—

"Boys, be firm as iron ; wait until you see the first spear, and then take good aim. Don't fire all at once. Keep aiming until you are sure of your man. Don't think of running away, for only your guns can save you."

Frank is with the *Ocean* on the right flank, and has a choice crew, and a good bulwark of black wooden shields. Manwa Sera has the *London Town*—which he has taken in charge instead of the *Glasgow*—on the left flank, the sides of the canoe bristling with guns, in the hands of tolerably steady men.

The monster canoe aims straight for my boat, as though it would run us down ; but, when within fifty yards off, swerves aside, and, when nearly opposite, the warriors above the manned prow let fly their spears, and on either side there is a noise of rushing bodies. But every sound is soon lost in the ripping, crackling musketry. For five minutes we are so absorbed in firing that we take no note of anything else ; but at the end of that time we are made aware that the enemy is reforming about 200 yards above us.

Our blood is up now. It is a murderous world, and we feel for the first time that we hate the filthy, vulturous ghouls who inhabit it. We therefore lift our anchors, and pursue them up-stream along the right bank, until rounding a point we see their villages. We make straight for the banks, and continue the fight in the village streets with those who have landed, hunt them out into the woods, and there only sound the retreat, having returned the daring cannibals the compliment of a visit.

While mustering my people for re-embarkation, one of the men came forward and said that in the principal village there was a "Meskiti," a "pembé"—a church, or temple, of ivory—and that ivory was "as abundant as fuel." In a few moments I stood before the ivory temple, which was merely a large circular roof supported by thirty-three tusks of ivory, erected over an idol 4 feet high, painted with camwood dye, a bright vermilion, with black eyes and beard and hair. The figure was very rude, still it was an unmistakable likeness of a man. The tusks being wanted by the Wangwana, they received permission to convey them into the canoes. One hundred other pieces of ivory were collected, in the shape of log wedges, long ivory war-horns, ivory

THE FIGHT BELOW THE CONFLUENCE OF THE ARUWIMI AND THE LIVINGSTONE RIVERS. [To face page 212

pestles to pound cassava into meal and herbs for spinach, ivory armlets and balls, and ivory mallets to beat the fig-bark into cloth.

The stores of beautifully carved paddles, 10 feet in length, some of which were iron-pointed, the enormous six-feet-long spears, which were designed more for ornament than use, the splendid long knives, like Persian kummars, and bright iron-mounted sheaths with broad belts of red buffalo and antelope-hide, barbed spears, from the light assegai to the heavy double-handed sword-spear, the tweezers, hammers, prickers, hole-burners, hairpins, fish-hooks, arm and leg-rings of iron and copper, iron beads and wrist-bands, iron bells, axes, war-hatchets, adzes, hoes, dibbers, &c., proved the people on the banks of this river to be clever, intelligent, and more advanced in the arts than any hitherto observed since we commenced our descent of the Livingstone. The architecture of their huts, however, was the same, except the conical structure they had erected over their idol. Their canoes were much larger than those of the Mwana Ntaba, above the Stanley Falls, which had crocodiles and lizards carved on them. Their skull-caps of basket-work, leopard, civet, and monkey skins, were similar to those that we had observed in Uregga. Their shields were like those of the Wariwa. There were various specimens of African wood-carving in great and small idols, stools of ingenious pattern, double benches, walking-staffs, spear-staffs, flutes, grain-mortars, mallets, drums, clubs, troughs, scoops and canoe-balers, paddles, porridge spoons, &c. Gourds also exhibited taste in ornamentation. Their earthenware was very superior, their pipes of an unusual pattern—in short, everything that is of use to a well-found African village exhibited remarkable intelligence and prosperity.

Evidences of cannibalism were numerous in the human and "soko" skulls that grinned on many poles, and the bones that were freely scattered in the neighbourhood, near the village garbage heaps and the river banks, where one might suppose hungry canoe-men to have enjoyed a cold collation on an ancient matron's arm. As the most positive and downright evidence, in my opinion, of this hideous practice, was the thin forearm of a person that was picked up near a fire, with certain scorched ribs which might have been tossed into the fire after being gnawed. It is true that it is but circumstantial evidence, yet we accepted them as indubitable proofs. Besides, we had been taunted with remarks that we would furnish them with meat supplies—for the words *meat* and *to-day* have but slight dialectic difference in many languages.

We embarked in our canoes at 5 P.M., and descending the affluent came to the confluence again, and then, hugging the right bank, appeared before other villages; but after our successful resistance to such a confederation of chiefs and the combined strength of three or four different tribes, it was not likely that one small settlement would risk an encounter. We anchored about 50 yards from the shore. Two old men advanced to the edge of the steep bank and rattled pebbles, which were enclosed in basket-work, towards us. We sat perfectly still for about five minutes regarding them, and then we endeavoured to open a conversation with them. We could understand but a few dozen words, which we had managed to pick up. We understood them, how-

PADDLE OF THE ARUWIMI CANNIBALS.

ever, to say that the river where we had just had the fight was called the Aruwimi, that the right branch of the great river was called Irondo, and the left, Rinda; that the district between the confluence of the Aruwimi and the Livingstone was Isangi, in Koruru. The country on the left bank was still Yambarri, or Yambari, but ahead, or below Yambarri, were the Baonda and the Wakunga; on the right bank, below them, were the Bemberri.

The direction of the Aruwimi was from east-north-east magnetic, or north-east true. It emptied into the Livingstone at a point three hundred and forty geographical miles north of Nyangwé. Though comparatively shallow and studded with islands, it is the most important affluent of the Livingstone from the countries east. I have no hesitation in pronouncing it to be the Wellé of Schweinfurth. The report that he received from the natives, that the Wellé at a long distance from the Monbuttu "widened into a boundless expanse of water," and that its general direction was west or north of west, ought not to receive greater credence than the report which the natives all along the Livingstone gave me, that the great river went "north, ever north." As we follow the Luama from its source to the great river, and know the utmost reach north of the Tanganika, and have touched more than once that central elevated region in whose bosom are found the Lakes Albert Muta-Nzigé, Alexandra, and Tanganika, we may be supposed to have a rational idea of the eastern and western watershed of the central regions. If we continue our suppositions, which are founded upon a long study of the hydrographical system of this region, we may suppose the Wellé to drain the most extreme north-eastern corner of the Livingstone basin, and, imitating the curve of the mighty river, to maintain a north-westerly and westerly direction for a degree, or perhaps two degrees, and then, skirting closely the watershed that separates the basin of the Livingstone from that of the south-western Nile, the Benué, and the Shari basins, to meet some obstructing hill, and be deflected south-west into the Livingstone. In the same manner as we suppose the course of the Wellé to be, the Luama proceeds north from Southern Goma to Umeué, then west, through Manyema to the Lualaba. The Urindi is reported to flow in the same manner, but the best example of this curious curve which belongs to the system of the Livingstone is the great river itself, which maintains a northerly course for over twelve degrees of latitude, a westerly course across three degrees of longitude, and a south-westerly or a diagonal course across ten degrees of longitude. The largest southern influent of the Livingstone flows 1100 miles northward before it turns west and south-west. The course of the Kwango and the Lumami are other evidences to prove that this extraordinary curve is a characteristic of the river system of the Livingstone and its feeders.

If other evidences were wanting to confirm this supposition, I might point to the cannibalistic propensities of the people, their superiority in the domestic arts of the African, the weapons and shields, their idols, their peculiar canoes, the stores of camwood, the prodigious height and girth of trees, the character of the vegetation—which resembles what the German traveller has written of the Monbuttu and Wellé valley.

At the same time one must not forget that there is a remarkable similarity between all the west coast tribes, from Lake Chad to Loanda, which proves, in my opinion, the non-existence of those Mountains of the Moon which have been drawn across Africa since Ptolemy's time. Schweinfurth crossed the watershed from the Nile side to the Wellé while scarcely observing the difference of altitude. In the same manner one might travel from Ituru to Unyanyembé without observing that he had crossed the water-parting that separates the extreme southern sources of the Nile from the extreme sources of Lake Tanganika's principal affluent.

We felt it to be unwise to stay long in the vicinity of such powerful, well-equipped, and warlike tribes. We therefore lifted anchor, and began to descend the stream; but as we turned away the savages lined the banks, beat their drums, shouted their war-cries, and performed for our edification the gymnastics of a true aboriginal fight. It never entered their heads that they had given us provocation, and had but lately charged us in mid-river with the fell purpose of destroying every soul, that we had behaved kindly to them, or that we had attempted, though ineffectually, to make friends with them. Had their canoes not fled up river, I verily believe that our turning away would have been the signal for another attack on us.

This last of the twenty-eight desperate combats which we had had with the insensate furies of savage-land began to inspire us with a suspicion of everything bearing the least semblance of man, and to infuse into our hearts something of that feeling which possibly the hard-pressed stag feels when, after distancing the hounds many times, and having resorted to many stratagems to avoid them, wearied and bathed with perspiration, he hears with terror and trembling the hideous and startling yells of the ever-pursuing pack. We also had laboured strenuously through ranks upon ranks of savages, scattered over a score of flotillas, had endured persistent attacks night and day while struggling through them, had resorted to all modes of defence, and yet at every curve of this fearful river the yells of the savages broke loud on our ears, the snake-like canoes darted forward impetuously to the attack, while the drums, and horns, and shouts raised fierce and deafening uproar. We were becoming exhausted. Yet we were still only on the middle line of the continent! We were also being weeded out by units and twos and threes. There were not thirty in the entire Expedition that had not received a wound. To continue this fearful life was not possible. Some day we should lie down, and offer our throats like lambs to the cannibal butchers.

It was getting near sunset, and, looking round for a suitable place to camp for the night, I observed that the river since the accession of the Aruwimi had spread to an immense width. Instead of consisting of a right and a left branch, separated by a single line of islands, there were now from three to six branches, separated from each other by series of long islands, densely clothed with woods, their ends overlapping one another. Common sense suggested that where there was such breadth there could be no cataracts. So, when almost inclined to despair, I pointed out the island channels to the people, and told them that Allah had provided means of escape. Near sunset we sheered off towards the islands, entered a dark channel about one hundred yards wide, and after an hour drew our canoes alongside, and, having fastened them, prepared to bivouac in the island forest.

Feb. 2.—Next day we clung to the channel; but as the islands lay sometimes diagonally across the stream, we finally emerged in view of the Bemberri, too late to return. Immediately they called up their people to war, with a terrible racket of drums; and about fifteen large canoes dashed out to meet us. But after the Aruwimi flotilla this number was contemptible; we drove them away, followed them to their villages, and compelled them to seek shelter in the woods. Then the word was given that every man should provide himself with bananas and cassava. This was done, and we re-embarked. Before, however, we could find another opening amongst the islands, other villages discovered us, and again a terrific dinning rose, which inspired even fishing-boys to acts of ferocious valour. These we permitted to exhibit for our benefit the utmost rage they were capable of, except actually to throw their spears. Whenever they threatened to launch their weapons, a furious demonstration with our long oars was sufficient to send them skimming away. They followed us three or four miles, sending out every now and then wailing notes, which, from the frequent recurrence of the word *meat*, we understood to be expressions of regret that they were unable to secure the "meat" which was running away from them.

Finally we discovered a channel flowing between a series

of islands, which we gladly entered, and our young tormentors turned back and left us to pursue our way alone. From Bemberri the course of the great river varied from north-west by north half north, north-north-west, north by west, and north-west. I missed the latitude on February 2.

The following entries are from my note book :—

Feb. 3.—General course of river from morning until noon, north-west. At noon ascertained our latitude to be north of the equator 1° 29′ 1″.

"We endeavoured to do our best to avoid conflict with the savages, and this required great judgment and constant watching of the channels. We happily succeeded, though a little after noon it became extremely doubtful, for it seems that we edged a little too much to the left bank in our eagerness to avoid all channels that might take us to the right. The Barundu, of whom we heard yesterday, sighted us, as we passed a gap between the islands, and instantly manned eighteen large war-canoes. But as we had obtained a start of them we pulled desperately down river among the islands, leading them a chase of eight miles or so, when they returned.

"Livingstone called floating down the Lualaba a foolhardy feat. So it has proved, indeed, and I pen these lines with half a feeling that they will never be read by any man; still, as we persist in floating down according to our destiny, I persist in writing, leaving events to an all-gracious Providence. Day and night we are stunned with the dreadful drumming which announces our arrival and presence on their waters. Either bank is equally powerful. To go from the right bank to the left bank is like jumping from the frying-pan into the fire. As we row down amongst these islands, between the savage countries on either side of us, it may well be said that we are 'running the gauntlet.'

"*Feb.* 4.—We had a glimpse of numerous villages between the island gaps, but we pushed rapidly through, and at noon had attained to north latitude 1° 45′ 40″. The general course of the river since noon yesterday has been north-north-west.

"*Feb.* 5.—At noon to-day we obtained by solar observation north latitude 1° 51′ 17″. General course of the river was north-north-west.

"*Feb.* 6.—A little before we sought our camp amid the islands, the river for the first time deflected west. All this morning its course was from west half south to west by north. Our observations at noon showed we had not made quite a mile of northing, for our north latitude was 1° 51′ 59″. The Livingstone is now from four to seven miles across from bank to bank. So far as we can see through a glass, the banks are very low, from 6 to 10 feet high, capped with woods. The islands are also densely wooded.

"We have had in this extraordinary journey by river all the terrors as well as pleasures of river life. We now glide down narrow streams, between palmy and spicy islands, whose sweet fragrance and vernal colour causes us to forget at moments our dangerous life. We have before us the winding shores of islands crowned with eternal spring-life and verdure. Teak and cotton-wood, the hyphene, borassus, wild date, and Guinea oil-palms, the tall serpent-like rattan, with its pretty, drooping feathery leaves; the bushy and many-rooted mangrove, the towering gum, the shea-butter tree, the *Ficus kotschyana*, the branchy *Tamar indica*, with an undergrowth of extraordinary variety. Along the banks, especially wherever there is a quiet nook, thrive dense growths of the *Arundo phragmites* grass, whose long, bright green leaves we hear rustle as we glide by before the breeze blowing up river; here and there the *Papyrus antiquorum*, or a specimen of the *Edemone mirabilis*, or Eschinomenæ. In the calm tepid waters of the little creeks that wind in mazy curves between low islands a wonderful variety of aquatic plants is discovered; various species of Nymphæa, with white or lavender-coloured flowers, and, woven with their slender stalks, the broad-leafed Vallisneria, and amongst them, modest and of a pretty green, the rosette-shaped *Pistia stratiotes*. In thick hedges bordering either side of the creeks are vigorous growths of ever-fresh-looking ferns.

"In the undergrowth, where the giant trees are wanting, we find the anona flourish best, their clusters of crimson fruit, growing at the base of the stalk, serving me for a tartish dessert, and their grains, commonly called "grains of paradise," being sought after by the bhang smokers of my Expedition to sweeten their breath and increase saliva. The leaves are always of a fresh green, and give one a true idea of a tropical forest and moist, warm climate. Not far off from these is the *Phrynium ramosissimum*, whose broad and long fronds serve to thatch the natives' huts and fishers' sheds, or to fold their cassava bread, or for platters and salt-baskets, or for storing the minnows or whitebait for market. You may also see here the *Strelitza vagina*, or the wild banana, or the violet-tree, and the oil-berry tree, the black ivory nut-tree, which might be made a valuable article of commerce; the *Semicarbus anacardium*, commonly called the marking-ink plant, the *Encephastos Aldensteini*, the ginger plant, the dragon's-blood tree, various species of the Verbenaceæ, such as the *Vitex umbrosa*, the physic nut-tree (*Jatrophe purgans*), which is frequently associated with Muzimus, especially by Wakerewé and Wajiji, and the brilliant bloom of a Loranthus or species of Liliaceæ in flower, will not fail to be noted as one dreamily glides by these unknown islets, full of treasures to bewitch a botanist, and wherein the enterprising merchant might find profit.

"Some other pleasures we have are in watching a sunny bank, where we may rest assured the crocodile lies dreaming of fish banquets, and whence he will rise and plunge with a startling splash; or in watching the tricks of some suspicious and watchful behemoth, whose roar has its volume redoubled as it is reverberated from shore to shore in these eerie wilds.

"Our terrors are numerous. First, the rocks and rapids, the plunging cataract and whirling pool, which fortunately are passed, and which we pray we shall not have to encounter again. Then the sudden storm, which now blows each day up river, and, first wrinkling the face of the river, soon raises heavy brown waves, like those of a lake, which, having already suffered from, we are careful to avoid; but the greatest danger, an ever-recurring one, is that which we have to encounter each time the wild howling cannibal aborigines observe us. Indeed, the sense of security is short-lived, our pleasure evanescent; but the sense of danger is always present, and pervades our minds whether in our sleeping or our waking hours.

"*Feb.* 7.—Obtained no latitude. It has been a tempestuous day. Great heavy swells rolled up river in our front, and the wind howled and shrieked so through the dismal glades that we became quite gloomy. To add to our troubles, our food is finished; we have no more, and to attempt to obtain it will cost human life. Empty stomachs serve to render the prospects in unknown and wild regions still darker. We have three asses with us; but then my people have grown to look at them as fellow-members of the Expedition. They say they will die first, but the faithful asses which have accompanied us so far the people say shall not be touched. So far so good: but what are we to do? Late at night the chiefs came to me and declared they must have food to-morrow. I told them they should have it, that from the first village we saw we should go and demand it.

"*Feb.* 8.—Thank God! An anxious day has terminated with tranquillity to long-disturbed minds. We are camped on a small jungle-covered islet in north latitude 1° 40′ 44″ by observation, and east longitude 21° 4′ by acct. Opposite, at 500 yards' distance, on the left bank, is the village of Rubunga, in Nganza. On the right bank, at 1700 yards' distance from us, is the large town of Gunji.

"Our course yesterday was west by south, and to-day west-south-west. We embarked at 7 A.M., and rowed past a very long wooded island, which lay on our left. At 8 A.M., we began to observe on the right bank a long hilly ridge, with cultivated slopes, and a dense population, which we later learned was called Upoto—or Mbapoto, as one man called it. I solemnly addressed my people, and, while telling them to prepare every weapon, gun, spear, axe, and knife, reminded them that it was an awful thing to commence hostilities, whether for food or anything else. They groaned in spirit, and asked me what they should do when their bowels yearned for something to satisfy its cravings; and though there was an abundance of copper, brass, iron, shells, beads, and cloth, nobody would sell even a small piece of cassava to them, or even look at them without manifesting a thirst for their blood.

"I had prepared the brightest and most showy wares close by me, and resolved to be as cunning and patient as a serpent in this intercourse. At 11 A.M. we sighted the village of Rubunga, and, giving instructions to Frank not to approach nearer to me than a quarter of a mile with the canoes, we rowed steadily down until within a few hundred yards of it, when we lay-to on our oars. Presently three canoes advanced to meet us without the usual savage demonstrations. Not even a drum was beaten, a horn blown, or a cry uttered. This was promising. We tried the words 'Sen-nen-neh!' 'Chare-reh!' in soft, mild, melodious strains. They ran away. Things appeared gloomy again. However, patience

"We had reserved one banana and a piece of cassava. We had our mouths and our stomachs with us. An appropriate gesture with the banana to the mouth, and a gentle fondling with a puckered stomach, would, we thought, be a manner of expressing extreme want, eloquent enough to penetrate the armoured body of a crocodile. We came opposite the village at 30 yards' distance, and dropped our stone anchor, and I stood up with my ragged old helmet pushed back far, that they might scrutinise my face, and the lines of suasion be properly seen. With the banana in one hand, and a gleaming armlet of copper and beads of various colours in the other, I began the pantomime. I once knew an idiot in Brusa, Asia Minor, who entreated me for a para in much the same dumb strain that I implored the assembled hundreds of Rubunga to relax that sullen sternness, that uncompromising aspect, that savage front, and yield to the captivating influence of fair and honest barter. I clashed the copper bracelets together, lovingly handled the bright gold-brown of the shining armlet, exposed with all my best grace of manner long necklaces of bright and clean *Cypræa moneta*, and allured their attention with beads of the brightest colours. Nor were the polished folds of yellow brass wire omitted; and again the banana was lifted to my open mouth. Then what suspense, what patience, what a saint-like air of resignation! Ah, yes! but I think I may be pardoned for all that degrading pantomime. I had a number of hungry, half-wild children; and through a cannibal world we had ploughed to reach these unsophisticated children of nature.

"We waited, and at length an old chief came down the high bank to the lower landing near some rocks. Other elders of the people in head-dresses of leopard and civet skin joined him soon, and then all sat down. The old chief nodded with his head. We raised our anchor, and with two strokes of the oars had run our boat ashore, and, snatching a string or two of cowries, I sprang on land, followed by the coxswain Uledi, and in a second I had seized the skinny hand of the old chief, and was pressing it hard for joy. Warm-hearted Uledi, who the moment before was breathing furious hate of all savages, and of the procrastinating old chief in particular, embraced him with a filial warmth. Young Saywa, and Murabo, and Shumari, prompt as tinder upon all occasions, grasped the lesser chiefs' hands, and devoted themselves with smiles and jovial frank bearing to conquer the last remnants of savage sullenness, and succeeded so well that in an incredibly short time the blood-brotherhood ceremony between the suddenly formed friends was solemnly entered into, and the irrevocable pact of peace and goodwill had been accomplished!

"The old chief pointed with his finger to the face of Frank, which shone white amongst the dusky bodies of his comrades, and I beckoned to him. The canoes were all to anchor 100 yards off shore, but Frank was required to respond to the chief of Rubunga's wish for friendship. We distributed presents to each native, and in return we received great bunches of mellow, ripe, and green bananas, as well as of fish. It was agreed between us that we should encamp on this little islet, on which we find ourselves to-night, with a feeling as though we were approaching home.

"Before leaving the chief of Rubunga's presence, I asked him the name of the river, in a mongrel mixture of Ki-swahili, Kinyamwezi, Kijiji, Ki-regga, and

Ki-Kusu. He understood after a while, and replied it was 'Ibari.' But after he had quite comprehended the drift of the question, he replied in a sonorous voice, '*Ikutu ya Kongo!*'

"There had really been no doubt in my mind since we had left the Stanley Falls that the terrible river would prove eventually to be the river of Congo-land, but it was very agreeable to be told so.

"We have received food sufficient to last us for this day. The native women require a longer time to muster courage to make the acquaintance of the strangers, and have postponed their visit until to-morrow. A grand market for our special benefit is to be held on this island. The drums of Rubunga will be beaten to-morrow morning, not for war, but to summon the aborigines to come forward with provisions to sell. In the meantime hunger has been expelled, the gnawing emptiness has been banished, and our long-harassed minds are at rest. May this happy friendship be the first of many more!"

CHAPTER X.

High art in tattooing—Suspicious friendliness—Friends or foes?—A treacherous attack—The fauna of the Livingstone—Among the "Houyhnhnms"—The "Yaha-ha-has"—Frank's courage and narrow escape—Our fight with the Bangala—The mirage on the river—The great tributary of the Livingstone—Among friends.

Feb. 9.—While we rested on the jungle-covered islet opposite Rubunga, we experienced that repose of spirits which only the happy few who know neither care nor anxiety can enjoy. For the first time for many weeks we had slept well. There was no simulation in the cheerful morning greetings which were passed from one man to another. That wide-eyed suspicious look and the swift searching glance of distrust had toned down, and an unreserved geniality pervaded the camp.

About 9 A.M. the first canoe arrived, and its occupants received warm and hearty welcome. Soon others arrived, while the big market-drum continued to hasten the natives from both banks—from Rubunga and Urangi on the left, and Gunji and Upoto on the right. In light, swift, elegant canoes, of the caique pattern, the people brought fresh and dried fish, snails, oysters, mussels, dried dogs'-meat, live dogs and goats, bananas, plantains, robes of grass cloth, cassava tubers, flour and bread of the consistence of sailor's "duff," spears, knives, axes, hatchets, bells, iron bracelets and girdles, in fact everything that is saleable or purchasable on the shores of the Livingstone. The knives were singular specimens of the African smith's art, being principally of a waving, sickle-shaped pattern, while the principal men carried brass-handled weapons, 18 inches long, double-edged, and rather wide-pointed, with two blood channels along the centre of the broad blade, while near the hilt the blade was pierced by two quarter-circular holes, while the top of the haft was ornamented with the fur of the otter.

The aborigines dress their hair with an art peculiar to the Warua and Waguha, which consists in wearing it in tufts on the back of the head, and fastening it with elegantly shaped iron hairpins—a fashion which also obtains among many kitchen maids in England. Tattooing is carried to excess, every portion of the skin bearing punctured marks, from the roots of the hair down to the knees. Their breasts are like hieroglyphic parchment charts, marked with *raised* figures, ledges, squares, circles, wavy lines, tuberose knots, rosettes, and every conceivable design. No colouring substance had been introduced into these incisions and punctures; the cuticle had simply been tortured and irritated by the injection of some irritants or air. Indeed, some of the glossy tubercules, which contained air, were as large as hens' eggs. As many as six thin ledges marked the foreheads from temple to temple, as many ran down each cheek, while from lower eyelid to base of septum curved wavy lines; the chin showed rosettes, the neck seemed goitrous with the large vesicular protuberances, while the front parts of their bodies

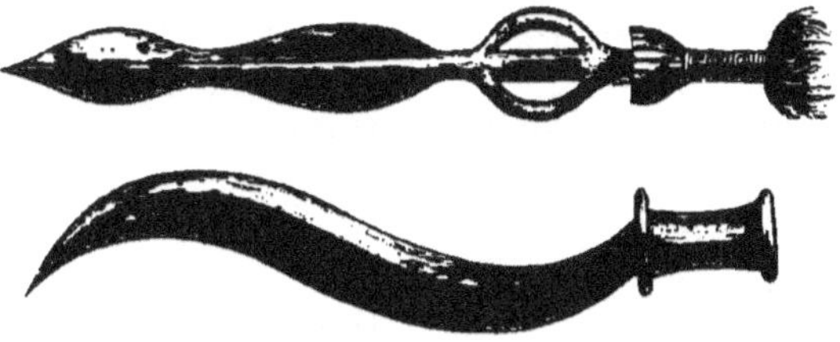

KNIVES, RUBUNGA.

afforded broad fields upon which the native artist had displayed the exuberant fertility of his genius. To such an extent is this fashion carried that the people are hideously deformed, many of them having quite unnatural features and necks.

To add to the atrocious bad taste of these aborigines, their necklaces consisted of human, gorilla, and crocodile teeth, in such quantity in many cases that little or nothing could be seen of the neck. A few possessed polished boars' tusks, with the points made to meet from each side.

Blood-brotherhood was a beastly cannibalistic ceremony with these people, yet much sought after, whether for the satisfaction of their thirst for blood, or that it involved an interchange of gifts, of which they must needs reap the most benefit. After an incision was made in each arm, both brothers bent their heads, and the aborigine was observed to suck with the greatest fervour, whether for love of blood or excess of friendship it would be difficult to say. Having discovered our liberality, they became arrant beggars, and difficult to satisfy. Copper was despised, but brass wire was gold—anything became purchasable with it except canoes.

The most curious objects we discovered at Rubunga were four ancient Portuguese muskets, at the sight of which the people of the Expedition raised a glad shout. These appeared to them certain signs that we had not lost the road, that the great river did really reach the sea, and that their master was not deluding them when he told them that some day they would see the sea.

In reply to our questions as to where they had obtained them, they said from men in canoes from Bankaro, Bangaro, Mangara, or, as the word finally settled down, from Mangala, who came once a year to buy ivory. These traders were black men, and they had never heard of white men or of Arabs. One or two of their people had visited Mangala, and from these great travellers I obtained the following list of places—which geographers will do well to study—which they had heard of as being down river:

Iringi.	Mpungu (river entering from left bank).
Mpakiwana.	Mangala.
Ukataraka.	Ibeko.
Marunja.	Iregweh.
Ikonogo.	Batekć.
Bubeka.	Ikumu.
Imemé.	Irebu.
Ikandawanda.	

The nations reported to be below Rubunga were Bakongo, Mberri, Wakomera, Wyyaka, Baurengeri, Mangala.

Feb. 10.—On the morning of the 10th of February natives from down river appeared to escort us, and our friends of Rubunga also despatched a canoe and five men to introduce us to Urangi. In about two hours we arrived at the very populous settlement of Urangi, consisting of several villages almost joining one another.

In order that there should be no possible chance of a rupture, we prepared to camp on a very long wooded island, on a beautiful green thoroughly shaded by forest patriarchs. Our appearance was the signal for a great number of the elegant canoes of this region to approach us. These ranged in length from 15 to 45 feet, and were manned by from one person to twenty men, according to their size. Beautifully carved and perfectly shaped, their crews, standing, and armed with powerful paddles of light wood, propelled them along at the rate of six knots an hour. They were as different in form and design from those monsters up river as the natives themselves were. It was very curious to watch this transition from one tribal peculiarity and custom to another. It was evident that these tribes never traded with those above. I doubt whether the people of Urangi and Rubunga are cannibals, though we obtained proof sufficient that human life is not a subject of concern with them, and the necklaces of human teeth which they wore were by no means assuring—they provoked morbid ideas.

We received a noisy and demonstrative welcome. They pressed on us in great numbers, which, considering our late eventful life, did not tend to promote that perfect feeling of security which we had briefly tasted at Rubunga. Still we bore it good-humouredly. If geniality, frankness, sociability are the best weapons with which to treat savage man, we showed ourselves adepts and practised professors of the art. I did not observe the least shadow of a frown, sulkiness, doubt, or suspicion on the face of any man, woman, or child connected with the Expedition. As for Frank and myself, our behaviour was characterized by an angelic benignity worthy of canonization. I sat smiling in the midst of a tattooed group, remarkable for their filed teeth and ugly gashed bodies, and bearing in their hands fearfully dangerous-looking naked knives or swords, with which the crowd might have hacked me to pieces before I could have even divined their intentions.

But presently murmurs were heard, and finally the camp was in an uproar. One man complained of his mat being stolen, another of his knife, another of his cloth, another of his store of beads; three or four spears were next abstracted: and finally, the thieving culminated in two guns being stolen. Fortunately, however, the thieves were apprehended before they had succeeded in effecting their escape. Then a new order of things was determined upon. We fell back upon the old rule of never forgetting that an unsophisticated savage was not trustworthy, except when your eyes were on him. We built a boma, and refused admission to the camp, but a market was fixed in a special place without, where, the natives were told, those who possessed articles for sale would find purchasers. The chiefs agreed to this, and friendship and fraternity were apparently as much in demand as before the little disturbance, since no one had been injured, and the losses had been borne without reprisals.

At 5 P.M. the great chief of Urangi made his presence known by sounding his double iron gong. This gong consisted of two long iron bell-shaped instruments, connected above by an iron handle, which, when beaten with a short stick with a ball of indiarubber at the end, produced very agreeable musical sounds. He received a kindly reception; and though he manifested no desire nor declared any intention of reciprocating our gift, he did not leave our camp dissatisfied with his present. He loudly proclaimed to the assembly on the river something to the effect that I was his brother: that peace and goodwill should prevail, and that everybody should behave, and "make plenty of trade." But on his departure his people became roguish and like wild children. Scores of canoes flitted here and there, up and down, along the front of the camp, which gave us opportunities of observing that every person was tattooed in the most abominable manner; that the coiffeur's art was carried to perfection; that human teeth were popular ornaments for the neck; that their own teeth were filed; that brass wire to an astonishing quantity had been brought to them by the Bangala; as they had coils of it upon their arms and legs, and ruffs of it resting on their shoulders; that while the men wore ample loin-coverings of grass cloth, their women went naked; that ivory was to be purchased here to any amount, and that palm-wine had affected the heads of a great many. We also discovered that Urangi possessed about a dozen muskets.

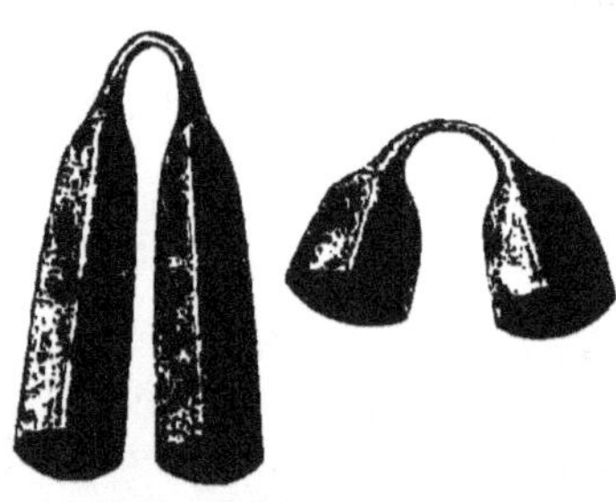
DOUBLE IRON BELLS OF URANGI.

From a friend of mine, who paid me much attention, I ascertained that three hours from Urangi inland was a large market-town, called Ngombé, whither the Barangi frequently went with fish, dried and fresh, to purchase cassava, bananas, ground nuts, and palm-oil; that palm-trees were as thick as a forest inland; that on the right bank below Gunji are three districts, Umangi, Ukeré, and Mpisa; that the river on the right side is known as Ukeré, while that which rolls by Urangi is called Iringi.

At sunset our strange friends departed, and paddled across river to their villages, very amiably disposed, if one might judge from smiles and pleasant nods of the head. At 8 P.M. a terrific drumming and some half a dozen musket-shots were heard from the Urangi villages. We supposed them to be dancing and enjoying their palm-wine, the delicious and much-esteemed *malofu*. Sometimes we heard, amid a deathly silence, also the voice of a man, who might be reading a proclamation or delivering a lecture, for all we understood. The voice was clearly audible, but the words were not. Finally, about midnight I slept.

Feb. 11.—An hour before dawn we were alert, preparing our morning meal, packing up, delivering instructions, and observing other customs preparatory to starting the Expedition anew on the voyage.

A little after sunrise our guides of Urangi, who had shown us the way from Rubunga, appeared, according to their promise to escort us to another tribe below. For their good nature we gave an earnest of our liberal purpose. We then embarked.

As we began to move from our camp we observed scores of canoes approaching us from Urangi, across the wide branch that separated our island from the villages. This was so natural that we paid no attention to it, yet we thought a greater number of men manned them than on the previous day. But for ten minutes we glided down smoothly and agreeably. Suddenly I heard a shot and a whistling of slugs in the neighbourhood of the boat. I turned my head, and observed the smoke of gunpowder drifting away from a native canoe. Yet we could scarcely realise that our friends had so soon become enemies, until one of my people cried out, "Master, one of our men is killed. The people are firing at us." Simultaneously with the shot I observed our guides had darted away in their canoe, and it dawned on my mind that the whole was a preconcerted arrangement.

Anxious for the safety of the Expedition, I permitted my canoes to float by me, and then formed them in line, the boat in the rear, and thus we began the fight. The natives advanced on us in gallant style, and after firing their heavily charged guns withdrew rapidly again to reload, and in the meantime the wooden assegais were launched with a marvellous dexterity, and the beautiful canoes skimmed about like flying fish here and there with bewildering evolutions and wonderful velocity and grace. Of course the shields were raised like bulwarks around our flotilla, and the fire from behind them was deadly; while though we in the boat were conspicuous marks, we could not be touched owing to our rapidity of fire. But they persistently followed us until the natives of the district of Mpakiwana heard the firing and rushed to the assault, and maintained it with a pertinacity that made us almost despair. About noon we discovered a channel leading among the islands, which we followed, soon becoming involved once more among the mazy laybrinths of the winding creeks.

Our course may be ascertained, if I state that a little above Urangi we were in north latitude 1° 36′ 0″, and at noon of the 11th, about twenty miles westward of the Urangi, we obtained north latitude 1° 41′ 0″

The islands are much more numerous below Rubunga, and are marvels of vegetation, producing greater varieties of the palm species than those above. Though gigantic trees of the class already mentioned are as numerous, they are much more shrouded by masses of palm-vegetation, vines, and creepers, from the observation of the river voyager. As the banks here rise only from 5 to 10 feet above the surface of the river, they are subject to inundation when the river is in flood, and in many parts there are swampy depressions, favourable to dense growths of rattan and young palms. These low islands are haunted by many pests. As we glided by them during the day, we were subject to the attacks of vicious gad-flies and the tsetsé, and at night mosquitoes were so abundant that we obtained but little sleep. The murmur of the vast multitude of these insects sounded during the night to our half-waked senses like the noise of advancing savages, and until the wee hours of the morning the continual flip-flap of branches of the fig-tree, with which the worried mortals had armed themselves, annoyed my drowsy ears.

We obtained just a glimpse of Ukatakura, or, as it is sometimes called, Ukaturaka, as we hastened from one island channel to another. We were followed by five or six canoes for a distance of five miles, but we finally escaped them.

Feb. 12.—The 12th of February was passed without alarm; the islands were still increasing in number; the river was immensely wide, extending over seven miles. We obtained once a distant view of a village on the right bank. Low islands of alluvial sand, which shot forth rich crops of the *Arundo phragmites* grass, *Papyrus antiquorum*, and many other varieties of the Cyperaceæ, became more numerous. These were the haunts of Marabu storks, Balearic cranes, the short-legged *Balæniceps Rex*, flamingoes, spur-winged geese, flocks of wild duck, divers, kingfishers, egrets, black as well as white ibis, and snipe. Any number of birds for meat might easily have been obtained, were it not that a single shot would have entailed a combat with musket-armed men. Our only hope of escape from this region was by avoiding ferocious man.

On one of these islands we saw an elephant with a pair of magnificent tusks, but he was as safe from us as though we had been unarmed; and on a reedy island of considerable length we saw a herd of red buffalo, which are smaller and very different generally from the black buffalo of the eastern half of the continent. But though we pined for meat, and were accustomed, in countries where strangers are not hunted for their lives, to devote much time to hunting, still we dared not fire. The lives of many men—our own and the natives'—depended on our forbearance.

The higher and more wooded islands swarm with baboons, the *Cynocephalus porcarius*, the night-waking lemur, and diminutive long-tailed monkeys. Once a beating of the bushes caused me to look quickly up, and I had just a glimpse of a large species of monkey of a bearded kind, standing up; but the current was inexorable, and we were at that time rowing rapidly, so that it was useless to hope to be able to find him.

The channels swarmed with Amphibia—the hippopotamus, crocodile, and monitor. Frequently at the lower end of islands, spits of white gleaming sand were observed, with two or three bloated and monstrous crocodiles basking on them, while smaller ones, at a respectful distance from the sires, imitated their lifelessness, until the splash of our oars caused them, sires and young alike, to hurry waddling to their deep homes.

A remarkable feature of the river was its immunity from snags. A few gigantic trees, it is true, were seen stranded on a gleaming islet of sand, but those dangerous obstacles of navigation, so frequent in American rivers, are very rare on the Livingstone. This may be accounted for, perhaps, by the fact that its bed is harder and more compact, and contains a less tenacious alluvium than the river beds of North America. Yet landslips are frequent, and the banks of islands exhibit many prostrate forest monarchs; but by steering a few feet beyond these our descent was never interrupted by any obstructing branch or snag.

Feb. 13.—On the morning of the 13th we passed either the mouth of a channel 500 yards wide, or a river—the Sankuru (?)—to our left. We certainly thought it was a mere island channel, until we became surprised at its great length, and still more surprised when, turning round a bend, we discovered ourselves in the presence of a large number of villages. It was too late to return. The great war-drums and horns thundered through the woods, and startled the wild echoes of many a forested isle. With an intuitive feeling that we should again "catch it," and become soon engaged in all the horrors of savage warfare, we prepared with all the skill in our power to defend ourselves. The women and children were told to lie down in the bottom of the canoes, and the spearmen to "stand by shields" to protect the riflemen. At this time we possessed only thirty-nine guns—nineteen Sniders and twenty muskets—besides my own rifles. When within 300 yards of the first settlement, we sheered off into mid-river and paddled slowly down in close line, the boat in the advance, with a vague sense that there would be no rest for us until we either sank into the grave or Providence should endow us with wings to enable us to vanish from this fearful savage world.

The first war-cries that rang out as the beautiful but cruel canoes skimmed towards us reminded me of the "Houyhynyms," for, to express correctly the neighing sounds of the warriors of Marunja, their cry ought to be spelled "Yaha-ha-ha." But in tone it was marvellously like a neighing chorus of several full-blooded stallions. Had I not been able to ascertain the names of these tribes, I should certainly have been justified in stating that after the "Ooh-hu-hus" we encountered the "Bo-bo-bos," and after a dire experience with the fierce "Bo-bo-bos" we met the terrible "Yaha-ha-has." Any traveller who should succeed me would be certain to remark upon the fidelity of the novel classification.

For my part I must confess to having been charmed into

a dangerous inactivity by the novelty of the human cries, so much so that, before I was on the alert, there were three canoes in front of me, and over the gunwales I saw nine bright musket barrels aimed at me. As my position was in the bow of the boat while leading the Expedition down river, I soon became the target for a few more, as the swift gliding canoes were propelled in a crescent form in our front. But, as on several other occasions, I was saved, because my very appearance startled them. Had I been a black man I should have long before been slain; but even in the midst of a battle, curiosity, stronger than hate or bloodthirstiness, arrested the sinewy arm which drew the bow, and delayed the flying spear. And now, while their thin flint hammers were at full cock, and the fingers pressing the triggers of the deadly muskets, the savages became absorbed in contemplating the silent and still form of a kind of being which to them must have appeared as strange as any unreal being the traditions of their fathers had attempted to describe. "*White!*"

Of course the slightest movement on my part would have been instantly followed by my death. Though it was unpleasant to sit and feel oneself to be a target for so many guns, yet it was the wisest plan. While I was the object of curiosity to a large party, Frank was no less the centre of attraction to a number of men that hovered on our left flank, and our asses shared with us the honour of being wonders to the aborigines. Katembo attempted to open a conversation with them, and by surprising them with the question if they were Marunja we obtained a knowledge as to whom we were indebted for these unpleasant honours. And I believe it was to Katembo that we owed the rupture of the charm of curiosity, for five minutes afterwards, when we had descended nearly two miles in silence below their villages, a vicious black aborigine fired and killed Rehani, one of our finest men. Instinctively the Wangwana raised their shields, and, rowing up swiftly to meet them, to defend the people like a hen her chickens, the boat opened its battery of small arms to avenge the death of Rehani, and in thirty minutes the seventy musket-armed canoes of the Marunja were retreating to a more respectful distance. After following us for five miles they abandoned the pursuit, and we happily saw no more of them.

At noon we obtained an observation, north latitude 1° 28′ 0″, while at noon of the 12th we were in north latitude 1° 36′ 0″. Our course among the islands had ranged from west half north to west-south-west.

After we had escaped the Marunja, we crept from channel to channel and creek to creek, which wound in and out between island groves, until night, when we encamped, to undergo the usual nightly tortures of the light-coloured mosquitoes of the Livingstone.

We had discovered on several islands, since leaving Urangi, small camps, consisting of, perhaps, a dozen small grass huts or sheds, which had, no doubt, been the temporary shelter erected by some trading tribe below, and, as we heard from the aborigines of Rubunga the power of the Mangala highly extolled, we came to the conclusion that upon arriving in the Bangala's country we should be freed from all strife and danger.

Feb. 14.—During the forenoon of the 14th of February, while anxiously looking out lest we should be taken by some erratic channels in view of other villages, we arrived at the end of an island, which, after some hesitation, we followed along the right. Two islands were to the right of us, and prevented us from observing the mainland. But after descending two miles we came in full view of a small settlement on the right bank. Too late to return, we crept along down river, hugging the island as closely as possible, in order to arrive at a channel before the natives should sight us. But, alas! even in the midst of our prayers for deliverance, sharp quick taps on a native kettledrum sent our blood bounding to the heart, and we listened in agony for the response. Presently one drum after another sounded the alarm, until the Titanic drums of war thundered the call to arms.

In very despair, I sprang to my feet, and, addressing my distressed and long-suffering followers, said, "It is of no use, my friends, to hope to escape these bloody pagans. Those drums mean war. Yet it is very possible these are the Bangala, in which case, being traders, they will have heard of the men by the sea, and a little present may satisfy the chiefs. Now, while I take the sun you prepare your guns, your powder and bullets, see that every shield is ready to lift at once, as soon as you see or hear one gun-shot. It is only in that way I can save you, for every pagan now, from here to the sea, is armed with a gun, and they are black like you, and they have a hundred guns to your one. If we must die, we will die with guns in our hands like men.

While I am speaking, and trying to make friendship with them, let no one speak or move."

We drew ashore at the little island, opposite the highest village, and at noon I obtained my observation north latitude 1° 7′ 0″. Meanwhile savage madness was being heated by the thunder of drums, canoes were mustering, guns were being loaded, spears and broadswords were being sharpened, all against us, merely because we were strangers, and afloat on their waters. Yet we had the will and the means to purchase amity. We were ready to submit to any tax, imposition, or insolent demand for the privilege of a peaceful passage. Except life, or one drop of our blood, we would sacrifice anything.

Slowly and silently we withdrew from the shelter of the island and began the descent of the stream. The boat took position in front, Frank's canoe, the *Ocean*, on the right, Manwa Sera's, *London Town*, to the left. Beyond Manwa Sera's canoe was the uninhabited island, the great length of which had ensnared us, and hedged us in to the conflict. From our right the enemy would appear with muskets and spears, and an unquenchable ferocity, unless we could mollify him.

We had left Observation Island about half a mile behind us when the prows of many canoes were seen to emerge out of the creek. I stood up and edged towards them, holding a long piece of red cloth in one hand, and a coil of brass wire in another. We rested on our oars, and the men quietly placed their paddles in their canoes, and sat up, watchful, but ready for contingencies. As we floated down, numbers of canoes advanced.

I hailed the natives, who were the most brilliantly decorated of any yet seen. At a distance they all appeared to wear something like English University caps, though of a white colour. There was a great deal of glitter and flash of metal, shining brass, copper, and bright steel among them.

The natives returned no answer to my hail; still I persisted, with the same artfulness of manner that had been so successful at Rubunga. I observed three or four canoes approaching Frank's vessel with a most suspicious air about them, and several of their canoes menacing him, at which Frank stood up and menaced them with his weapon. I thought the act premature, and ordered him to sit down, and to look away from them. I again raised the crimson cloth and wire, and by pantomime offered to give it to those in front, whom I was previously addressing; but almost immediately those natives who had threatened Frank fired into my boat, wounding three of my young crew—Mambu, Murabo, and Jaffari—and two more natives fired into Frank's canoe, wounding two—Hatib and Muftah. The missiles fired into us were jagged pieces of iron and copper ore precisely similar to those which the Ashantees employed. After this murderous outrage there was no effort made to secure peace. The shields were lifted, and proved capital defences against the hail of slugs. Boat, shields, and canoes were pitted, but only a few shields were perforated.

The conflict began in earnest, and lasted so long that ammunition had to be redistributed. We perceived that, as the conflict continued, every village sent out its quota. About two o'clock a canoe advanced with a swaggering air, its crew evidently intoxicated, and fired at us when within thirty yards. The boat instantly swept down to it and captured it, but the crew sprang into the river, and, being capital swimmers, were saved by a timely arrival of their friends. At three o'clock I counted sixty-three opposed to us. Some of the Bangala—which they disclosed themselves by their peculiar cries, "Yaha-ha-ha, Ya Bangala!" "Ya Bangala! Yaha-ha-ha!"—distinguished themselves by an audacity and courage that, for our own sakes, I was glad to see was not general. Especially one young chief, distinguished by his head-dress of white goat-skin, and a short mantle of the same material, and wreaths of thick brass wire on neck, arms and legs, sufficient, indeed, to have protected those parts from slugs, and proving him to be a man of consequence. His canoe mates were ten in number; and his steersman, by his adroitness and dexterity, managed the canoe so well that after he and his mates had fired their guns, he instantly presented its prow and only a thin line of upright figures to our aim. Each time he dashed up to deliver his fire all the canoes of his countrymen seemed stimulated by his example to emulate him. And, allowing five guns on an average to each of the sixty-three canoes, there were 315 muskets opposed to our forty-four. Their mistake was in supposing their slugs to have the same penetrative effect and long range as our missiles had. Only a few of the boldest approached, after they had experienced our fire, within a hundred yards. The young chief already mentioned frequently charged to within fifty yards, and delivered a smashing charge of missiles, almost all of which were either too low or too high. Finally Manwa Sera wounded him with a Snider bullet in the thigh. The brave fellow coolly, and in presence of us all, took a piece of cloth and deliberately bandaged it, and then calmly retreated towards shore. The action was so noble and graceful that orders were given to let him withdraw unmolested. After his departure the firing became desultory, and at 5.30 P.M. our antagonists retired, leaving us to attend to our wounded, and to give three hearty cheers at our success. This was our thirty-first fight on the terrible river—the last but one and certainly the most determined conflict that we had endured.

My gossipy friend at Urangi had stated to me that the Bangala, when they visited his country, were in the habit of carrying things with a high hand, that they frequently indulged in shooting in the most indiscriminate manner at everything if angered, that they were very "hot." But I never expected they would have indulged their "hot-headedness" at the expense of people who might be called relations of those who had supplied them with guns and powder. It is evident, however, to me that, enterprising as the Bangala are, they have never ascended the Livingstone higher than Upoto, otherwise they must certainly have been compelled to measure their strength against the cannibals of the Aruwimi.

The Bangala may be said to be the Ashantees of the Livingstone River, though their country has comparatively but a small populated river front. Their villages cover at intervals—of a mile or half a mile—a line of ten miles. They trade with Ikengo and Irebu down the river all the ivory they have purchased from Upoto, Gunji, Mpisa, Ukeré, Rubunga, Urangi, Mpakiwana, and Marunja. I observed soon after the fight began that many canoes emerged out of a river coming from a northerly direction. For a long period the river of Bangala has appeared on West African maps as the Bancaro river. The word Bangala, which may be pronounced Bangara, Bankara, or Bankaro, signifies the people of Mangala or Mangara, Mankara or Mankaro. I have simply adopted the more popular term.

Unquestionably the Bangala are a very superior tribe. I regret very much the singular antipathy they entertain towards strangers, which no doubt they will continue to show until, like the Ashantees, they have been taught by two or three sharp fights to lessen their pretensions to make targets of aborigines and strangers. While the Bangala are permitted to pass Ikengo to Irebu, the people of Ikengo and Irebu are not privileged to ascend the river beyond Bangala.

We continued our journey on this eventful day until an hour after sunset, when we proceeded to establish a camp at the head of a narrow tortuous channel, which lost itself amid the clusters of small islets.

Feb. 15.—On the 15th, at noon, we reached north latitude 0° 58′ 0″. The strong winds which at this season blow daily up river impeded our journey greatly. They generally began at 8 A.M. and lasted until 3 P.M. When narrow channels were open to us we were enabled to proceed without interruption, but when exposed to broad open streams the waves rose as high as 2 feet, and were a source of considerable danger. Indeed, from the regularity and increased force of the winds, I half suspected at the time that the Livingstone emptied into some vast lake such as the Victoria Nyanza. The mean temperature in the shade seldom exceeds 74° Fahr., and the climate, though not dry, was far more agreeable than the clammy humidity characteristic of the east coast. The difference between the heat in this elevated region and that of the east coast was such that, while it was dangerous to travel in the sun without a sun-umbrella near the sea on the east coast, a light double-cotton cloth cap saved me from feeling any inconvenience when standing up in the boat under a bright glaring sun and cloudless sky. While sitting down in the boat, a few minutes was sufficient to convince me it was dangerous without an umbrella, even here. While at work at the Stanley Falls the umbrella was not used. The nights were uncomfortable without a blanket, and sometimes even two were desirable.

The winds which prevail at this season of the year are from the south-west, or south, which means from the temperate latitude of the South Atlantic, and slightly chilled in their passage over the western ranges. In the early morning the thermometer was often as low as 64°. From 10 A.M. to 4 P.M. it ranged from 75° to 85° Fahr. in the shade; from 4 P.M. to sunset it ranged from 72° to 80°. From the 12th January until the 5th March we experienced no rain.

One remarkable fact connected with our life in this region is, that though we endured more anxiety of mind and more strain on the body, were subject to constant peril, and fared harder (being compelled for weeks to subsist on green bananas, cassava, and sugarless tea, and those frequently in scanty quantities), we—Frank and I—enjoyed better health on the Livingstone than at any other period of the journey; but whether this unusual health might not be attributed to having become more acclimatized is a question.

The mirage on the Livingstone was often ludicrously deceptive, playing on our fears at a most trying period, in a manner which plunged us from a temporary enjoyment of our immunity from attack into a state of suspicion and alarm, which probably, in nine cases out of ten, arose out of the exaggerated proportions given to a flock of pelicans or wild geese, which to our nerves, then in a high state of tension, appeared to be a very host of tall warriors. A young crocodile basking on a sandy spit appeared to be as large as a canoe, and an ancient and bleached tree a ship.

Feb. 17.—At noon of the 17th we had reached north latitude 0° 18′ 41″, our course during the 16th and 17th having been south-west, but a little before sunset the immense river was gradually deflecting to south.

Since the 10th we had been unable to purchase food. The natives had appeared to be so unapproachable, that again the questions naturally arose in each mind, "Where shall we obtain food?" "What shall we do?" "What will be the end of all this?" "Whither, oh whither are we going?" My poor people had been elevated to a high pitch of exultation when they had first seen the four muskets at Rubunga. They regarded them as the beginning of the end. But now? "Ah, whither are we going on this cruel, cruel river?"

Yet they bore the dire period with Spartan stoicism. They were convinced that, had it been in my power, they should never have suffered from scarcity. They had become trained to rely on my judgment and discretion, and with a child-like faith they trusted me. Knowing this but too well, my anxiety to show myself worthy of their love and duty was increased. I might delay procuring food for their safety.

but human beings cannot live on air. But where should I get it, when the mere sight of us put the natives into a rage for murder? How was food to be obtained if the sound of our voices was followed instantly with deadly missiles?

I quote the following from my note-book:—

"*Feb.* 18, 1877.—For three days we have been permitted, through the mercy of God, to descend this great river uninterrupted by savage clamour or ferocity. Winds during two days seriously impeded us, and were a cause for anxiety, but yesterday was fine and calm, and the river like a sheet of burnished glass; we therefore made good progress. In the afternoon we encountered a native trading expedition from Ikengo in three canoes, one of which was manned by fifteen paddlers, clothed in robes of crimson blanket cloth. We hailed them, but they refused to answer us. This sight makes me believe the river must be pretty free of cataracts, and it may be that there are no more than the Sundi cataract, and the Falls of Yellalla, reported by Tuckey in 1816, otherwise I cannot account for the ascent of three trading vessels, and such extensive possession of cloth and guns, so far up the river.

"Since the 10th February we have been unable to purchase food, or indeed approach a settlement for any amicable purpose. The aborigines have been so hostile, that even fishing-canoes have fired at us as though we were harmless game. God alone knows how we shall prosper below. But let come what may, I have purposed to attempt communicating with the natives to-morrow. A violent death will be preferable to death by starvation.

"At 7 A.M. we were on the Equator again, and at noon I obtained an observation which showed we were 0° 17′ 59″ south latitude, as our course has been nearly straight south since yesterday 5 P.M.

"*Feb.* 19, 1877.—This morning we regarded each other as fated victims of protracted famine, or the rage of savages, like those of Mangala. But as we feared famine most, we resolved to confront the natives again. At 10 A.M., while we were descending the Livingstone along the left bank, we discovered an enormous river, considerably over a thousand yards wide, with a strong current, and deep, of the colour of black tea. This is the largest influent yet discovered, and after joining the Livingstone it appeared to command the left half to itself—it strangely refuses to amalgamate with the Livingstone, and the divisional line between them is plainly marked by a zigzag ripple, as though the two great streams contended with one another for the mastery. Even the Aruwimi and the Lowwa united would not greatly exceed this giant influent. Its strong current and black water contrast very strongly with the whitey-brown Livingstone. On the upper side of the confluence is situate Ibonga, but the natives, though not openly hostile, replied to us with the peculiar war-cries 'Yaha-ha-ha!'

"We continued our journey, though grievously hungry, past Bwena and Inguba, doing our utmost to induce the staring fishermen to communicate with us, without any success. They became at once officiously busy with guns, and dangerously active. We arrived at Ikengo, and as we were almost despairing, we proceeded to a small island opposite this settlement and prepared to encamp. Soon a canoe with seven men came dashing across, and we prepared our moneys for exhibition. They unhesitatingly advanced, and ran their canoe alongside us. We were rapturously joyful, and returned them a most cordial welcome, as the act was a most auspicious sign of confidence. We were liberal, and the natives fearlessly accepted our presents, and from this giving of gifts we proceeded to seal this incipient friendship with our blood with all due ceremony.

"After an hour's stay with us they returned to communicate with their countrymen, leaving one young fellow with us, which was another act of grace. Soon from a village below Ikengo two more canoes came up with two chiefs, who were extremely insolent and provoking, though after nearly two and a half years' experience of African manners we were not to be put out of temper because two drunken savages chose to be overbearing.

"It is strange, if we consider of what small things pride is born. The European is proud of his pale colour, and almost all native Africans appear to be proud because they are black. Pride arises most naturally from a full stomach. Esau, while hungry, forgot his birthright and heritage, because of weakened vitals. I forgot mine because my stomach had collapsed through emptiness. The arrogance of the two chiefs of Ikengo was nourished by a sense of fulness. I presume, were the contents of their stomachs analysed, we should find them consist of undigested manioc, banana, with a copious quantity of fluid. What virtues lie in these that they should be proud? Their bodies were shrouded with a grass cloth, greasy and black from wear. Their weapons were flintlocks loaded with three inches of powder and three of slugs. Yet they were insufferably rude!

"By-and-by they cooled down. We got them to sit and talk, and we laughed together, and were apparently the best of friends. Of all the things which struck their fancy, my note-book, which they called 'tara-tara,' or looking-glass, appeared to them to be the most wonderful. They believed it possessed manifold virtues, and that it came from above. Would I, could I, sell it to them? It would have found a ready sale. But as it contains records of disaster by flood and fire, charts of rivers and creeks and islands, sketches of men and manners, notes upon a thousand objects, I could not part with it even for a tusk of ivory

"They got angry and sulky again. It was like playing with and coaxing spoiled children. We amused them in various ways, and they finally became composed, and were conquered by good nature. With a generous scorn of return gifts, they presented me with a gourdful of palm-wine. But I begged so earnestly for food that they sent their canoes back, and, while they sat down by my side, it devolved upon me until their return to fascinate and charm them with benignant gestures and broken talk. About 3 P.M. provisions came in basketfuls of cassava tubers, bananas, and long plantains, and the two chiefs made me rich by their liberality, while the people began also to thaw from that stupor into which impending famine had plunged them. At sunset our two friends, with whom I had laboured with a zealot's enthusiasm, retired, each leaving a spear as a pledge with me that they would return to-morrow, and renew our friendly intercourse, with canoe-loads of provisions.

"*Feb.* 20, 1877.—My two friends, drunk no longer, brought most liberal supplies with them of cassava tubers, cassava loaves, flour, maize, plantains, and bananas, and two small goats, besides two large gourdfuls of palm-wine, and, what was better, they had induced their countrymen to respond to the demand for food. We held a market on Mwangangala Island, at which there was no scarcity of supplies; black pigs, goats, sheep, bananas, plantains, cassava bread, flour, maize, sweet potatoes, yams, and fish being the principal things brought for sale.

"The tall chief of Bwena and the chief of Inguba, influenced by the two chiefs of Ikengo, also thawed, and announced their coming by sounding those curious double bell-gongs, and blowing long horns of ivory, the notes of which distance made quite harmonious. During the whole of this day life was most enjoyable, intercourse unreservedly friendly, and though most of the people were armed with guns there was no manifestation of the least desire to be uncivil, rude, or hostile, which inspired us once more with a feeling of security to which we had been strangers since leaving Urangi.

"From my friends I learned that the name of the great river above Bwena is called Ikelemba. When I asked them which was the largest river, that which flowed by Mangala, or that which came from the south-east, they replied that though Ikelemba river was very large it was not equal to the 'big river.'

"They also gave me the following bit of geography, which, though a little inaccurate, is interesting:—

Left Bank.

From Ikengo, in Nkonda, to
Ubangi to Irebu . . . 1 day.
Float down by Irebu. . 3 days.
Thence to Ukweré . . 1 day.
" " Nkoko Ngombé 1 "
" " Butunu . . 1 "
" " Usini . . . 1 "
" " Mpumba . . 7 hours.
" " Nkunda . . 3 days.
" " Bolobo . . . 4 "

Isangu to Mankonno . . 4 hours.
" " Chumbiri . . 4 "
" " Misongo . . 4 "
" " Nkunda . . 10 days.
" " First Cataract (Livingstone Falls) . . 1 day.

Right Bank.

Ubangi . . . . . . 7 hours.

From Bolobo to Mompurengi . . . . 7 hours.
Thence to Isangu . . 7 "

"The Barumbé are a powerful tribe south-east of Ikengo, left bank. They are probably a sub-tribe of Barua. Bunga is on the right bank. Ubangi is a country which commences opposite Ikengo on the right bank and faces Irebu. Not a single name, except Bankaro, can I recognize of all that is published on Stanford's library map of Africa which I possess. It is clear, then, that above the cataract, which is said to be about thirty days from Ikengo, nothing was ever known by Europeans. I wonder whether this cataract is the Sundi cataract reported by Tuckey? The distance, which the natives give as 30 days, may be but 15 days according to our rate of travel.

"Every weapon these natives possess is decorated with fine brass wire and brass tacks. Their knives are beautiful weapons, of a bill-hook pattern, the handles of which are also profusely decorated with an amount of brass-work and skill that places them very high among the clever tribes. These knives are carried in broad sheaths of red buffalo-hide, and are suspended by a belt of the same material. Besides an antique flintlock musket, each warrior is armed with from four to five light and long assegais, with staves being of the *Curtisia faginea*, and a bill-hook sword. They are a finely-formed people, of a chocolate brown, very partial to camwood powder and palm oil. Snuff is very freely taken, and their tobacco is most pungent.

"*Feb.* 21.—This afternoon at 2 P.M. we continued our journey. Eight canoes accompanied us some distance, and then parted from us, with many demonstrations of friendship. The river flows from Ikengo south-westerly, the flood of the Ikelemba retaining its dark colour, and spreading over a breadth of 3000 yards; the Livingstone's pure whitey-grey waters flow over a breadth of about 5000 yards, in many broad channels."

THE ATTACK OF THE SIXTY-THREE CANOES OF THE PIRATICAL BANGALA.

[To face page 240.

CHAPTER XI.

Running the gauntlet—Kindly solitudes—Amina's death—The humanizing effects of trade apparent—"The most plausible rogue of all Africa"—The king of Chumbiri; his hospitality, wives, possessions, and cunning—Making up a language—Pythons—The Ibari Nkutu or the Kwango—Treacherous guides—The Stanley Pool—Chief Itsi of Ntamo—We have to give up our big goat—River observations.

Feb. 22.—From the left bank we crossed to the right, on the morning of the 22nd, and, clinging to the wooded shores of Ubangi, had reached at noon south latitude 0° 51′ 13″. Two hours later we came to where the great river contracted to a breath of 3000 yards, flowing between two low rocky points, both of which were populous, well cultivated, and rich with banana plantations. Below these points the river slowly widened again, and islands well wooded, as above river, rose into view, until by their number they formed once more intricate channels and winding creeks.

Desirous of testing the character of the natives, we pulled across to the left bank, until, meeting with a small party of fishermen, we were again driven by their ferocity to seek the untravelled and unpopulated island wildernesses. It was rather amusing than otherwise to observe the readiness of the savages of Irebu to fire their guns at us. They appeared to think that we were human waifs without parentage, guardianship, or means of protection, for their audacity was excessive. One canoe with only four men dashed down at us from behind an island close to the left bank, and fired point-blank from a distance of 100 yards. Another party ran along a spit of sand and coolly waited our approach on their knees, and, though we sheered off to a distance of 200 yards from them, they poured a harmless volley of slugs towards us, at which Baraka, the humourist, said that the pagans caused us to "eat more iron than grain."

Such frantic creatures, however, could not tempt us to fight them. The river was wide enough, channels innumerable afforded us means of escaping from their mad ferocity, and if poor purblind nature was so excessively arrogant, Providence had kindly supplied us with crooked by-ways and unfrequented paths of water which we might pursue unmolested.

Feb. 23.—At noon of the 23rd we had reached 1° 22′ 15″ south latitude. Strong gales met us during each day. The islands were innumerable, creeks and channels winding in and out amongst the silent scenes. But though their general appearance was much the same, almost uniform in outline and size, the islands never became commonplace. Was it from gratitude at the security they afforded us from the ruthless people of these regions? I do not know, but every bosky island into whose dark depths, shadowed by impervious roofs of foliage, we gazed had about it something kindly and prepossessing. Did we love them because, from being hunted by our kind, and ostracized from communities of men, we had come to regard them as our homes? I cannot tell, but I shall ever and for ever remember them. Ah, had I but space, how I would revel in descriptions of their treasures and their delights! Even with their gad-flies and their tsetsé, their mosquitoes and their ants, I love them. There was no treachery or guile in their honest depths; the lurking assassin feared their twilight gloom; the savage dared not penetrate their shades without a feeling of horror; but to us they were refuges in our distress, and their solitudes healed our woes. How true the words, "Affliction cometh not out of the dust, nor doth trouble spring out of the ground." Innocence and peace dwelt in the wilderness alone. Outside of them glared the fierce-eyed savage, with malice and rage in his heart, and deadly weapons in his hand.

To us, then, these untenanted islets, with their "breadths of tropic shade, and palms in clusters," seemed verily "knots of paradise." Like hunted beasts of the chase, we sought the gloom and solitude of the wilds. Along the meandering and embowered creeks, hugging the shadows of the o'erarching woods, we sought for that safety which man refused us.

Feb. 24.—The great river grew sea-like in breadth below Irebu on the morning of the 24th; indeed, it might have been 100 miles in breadth for aught we knew, deep-buried as we were among the islands. Yet there were broad and deep channels on every side of us, as well as narrow creeks between lengthy islands. The volume of water appeared exhaustless, though distributed over such an enormous width. There was water sufficient to float the most powerful steamers that float in the Mississippi. Here and there amongst the verdured isles gleamed broad humps of white sand, but on either side were streams several hundred yards wide, with as much as three fathoms' depth of water in the channels.

At noon we reached south latitude 1° 37′ 22″. The Mompurengi natives appeared on an island and expressed their feelings by discharging two guns at us, which we did not resent, but steadily held on our way. An hour afterwards faithful Amina, wife of Kachéché, breathed her last, making a most affecting end.

Being told by Kachéché that his poor wife was dying, I drew my boat alongside of the canoe she was lying in. She was quite sensible, but very weak. "Ah, master!" she said, "I shall never see the sea again. Your child Amina is dying. I have so wished to see the cocoanuts and the mangoes; but no—Amina is dying—dying in a pagan land. She will never see Zanzibar. The master has been good to his children, and Amina remembers it. It is a bad world, master, and you have lost your way in it. Good-bye, master; do not forget poor little Amina!"

While floating down, we dressed Amina in her shroud, and laid her tenderly out, and at sunset consigned her body to the depths of the silent river.

Feb. 25.—The morning of the 25th saw us once again on the broad stream floating down. We got a view of the mainland to the right, and discovered it to be very low. We hurried away into the island creeks, and floated down amongst many reedy, grassy islets, the haunt of bold hippopotami, one of which made a rush at a canoe with open mouth, but contented himself fortunately with a paddle, which he crunched into splinters.

At noon we had reached south latitude 1° 58′ 12″. About 4 P.M. we came to what appeared to be a river, 1500 yards wide, issuing from north-north-east, while the course that we had followed was from the north-east during the afternoon. It was quite free from islets, and this made me suspect it was a separate river. The main river was here about six miles wide.

Feb. 26.—During our voyage on the 26th, the grassy islets became more frequent, inhabited by the flamingo, pelican, stork, whydahs, ibis, geese, ducks, &c. The salt-makers find a great source of wealth in the grasses; and the smoke of their fires floated over the country in clouds.

At 10 A.M. the Levy Hills rose into view about two miles beyond the river on the left bank, which as we neared Kutumpuku approached the river, and formed a ridge. Instantly the sight of the approaching hills suggested cataracts and the memories of the terrific struggles we had undergone in passing the Stanley Falls were then brought vividly to our mind. What should we do with our sadly weakened force, were we to experience the same horrible scenes again?

At noon I took an observation and ascertained that we were in south latitude 2° 23′ 14″. Edging off towards the right bank, we came to a creek, which from the immense number of those amphibious animals, I have called "Hippopotamus Creek." Grass-covered islets, innumerable to us as we passed by them, were on either side. When about half-way through this creek we encountered seven canoes, loaded with men, about to proceed to their fishing haunts. Our sudden meeting occasioned a panic among the natives, and as man had hitherto been a dreaded object, it occasioned us also not a little uneasiness. Fortunately, however, they retreated in haste, uttering their fearful "Yaha-ha-has," and we steadily pursued our way down river, and about 3 P.M. emerged in view of the united stream, 4000 yards wide, contracted by the steep cultivated slopes of Bolobo on the left, and by a beautiful high upland—which had gradually been lifting from the level plains—on the right bank.

For a moment, as we issued in view of the stream, with scores of native canoes passing backwards and forwards, either fishing or proceeding to the grassy islets to their fish-sheds and salt-making, we feared that we should have another conflict; but though they looked at us wonderingly, there was no demonstration of hostility. One man in a canoe, in answer to our question, replied that the bold heights 200 feet above the river, which swarmed with villages, was Bolobo. Being so near the border of the savage lands above, we thought it safer to wait yet one more day before attempting further intercourse with them.

Feb. 27.—On the 27th, during the morning, we were still among islets and waving branches, but towards the afternoon the islets had disappeared, and we were in view of a magnificent breadth of four miles of clear water. On our left the cultivated uplands of Bolobo had become elevated into a line of wooded hills, and on our right the wall of the brown grassy upland rose high and steep, broken against the sky-line into cones.

Gradually the shores contracted, until at 3 P.M. the right bank deflected to a south-east course, and finally shot out a long rocky point, which to us, accustomed to an enormous breadth of river, appeared as though it were the commencement of a cataract. We approached it with the utmost caution, but on arriving near it we discovered that the mirage had exaggerated its length and height, for between it and the left bank were at least 2500 yards of deep water.

The time had now come when we could no longer sneak amongst reedy islets, or wander in secret amongst wildernesses of water; we must once more confront man. The native, as we had ascertained opposite Bolobo, was not the destructive infuriate of Irebu or Mompurengi, or the frantic brute of Mangala and Marunja. He appeared to be toning down into the MAN, and to understand that others of his species inhabited this globe. At least, we hoped so. We wished to test the accuracy of this belief, and now eagerly searched for opportunities to exchange greetings, and to claim kindred with him. As we had industriously collected a copious vocabulary of African languages, we felt a certain confidence that we had been sufficiently initiated into the science of aboriginal language to be able to begin practising it.

Behind the rocky point were three natives fishing for minnows with hand-nets. We lay-to on our oars and accosted them. They replied to us clearly and calmly. There was none of that fierce fluster and bluster and wild excitement that we had come to recognize as the preliminary symptoms of a conflict. The word *ndu*—brother—was more frequent. To our overtures of friendship there was a visible inclination of assent; there was a manifest desire to accept our conciliatory sentiments; for we received conciliatory responses. Who could doubt a pacific conclusion to the negotiations? Our tact and diplomacy had been educated in a rough school of adversity. Once the attention of the natives had been arrested, and their confidence obtained, we had never failed to come to a friendly understanding.

They showed us a camping-place at the base of the brown

grassy upland, in the midst of a thin grove of trees. They readily subscribed to all the requirements of friendship, blood-brotherhood, and an exchange of a few small gifts. Two of them then crossed the river to Chumbiri, whose green wooded slopes and fields, and villages and landing-place, were visible, to tell the king of Chumbiri that peaceable strangers desired friendship with him. They appeared to have described us to him as most engaging people, and to have obtained his cordial co-operation and sympathy in a very short time, for soon three canoes appeared conveying about forty men, under three of his sons, who bore to us the

THE KING OF CHUMBIRI.

royal spear, and several royal gifts, such as palm-wine, a goat, bananas, and a chicken to us, and a hearty welcome from the old king, their father, with the addition of a promise that he would call himself the next day.

Feb. 28.—About 9 A.M. of the 28th the king of Chumbiri appeared with *éclat.* Five canoes filled with musketeers escorted him.

Though the sketch above is an admirable likeness of him, it may be well also to append a verbal description. A small-eyed man of about fifty or thereabout, with a well-formed nose, but wide nostrils and thin lips, clean-shaved, or rather clean-plucked, with a quiet yet sociable demeanour, ceremonious, and mild-voiced, with the instincts of a greedy trader cropping out of him at all points, and cunning beyond measure. The type of his curious hat may be seen on the head of any Armenian priest. It was formed out of close-plaited hyphene-palm fibre, sufficiently durable to outlast his life, though he might live a century. From his left shoulder, across his chest, was suspended the sword of the bill-hook pattern, already described in the passages about Ikengo. Above his shoulder stood upright the bristles of an elephant's tail. His hand was armed with a buffalo's tail, made into a fly-flapper, to whisk mosquitoes and gnats off the royal face. To his wrist were attached the odds and ends which the laws of superstition had enjoined upon him, such as charm-gourds, charm-powders in bits of red and black flannel, and a collection of wooden antiquities, besides a snuff-gourd and a parcel of tobacco-leaves.

The king's people were apparently very loyal and devoted to him, and his sons showed remarkable submissiveness. The

GREAT PIPE OF KING OF CHUMBIRI.

little snuff-gourd was in constant requisition, and he took inmoderate quantities, inhaling a quarter of a tea-spoonful at a time from the palm of his hand, to which he pressed his poor nose until it seemed to be forced into his forehead. Immediately after, one of his filially-affectionate children would fill his long chibouque, which was 6 feet in length, decorated with brass tacks and tassels of braided cloth. The bowl was of iron, and large enough to contain half an ounce of tobacco. He would then take two or three long-drawn whiffs, until his cheeks were distended like two hemispheres, and fumigate his charms thoroughly with the smoke. His sons then relieved him of the pipe, at which he snapped his fingers—and distended their cheeks into hemispherical protuberances in like manner, and also in the same way fumigated their little charms; and so the chibouque of peace and sociability went the round of the circle, as though it was a council of Sioux about to hold a pow-wow, and as the pipe passed round there was an interchange of finger-snaps in a decorous, grave, and ceremonious style.

Our intercourse with the king was very friendly, and it was apparent that we were mutually pleased. The only fault that I, as a stranger, could find in him was an excessive cunning, which approached to the sublime. He had evidently cultivated fraud and duplicity as an art, yet he was suave and wheedling. Could I complain? Never were people so willing to be victimized. Had we been warned that he would victimize us, I do not think that we should have refused his friendship.

An invitation was extended to us to make his own village our home. We were hungry; and no doubt we were approaching cataracts. It would be welcome knowledge to know what to expect below in that broad defile filled by the great river; what peoples, countries, tribes, villages, rivers we should see; if the tribes were amenable to reason in the unknown country; if white men had ever been heard of; if there were cataracts below, and if they were passable. We accepted the invitation, and crossed the river, drums and double bell-gongs sounding the peaceful advance of our flotilla upon Chumbiri.

We were proud of our reception by the dames of Chumbiri. Loyal and submissive to their king, they exhibited kindly attentions to the strangers. We held a grand market, and won the natives' hearts by our liberality. Back rations for several days were due to our people, and, filled with an extravagant delight—even as Frank and I were—they expended their ration moneys with a recklessness of consequences which only the novelty of the situation explained. We had arrived at port, and weather-beaten voyagers are generally free with their moneys upon such occasions.

The dames at Chumbiri were worth seeing, even to us, who were sated with the thousand curious things we had met in our long travels. They were also pretty, of a rich brown colour many of them, large-eyed, and finely formed, with a graceful curve of shoulder I had not often observed. But they were slaves of fashion. Six-tenths of the females wore brass collars 2 inches in diameter; three-tenths had them $2\frac{1}{2}$ inches in diameter; one-tenth were oppressed with collars 3 inches in diameter; which completely covered the neck, and nearly reached the shoulder ends. Fancy the weight of 30 lbs. of brass, soldered permanently round the neck! Yet these oppressed women were the favourite wives of Chumbiri! And they rejoiced in their oppression!

I believe that Chumbiri—who, as I said, was a keen and enterprising trader, the first aboriginal African that might be compared to a Parsee—as soon as he obtained any brass wire, melted it and forged it into brass collars for his wives. That the collars were not larger may be attributed, perhaps, to his poverty. He boasted to me he possessed "four tens" of wives, and each wife was collared permanently in thick brass. I made a rough calculation, and I estimated that his wives bore about their necks until death at least 800 lbs. of brass; his daughters—he had six—120 lbs.; his favourite female slaves about 200 lbs. Add 6 lbs. of brass wire to each wife and daughter for arm and leg ornaments, and one is astonished

ONE OF THE KING'S WIVES AT CHUMBIRI.

to discover that Chumbiri possesses a portable store of 1396 lbs. of brass.

I asked of Chumbiri what he did with the brass on the neck of a dead wife. Chumbiri smiled. Cunning rogue: he regarded me benevolently, as though he loved me for the searching question. Significantly he drew his finger across his throat.

The warriors and young men are distinguished for a characteristic style of hair-dressing, which belongs to Uyanzi alone. It is arranged into four separate plaits, two of which overhang the forehead like lovers' curls. Another special mark of Uyanzi are two tattooed lines over the forehead. In whatever part of the lower Livingstone these peculiarities of style may be seen, they are indubitably Wy-yanzi, or natives of Uyanzi.

The country of Uyanzi embraces many small districts, and extends along the left bank of the great river, from

Bolobo, in south latitude 2° 23′ 14″, to the confluence of the Ibari Nkutu, or river of Nkutu, and the Livingstone, in 3° 14′ south latitude. The principal districts are Bolobo, Isangu, Chumbiri, Musevoka, Misongo, and Ibaka. Opposite is the country of the Batekė, a wilder tribe than the Wy-yanzi, some of the more eastern of whom are professed cannibals. To the north is the cannibal tribe of the Wanfuninga, of ferocious repute, and dreaded by the Wy-yanzi and Batekė.

The language of Uyanzi seemed to us to be a mixture of almost all Central African dialects. Our great stock of native words in all dialects proved of immense use to me; and in three days I discovered, after classifying and comparing the words heard from the Wy-yanzi with other African words, that I was tolerably proficient, at least for all practical purposes, in the Kiyanzi dialect.

Mar. 7.—On the 7th March we parted from the friendly king of Chumbiri, with an escort of forty-five men, in three canoes under the leadership of his eldest son, who was instructed by his father to accompany us as far as the pool, now called Stanley Pool, because of an incident which will be described hereafter.

For some reason we crossed the river, and camped on the right bank, two miles below Chumbiri. At midnight the Wy-yanzi awoke us all by the fervour with which they implored their fetishes to guide us safely from camp to camp, which they named. As they had been very successful in charming away the rain with which we had been threatened the evening before, our people were delighted to hear them pray for success, having an implicit faith in them.

Just below our camp the river contracted to 2500 yards, between two high hilly banks, and 400 to 600 feet high.

Mar. 8.—A violent rain-storm began at 8 A.M. of the 8th, which lasted four hours. We then made a start, but after an hour of our company the escort lagged behind, but told us to continue our journey, as they would overtake us. Though I strongly suspected that the Wy-yanzi intended to abandon us, we could find no reasonable cause to doubt them, and therefore proceeded without them until near sunset. We camped in the midst of a dense jungly forest. About an hour after, the camp was alarmed by the shrieks of a boy, who was about to be attacked by a python, which vanished in the woods when the people rushed to the rescue. The boy said he had hailed it at first, imagining it to be one of his friends. In half an hour the python, or another one, was discovered in a different part of the camp, about to embrace a woman in its folds; but this time, after tremendous excitement, the monster was despatched. It measured only 13 feet 6 inches in length, and 15 inches round the thickest part of the body.

Mar. 9.—At early dawn we continued our journey along the right bank, and about 7 A.M. discovered a rapid river about two hundred and fifty yards wide, having two mouths, to which I have given the name of Lawson River, after

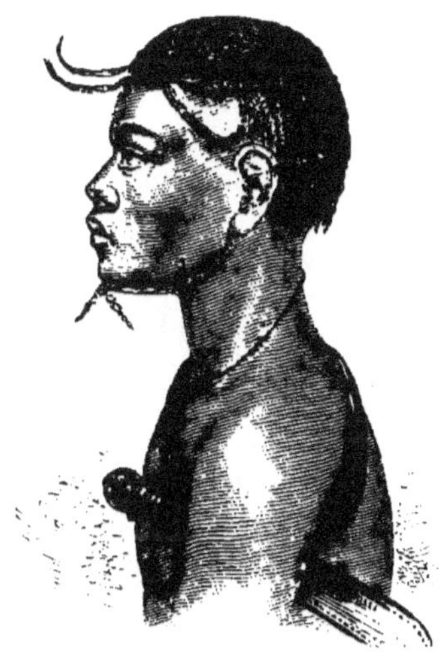

SON OF THE KING OF CHUMBIRI.

Mr. Edward Levy Lawson. The water was of a very light colour.

The water of the Ikelemba river, which enters the Livingstone above Ikengo in about 12′ south latitude, did not commingle with that of its great recipient until both had flowed side by side in the same bed for about 130 miles, or near Bolobo. Its strong-tea-coloured water had now quite changed the complexion of the Livingstone; for, while above Bolobo it had a clear whitey-grey colour, it was now of a deep brown. The other tea-coloured rivers, such as the Ruiki, Kasuku, and Black, above the Stanley Falls, had soon become absorbed by the waters of the Livingstone.

Below the last affluent the Livingstone narrowed to 1500 yards, and flowed with a perceptibly quickened current through the deep chasm in the table-land, the slopes of which were mostly uninhabited; but on the summit near the verge, on either side, villages, banana plantations, and other signs of population were visible.

I tossed my lead into the stream in this comparatively narrow channel, and obtained at the first cast 158 feet; half an hour afterwards I obtained 163: a third time, 79 feet.

On our left, in south latitude 3° 14′ 4″, we came to the Ibari (river) Nkutu, issuing from east-north-east through a deepening cleft in the table-land, and 450 yards wide at the mouth, a powerful and deep river. There is no doubt that this Ibari-Nkutu is the Coango or Kwango of the Portuguese, the sources of which Livingstone crossed, on his way to Loanda in 1854, and which takes its rise in the watershed that separates the basin of the great river from that of the Zambezi.

Six miles below the confluence of the Nkutu river with the Livingstone we drew our vessels close to a large and thick grove, to cook breakfast, and with a faint hope that in the meantime our guides would appear. Fires were kindled, and the women were attending to the porridge of cassava flour for their husbands. Frank and I were hungrily awaiting our cook's voice to announce our meal ready, when, close to us, several loud musket-shots startled us all, and six of our men fell wounded. Though we were taken considerably at a disadvantage, long habit had taught us how to defend ourselves in a bush, and a desperate fight began, and lasted an hour, ending in the retreat of the savages, but leaving us with fourteen of our men wounded. This was our thirty-second fight, and last.

After the wounded had been tended, and breakfast despatched, we proceeded down river, and two miles below we discovered the settlement to which our late antagonists belonged. But we continued our journey until 2 P.M., when, coming to a small island, we disembarked. At 4 P.M. our long absent guides appeared, and, as they were disinclined to halt, we followed them down river, until they stopped at a large settlement called Mwana Ibaka, which occupied a low semi-circular terrace at the base of tall hills. Imagining that there was not the slightest fear of a rupture after being heralded by our friends, we steered for the shore; but as we approached, the shore swarmed with hundreds of excited men, with brass-banded muskets in their hands. Through sheer surprise at the frantic savagery so suddenly displayed, we floated down dangerously near the aiming men, before we observed that our guides were making violent gestures for us to move off. This recalled us to our senses, and we rowed away before the fierce people had drawn trigger. Three miles below we encamped on the right bank, and at sunset our guides appeared, but halted on the left bank.

Mar. 10.—On the morning of the 10th, at 6 A.M., the downward voyage was continued, between lofty and picturesque shores, here bold and precipitous, there wooded from base to summit—here great hill shoulders sloping abruptly to the edge of the deep river, there retreating into wooded valleys between opposing ridges. Our guides overtook us, but they would hold no conversation with us, until, arriving at the woods of Ndande-Njoko, at 10 A.M., they changed their minds, crossed over to the right bank, and halted for breakfast. We also stopped, and renewed our intercourse with them, while they began vehemently to excuse themselves from being the cause of Mwana Ibaka's outrageously wild conduct, and of not warning us of the murderous community which had attacked us in the grove the day previous, and which had caused us such a grievous loss. We excused them gladly, and then took an opportunity of promising more brass wire to them if they would accompany us to the cataract; but our friends required it in advance. But having already been paid at Chumbiri most bounteously for services which they had as yet shown no disposition to give, and as we felt assured they would not fulfil any new engagement, we resolved to depend upon ourselves.

When I came to reflect upon the manner we had been treated above river by the cannibals who had netted us in at the Sixth Cataract of the Stanley Falls, and the extraordinarily cunning king of Chumbiri and his sons, I perceived that the conduct of both had alike sprung from contempt of people of whom they knew nothing. Though I have seen five hundred African chiefs, it may not be amiss to record here my firm belief that the mild-voiced king of Chumbiri is the most plausible rogue of all Africa.

Near sunset we camped in a little cove below precipitous red cliffs, which had contracted the river to 1000 yards in width. The upper parts of these cliffs consisted of hard grey sandstone, overlying a soft red sandstone.

Mar. 11.—The 11th of March was passed without further incident than the usual storm—south-wester—which blew almost every day, and often made the river dangerous to low-board river canoes. The river was very deep, and flowed with a current of 3 knots an hour, and varied in width from 1000 to 1400 yards, pent in by the steep but wooded slopes of the hilly ridges that rose to the height of 600 feet above us. Red buffaloes and small antelope were abundant on the right bank, but not even a shot dared we fire, lest it might startle some frenzied savage to sound the call to war, and so alarm the people at the cataract the terrors of which we were constantly exaggerating in our thoughts.

Mar. 12.—About 11 A.M. of the 12th, the river gradually expanded from 1400 yards to 2500 yards, which admitted us in view of a mighty breadth of river, which the men at once, with happy appropriateness, termed "a pool." Sandy islands rose in front of us like a sea-beach, and on the right towered a long row of cliffs, white and glistening, so like the cliffs of Dover that Frank at once exclaimed that it was a bit of England. The grassy table-land above the cliffs appeared as green as a lawn, and so much reminded Frank of Kentish Downs that he exclaimed enthusiastically, "I feel we are nearing home."

While taking an observation at noon of the position, Frank, with my glass in his hand, ascended the highest part of the large sandy dune that had been deposited by the mighty river, and took a survey of its strange and sudden expansion, and after he came back he said, "Why, I declare, sir, this place is just like a pool; as broad as it is long. There are mountains all round it, and it appears to me almost circular." *

"Well, if it is a pool, we must distinguish it by some name. Give me a suitable name for it, Frank."

"Why not call it 'Stanley Pool,' and these cliffs 'Dover Cliffs'? For no traveller who may come here again will fail to recognize the cliffs by that name."

Subsequent events brought these words vividly to my recollection, and in accordance with Frank's suggestion I

* Frank described the crater of an extinct volcano, which is six miles in length and four miles wide, as described more in detail subsequently.

have named this lake-like expansion of the river from Dover Cliffs to the first cataract of the Livingstone Falls—embracing about thirty square miles—the Stanley Pool. The latitude of the entrance from above to the pool was ascertained to be 4° 3′ south latitude.

The left shore is occupied by the populous settlements of Nshasa, Nkunda, and Ntamo. The right is inhabited by the wild Bateké, who are generally accused of being cannibals.

Soon after we began our descent of the pool, skirting the right shore, we observed a chalky mount, near which were two or three columns of the same material. From a cove just below emerged two or three Batcké canoes, the crews of which, after collecting their faculties, consented to show us the cataract, the noise of which, as they attempted to describe it, elicited roars of laughter from the members of the Expedition. This outburst of loud merriment conquered all reluctance on the part of the Batcké to accompany us.

After winding in and out of many creeks which were very shallow, we approached the village of Mankoneh, the chief of the Batcké. His people during the daytime are generally scattered over these sandy dunes of the Stanley Pool attending to their nets and fish-snares, and to protect themselves from the hot sun always take with them several large mats to form sheds. Mankoneh, to our great delight, was a bluff, hearty, genial soul, who expressed unbounded pleasure at seeing us; he also volunteered to guide us to the falls. He was curious to know how we proposed travelling after arriving near them, for it was impossible, he said, to descend the falls. By a ludicrous pantomime he led us to understand that they were something very fearful.

A few hundred yards below his village the pool sharply contracted, and the shore of Ntamo—a projecting point from the crescent-shaped ridge beyond—appeared at a distance of 2000 yards. It was then that we heard for the first time the low and sullen thunder of the first cataract of the Livingstone Falls.

Slowly Mankoneh, in his canoe, glided down towards it, and louder it grew on the ears, until when within one hundred yards of the first line of broken water he pointed forward, and warned us not to proceed farther. We made for the shore, and found ourselves on a narrow ledge-like terrace bristling with great blocks of granite, amidst a jungly tangle, which grew at the base of high hills. Here, after a short busy period with axe and machete, we constructed a rude camp. The only level spot was not six feet square.

Mankoneh, the Batekè chief, pointed out to us the village of Itsi, the chief of Ntamo, which is situate on the left bank, in a line with the beginning of the first cataract, and spoke of Itsi with great respect, as though he were very powerful.

About 5 P.M. a small canoe was observed to cross over to our side from the left bank, a mile above the falls. The canoe-men, through the representations of our hearty friend Mankoneh, were soon induced to land in our camp to converse with the white men, and before long we had succeeded in making them feel quite at home with us. As they were in a quiver of anxious desire to impart to the chief Itsi all the wonderful things they had witnessed with us, they departed about sunset, solemnly promising we should see the famous Itsi of Ntamo next morning.

Lashing our canoes firmly lest an accident should happen during the night, we turned to our rude huts to sleep in peace. We were all very hungry, as we had been able to purchase nothing from the natives since leaving Chumbiri five days before, and we had been more than usually improvident, having placed far too much reliance on the representations so profusely made to us by the mild-voiced but cunning king of Chumbiri. From very shame I refrain from publishing the stores of goods with which I purchased the glib promises of assistance from Chumbiri, not one of which were realized.

Mar. 13.—Morning of the 13th of March found us, from the early hours of dawn, anxiously waiting the arrival of Itsi of Ntamo and the reappearance of Mankoneh. From our camp we might easily with a glass note any movement on the other bank. At 9 A.M.—Itsi evidently was not an early riser—a large canoe and two consorts, laden with men, were seen propelled up stream along the left bank, and a mile above the landing-place to cross the river at a furious pace. The rows of upright figures, with long paddles, bending their bodies forward in unison, and their voices rising in a swelling chorus to the sound of the steady beat of a large drum, formed a pretty and inspiring sight. Arriving at the right bank, with a perfect recklessness of the vicinity of the falls, they dashed down towards our camp at the rate of six knots an hour. The large war-canoe, though not quite equal to the monster of the Aruwimi in size, was a noble vessel, and Itsi, who was seated in state "mid-ship," with several grey-headed elders near him, was conscious, when he saw our admiration, that he had created a favourable impression. She measured 85 feet 7 inches in length, 4 feet in width, and was 3 feet 3 inches deep. Her crew consisted of sixty paddlers and four steersmen, and she carried twenty-two passengers, close-packed, besides, making a total of eighty-six persons. The other two canoes carried ninety-two persons altogether. We cordially invited Itsi and his people to our camp, to which they willingly responded. Some grass, fresh cut, in anticipation of the visit of our honourable friends, had been strewn over a cleared space close to the stream, and our best mats spread over it.

There were four or five grey-headed elders present, one of whom was introduced as Itsi. He laughed heartily, and it was not long before we were on a familiar footing. They then broached the subject of blood-brotherhood. We were willing, but they wished to defer the ceremony until they had first shown their friendly feelings to us. Accordingly the old man handed over to me ten loaves of cassava bread, or cassava pudding, fifty tubers of cassava, three bunches of bananas, a dozen sweet potatoes, some sugar-cane, three fowls, and a diminutive goat. A young man of about twenty-six years made Frank's acquaintance by presenting to him double the quantity I received. This liberality drew my attention to him. His face was dotted with round spots of soot-and-oil mixture. From his shoulders depended a long cloth of check pattern, while over one shoulder was a belt, to which was attached a queer medley of small gourds containing snuff and various charms, which he called his Inkisi. In return for the bounteous stores of provisions given to Frank and myself, as they were cotton- or grass-cloth-wearing people, we made up a bundle of cloths for each of the principals, which they refused, to our surprise. We then begged to know what they desired, that we might show our appreciation of their kindness, and seal the bond of brotherhood with our blood.

The young man now declared himself to be Itsi, the king of Ntamo; the elder, who had previously been passed off for the king, being only an ancient councillor.

It was a surprise, but not an unpleasant one, though

there was nothing very regal or majestic about him, unless one may so call his munificent bounty to Frank, as compared to the old man's to me. We finally prevailed upon Itsi to inform us what gift would be pleasing to him.

He said, "I want only that big goat; if you give me that, I shall want nothing more."

The "big goat" which he so earnestly required was the last of six couples I had purchased in Uregga for the purpose of presentation to an eminent English lady, in accordance with a promise I had made to her four years previously. All the others had perished from heat apoplexy, sickness, and want of proper care, which the terrible life we had led had prevented us from supplying. This "big goat" and a lion-like ram, gigantic specimens of the domestic animals of Manyema and Uregga, were all that survived. They had both become quite attached to us, and were valued companions of a most eventful journey of 1100 miles. I refused it, but offered to double the cloths. Whereupon Itsi sulked, and prepared to depart, not, however, before hinting that we should find it difficult to obtain food if he vetoed the sale of provisions. We coaxed him back again to his seat, and offered him one of the asses.

The possession of such a "gigantic" animal as an ass, which was to him of all domestic animals a veritable Titanosaurus, was a great temptation; but the shuddering women, who feared being eaten by it, caused him to decline the honour of the gift. He now offered three goats for what appeared to him to be the "largest" goat in Africa, and boasted of his goodness, and how his friendship would be serviceable to me, whereas, if he parted in anger, why, we should be entirely at his mercy. The goat was therefore transferred to his canoe, and Itsi departed for Ntamo as though he were in possession of a new wonder.

Our provisions were only sufficient to prove what appetites we possessed, and not to assuage them: all were consumed in a few minutes, and we were left with only hopes of obtaining a little more on the next day.

Mar. 14.—On the 14th Itsi appeared with his war-canoe at 9 A.M., bringing three goats and twenty loaves of cassava bread and a few tubers, and an hour afterwards Nchuvira, king of Nkunda, Mankoneh, chief of the Bateké fishermen near the Stanley Pool, and the king of Nshasa, at the south-east end of the Stanley Pool, arrived at our camp with several canoe crews. Each of the petty sovereigns of the districts in our neighbourhood contributed a little, but altogether we were only able to distribute to each person 2 lbs. of eatable provisions. Every chief was eager for a present, with which he was gratified, and solemn covenants of peace were entered into between the whites and the blacks. The treaty with Itsi was exceedingly ceremonious, and involved the exchange of charms. Itsi transferred to me, for my protection through life, a small gourdful of a curious powder, which had rather a saline taste, and I delivered over to him, as the white man's charm against all evil, a half-ounce vial of magnesia; further, a small scratch in Frank's arm, and another in Itsi's arm, supplied blood sufficient to unite us in one and indivisible bond of fraternity. After this we were left alone.

An observation by boiling-point, above the First Cataract of the Livingstone Falls, disclosed to us an altitude of 1147 feet above the ocean. At Nyangwé the river was 2077 feet. In 1235 miles therefore there had been only a reduction of 930 feet, divided as follows:—

	Feet.	Distance in Miles.	Fall per Mile.
Nyangwé	2077	327	20 inches.
4 miles below seventh cataract, Stanley Falls	1511		
	Feet 566		
4 miles below seventh cataract, Stanley Falls	1511	898 River uninterrupted.	5 inches nearly.
River at Ntamo, above first cataract, Livingstone Falls	1147		
	Feet 364		

CHAPTER XII.

The struggle with the river renewed—Passing the "Father"—In the "Cauldron"—Poor Kalulu!—Soudi's strange adventures—At the "Whirlpool Narrows"—Lady Alice Rapids—Our escape from death—"Isles of Eden"—Thieves amongst us—The Inkisi Falls—The canoes dragged over the mountain—Trade along the Livingstone—Ulcers and entozoa—An artful compound.

Mar. 15.—The wide wild land which, by means of the greatest river of Africa, we have pierced, is now about to be presented in a milder aspect than that which has filled the preceding pages with records of desperate conflicts and furious onslaughts of savage men. The people no longer resist our advance. Trade has tamed their natural ferocity, until they no longer resent our approach with the fury of beasts of prey.

It is the dread river itself of which we shall have now to complain. It is no longer the stately stream whose mystic beauty, noble grandeur, and gentle uninterrupted flow along a course of nearly nine hundred miles, ever fascinated us, despite the savagery of its peopled shores, but a furious river rushing down a steep bed obstructed by reefs of lava, projected barriers of rock, lines of immense boulders, winding in crooked course through deep chasms, and dropping down over terraces in a long series of falls, cataracts, and rapids. Our frequent contests with the savages culminated in tragic struggles with the mighty river as it rushed and roared through the deep, yawning pass that leads from the broad table-land down to the Atlantic Ocean.

Those voiceless and lone streams meandering between the thousand isles of the Livingstone; those calm and silent wildernesses of water over which we had poured our griefs and wailed in our sorrow; those woody solitudes, where nightly we had sought to soothe our fevered brows, into whose depths we breathed our vows; that sea-like amplitude of water which had proved our refuge in distress, weird in its stillness, and solemn in its mystery, are now exchanged for the cliff-lined gorge, through which with inconceivable fury the Livingstone sweeps with foaming billows into the broad Congo, which, at a distance of only 155 geographical miles, is nearly 1100 feet below the summit of the first fall.

Mar. 16.—On the 16th of March, having explored as far as the Gordon-Bennett River, and obtained a clear idea of our situation during the 15th, we began our labours with energy. Goods, asses, women, and children, with the guard under Frank, first moved overland to a temporary halting-place near the confluence. Then manning the boat, I led the canoe-men from point to point along the right bank, over the first rapids. We had some skilful work to perform to avoid being swept away by the velocity of the current; but whenever we came to rocks we held the rattan hawsers in our hands, and, allowing the stream to take them beyond these dangerous points, brought them into the sheltered lee. Had a hawser parted nothing could have saved the canoe or the men in it, for at the confluence of the Gordon-Bennett with the great river the entire river leaps headlong into an abyss of waves and foam. Arriving in the Gordon-Bennett, we transported the Expedition across, and then our labours ended at 5 P.M. for the day.

Itsi of Ntamo had informed us there were only three cataracts, which he called the "Child," the "Mother," and the "Father." The "Child" was a two hundred yards' stretch of broken water; and the "Mother," consisting of half a mile of dangerous rapids, we had succeeded in passing, and had pushed beyond it by crossing the upper branch of the Gordon-Bennett, which was an impetuous stream, 75 yards wide, with big cataracts of its own higher up. But the "Father" is the wildest stretch of river that I have ever seen. Take a strip of sea blown over by a hurricane, four miles in length and half a mile in breadth, and a pretty accurate conception of its leaping waves may be obtained. Some of the troughs were 100 yards in length, and from one to the other the mad river plunged. There was first a rush down into the bottom of an immense trough, and then, by its sheer force, the enormous volume would lift itself upward steeply until, gathering itself into a ridge, it suddenly hurled itself 20 or 30 feet straight upward, before rolling down into another trough. If I looked up or down along this angry scene, every interval of 50 or 100 yards of it was marked by wave-towers—their collapse into foam and spray, the mad clash of watery hills, bounding mounds and heaving billows, while the base of either bank, consisting of a long line of piled boulders of massive size, was buried in the tempestuous surf. The roar was tremendous and deafening. I can only compare it to the thunder of an express train through a rock tunnel. To speak to my neighbour, I had to bawl in his ear.

The most powerful ocean steamer, going at full speed on this portion of the river, would be as helpless as a cockle-boat. I attempted three times, by watching some tree floated down from above, to ascertain the rate of the wild current, by observing the time it occupied in passing between two given points, from which I estimate it to be about thirty miles an hour!

Mar. 17.—On the 17th, after cutting brushwood and laying it over a path of 800 yards in length, we crossed from the upper branch of the Gordon-Bennett to the lower branch, which was of equal breadth, but 20 feet below it. This enabled us the next day to float down to the confluence of the lower branch with the Livingstone. We could do no more on this day; the people were fainting from lack of food.

Mar. 18.—On the 18th, through the goodwill of Mankoneh, the chief of the Bateké, we were enabled to trade with the aborigines, a wild and degraded tribe, subsisting principally on fish and cassava. A goat was not to be obtained at any price, and for a chicken they demanded a gun! Cassava, however, was abundant.

From the confluence we formed another brush-covered road, and hauled the canoes over another 800 yards into a creek, which enabled us to reach, on the 20th, a wide sand-bar that blocked its passage into the great river. The sand-bar, in its turn, enabled us to reach the now moderated stream, below the influence of the roaring "Father," and to proceed by towing and punting half a mile below to an inlet in the rocky shore.

Gampa, the young chief of this district, became very friendly, and visited us each day with small gifts of cassava bread, a few bananas, and a small gourd of palm-wine.

Mar. 21.—On the 21st and the two days following we were engaged in hauling our vessels overland, a distance of three-quarters of a mile, over a broad rocky point, into a bay-like formation. Gampa and his people nerved us to prosecute our labours by declaring that there was only one

VIEW OF THE RIGHT BRANCH, FIRST CATARACT, OF THE LIVINGSTONE FALLS, FROM FOUR MILES BELOW JUEMBA ISLAND.

[To face page 262.

small cataract below. Full of hope, we halted on the 24th to rest the wearied people, and in the meantime to trade for food.

Mar. 25.—The 25th saw us at work at dawn in a bad piece of river, which is significantly styled the "Cauldron." Our best canoe, 75 feet long, 3 feet wide, by 21 inches deep, the famous *London Town*, commanded by Manwa Sera, was torn from the hands of fifty men, and swept away in the early morning down to destruction. In the afternoon, the *Glasgow*, parting her cables, was swept away, drawn nearly into mid-river, returned up river half a mile, again drawn into the depths, ejected into a bay near where Frank was

OVER ROCKY POINT CLOSE TO GAMPA'S.

camped, and, to our great joy, finally recovered. Accidents were numerous; the glazed trap rocks, washed by the ever-rising tidal-like waves, were very slippery, occasioning dangerous falls to the men. One man dislocated his shoulder, another was bruised on the hips, and another had a severe contusion of the head. Too careless of my safety in my eagerness and anxiety, I fell down, feet first, into a chasm 30 feet deep between two enormous boulders, but fortunately escaped with only a few rib bruises, though for a short time I was half stunned.

Mar. 27.—On the 27th we happily succeeded in passing the fearful Cauldron, but during our last efforts the *Crocodile*, 85 feet 3 inches long, was swept away into the centre of the Cauldron, heaved upward, whirled round with quick gyrations, and finally shot into the bay north of Rocky Island, where it was at last secured. The next day we dropped down stream, and reached the western end of the bay above Rocky Island Falls.

Leaving Frank Pocock as usual in charge of the camp and goods, I mustered ninety men—most of the others being stiff from wounds received in the fight at Mwana Ibaka and other places—and proceeded, by making a wooden tramway with sleepers and rollers, to pass Rocky Island Falls. Mpwapwa and Shumari, of the boat's crew, were sent to explore meanwhile, for another inlet or recess in the right bank. By 2 P.M. we were below the falls, and my two young men had returned, reporting that a mile or so below there was a fine camp, with a broad strip of sand lining a bay. This animated us to improve the afternoon hours by attempting to reach it. The seventeen canoes now left to us were manned according to their capacity. As I was about to embark in my boat to lead the way, I turned to the people to give my last instructions—which were, to follow me, clinging to the right bank, and by no means to venture into mid-river into the current. While delivering my instructions, I observed Kalulu in the *Crocodile*, which was made out of the *Bassia Parkii* tree, a hard heavy wood, but admirable for canoes. When I asked him what he wanted in the canoe, he replied, with a deprecating smile and an expostulating tone, "I can pull, sir; see!" "Ah, very well," I answered.

The boat-boys took their seats, and, skirting closely the cliffy shore, we rowed down stream, while I stood in the bow of the boat, guiding the coxswain, Uledi, with my hand. The river was not more than 450 yards wide; but one cast of the sounding-lead close to the bank obtained a depth of 138 feet. The river was rapid, with certainly a 7-knot current, with a smooth greasy surface, now and then an eddy, a gurgle, and gentle heave, but not dangerous to people in possession of their wits. In a very few moments we had descended the mile stretch, and before us, 600 yards off, roared the furious falls since distinguished by the name "Kalulu."

With a little effort we succeeded in rounding the point and entering the bay above the falls, and reaching a pretty camping-place on a sandy beach. The first, second, and third canoes arrived soon after me, and I was beginning to congratulate myself on having completed a good day's work, when to my horror I saw the *Crocodile* in mid-river far below

AT WORK PASSING THE LOWER END OF THE FIRST CATARACT OF THE LIVINGSTONE FALLS, NEAR LOCKY ISLAND.

[To face page 264.

the point which we had rounded, gliding with the speed of an arrow towards the falls over the treacherous calm water. Human strength availed nothing now, and we watched it in agony, for I had three favourites in her—Kalulu, Mauredi, and Ferajji; and of the others, two, Rehani Makua and Wadi Jumah, were also very good men. It soon reached the island which cleft the falls, and was swept down the left branch. We saw it whirled round three or four times, then plunged down into the depths, out of which the stern presently emerged pointed upward, and we knew then that Kalulu and his canoe-mates were no more.

DEATH OF KALULU.

Fast upon this terrible catastrophe, before we could begin to bewail their loss, another canoe with two men in it darted past the point, borne by irresistibly on the placid but swift current to apparent, nay, almost certain destruction. I despatched my boat's crew up along the cliffs to warn the forgetful people that in mid-stream was certain death, and shouted out commands for the two men to strike for the left shore. The steersman by a strange chance shot his canoe over the falls, and, dexterously edging his canoe towards the left shore a mile below, he and his companion contrived to spring ashore and were saved. As we observed them clamber over the rocks to approach a point opposite us, and finally sit down, regarding us in silence across the river, our pity and love gushed strong towards them, but we could utter nothing of it. The roar of the falls completely mocked and overpowered the feeble human voice.

Before the boat's crew could well reach the descending canoes, the boulders being very large and offering great obstacles to rapid progress, a third canoe—but a small and light one—with only one man, the brave lad Soudi, who escaped from the spears of the Wanyaturu assassins in 1875, darted by, and cried out, as he perceived himself to be drifting helplessly towards the falls, "La il Allah, il Allah" (There is but one God), "I am lost, Master!" He was then seen to address himself to what fate had in store for him. We watched him for a few moments, and then saw him drop. Out of the shadow of the fall he presently emerged, dropping from terrace to terrace, precipitated down, then whirled round, caught by great heavy waves, which whisked him to right and left, and struck madly at him, and yet his canoe did not sink, but he and it were swept behind the lower end of the island, and then darkness fell upon the day of horror. Nine men lost in one afternoon!

This last accident, I was told, was caused by the faithlessness of the crew. One man, utterly unnerved by his fear of the river, ran away and hid in the bushes; the two others lost their hold of the tow-ropes, and thus their comrade was carried into the swift centre.

Mar. 30.—On the 30th of March a messenger was despatched to Frank to superintend the transport of the goods overland to where I had arrived with the boat. The natives continued to be very amiable, and food was abundant and cheap. They visited our camp from morning to night, bringing their produce from a great distance. They are a very gentle and harmless tribe the Western Bateké, and distinguishable by four cicatrices down each cheek. They are also remarkable for their numerous bird-snares—bird lime being furnished by the *Ficus sycamorus*—and traps. About sunset a wide-spreading flock of large birds like parrots passed north-east over our camp, occupying nearly half an hour in passing. They were at too great an altitude to be recognized. Lead-coloured water-snakes were very numerous, the largest being about 7 feet in length and 2½ inches in diameter.

Confined within the deep narrow valley of the river, the hills rising to the height of about 800 feet above us, and exposed to the continued uproar of the river, we became almost stunned during our stay of the 31st.

April 1.—On the 1st of April we cleared the Kalulu Falls, and camped on the right bank below them. Our two absentees on the left side had followed us, and were signalling frequently to us, but we were helpless. The next day we descended a mile and a half of rapids, and in the passage one more canoe was lost, which reduced our flotilla to thirteen vessels.

About 2 P.M., to the general joy, appeared young Soudi and our two absentees, who the day before had been signalling us from the opposite side of the river!

Soudi's adventures had been very strange. He had been swept down over the upper and lower Kalulu Falls and the intermediate rapids, and had been whirled round so often that he became confused. "But clinging to my canoe," he said, "the wild river carried me down and down, and down from place to place, sometimes near a rock, and sometimes near the middle of the stream, until an hour after dark, when I saw it was near a rock; I jumped out, and, catching my canoe, drew it on shore. I had scarcely finished when my arms were seized, and I was bound by two men, who hurried me up to the top of the mountain, and then for an hour over the high land, until we came to a village. They then pushed me into a house, where they lit a fire, and when it was bright they stripped me naked and examined me. Though I pretended not to understand them, I knew enough to know that they were proud of their prize. They spoke kindly to me, and gave me plenty to eat; and while one of them slept, the other watched sharp lest I should run away. In the morning it was rumoured over the village that a handsome slave was captured from a strange tribe, and many people came to see me, one of whom had seen us at Ntamo and recognized me. This man immediately charged the two men with having stolen one of the white man's men, and he drew such a picture of you, master, with large eyes of fire and long hair, who owned a gun that shot all day, that all the people became frightened, and compelled the two men to take me back to where they had found me. They at once returned me my clothes, and brought me to the place near where I had tied my canoe. They then released me, saying, 'Go to your king: here is food for you; and do not tell him what we have done to you; but tell him you met friends who saved you, and it shall be well with us.'"

The other two men, seeking for means to cross the river, met Soudi sitting by his canoe. The three became so encouraged at one another's presence that they resolved to cross the river rather than endure further anxiety in a strange land. Despair gave them courage, and though the river was rapid, they succeeded in crossing a mile below the place they had started from, without accident.

April 3.—On the 3rd of April we descended another mile and a half of dangerous rapids, during which several accidents occurred. One canoe was upset which contained fifty tusks of ivory and a sack of beads. Four men had narrow escapes from drowning, but Uledi, my coxswain, saved them. I myself tumbled headlong into a small basin, and saved myself with difficulty from being swept away by the receding tide.

Our system of progress was to begin each day with Frank leading the Expedition overland to a camp at the head of some inlet, cove, or recess, near rapids or falls, where, with the older men, women, and children, he constructed a camp; the working party, consisting of the younger men, returning to assist me with the canoes down to the new camp. Anxious for the safety of the people, I superintended the river work myself, and each day led the way in the boat. On approaching rapids I selected three or four of the boat's crew (and always Uledi, the coxswain), and clambered along the great rocks piled along the base of the steeply sloping hills, until I had examined the scene. If the rapids or fall were deemed impassable by water, I planned the shortest and safest route across the projecting points, and then, mustering the people, strewed a broad track with bushes, over which, as soon as completed, we set to work to haul our vessels beyond the dangerous water, when we lowered them into the water, and pursued our way to camp, where Frank would be ready to give me welcome, and such a meal as the country afforded.

At Gamfwé's the natives sold us abundance of bread, or rolls of pudding, of cassava flour, maize, cassava leaves, water-cresses, and a small Strychnos fruit and, for the first time, lemons. Fowls were very dear, and a goat was too expensive a luxury in our now rapidly impoverishing state.

April 8.—On the 8th we descended from Gamfwé's to "Whirlpool Narrows," opposite Umvilingya. When near there we perceived that the eddy tides, which rushed up river along the bank, required very delicate and skilful manœuvring. I experimented on the boat first, and attempted to haul her by cables round a rocky point from the bay near Whirlpool Narrows. Twice they snapped ropes and cables, and the second time the boat flew up river, borne on the crests of brown waves, with only Uledi and two men in her. Presently she wheeled into the bay, following the course of the eddy, and Uledi brought her in-shore. The third time we tried the operation with six cables of twisted rattan, about 200 feet in length, with five men to each cable. The rocks rose singly in precipitous masses 50 feet above the river, and this extreme height increased the difficulty and rendered footing precarious, for furious eddies of past pages had drilled deep circular pits, like ovens, in them, 4, 6, even 10 feet deep. However, with the utmost patience we succeeded in rounding these enormous blocks, and hauling the boat against the uneasy eddy tide to where the river resumed its natural downward flow. Below this, as I learned, were some two miles of boisterous water; but mid-river, though foaming in places, was not what we considered dangerous. We therefore resolved to risk it in mid-stream, and the boat's crew, never backward when they knew what lay in front of them, manned the boat, and in fifteen minutes we had taken her into a small creek near Umvilingya's landing, which ran up river between a ridge of rocks and the right bank. This act instilled courage into the canoe-men, and the boat-boys having voluntered to act as steersmen, with Frank as leader, all manned the canoes next morning, and succeeded in reaching my camp in good time without accident, though one canoe was taken within 200 yards of Round Island Falls, between Isameh's and Umvilingya's.

At this place Frank and I treated ourselves to a pig, which we purchased from the chief Umvilingya for four cloths, we having been more than two weeks without meat.

April 10.—On the 10th, having, because of illness, entrusted the boat to Manwa Sera and Uledi, they managed to get her jammed between two rocks near the entrance to Gavubu's Cove, and, as the after-section was sunk for a time, it appeared that the faithful craft would be lost here after her long and wonderful journey. Springing from my bed upon hearing of the threatened calamity, I mustered twenty active men and hastened to the scene, and soon, by inspiring every man to do his best, we were able to lift her out of her dangerous position, and take her to camp apparently uninjured.

April 11.—The lower end of Gavubu's Cove was reached on the 11th, and the next day by noon the land party and canoes were taken safely to the lower end of Gamfwé's Bay. As our means were rapidly diminishing in this protracted struggle we maintained against the natural obstacles to our journey, we could only hope to reach the sea by resolute and continual industry during every hour of daylight. I accordingly instructed the canoe-men to be ready to follow me, as soon as they should be informed by a messenger that the boat had safely arrived in camp.

The commencement of "Lady Alice Rapids" was marked by a broad fall, and an interruption to the rapidly rushing river by a narrow ridgy islet of great rocks, which caused the obstructed stream to toss its waters in lateral waves against the centre, where they met waves from the right bank, and overlapping formed a lengthy dyke of foaming water.

Strong cane cables were lashed to the bow and stern, and three men were detailed to each, while five men assisted me in the boat. A month's experience of this kind of work had made us skilful and bold. But the rapids were more powerful, the river was much more contracted, and the impediments were greater than usual. On our right was an upright wall of massive boulders terminating in a narrow terrace 300 feet high; behind the terrace, at a little distance, rose the rude hills to the height of 1200 feet above the river; above the hills rolled the table-land. On our left, 400 yards from the bouldery wall, rose a lengthy and stupendous cliff line topped by a broad belt of forest, and at its base rose three rocky islets, one below another, against which the river dashed itself, disparting with a roaring surge.

We had scarcely ventured near the top of the rapids when, by a careless slackening of the stern cable, the current swept the boat from the hands of that portion of her crew whose duty it was to lower her carefully and cautiously down the fall, to the narrow line of ebb flood below the rocky projection. Away into the centre of the angry, foaming, billowy stream the boat darted, dragging one man into the maddened flood, to whom, despite our awful position, I was able to lend a hand and lift into the boat.

"Oars, my boys, and be steady! Uledi, to the helm!" were all the instructions I was able to shout, after which, standing at the bow of the boat, I guided the coxswain with my hand; for now, as we rode downwards furiously on the crests of the proud waves, the human voice was weak against the overwhelming thunder of the angry river. Oars were only useful to assist the helm, for we were flying at a terrific speed past the series of boulders which strangled the river. Never did the rocks assume such hardness, such solemn grimness and bigness, never were they invested with such terrors and such grandeur of height, as while we were the cruel sport and prey of the brown-black waves, which whirled us round like a spinning top, swung us aside, almost engulfed us in the rapidly subsiding troughs, and then hurled us upon the white, rageful crests of others. Ah! with what feelings we regarded this awful power which the great river had now developed! How we cringed under its imperious, compelling, and irresistible force! What lightning retrospects we cast upon our past lives! How impotent we felt before it!

"La il Allah, il Allah!" screamed young Mabruki. "We are lost!—yes, we are lost!"

After two miles we were abreast of the bay, or indentation, at which we had hoped to camp, but the strong river mocked our efforts to gain it. The flood was resolved we should taste the bitterness of death. A sudden rumbling noise, like the deadened sound of an earthquake, caused us to look below, and we saw the river heaved bodily upward, as though a volcano was about to belch around us. Up to the summit of this watery mound we were impelled; and then, divining what was about to take place, I shouted out, "Pull, men, for your lives!" A few frantic strokes drove us to the lower side of the mound, and before it had finished subsiding, and had begun its usual fatal circling, we were precipitated over a small fall, and sweeping down towards the inlet into which the Nkenké Cataract tumbled, below the lowest lines of breakers of the Lady Alice Rapids. Once or twice we were flung scornfully aside, and spun around contemptuously, as though we were too insignificant to be wrecked; then, availing ourselves of a calm moment, we resumed our oars, and soon entering the ebb-tide, rowed up river and reached the sandy beach at the junction of the Nkenké with the Livingstone. Arriving on shore, I despatched Uledi and young Shumari to run to meet the despairing people above, who had long before this been alarmed by the boat-boys, whose carelessness had brought about this accident, and by the sympathizing natives who had seen us, as they reported, sink in the whirlpools. In about an hour a straggling line of anxious souls appeared; and all that love of life and living things, with the full sense of the worth of living, returned to my heart, as my faithful followers rushed up one after another with their exuberant welcome to life which gushed out of them in gesture, feature, and voice. And Frank, my amiable and trusty Frank, was neither last nor least in his professions of love and sympathy, and gratitude to Him who had saved us from a watery grave.

The land party then returned with Frank to remove the goods to our new camp, and by night my tent was pitched within a hundred yards of the cataract mouth of the Nkenké. We had four cataracts in view of us: the great river which emptied itself into the bay-like expanse from the last line of the Lady Alice Rapids; two miles below, the river fell again, in a foamy line of waves; from the tall cliffs south of us tumbled a river 400 feet into the great river; and on our right, 100 yards off, the Nkenké rushed down steeply like an enormous cascade from the height of 1000 feet. The noise of the Nkenké torrent resembled the roar of an express train over an iron bridge; that of Cataract River, taking its 400-feet leap from the cliffs, was like the rumble of distant thunder; the "Lady Alice's" last line of breakers, and its fuming and fretting flanks, was heard only as the swash of waves against a ship's prow when driven by a spanking breeze against a cross sea; while the cataract below lent its dull boom to swell the chorus of angry and falling rivers, which filled our ears with their terrific uproar.

Very different was this scene of towering cliffs and lofty mountain walls, which daily discharged the falling streams from the vast uplands above and buried us within the deafening chasm, to that glassy flow of the Livingstone by the black eerie forests of Usongora Meno and Kasera, and through the upper lands of the cannibal Wenya, where a single tremulous wave was a rarity. We now, surrounded by the daily terrors and hope-killing shocks of these apparently endless cataracts, and the loud boom of their baleful fury, remembered, with regretful hearts, the Sabbath stillness and dreamy serenity of those days. Beautiful was it then to glide among the lazy creeks of the spicy and palm-growing isles, where the broad-leafed Amomum vied in greenness with the drooping fronds of the Phrynium, where the myrrh and bdellium shrubs exhaled their fragrance side

THE NKENKÉ RIVER ENTERING THE LIVINGSTONE BELOW THE LADY ALICE RAPIDS.

by side with the wild cassia, where the capsicum with its red-hot berries rose in embowering masses, and the Ipomœa's purple buds gemmed with colour the tall stem of some sturdy tree. Environed by most dismal prospects, for ever dinned by terrific sound, at all points confronted by the most hopeless outlook, we think that an Eden which we have left behind, and this a watery hell wherein we now are.

Though our involuntary descent of the Lady Alice Rapids from Gamfwé's Bay to Nkenké River Bay—a distance of three miles—occupied us but fifteen minutes, it was a work of four days, viz. from the 13th to the 16th inclusive, to lower the canoes by cables. Experience of the vast force of the flood, and the brittleness of the rattan cables, had compelled us to fasten eight cables to each canoe, and to detail five men to each cable for the passage of the rapids. Yet, with all our precautions, almost each hour was marked with its special accident to man or canoe. One canoe, with a man named Nubi in it, was torn from the hands of forty men, swept down two miles, and sunk in the great whirlpool. Nubi clung to his vessel, until taken down a second time, when he and the canoe were ejected fifty yards apart, but being an expert swimmer he regained it in the Nkenké basin, and astride of its keel was circling round with the strong ebb tide, when he was saved by the dashing Uledi and his young brother Shumari.

While returning to my labours along the bouldery heap which lined the narrow terrace opposite the islets, I observed another canoe, which contained the chief Wadi Rehani and two of my boat-bearers, Chiwonda and Muscati, drifting down helplessly near the verge of some slack water. The three men were confused, and benumbed with terror at the roar and hissing of the rapids. Being comparatively close to them, on the edge of a high crag, I suddenly shot out my voice with the full power of my lungs, in sharp, quick accents of command to paddle ashore, and the effect was wonderful. It awoke them like soldiers to the call of duty, and after five minutes' energetic use of their paddles they were saved. I have often been struck at the power of a quick, decisive tone. It appears to have an electric effect, riding rough-shod over all fears, indecision, and tremor, and, just as in this instance, I had frequently up river, when the people were inclined to get panic-stricken, or to despair, restored them to a sense of duty by affecting the sharp-cutting, steel-like, and imperious tone of voice, which seemed to be as much of a compelling power as powder to a bullet. But it should be remembered that a too frequent use of it spoils its effect.

April 18.—On the 18th we descended from Nkenké Bay to a lengthy indentation behind two islands above Msumbula. In shooting the rapids one canoe was wrecked, but fortunately a large canoe which had been lost up river was recovered by paying a small present to the amiable Bateké fishermen. At this camp we discovered that our people were

"LADY ALICE" OVER THE FALLS.

[To face page 274

robbing me in the most shameless manner, and I was indebted for this discovery to Frank, whose duty as camp-keeper and leader of the land party gave him opportunities for detecting the rapid diminution of our stores. A search was instituted without warning, and a hundredweight or two of purloined beads and shells were discovered. The boldest thief, fearing punishment, absconded, and never returned.

April 19, 21.—The next day, after Frank had transported the goods and moved his party to a new camp, we descended two miles of dangerous rapids and whirlpools, and on the 20th I led the way in my boat and proceeded a distance of four miles, forming camp behind some small islets, near which the river expanded to a width of about eight hundred yards. By three in the afternoon the land party had also arrived. On the 21st we dropped down, without difficulty, a distance of two miles, and camped for the first time in Babwendé territory.

Nsangu, a village of the Basessé, was opposite, crowning with its palms and fields a hilly terrace, projected from the mountain range, at whose richly wooded slopes or cliffy front, based with a long line of great boulders, we each day looked from the right bank of the river. The villagers sent a deputation to us with palm-wine and a small gift of cassava tubers. Upon asking them if there were any more cataracts they replied that there was only one, and they exaggerated it so much that the very report struck terror and dismay into our people. They described it as falling from a height greater than the position on which their village was situated, which drew exclamations of despair from my followers. I, on the other hand, rather rejoiced at this, as I believed it might be "Tuckey's Cataract," which seemed to be eternally receding as we advanced. While the Bateké above had constantly held out flattering prospects of "only one more" cataract, I had believed that one to be Tuckey's Cataract, because map-makers have laid down a great navigable reach of river between Tuckey's upper cataract and the Yellala Falls—hence our object in clinging to the river, despite all obstacles, until that ever-receding cataract was reached.

The distance we had laboured through from the 16th of March to the 21st of April inclusive, a period of thirty-seven days, was only 34 miles! Since the Basessé fishermen, "who ought to know" we said, declared there was only this tremendous cataract, with a fall of several hundred feet, below us, we resolved to persevere until we had passed it.

April 22, 23.—During the 22nd and 23rd we descended from opposite Nsangu, a distance of five miles, to below Rocky Island Falls, and during the three following days we were engaged in the descent of a six-mile stretch, which enabled us to approach the "terrific" falls described by the Basessé at Nsangu. Arriving at camp with my canoe party, I instantly took my boat's crew and explored the ground. The "Falls" are called Inkisi, or the "Charm"; they have no clear drop, but the river, being forced through a chasm only 500 yards wide, is flanked by curling waves of destructive fury, which meet in the centre, overlap, and strike each other, while below is an absolute chaos of mad waters, leaping waves, deep troughs, contending watery ridges, tumbling and tossing for a distance of two miles. The commencement of this gorge is a lengthy island which seems to have been a portion or slice of the table-land fallen flat, as it were, from a height of 1000 feet. More geologically speaking, it is a mile-long fragment of the gneissic substructure of the table-land which appears to have suddenly subsided, retaining its original horizontal stratification. On the sides, however, the heaps of ruin, thick slabs, and blocks of trap rock bear witness to that sudden collapsing from beneath which undoubtedly formed this chasm.

The natives above Inkisi descended from their breezy homes on the table-land to visit the strangers. They were burning to know what we intended to do to extricate ourselves from the embarrassing position in which we found ourselves before these falls. I had already explored the ground personally twice over, and had planned a dozen ways to get over the tremendous obstacle. I had also ascended to the table-land to take a more general view of the situation. Before replying to their questions, I asked if there was another cataract below. "No," said they, "at least only a little one, which you can pass without trouble."

"Ah," thought I to myself, "this great cataract then must be Tuckey's Cataract, and the 'little one,' I suppose, was too contemptible an affair to be noticed, or perhaps it was covered over by high water, for map-makers have a clear, wide—three miles wide—stream to the falls of Yellala. Good! I will haul my canoes up the mountain and pass over the table-land, as I must now cling to this river to the end, having followed it so long."

My resolution was soon communicated to my followers, who looked perfectly blank at the proposition. The natives heard me, and, seeing the silence and reluctance of the people, they asked the cause, and I told them it was because I intended to drag our vessels up the mountain.

"Up the mountain!" they repeated, turning their eyes towards the towering height, which was shagged with trees and bristling with crags and hill fragments, with an unspeakable look of horror. They appeared to fancy the world was coming to an end, or some unnatural commotion would take place, for they stared at me with lengthened faces. Then, without a word, they climbed the stiff ascent of 1200 feet, and securing their black pigs, fowls, or goats in their houses, spread the report far and wide that the white man intended to fly his canoes over the mountains.

On the other hand, the amiable Basessé, on the left table-land across the river, had gathered in hundreds on the cliffs overlooking the Inkisi Falls, in expectation of seeing a catastrophe, which certainly would have been worth seeing had we been so suicidally inclined as to venture over the falls in our canoes—for that undoubtedly was their idea. It was strange with what poor wits the aborigines of these new and exhumed regions credited us. These people believed we should be guilty of this last freak of madness just as the Wana Mpungu believed we should blindly stumble into their game-nets, and the Wy-yanzi of Chumbiri believed that, having been cheated out of 300 dollars' worth of goods, we should, upon the mere asking, be cheated again. Indeed, I observe that, wherever I go, savage and civilized man alike are too apt to despise each other at first, and that, when finally awakened to some sense of consideration for each other, they proceed to the other extreme, and invest one another with more attributes than they really possess.

Having decided upon the project, it only remained to make a road and to begin, but in order to obtain the assistance of the aborigines, which I was anxious for in order to relieve my people from much of the fatigue, the first day all hands were mustered for road making. Our numerous axes, which we had purchased in Manyema and in Uregga, came into very efficient use now, for, by night, a bush-strewn path 1500 yards in length had been constructed.

April 26.—By 8 A.M. of the 26th our exploring-boat and a small canoe were on the summit of the table-land at a new camp we had formed. As the feat was performed without ostentation and, it need not be told, without any unnatural commotion or event—the pigs had not been frightened, the fowls had not cackled uneasily, goats had not disappeared, women had not given birth to monsters—the native chiefs were in a state of agreeable wonder and complimentary admiration of our industry suitable for the commencement of negotiations, and after an hour's "talk" and convivial drinking of palm-wine they agreed, for a gift of forty cloths, to bring six hundred men to assist us to haul up the monster canoes we possessed, two or three of which were of heavy teak, over 70 feet in length, and weighing over three tons. A large number of my men were then detailed to cut rattan canes as a substitute for ropes, and as many were brittle and easily broken, this involved frequent delays. Six men under Kachéché were also despatched overland to a distance of ten miles to explore the river, and to prepare the natives for our appearance.

April 28.—By the evening of the 28th all our vessels were safe on the highest part of the table-land. Having become satisfied that all was going well in camp, and that Manwa Sera and his men were capable of superintending it, with the aid of the natives, I resolved to take Frank and the boat's crew, women, and children, and goods of the Expedition, to the frontier of Nzabi, and establish a camp near the river, at a point where we should again resume our toil in the deep defile through which the mighty river stormed along its winding course.

The Babwendé natives were exceeding friendly, even more so than the amiable Bateké. Gunpowder was abundant with them, and every male capable of carrying a gun possessed one, often more. Delft ware and British crockery were also observed in their hands, such as plates, mugs, shallow dishes, wash-basins, galvanized iron spoons, Birmingham cutlery, and other articles of European manufacture obtained through the native markets, which are held in an open space between each district. For example, Nzabi district holds a market on a Monday, and Babwendé from Zinga, Mowa farther down, and Inkisi, and Basessé, from across the river attend, as there is a ferry below Zinga, and articles such as European salt, gunpowder, guns, cloth, crockery, glass, and iron ware, of which the currency consists, are bartered for produce such as ground-nuts, palm-oil, palm-nuts, palm-wine, cassava bread and tubers, yams, maize, sugar-cane, beans, native earthenware, onions, lemons, bananas, guavas, sweet limes, pine-apples, black pigs, goats, fowls, eggs, ivory, and a few slaves, who are generally Bateké or Northern Basundi. On Tuesday the district above Inkisi Falls holds its market, at which Mowa, Nzabi, and the district above Inkisi attend. On Wednesday the Umvilingya, Lemba, and Nsangu districts hold a market. On Thursday most of the Babwendé cross the river over to Nsangu, and the Basessé have the honour of holding a market on their own soil. On Friday the market is again held at Nzabi, and the series runs its course in the same order. Thus, without trading caravans or commercial expeditions, the aborigines of these districts are well supplied with almost all they require without the trouble and danger of proceeding to the coast. From district to district, market to market, and hand to hand, European fabrics and wares are conveyed along both sides of the rivers, and along the paths of traffic, until finally the districts of Ntamo, Nkunda, and Nshasa obtain them. These then man their large canoes and transfer them to Ibaka, Misongo, Chumbiri, and Bolobo, and purchase ivory, and now and then a slave, while Ibaka, Misongo, Chumbiri, and Bolobo transport the European fabrics and wares to Irebu, Mompurengi, Ubangi, and Ikengo, and Ikengo conveys them to the fierce Bangala, and the Bangala to the Marunja, Mpakiwana, Urangi, Rubunga in Nganza Gunji, and finally to Upoto—the present ultimate reach of anything arriving from the west coast. By this mode of traffic a keg of powder landed at Funta, Ambriz, Ambrizette, or Kinsembo, requires about five years to reach the Bangala. The first musket was landed in Angola in about the latter part of the fifteenth century, for Diogo Cão only discovered the mouth of the Congo in 1485. It has taken 390 years for four muskets to arrive at Rubunga in Nganza, 965 miles from Point de Padrão, where Diogo Cão erected his memorial column in honour of the discovery of the Congo.

We discovered cloth to be so abundant amongst the Babwendé that it was against our conscience to purchase even a fowl, for naturally the nearer we approached civilization cloth became cheaper in value, until finally a fowl cost four yards of our thick sheeting! Frank and I therefore lived upon the same provisions as our people. Our store of sugar had run out in Uregga, our coffee was finished at Vinya Njara, and at Inkisi Falls our tea, alas! alas! came to an end. To guard against contingencies—for I thought it possible that, however desperately we strove to proceed towards the Western Ocean, we might have been compelled to return to Nyangwé—I had left at Nyangwé, in charge of Abed bin Salem, three tins of tea and a few other small things. At this juncture, how we wished for them!

Yet we could have well parted with a large stock of tea, coffee, and sugar in order to obtain a pair of shoes apiece. Though I had kept one pair of worn-out shoes by me, my last new pair had been put on in the jungles of doleful Uregga, and now six weeks' rough wear over the gritty iron and clink-stone, trap, and granite blocks along the river had ground through soles and uppers, until I began to feel anxious. As for Frank, he had been wearing sandals made out of my leather portmanteaus, and slippers out of our gutta-percha pontoon; but climbing over the rocks and rugged steeps wore them to tatters in such quick succession, that it was with the utmost difficulty that I was enabled, by appealing to the pride of the white man, to induce him to persevere in the manufacture of sandals for his own use. Frequently, on suddenly arriving in camp from my wearying labours, I would discover him with naked feet, and would reprove him for shamelessly exposing his white feet to the vulgar gaze of the aborigines! In Europe this would not be considered indelicate, but in barbarous Africa the feet should be covered as much as the body; for there is a small modicum of superiority shown even in clothing the feet. Not only on moral grounds did I urge him to cover his feet, but also for his own comfort and health; for the great cataract gorge and table-land above it, besides abounding in ants, mosquitoes, and vermin, are infested with three dangerous insects, which prey upon the lower limbs of man—the "jigga" from Brazil, the guinea-worm, and an entozoon, which, depositing its eggs in the muscles, produces a number of short, fat worms and severe tumours. I also discovered, from the examples in my camp, that the least abrasion of the skin was likely, if not covered, to result in an ulcer. My own person testified to this, for an injury to the thumb of my left hand, injured by a fall on the rocks at Gamfwé's, had culminated in a painful wound, which I daily cauterized; but though bathed, burned, plastered, and bandaged twice a day, I had been at this time a sufferer for over a month.

At this period we were all extremely liable to disease, for our system was impoverished. Four of my people suffered from chronic dysentery and eight from large and painful ulcers; the itch disease was rabid—about a dozen of the men were fearful objects of its virulence, though they were not incapacited from duty—and there were two victims of a low fever which no medicine seemed to relieve.

In the absence of positive knowledge as to how long we might be toiling in the cataracts, we were all compelled to be extremely economical. Goat and pig meat were such luxuries that we declined to think of them as being possible with our means; tea, coffee, sugar, sardines, were fast receding into the memory-land of past pleasures, and chickens had reached such prices that they were rare in our camp. We possessed one ram from far Uregga, and Mirambo, the black riding-ass—the other two asses had died a few weeks before—but we should have deserved the name of cannibals had we dared to think of sacrificing the pets of the camp. Therefore—by the will of the gods—contentment had to be found in boiled "duff," or cold cassava bread, ground-nuts, or pea-nuts, yams, and green bananas. To make such strange food palatable was an art that we possessed in a higher degree than our poor comrades. They were supplied with the same materials as we ourselves, but the preparation was different. My dark followers simply dried their cassava, and then pounding it made the meal into porridge. Ground-nuts they threw into the ashes, and when sufficiently baked ate them like hungry men.

For me such food was too crude: besides, my stomach, called to sustain a brain and body strained to the utmost by responsibilities, required that some civility should be shown to it. Necessity roused my faculties, and a jaded stomach goaded my inventive powers to a high pitch. I called my faithful cook, told him to clean and wash mortar and pestle for the preparation of a "high art" dish. Frank approached also to receive instructions, so that, in my absence, he might remind Marzouk, the cook, of each particular. First we rinsed in clear cold brook-water from the ravines some choice cassava or manioc tops, and these were placed in the water to be bruised. Marzouk understood this part very well, and soon pounded them to the consistence of a green porridge.

To this I then added fifty shelled nuts of the *Arachis hypogæa*, three small specimens of the *Dioscorea alata* boiled and sliced cold, a tablespoonful of oil extracted from the *Arachis hypogæa*, a tablespoonful of wine of the *Elais Guineensis*, a little salt, and sufficient powdered capsicum. This imposing and admirable mixture was pounded together, fried, and brought into the tent, along with toasted cassava pudding, hot and steaming, on the only Delft plate we possessed. Within a few minutes our breakfast was spread out on the medicine chest which served me for a table, and at once a keen appetite was inspired by the grateful smell of my artful compound. After invoking a short blessing, Frank and I rejoiced our souls and stomachs with the savoury mess, and flattered ourselves that, though British paupers and Sing-Sing convicts might fare better perhaps, thankful content crowned our hermit repast.

CHAPTER XIII.

Glorious timber—Cutting canoes—Frank suffers from ulcers—The episode of the fetished axe—Rain-gauge readings—The rise of the river—"Goee-Gooes"—The *Lady Alice* breached for the first time—A painful discovery: Uledi's theft—His trial and release—The burning of Shakespeare—The bees of Massassa—Local superstitions—Frank's cheery character.

April 29.—On the morning of the 29th of April, after giving the necessary instructions to Manwa Sera and his brother chiefs, and obtaining the promise of the Babwendé elders that they would do their utmost to help in transporting the vessels over the three miles of ground between Inkisi Falls and Nzabi, I led the caravan, loaded with the goods, down to a cove at the upper end of Nzabi. After erecting a rude camp, the more active men were directed to reascend the table-land to their duty, and in the afternoon two men were despatched to the old chief of Nzabi, desiring him to come and visit me. Meanwhile I explored a thick forest of tall trees, that flourished to an immense height along a narrow terrace, and up the steep slopes of Nzabi. For though cliffs were frequent on the left side of the river, a steep wooded slope distinguished the right side, especially along the whole front of Nzabi. As I wandered about among the gigantic trees, the thought struck me that, while the working parties and natives were hauling our vessels a distance of three miles over the table-land, a new canoe might be built to replace one of the nine which had been lost; but in order to obviate any rupture with our new friends, I resolved to wait until the next day, when the subject could be broached to the king.

Meanwhile, with Uledi, the coxswain, young Shumari, his brother, and their cousin Saywa, I went about, tape-line in hand, surveying the glorious timber, and from my note-book I take the following particulars, jotted down during the ramble:—

"Three specimens of cotton-wood. The largest, close to the cove, measured in girth 13 feet 6 inches; trunk unbranched for about 60 feet; its cotton used as tinder by the Babwendé. Eight specimens of the *Bassia Parkii*—or Shea butter-tree; bark rough, and $1\frac{1}{2}$ inch thick; exudes a yellowish-white sticky matter, which my boat-boys called its "milk": splendid timber, core dark and very hard; outside wood from two to three inches deep and whiter, easily worked; largest measured 12 feet round; height of unbranched stem, 55 feet: others measured 10, 11·9, 10 and $10\frac{1}{2}$ feet. Ten specimens of the *Ficus Kotschyana*—or Mku, as Uledi called it; bark half an inch thick; largest, 13 feet in girth. Many specimens of African silver beech, African ash, wild olive, *Zygia* sp., or Mkundi—largest, 24 feet circumferential measurement—acacia, catechu (?), *Grewia* sp., Mkuma; good timber tree, for small canoes. A glorious *Tamarindus Indica*, with amplitude of crown branching far, and dense; 9 feet round. Several specimens of Rubiaceæ and Sterculiaceæ, candleberry-tree, the *Lophira alata*, Balsomodendrons, *Landolphia florida* (?), an india-rubber-producing creeper in very large numbers. Proteas, several Loranthaceæ, ivory button or nut-trees, wild betel, *Anacardium occidentale*, or cashew-tree, cola-nut-tree, wild mango-tree, *Jatropha curcas* (physic-nut tree), Kigelias, several *Acacia Arabicas* near the river, within a few feet of the cove, and other gums. *Euphorbia antiquorum* and *E. Caput-Medusæ* on the craggy ground above the cove. Orchids upon humus-covered granite fragments, and far aloft in the forks of trees; as well as several species of ferns and aloes, and wild pine-apples upon the rock-strewn slopes."

Though there were a number of large and noble trees to choose from, I fixed upon a species of Burseraceæ, Boswellia, or gum-frankincense tree, 10 feet round at the base, and with 40 feet of branchless stem, which grew about a hundred yards from our camp. We "blazed" very many of the largest species with our hatchets, in order to discover the most suitable for lightness and softness, with sufficient strength, and the "ubani" or "lubani" as the Wangwana called it was pronounced the best. I discovered that the largest trees grew on the narrow terrace, which was from one hundred to two hundred yards wide, and about forty feet above the river; but this Boswellia grew about fifty yards above the terrace on the slope; from this the slope rose to the height of 1000 feet, at an angle of 45°, densely covered along its whole length with magnificent timber.

April 30.—The next day the chief came. He was a fine genial old man, bald-headed and jovial-featured; and would have made an admirable Uncle Tom. It was not long before we perfectly understood each other. He gave me permission to choose any of the largest trees in his country, and promised to visit me each day while in the cove. Meanwhile, as an earnest of his friendship, he begged my acceptance of a gourdful of palm-wine, and some ripe plantains, guavas, and papaws.

May 1.—On the 1st May, Uledi, with a cry of "Bismillah!" at the first blow, struck his axe into the tree, and two others chimed in, and in two hours, with a roaring crash which made the deep gorge of the river return a thundering echo, the ubani fell; but, alas! it fell across a gigantic granite rock, about thirty feet square. And then began the work of rolling the great tree by means of enormous levers, with cables of ficus attached to the end, and the suspended weight of fifteen people, and by noon, to the astonishment of the natives, it was lengthways along the ground. I measured out the log, 37 feet 5 inches; depth, 2 feet; breadth, 2 feet 8 inches, and out of this we carved the *Stanley* canoe, in place of the unfortunate *Stanley* which had been irretrievably lost on the 1st of April. In order to ensure both speed and systematic work, each of the boat's crew, who were now converted into shipbuilders, was allotted $3\frac{1}{2}$ feet as his share, with a promise of reward proportionate to the skill and energy which he displayed. It was refreshing to see, during the whole time he was employed on it, how Uledi swung his axe like a proficient workman who loved his work. He never gave a half-hearted stroke, but drove his axe into the tree with a vigour which was delightful to regard, eliciting the admiration of the aborigines, who would stand round us for hours wondering at the fact that there lived a man who could thus lend every fibre of his body to mere work, and was an enthusiast to duty. On the 8th the canoe was finished, except for a few finishing touches, which were entrusted to the chief carpenter of the Expedition, Salaam Allah.

Having yet a few days to spare, we cut another huge tree down—a teak—to replace the little *Jason* that Soudi Turu had lost at Kalulu Falls, which occupied us until the 16th, with fifteen men employed. It measured, when completed, 45 feet long, 2 feet 2 inches beam, and 18 inches deep, and was flat-bottomed, after the model of the Wy-yanzi canoes.

May 15.—In the meantime Manwa Sera was steadily advancing each day from 500 to 800 yards, according to the nature of the ground, and by the evening of the 15th was in our camp to receive a hearty meed of praise for the completion of his task. It was singular, however, how quickly the people became demoralized the moment I turned away. The natives brought various complaints of robbery of fowls and spoliation of cassava gardens against them, and one, Saburi

THE NEW CANOES, THE "LIVINGSTONE" AND THE "STANLEY."

Rehani, was a prisoner in their hands, or, in other words, was liable to be sold by them unless redeemed by me. I spent an entire day in the negotiation of his freedom, but finally he was purchased by me for 150 dollars' worth of cloth, which most wofully diminished my stock. Naturally this excessive price paid for the release of a thief drew most energetic threats from me should any crime of this nature be repeated. But my men had borne themselves in the most admirable manner since leaving Uguha, and, after crossing through a furnace of fire side by side with me, it would have been unnatural for me to have judged them very severely. At the same time the evil-dispositioned were not to be allowed to sacrifice the lives of their fellows either by slow hunger or in violent conflicts for their sakes. Frequent redemptions of thieves from the hands of those they had spoliated would at this period have ended in beggary and starvation. It was therefore explained, for the fiftieth time, that persons arrested by the natives while in the act of stealing would be left in their hands.

May 16.—During the afternoon of the 16th we embarked the goods, and the canoe-men, skirting the base of the rocky line, descended one mile to Nzabi Creek, which proved a calm haven, separated from the river by a rugged line of massive blocks, and after we had entered by the narrow entrance we obtained a view of the wide mouth of a ravine, which was like a deep indentation in the mountain line. From base to summit the table-land was wooded, and very many noble bombax and straight-shafted teaks rose above the grove in this happy and picturesque mountain fold.

After such a gigantic task as that of hauling the canoes up 1200 feet of a steep slope, and over three miles of ground, and then lowering them 1200 feet into the river again, the people deserved a rest. In the meantime, as absolute idleness would have been subversive of that energy which had to characterize us during this period, we set to work cutting down a teak-tree, and for this job selected forty men, twenty of whom were allotted to Frank for nightwork, and twenty I reserved for a day party. The tree was 13 feet 3 inches in circumference, and when prostrate we possessed a clear branchless log 55 feet in length.

It was at this period that Frank began to be troubled with a small pimple on each foot, and even then he neglected the advice I persisted in giving him to protect them from being tainted by the poisonous fœtor which flies extracted from the exposed sores of the Wangwana. There was one poor fellow in our camp named Feruzi who was now in the seventh month of this virulent disease, and was a frightful object. Both of his feet were almost in a state of mortification, and the leg bones were attacked. That part of the camp devoted to the victims of this ulcerous disease was prudently avoided by the natives, many of whom bore the scars of ancient ulcers. Safeni, my coxswain on the Victoria Nyanza, and who was also the second in rank and influence among the chiefs, adopted a very singular treatment, which I must confess was also wonderfully successful. This medicine consisted of a mixture of powder of copper and child's urine painted over the wound with a feather twice a day.

over which he placed some fine cotton. In six weeks five patients recovered completely. The Babwendé have recourse to green herb poultices, and some of their medicines were sold to us for the sick, but I failed to observe any improvement. One kind, however, which was the powdered core of some tree, appeared to have a soothing effect.

The old chief of Nzabi informed us, to our astonishment that five falls were still below us, which he called Njari Nseto, Njari Kwa Mowa, or river at Mowa, Njari Zinga, or river opposite Zinga, Njari Mbelo, or Mbelo's river, and Njari Suki, or Suki's river, the Babwendé term for river being Njari.

May 18.—On the 18th five of our axes required to be repaired, and Kachéché, who had some days before returned from his explorations below, and confirmed the news given to us by Nzabi's chief, was sent above to the table-land to seek a smithy. As a market-place is like a stock exchange to the natives of this region, most of the blacksmiths were absent, and Kachéché had proceeded for a long distance into the interior, when he came across a tribe north of Nzabi, armed with bows and arrows, and who were called Bizu-Nseké. A few seconds' acquaintance with them sufficed to prove to Kachéché that he had overstepped the boundaries of the peaceable, and accordingly he and his fellows fled for their lives, not unquickened by flying arrows. When almost in despair of discovering a native mechanic, he at last came to a forge between Mowa and Nzabi, the owner of which undertook the job of repairing the axes.

The blacksmith's children were playing about close to the anvil while he was at work, and it happened that a piece of glowing hot iron to be welded to an axe flew off on being struck and seared a child's breast, whereupon the father got into a fearful rage and beat the war-drum, which soon mustered scores of his countrymen prepared for battle, but as yet quite ignorant of the cause. Kachéché, however, was a man of tact, and, knowing himself innocent, folded his hands, and appealed to the good sense of the people. But the angered father averred that the axe was fetish, and that as Kachéché had brought the fetished instrument he was guilty of malevolence, for only the property of an evilly disposed person could have wrought such hurt to an innocent child. While the argument was at its height the chief of Nzabi happily appeared on his way home from Mowa market, and through his influence the affair was compromised by Kachéché promising to pay fifteen cowries extra to the blacksmith. Hearty laughing, a convivial drink all round of palm-wine, hand-shakes, and many terrible stories of fetish wonders dispelled the little black cloud.

May 22.—On the 22nd of May the magnificent teak canoe *Livingstone*, perfectly complete, was launched with the aid of one hundred happy and good-humoured natives, into the Nzabi Creek, in presence of the Nzabi chief and his three wives. In order to prove its capacity we embarked forty-six people, which only brought its gunwales within six inches of the water. Its measurements were 54 feet in length, 2 feet 4 inches deep, and 3 feet 2 inches wide. With the completion of this third canoe, our flotilla now consisted of twelve large canoes and one boat, the whole being of sufficient capacity to transport the Expedition should we ever be fortunate enough in arriving at that "Tuckey's Cataract" of which I was in search.

The rainy days of this season, which began at the change of the fifth moon, were as follows:—

Year	Month	Day	Remarks
1877.	Feb.	24	Short shower.
	,,	27	,,
	,,	28	,, ,,
	March	2	,, ,,
	,,	5	Severe ,,
	,,	7	,, ,,
	,,	8	6 hours.
	,,	9	4 ,,
	April	3	From 2 to 6 hours' showers during the early morning.
	,,	4	
	,,	5	
	,,	6	
	,,	7	
	,,	11	Long showers from the afternoon into the night.
	,,	12	
	,,	13	
	,,	14	
	,,	15	
	,,	16	
	,,	17	
	,,	18	
1877.	April	19	Rain during night.
	,,	20	,, ,, ,,
	,,	21	,, ,, ,,
	,,	23	,, ,, ,,
	,,	25	Severe ,, ,,
	,,	26	,, ,, ,,
	,,	27	,, ,, ,,
	,,	28	,, ,, ,,
	May	1	,, ,, morning.
	,,	3	,, all day.
	,,	4	6 hours.
	,,	10	5 ,,
	,,	15	Noon.
	,,	16	Afternoon.
	,,	17	,,
	,,	19	Night.
	,,	20	,,
	,,	21	4 hours, forenoon.

Between the 15th of November and the 16th of January I recorded thirty-two rainy days, the total rainfall being of 115 hours' duration. Between the 16th of January and the 24th of February no rain fell, but between the 24th of February and the 21st of May there was a total of thirty-nine rainy days. This interval composed the later or greater Masika, or monsoon.

On the 26th of April I observed the river begin to rise, but moving from Inkisi Falls to Nzabi Cove on April the 29th, I had better opportunities of testing the rate of the rise while cutting out my canoe, viz. until the afternoon of the 16th of May.

My notes regarding the rise were as follows:—

1877. April	30	3 inches
May	1	3 "
"	2	4 "
"	3	4 "
"	4	4½ "
"	5	5 "
"	6	5¼ "
"	7	8 "
"	8	9 "
"	9	9 "
"	10	9½ "
"	11	10 "
"	12	11 "
"	13	13 "
"	14	13 "
"	15	12 "
"	16	11½ "
		135¼ "

or 11 feet 3¼ inches within 17 days.

At Nzabi Creek the registered rise was as follows:—

1877. May	17	10 inches.
"	18	10 "
"	19	9 "
"	20	8½ "
"	21	7 "
"	22	6 "
		50½ " = 4 feet 6½ inches.

During these storms of rain, the thunder-claps were fully as loud as those on the Victoria Nyanza during the rainy season of 1875, and the lightning fully as fierce, being quivering, flaring pennants of flame, accompanied by bursting shocks, in apparently such close proximity that we felt frequently half stunned by the sound, and dazed by the coruscating displays of the electric flame. The deep chasm in which we were pent while the season was at its height increased the sound and re-echoed it from side to side, until each thunder-clap was protracted like a file-fire of artillery. Our position at Nzabi Cove was by no means enviable or desirable, though our experiences did not nearly realize all that we had anticipated. As we were encamped on a low terrace, which was only 30 feet above the river when we first arrived, we feared that, at a period when it was rising so rapidly, a sudden increase of 20 or 30 feet was quite "on the cards," from what we remembered of the sudden creation of rivers in Ugogo, where a few moments before, dry, sandy water-courses were alone visible. The increasing fury of the mighty stream, the deepening roar of the falls, the formation of new rapids, the booming chorus of a score of torrents precipitated in leaping columns from the summit of the opposite cliffs a height of 400 feet into the river, the continuous rain, the vivid flashes of lightning, and the loud thunder which crackled and burst overhead with overwhelming effect, sufficed to keep alive the anticipation of terrors happily never realized.

May 23.—The chief of Nzabi received in return for his fine trees and the cordial assistance and uniform kindness he had extended to us, a gift of goods, which exceeded even his hopes. The people were sufficiently rested after this agreeable interlude to resume the dangerous passage of the cataracts, and on the 23rd we made a movement down to the west end of Nzabi Creek, and began hauling the canoes over the rocky ridge which separated us from another small creek lower down. The next day we were also clear of the lower creek, and descended a mile, by which feat we had succeeded in getting below the Nséto Falls.

May 25.—On the 25th, Frank Pocock, being too lame, from his ulcers, to travel overland, the conduct of the canoe-party was given to Manwa Sera and Chowpereh, and the care of the boat to Uledi, the coxswain. Besides Frank, there were thirteen persons afflicted with ulcerous sores, dysentery, and general debility; upon whom, on account of their utter inability to travel by land or climb over the rocks, the humourist Baraka had bestowed, out of his fertile brain, the sobriquet of Goee-Goee, a term quite untranslatable as regards its descriptive humour, though "despairing, forlorn, good-for-nothings" would be a tolerably fair equivalent. With decent, sober Christian souls the party would have been distinguished as the "sick list"; but Baraka was not a Christian, but a reckless good-natured *gamin*, of Mohammedan tendencies. Turning to Frank, he said to him, with a broad grin, "Ah, ha! is our little master become a Goee-Goee too? Inshallah! we shall all become Goee-Goees now, if our masters get on the list." Frank laughingly assented, and hobbled to the boat to take a seat.

I led the active members of the Expedition and the women and children up the mountain from the lower Nzabi Creek, and, having well surmounted the table-land, struck west from Nzabi to Mowa, a distance of three miles. The plateau was a rolling country, and extremely picturesque in the populated part which bordered the river, thickly sprinkled with clusters of the guinea-palm and plantain groves, under which nestled the elegant huts of the Babwendé. This palm furnishes the natives with a delicious wine, and also with a yellow butter, which may be turned

VIEW FROM THE TABLE-LAND NEAR MOWA.

into a good burning oil, an unguent for the body, or an oil for stewing their provisions, bananas, yams, or potatoes; or served up with herbs, chicken, and chilies, for "palm-oil chop"; or as an excellent sop, when hot, for their cassava pudding.

At the third mile we turned down a broad and steep ravine, escorted by scores of gentle and kind people, and descended to the debouchure of a mountain brook, which empties into a deep bay-like indentation below the lower Mowa Falls. As we approached the bottom the Mowa became visible. It consists of a ledge of igneous rocks,

CUTTING OUT THE NEW "LIVINGSTONE" CANOE.

[*To face page* 282.

pumice and ironstone, rising 20 feet or so above the water, and though extending nearly three-fourths across, is pierced by various narrow clefts which discharge as many streams into the bay below. At the left side, between the end of the ledge and the perpendicular cliffs of iron-tinted rock, the river contracts, and in mighty waves leaps down with a terrific, torrent-like rush, whirling pools, and heaving mounds. From the debouchure of the brook by which we enter upon the scene to the cliffs across is about 1800 yards; the ledge of the Mowa rocks above it extends probably 800 yards, while the river beyond occupied perhaps 500 yards. The streams from the great river which falls into the bay through the gaps of the ledge have a drop of 12 feet; the great river itself has no decided fall, but, as already described, is a mere rush, with the usual tempestuous scene.

We occupied a beautiful camping place above the Mowa, on a long stretch of pure white river sand, under the shadow of such an upright and high cliff that the sunshine did not visit us until 9 A.M. I travelled up over the rocks until I reached a point at the base of which the Upper Mowa rapids broke out into waves, with intervals of unruffled glassy slope, and here I stood for an hour, pondering unspeakable things, as I listened to the moan and plaint of the tortured river. Far away below me extended the great cleft of the table-land, of savagely stern aspect, unmarked by aught to relieve its awful lonely wildness, with mountain lines on the right and on the left rising to 1500 feet, and sheer, for half their height, from unknown depths of water. The stately ranks of tall trees that had dignified the right side of the river at Nzabi up to the summit of the table-land, are exchanged from the Mowa down to Mpakambendi, for clear rock walls of from 300 to 600 feet high, buttressed by a thin line of boulders or splintered rock slabs of massive size.

One of the boys announced the boat coming. It soon appeared, Frank standing up in the bow, and Uledi, as usual, at the helm; but as this was the first time Frank had played the pioneer over cataracts, I observed he was a little confused—he waved his hand too often, and thereby confused the steersman—in consequence of which it was guided over the very worst part of the rapids, and though we signalled with cloth we were unheeded, and the boat, whose timbers had never been fractured before, now plunged over a rock, which crashed a hole 6 inches in diameter in her stern, and nearly sent Frank headlong over the bow. Naturally there was a moment of excitement, but by dint of shouting, frantic gestures, and energy on the part of the crew, the poor wounded boat was brought towards shore, with her bow in the air and her stern buried.

"Ah, Frank! Frank! Frank!" I cried, "my boat, my poor boat, after so many thousands of miles, so many cataracts, to receive such a blow as this on a contemptible bit of rapids like the Upper Mowa!" I could have wept aloud: but the leader of an Expedition has but little leisure for tears, or sentiment, so I turned to repair her, and this, with the aid of Frank, I was enabled to do most effectually in one day.

May 27.—All the canoes arrived successfully during the 25th and 26th without accident. On the 27th, after first conveying the goods of the Expedition and forming a new camp, below the Lower and Greater Mowa Falls, on a projection of terrace extending from the debouchure of the Mowa Brook, which overhung the Mowa Cove, we dropped our canoes down along the bank and through a cleft in the ledge already described, and by 3 P.M. had passed the Great Mowa Falls, and everybody was safe in camp.

An event occurred this day which I shall never forget. I would gladly leave it out, but as the historian of the journey, I may not do so. It touches human nature, and reveals its weakness, despite the possession of grand and noble, even matchless, qualities. The incident relates to Uledi, the coxswain of the *Lady Alice*, the best soldier, sailor, and artisan, and the most faithful servant, of the Expedition. Up to this date Uledi had saved thirteen persons from drowning. Simply because I wished it he had risked his own life to save the lives of others; and this heroic obedience, though it did not really elevate him much above the other first-class men of the Expedition, such as Manwa Sera the chief, Safeni the councillor, Wadi Rehani the storekeeper, and Kachéché the detective, had endeared him to me above all the rest. Uledi was not a handsome man; his face was marred by traces of the small-pox, and his nostrils were a little too dilated for beauty; but "handsome is that handsome does." He was not a tall man; he was short, and of compact frame; but every ounce of his strength he devoted to my service. I never sought in him for the fine sentiments which elevate men into heroes; but the rude man, with his untutored, half-savage nature, was always at my service. He was a devotee to his duty, and as such he was ennobled; he was affectionately obedient, as such he was beloved; he had risked his life many times, for creatures who would never have risked their own for his; as such he was honoured. Yet—this ennobled, beloved and honoured servant—ah! I regret to speak of him in such terms—*robbed me*.

After we had all reached camp, the boy Majwara came to me in the waning afternoon, and reported that in the transport of goods from the Upper Mowa camp a sack of beads had been ripped open, and a considerable quantity of the beads abstracted.

Beads abstracted! at such a period, when every bead is of more value to me than its bulk in gold or gems, when the lives of so many people depend upon the strictest economy, when I have punished myself by the most rigid abstinence from meat in order to feed the people!

"Who was the thief, Majwara? Speak, and I will make an example of him."

He was not sure, but he thought it must be Uledi. "*Uledi!* not Uledi the coxswain?"

"Yes," Majwara replied timidly.

Uledi was called, and while he was kept waiting Kachéché was called and told in Uledi's presence—while I watched his face—to seize upon everything belonging to him and his wife, and to produce everything before me unopened. Uledi was asked to confess if he possessed any beads to which he had no right. He replied: "None." Kachéché was then told to open his mat, and in the mat were discovered over five pounds of the fine Sami Sami beads, sufficient for nearly two days' provisions for the whole Expedition! He was placed under guard.

At sunset, after the Mowa natives had retired, the people of the Expedition—men, women, and children—were mustered. I addressed them seriously. For a long time, I said, both Frank and I had seen it necessary to exercise the strictest economy, and had sacrificed for the general good all our rights and privileges of investing moneys from the general store towards our own comfort, and had simply considered ourselves in the light of stewards of the goods for the public benefit. But it had been obvious to us for some time that the goods were rapidly diminishing during their transit from camp to camp over the rocks and table-land, and we had found it totally impossible to protect the goods from peculation, or to animate the people with our own fears that we should be reduced to starvation long before reaching the sea at the present rate of consumption. Entreaties we had perceived to be of no avail. There were some amongst them, it appeared, who through greed were resolved to cause everybody to suffer; yet if people died through hunger there was not the slightest doubt but that the dying would impute blame to us for having reduced them to such straits. To prevent the calamity which would surely follow absolute poverty, it was our duty to see that some measures should be adopted to punish those who would provoke such frightful suffering. A man had been found that afternoon with a large stock of beads, which he had filched from the general store—that man was Uledi. What ought to be done with him?

After much urging, Manwa Sera, the chief, said that it was a very hard case, seeing it was Uledi. Had it been any of the Goee-Goees, men who had for months been tenderly cared for, who had not toiled from morn to eve in the cataracts, nor borne the fatigue and toil of the day; who had never been distinguished for worth, but were always a shiftless and cowardly set, he would have given his vote for drowning him by hanging a great stone to his neck and pitching him into the river; but as it happened to be Uledi, he therefore proposed that he should receive a thorough flogging, to deter others from repeating the crime. The votes of the chiefs were in accord with Manwa Sera's, and three-fourths of the people cried out for "flogging."

Then I turned to the boat's crew, and said, "Now, you boys, you who know Uledi so well, and have followed him like children through a hundred rough scenes, speak, what shall be done to him?"

Mpwapwa, whose duty was to watch the boat in camp, and who was one of the most reliable and steady men, replied, "Well, master, it is a hard question. Uledi is like our elder brother, and to give our voice for punishing him would be like asking you to punish ourselves. But the fathers of the people have demanded that he shall be beaten, and I am only like a boy among them. Yet, master, for our sakes beat him only just a little. Mpwapwa has said."

PASSING NSÉTO FALLS.

[To face page 296.

"And you, Marzouk—Uledi's companion on the rock at the fourth cataract of the Stanley Falls—what do you say?"

"Verily, master, Mpwapwa has spoken what my tongue would have uttered, yet I would say, remember it is Uledi."

"And you, Shumari, who are Uledi's brother, what punishment shall I mete to this thief who would starve everybody, you and me?"

"Ah, dear master, your words are as lead. Spare him! It is true Uledi has stolen, and he has done very wrong. He is always stealing, and I have scolded him often for it. I have never stolen. No man can accuse me of taking that which did not belong to me, and I am but a boy, and Uledi is my elder. But please, master, as the chiefs say he must be flogged, give me half of it; and knowing it is for Uledi's sake I shall not feel it."

"Now, Saywa, you are his cousin, what do you say? Ought not Uledi to receive the severest punishment to prevent others from stealing?"

"Will the master give his slave liberty to speak?"

"Yes, say all that is in your heart, Saywa."

Young Saywa advanced, and kneeling, seized my feet and embraced them, and then said:—

"The master is wise. All things that happen he writes in a book. Each day there is something written. We, black men, know nothing, neither have we any memory. What we saw yesterday is to-day forgotten. Yet the master forgets nothing. Perhaps if the master will look into his books he may see something in it about Uledi. How Uledi behaved on Lake Tanganika; how he rescued Zaidi from the cataract; how he has saved many men whose names I cannot remember from the river, Bill Alli, Mabruki, Kom-Kusi, and others; how he worked harder on the canoes than any three men; how he has been the first to listen to your voice always; how he has been the father of the boat-boys, and many other things. With Uledi, master, the boat-boys are good, and ready; without him they are nothing. Uledi is Shumari's brother. If Uledi is bad, Shumari is good. Uledi is my cousin. If, as the chiefs say, Uledi should be punished, Shumari says he will take a half of the punishment; then give Saywa the other half, and set Uledi free. Saywa has spoken."

"Very well," I said. "Uledi, by the voice of the people,

is condemned, but as Shumari and Saywa have promised to take the punishment on themselves, Uledi is set free, and Shumari and Saywa are pardoned."

Uledi, upon being released, advanced and said, "Master, it was not Uledi who stole. It was the devil which entered into his heart. Uledi will be good in future, and if he pleased his master before he will please his master much more in time to come."

May 28.—On the 28th the natives appeared in camp by the hundred, to wonder, and barter, and be amused. Mowa is divided into two districts, governed by four kings. The brook, which empties into the cove, separates the two districts, which united are not more than eight square miles. The two principal chiefs are Manwana and Kintu.* Each vied with the other in supplying Frank and myself with palm-wine, cassava bread, and bananas, in the hope, of course, of receiving munificent gifts in return, for the natives of this region are too poor to make gratuitous gifts to the Mundelé, or merchant, as I was called, who is supposed to be a rich man, and who ought by all natural laws to respond liberally to their gifts. Yet the Babwendé are not illiberal, and my people gave them great credit for hospitality. They invariably, if any of the Wangwana passed them during their drinking bouts, proffered a glassful of their wine and some cassava bread.

The Babwendé have one peculiarity which is rather startling at first to a stranger. When, for instance, they have visited the camp bringing with them small gifts of wine and bread, and having seated themselves for a sociable chat, they suddenly begin grinding their teeth, as though in a mad rage! After a while we discovered that it was only a habit of the Babwendé and the Bakongo.

Many of the Babwendé from below Nzabi, as far as Manyanga, have been once in their lives to the sea, to the ports of Kinsembo, Kinzau, Mkura, Mkunga, Mbala, and a few had been to Embomma. They are consequently amiable, and disposed to be civil to strangers, though very little is required to stir them to fighting pitch, and to discharge their heavily loaded guns at strangers or at one another. The theft of the smallest article, or a squabble with a native, would

* It is rather singular that at such a vast distance from Uganda I should find the name of the Lost Patriarch, so celebrated in the traditional history of that country.

be at once resented. Writing on paper, taking observations, sketching or taking notes, or the performance of any act new or curious to them, is sufficient to excite them to hostilities.

On the third day of our stay at Mowa, feeling quite comfortable amongst the people, on account of their friendly bearing, I began to write down in my note-book the terms for articles in order to improve my already copious vocabulary of native words. I had proceeded only a few minutes when I observed a strange commotion amongst the people who had been flocking about me, and presently they ran away. In a short time we heard war-cries ringing loudly and shrilly over the table-land. Two hours afterwards, a long line of warriors, armed with muskets, were seen descending the table-land and advancing towards our camp. There may have been between five hundred and six hundred of them. We, on the other hand, had made but few preparations except such as would justify us replying to them in the event of the actual commencement of hostilities. But I had made many firm friends amongst them, and I firmly believed that I would be able to avert an open rupture.

When they had assembled at about a hundred yards in front of our camp, Safeni and I walked up towards them, and sat down midway. Some half-dozen of the Mowa people came near and the shauri began.

"What is the matter, my friends?" I asked. "Why do you come with guns in your hands in such numbers, as though you were coming to fight? Fight! Fight us, your friends! Tut! this is some great mistake, surely."

"Mundelé," replied one of them, a tall fellow with a mop-head which reminded me of Mwana Saramba, who had accompanied me round Lake Victoria—"our people saw you yesterday make marks on some tara-tara" (paper). "This is very bad. Our country will waste, our goats will die, our bananas will rot, and our women will dry up. What have we done to you, that you should wish to kill us? We have sold you food, and we have brought you wine, each day. Your people are allowed to wander where they please, without trouble. Why is the Mundelé so wicked? We have gathered together to fight you, if you do not burn that tara-tara now before our eyes. If you burn it we go away and shall be friends as heretofore."

I told them to rest there, and left Safeni in their hands as a pledge that I should return. My tent was not fifty yards from the spot, but while going towards it my brain was busy in devising some plan to foil this superstitious madness. My note-book contained a vast number of valuable notes; plans of falls, creeks, villages, sketches of localities, ethnological and philological details, sufficient to fill two octavo volumes—everything was of general interest to the public. I could not sacrifice it to the childish caprice of savages. As I was rummaging my book box, I came across a volume of Shakespeare (Chandos Edition), much worn and well thumbed, and which was of the same size as my field-book; its cover was similar also, and it might be passed for the note-book provided that no one remembered its appearance too well. I took it to them.

"Is this the tara-tara, friends, that you wish burnt?"

"Yes, yes, that is it!"

"Well, take it, and burn it or keep it."

"M—m. No, no, no. We will not touch it. It is fetish. You must burn it."

"I! Well, let it be so. I will do anything to please my good friends of Mowa."

We walked to the nearest fire. I breathed a regretful farewell to my genial companion, which during many weary hours of night had assisted to relieve my mind when oppressed by almost intolerable woes, and then gravely consigned the innocent Shakespeare to the flames, heaping the brush-fuel over it with ceremonious care.

"Ah-h-h," breathed tne poor deluded natives, sighing their relief. "The Mundelé is good—is very good. He loves his Mowa friends. There is no trouble now, Mundelé. The Mowa people are not bad." And something approaching to a cheer was shouted among them, which terminated the episode of the Burning of Shakespeare.

The boat had been in a leaky condition ever since she had received the shock at the Upper Mowa, and her constant portage by the falls of the Livingstone, the constant change from dry heat to wet, had almost ruined her, yet we persisted in caulking and repairing her. Some of the natives, observing my anxiety to render her water-tight, offered to bring me a substance which, they said, would be effectual for the purpose. In a few hours they had brought me a mixture of india-rubber and palm-butter. We experimented with it instantly, but it was a very poor substitute for pitch, and I expressed my dissatisfaction with it.

THE CIRCUMNAVIGATORS OF THE VICTORIA NYANZA AND LAKE TANGANIKA, AND EXPLORERS OF THE ALEXANDRA NILE AND LIVINGSTONE (CONGO) RIVER.

[*To face page 300.*

June 1.—Then a nephew of Manwana offered to show his friend Kachéché something else which would be much better. Accordingly, the next morning, at 10 A.M. of the 1st of June, Kachéché and the native brought about thirty pounds of bees-wax, a very dark substance, which, had it not been for the diminutive bees which clung to it, might have been mistaken for pitch. Subsequently I proceeded myself to the source of the supply, and discovered about a hundredweight of bees-wax attached to a lofty fragment of rock near Massassa Falls. These bees are of a dark brown colour, short and dumpy, about one-half the length of the ordinary honey-bee. At several places between Massassa and Mowa there were similar large secretions of wax on the cliffy rocks.

Another valuable article of commerce besides the bees-wax and india-rubber found here was the gum copal—not, however, amongst the possessions of the natives. We were first attracted to it at Kalulu Falls by the great quantities discovered between the rocks. One man collected about fifty pounds of it, under the impression that he would be able, on reaching the coast, to sell it for a few pice. Poor fellow! He had but little idea of what was in store for him and all of us, before we should arrive at the sea. The appearance of the substance proved that it had been long immersed in water. My own opinion is that it is fossilized gum carried down by the Livingstone river. On Cheandoah Island, a cake 15 lbs. in weight was discovered, besides many small pieces of two or three pounds' weight, of the mellow red and pale white variety.

The Babwendé are too rich in palm-oil to employ the gum, frankincense, and myrrh, and the other resins of the Burseraceæ, as the Waregga and natives of Karuru do, for lights. Of india-rubber the Mowa possess large quantities, as their wooded ravines and the right slopes of the great river furnish them with inexhaustible supplies. One enterprising fellow carried one load of it to sell to the Ba-Zombo, but he received so little cloth for it that he repented of the speculation.

The commercial enterprise of the Babwendé has never recovered from the effects of the melancholy termination to a great caravan which they despatched some years ago. A disease which they say attacked the bowels broke out among them, and but few returned to their native land. The

Basundi, who live to the west-north-west of Mowa, seldom venture near the verge of the Livingstone's chasm, from which the loud waters send up sometimes an appalling volume of sound. Should the wind bear the noise of the falls to their ears while at the *zandu*, or market, they place their hands over their ears and immediately withdraw, or should they by accident wander near the river, and from some point observe it, they instantly veil their eyes and hurry away.

One of the first customs obtaining among this tribe which first attracts the traveller's attention is that of mourning. The heavily loaded muskets are announcing their grief at all hours, and a statistician would find it an easy matter to ascertain the death-rate of any of these districts, as well as the sex and age of the deceased, by reckoning the number of shots fired. Six announce a child's death, ten that of a woman, and fifteen that of a man, the fire being directed at the bananas and palms, in the belief that the death was either caused by bad bananas or through some fault in the palm-juice.

In Mowa Cove are kept about a dozen small fishing canoes, which are cut out of the soft and light Rubiaceæ. For besides the cane-nets which are towing at the mouth of the several narrow falls over the Mowa rock-ledge, each night the Mowa fishermen enter their canoes with cord nets, and ply about the little cove to catch the whitebait, which they attract by torch-lights. Also, like sailing skippers whistling for a breeze, the natives appear to think that whistling charms the minnows, and all night long may be heard the peculiar sounds.

A traveller in these regions, where the people are so superstitious, is liable at any moment to be the object of popular fury. Aneurism might strike down a person while trading in his camp, or while standing carelessly upon a rock he might fall and meet an instantaneous death ; a disease like cholera or typhus might attack a settlement, a fatal accident with a gun cause loss of life, or apoplexy overtake a gormandizing chief, but everything would be charged to the malevolent influence of the traveller. Indeed, they are rather partial to "wars," it appears to me. An accident happened to a Mowa man at the Zinga Falls, and the Zinga district had at once to muster its warriors to resist an invasion from Mowa. A Zinga chief named Ndala owed a Mowa elder twenty-five cloths, but the credit he had received for one moon he extended to two, and at the end of two moons, being still unable to pay, he was fiercely attacked by the natives of Mowa.

June 2.—An exploration of the river as far as the Zinga Falls—which is two miles below Mowa—made by Manwa Sera, comforted us, for he reported that the river between Mowa and Zinga was not so difficult as many parts we had successfully passed, and that with a little caution no great danger was to be apprehended. On the 2nd of June I proceeded with him as far as Massassa Falls, along the summit of the lofty precipices. At Massassa terminates the comparatively narrow-walled channel, through which the river tumbles uneasily from the Mowa Falls and the lower basin down (by the Massassa Falls) into the Bolo-bolo—"quiet-quiet"—basin. On account of the great width of the Mowa basin, 1800 yards, the river rolls from above through its 500-yards-wide cleft in the ledge, streams along in a furious billowy course for a mile, and at Massessé seems to slack its current. Here the river, heaving upward, discharges a portion of its volume backward along its flanks, which, sweeping along the base of the Mowa cliffs, flows upstream until it enters the Mowa Cove. Then, after darting into the tongue-like cove like a tidal flow, it quickly subsides, and retreating along the base of the Mowa ledge, after a circuit of two miles, meets with the great falls and billowy rapids, where there is a wild contention between the two opposing currents. From Massessé the river resumes its rapid flow downwards, ruffled at projections into waves, but generally with an apparently calm face, though curling and gurgling ominously, until, approaching Massassa Point, one mile below Massessé, it drives against outstanding boulders, rises into curling waves on either side, which meet in mid-river 200 yards below: crest strikes crest, wave meets wave, and mutually overlap and wrestle, then subside, then heave aloft again in deep-brown surge and sounding tops. A half-mile length of wild waters rolls thus to Bolo-bolo basin, where they are finally gathered into a tranquil pool—hence the name.

While standing upon the summit of the high cliff-walls which encircle the crater-like pool, the frantic Massassa appears tame. Even wilder Zinga, one and a half miles below, and Ingulufi below that, are reduced to mere whitey flakes of water. If we step down, however, close to them, they become terrible enough to those purposing to try their terrors in a canoe.

Half-way to the Zinga Falls from Massassa, in the middle of the concave cliffs, falls the Edwin Arnold River, in a long cascade-like descent from the height of the table-land, with a sheer drop of 300 feet. While it rolls calmly above, this river has a width of 50 yards, and an average depth of 3 feet.

As usual, Frank Pocock and I spent our evening together in my tent. The ulcers by which he was afflicted had by this time become most virulent. Though he doctored them assiduously, he was unable to travel about in active superintendence of the men; yet he was seldom idle. Bead-bags required sewing, tents patching, and clothes becoming tattered needed repairing, and while he was at work his fine voice broke out into song, or some hymn such as he was accustomed to sing in Rochester Church. Joyous and light-hearted as a linnet, Frank indulged for ever in song, and this night the crippled man sang his best, raising his sweet voice in melody, lightening my heart, and for the time dispelling my anxieties. In my troubles his face was my cheer; his English voice recalled me to my aims, and out of his brave bold heart he uttered, in my own language, words of comfort to my thirsty ears. Thirty-four months had we lived together, and hearty throughout had been his assistance, and true had been his service. The servant had long ago merged into the companion; the companion had soon become a friend. At these nightly chats, when face looked into face, and the true eyes beamed with friendly warmth, and the kindly voice replied with animation, many were the airy castles we built together, and many were the brilliant prospects we hopefully sketched. Alas! alas!

THE MASASSA FALLS, AND THE ENTRANCE INTO POCOCK BASIN, OR BOLOBOLO POOL. [*To face page* 304.

CHAPTER XIV.

"I fruitless mourn to him who cannot hear,
And weep the more because I weep in vain."
GRAY.

Leaving Mowa—The whirling pools of Mowa—The *Jason* swept over the falls—The "Little Master" drowned—Too brave!—"Ah, Uledi, had you but saved him!"—The sympathy of the savages.

June 3.—The fatal 3rd of June found us refreshed after our halt of seven days, and prepared to leave Mowa to proceed to Zinga, there to establish a new camp above its great cataract, while the canoes should be leisurely taken down with such caution as circumstances demanded. Kachéché and Wadi Rehani, the store-keeper, who, in the absence of Frank, were deputed to look after the land party, mustered their following at break of day, which consisted of such invalids as were able to travel by land, the women and children, and sixty men carrying the stores, tents, and equipments of the Expedition.

Meanwhile, it was my duty to endeavour to reach Zinga—only two miles off by river, while the circuitous route by land was fully three miles—in advance of the land party, in order to prepare the aborigines for the reception of the Expedition. As I set out from Mowa Cove, Frank crawled on hands and knees to a rock overlooking the river to watch us depart, and the same feeling attracted Manwa Sera and the natives to the spot. Clinging close to the rock-lined shore, we rowed out of the cove, in full view of the river and all its terrors. For three-fourths of a mile to our left the river stormed down with long lines of brown billows. Arriving at Massessé Point, or the neck of the walled channel which separates Pocock Basin below from Mowa Basin, the river relaxed its downward current, and discharged fully a sixth of its volume to the right, which, flowing against the sharp edges and projections of the Mowa cliffs, raised many a line of low waves, and rolling towards us obliged us to hug the cliffs and take to our cables. But the base of the cliffs in many places afforded no means of foothold, and, after a long and patient attempt at passing those sharp angles, we were compelled to abandon it and endeavour to breast the strong current of the eddy with our oars. While, however, there was a strong current running against the base of the Mowa cliffs and washing its boulders, there was also a slope towards the vicinity of the giant billows discharged from the cataract; and though we strenuously strove to keep midway between the cliffs and the torrent-like career of the stream to the left, it became evident to us that we were perceptibly approaching it. Then a wild thought flashed across my mind that it would be better to edge along with it than to contend against the eddy with our heavy, leaky boat, and we permitted ourselves to be carried near its vicinity with that intention; but on nearing the rushing stream we observed in time that this was madness, for a line of whirlpools constantly plays between the eddy and the down stream, caused by the shock of the opposing currents. The down stream is raised like a ridge, its crest marked by ever-leaping waves, shedding a great volume over its flanks, which comes rushing to meet that which is ejected by the eddy. The meeting of these two forces causes one to overlap the other, and in the conflict one advances or recedes continually, and the baffled volumes create vortices, around which are wheeling bodies of water of great velocity, until the cavities are filled, when the whole becomes replaced by watery masses rising like mounds. Every minute in endless and rapid succession these scenes transpire. Such a one commenced before our terrified eyes. A whirlpool had ceased revolving for a brief moment, and in its place there rose one of those mounds whose rising volumes and horrid noise inspired the desire to flee the scene. Fearing we should be unable to escape, I doffed coat, shoes, and belt, and motioning to Uledi to keep off, I shouted to the boat's crew to do their best or die. Even had my actions not been sufficiently significant of our dangerous position, the stunning uproar would have informed them that we had been rash to approach the terrible scene. Therefore, following the upheaved and ejected waters, we retreated from the aqueous mound, for in its sudden subsidence lay danger, but were halted on the verge of the fatal pit which had now begun to replace the mound, and which angrily yawned behind the stern of our boat. Desperately we rowed, happily maintaining our position until a second convulsion occurred, by the efflux of which we finally escaped.

The boat was by this time half full of water. Our repairs were found to have been utterly insufficient, and we resolved therefore upon returning to camp to renew the attempt in the new *Jason*, as its swiftness would enable us to force our way against the current of the eddy, and reach Massassa. When we returned to Mowa it was ten o'clock, and the boat-boys were fatigued with their desperate exertions, and, probably unwilling to risk the terrors of the river without fortifying themselves, had scattered to search for food. But, unable to control my anxiety about the reception of the Expedition by the Zinga chiefs, I concluded that, in the absence of Frank, it would be unwise to delay appearing at the new camp and secure their goodwill while we should be engaged with the passage of the several falls.

I accordingly delivered my instructions to Manwa Sera, who had always shown himself a trustworthy man, saying, "When the boat's crew have returned, give them that best light canoe—the *Jason*; tie ropes along the sides, with strong cables at each end. Tell them to keep close to the Mowa side, and pick their way carefully down river, until they come to Massassa. On arriving there Uledi will be able to judge whether it can be passed in a canoe, or whether we shall have to take the canoes over the rocks. Above all things tell him to be careful, and not to play with the river."

Turning to Frank, I told him I should hurry to Zinga, and after arranging with the chiefs would send him his breakfast and hammock; and if I found the men still there I would detail six to carry him; if the men were not there he might, upon the arrival of the hammock, take the first men he saw, and follow me overland.

It was high noon when I arrived at our new camp, which was constructed on Zinga Point, about a hundred feet above the great cataract. There were four kings present, and hundreds of natives, all curious to view the Mundelé. Though somewhat noisy in their greetings, we were soon on an amicable footing, especially when a young fellow named Lazala began to ask me if I were "Ingiliz, Francees, Dytche, or Portigase." Lazala further named many seaport towns he had visited, and discharged his knowledge of the manners and customs of the whites by the sea with a refreshing volubility. The great waves along the sea-beach he described in a characteristic manner as being "Mputu, putuputu, just like the big waves of Zinga!" Whereupon a fast and sure friendship was soon established, which was never broken.

At 1 P.M. breakfast was despatched to Frank, through Majwara, Benni, and Kassim, and men were sent with a net-hammock.

The Zinga kings and most of their people had ascended to their homes above, on the plateau; and in my camp there were about fourteen able-bodied men besides the sick and women. And about three o'clock I took my seat on a high rock above the falls, to watch for Uledi, as from the Zinga Point, with a field-glass, I was enabled to view the river across Bolo-bolo basin, both Massassa Falls and Massessé Rapids, and nearly up to the Upper Mowa Falls. I was not long in my position before I observed something long and dark rolling and tumbling about in the fierce waves of Massassa. It was a capsized canoe, and I detected the forms of several men clinging to it!

I instantly despatched Kachéché, Wadi Rehani, and ten men, with cane-ropes, to take position in the bight in Bolo-bolo, near which I knew, by the direction of the waves, the current would carry them before sweeping them down towards Zinga. Meanwhile I watched the wrecked men as they floated through the basin. I saw them struggling to right the canoe. I saw them lift themselves on the keel, and paddling for dear life towards shore, to avoid the terrible cataract of Zinga. Finally, as they approached the land, I saw them leap from the wreck into the river, and swim ashore, and presently the unfortunate *Jason*, which they had but a moment before abandoned, swept by me with the speed of an arrow, and over the cataract, into the great waves and the soundless depths of whirlpools, and so away out of sight.

Bad news travels fast. Kachéché, breathless with haste and livid with horror, announced that out of the eleven men who had embarked in the canoe at Mowa, eight only were saved.

"Three are lost!—and—*one of them is the little master!*"

"*The little master*, Kachéché?" I gasped. "Surely not the little master?"

"Yes, he is lost, master!"

"But how came he in the canoe?" I asked, turning to Uledi and his dripping comrades, who had now come up, and were still brown-faced with their late terrors. "Speak, Uledi, how came he — a cripple — to venture into the canoe?"

In response to many and searching questions I obtained the following account.

As Uledi and his comrades were about to push off, Frank had crawled up near the river and bade them stop and place him in. Uledi expostulated with him, upon the ground that I had not mentioned anything about taking him, and Manwa Sera, in charge of the canoes, hurried up and coaxingly tried to persuade him not to venture, as the river was bad; but he repelled them with all a sick man's impatience, and compelled the crew to lift him into the canoe. The *Jason*, being swift and well-manned, was propelled against the eddy with ease, and in half an hour it was racing over the small rapids of Massessé down river. As they approached Massassa, which was only a mile below Massessé, the booming of the cataract made Uledi anxious not to venture too near, until he had viewed the falls, and for that purpose, with Frank's permission, he skirted the intermediate cliffs, until they came to a little cove just above the Massassa, where the crew held on to the rocks. Uledi soon climbed upward and proceeded to the rocks overhanging the fall, where he was enabled to view the extent of the danger at a glance. After only a few minutes' absence he returned to Frank, who was still seated in the bottom of the canoe, and addressing him said:—

"Little master, it is impossible to shoot the falls, no canoe or boat can do it and live."

"Bah!" said Frank contemptuously, "did I not see as we came down a strip of calm water on the left which by striking across river we could easily reach?"

"But, master, this fall is not directly across river, it is almost up and down (diagonally); the lower part on the left being much farther than that which is on the right, and which begins to break close by here. I tell you the truth," rejoined Uledi, as Frank shook his head sceptically, "little master, I have looked at all the fall, and I can see no way by water; it will be death to make the trial."

"Well," said Frank, "what shall we do?"

"We must send to the master," replied Uledi, "and tell

him that we have brought our canoe to Massassa. Meantime we can tie up our canoe here until he comes."

"And what is to become of me?" asked Frank.

"We will not be long before we are back with a kitanda" (hammock), "and you will reach camp by night."

"What, carry me about the country like a worthless Goee-Goee," he replied, "for all the natives to stare at me! No, indeed! Anyhow, I must wait here all day without food, eh?"

"It will not be long, master; in a quarter of an hour I can reach camp, and in another half I can be back, bringing food and hammock."

"Oh, it's all mighty fine," replied Frank, his temper rising at the idea of being carried, which he supposed would cause him to be made a laughing-stock to everybody. "I don't believe this fall is as bad as you say it is. The noise is not like that of the fall which we have passed, and I feel sure if I went to look at it myself I would soon find a way."

"Well, if you doubt me, send Mpwapwa and Shumari and Marzouk to see, and if they say there is a road I will try it if you command me."

Then Frank despatched two of them to examine, and after a few moments they returned, saying it was impassable by water.

Frank laughed bitterly, and said, "I knew what you would say. The Wangwana are always cowardly in the water; the least little ripple has before this been magnified into a great wave. If I had only four white men with me I would soon show you whether we could pass it or not."

Frank referred, no doubt, to his companions on the Medway or Thames, as by profession he was a bargeman or waterman, and being a capital swimmer had many a time exhibited to the admiring people, especially at Nzabi creek, his skill in the art of swimming and diving. At the death of Kalulu he expressed great surprise that not one of the five then lost had been saved, and declared his conviction that Kalulu Falls would never have drowned him, upon which I had described a whirlpool to him, and when, with an apparent instinct for the water, he sought occasions to exhibit his dexterity, I had cautioned him against being too venturesome, and kept him to his land duties. The success of Nubi, who was also a good swimmer, at the whirlpool of the Lady Alice Rapids, confirmed him in his idea that a perfect swimmer ran no danger from them. At this moment he forgot all my caution, and probably his high spirit had secretly despised it. But he was also goading brave men to their and his own destruction. His infirmity manifested itself in jeering at the men for whom with me he had not sufficient adjectives at command to describe their sterling worth; for he, as well as I, was well aware of Uledi's daring, and of his heroic exploit at the Fifth Cataract of the Stanley Falls he was himself a witness. Poor Frank, had some good angel but warned me of this scene, how easily he had been saved!

"Little master," said the coxswain gravely, stung to the quick, "neither white men nor black men can go down this river alive, and I do not think it right that you should say we are afraid. As for me, I think you ought to know me better. See! I hold out both hands, and all my fingers will not count the number of lives I have saved on this river. How then can you say, master, I show fear?"

"Well, if you do not, the others do," retorted Frank.

"Neither are they nor am I afraid. We believe the river to be impassable in a canoe. I have only to beckon to my men, and they will follow me to death—and it is death to go down this cataract. We are now ready to hear you command us to go, and we want your promise that if anything happens, and our master asks, 'Why did you do it?' that you will bear the blame."

"No, I will not order you. I will have nothing to do with it. You are the chief in this canoe. If you like to go—go, and I will say you are men, and not afraid of the water. If not, stay, and I shall know it is because you are afraid. It appears to me easy enough, and I can advise you. I don't see what could happen."

Thus challenging the people to show their mettle, poor Frank steadily hastened his fate.

Uledi then turned to the crew, and said, "Boys, our little master is saying that we are afraid of death. I know there is death in the cataract, but come, let us show him that black men fear death as little as white men. What do you say?"

"A man can but die once." "Who can contend with his fate?" "Our fate is in the hands of God!" were the various answers he received.

"Enough, take your seats," Uledi said.

"You are men!" cried Frank, delighted at the idea of soon reaching camp.

"Bismillah" ("in the name of God"), "let go the rocks, and shove off!" cried the coxswain.

"Bismillah!" echoed the crew, and they pushed away from the friendly cove.

In a few seconds they had entered the river; and, in obedience to Frank, Uledi steered his craft for the left side of the river. But it soon became clear that they could not reach it. There was a greasy slipperiness about the water that was delusive, and it was irresistibly bearing them broadside over the falls; and observing this, Uledi turned the prow, and boldly bore down for the centre. Roused from his seat by the increasing thunder of the fearful waters, Frank rose to his feet, and looked over the heads of those in front, and now the full danger of his situation seemed to burst on him. But too late! They had reached the fall, and plunged headlong amid the waves and spray. The angry waters rose and leaped into their vessel, spun them round as though on a pivot, and so down over the curling, dancing, leaping crests they were borne, to the whirlpools which yawned below. Ah! then came the moment of anguish, regret and terror.

"Hold on to the canoe, my men; seize a rope, each one," said he, while tearing his flannel shirt away. Before he could prepare himself, the canoe was drawn down into the abyss, and the whirling, flying waters closed over all. When the vacuum was filled, a great body of water was belched upwards, and the canoe was disgorged into the bright sunlight, with several gasping men clinging to it. When they had drifted a little distance away from the scene, and had collected their faculties, they found there were only eight of them alive; and, alas for us who were left to bewail his sudden doom! there was no white face among them. But presently, close to them, another commotion, another heave and belching of waters, and out of them the insensible form of the "little master" appeared, and they heard a loud moan from him. Then Uledi, forgetting his late escape from the whirling pit, flung out his arms, and struck gallantly towards him, but another pool sucked them both in, and the waves closed over them before he could reach him; and for the second time the brave coxswain emerged, faint and weary—but Frank Pocock was seen no more.

"My brave, honest, kindly-natured Frank, have you left me so? Oh, my long-tried friend, what fatal rashness! Ah,

Uledi, had you but saved him, I should have made you a rich man."

"Our fate is in the hands of God, master," replied he, sadly and wearily.

Various were the opinions ventured upon the cause which occasioned the loss of such an expert swimmer. Baraka, with some reason, suggested that Frank's instinctive impulse would have been to swim upward, and that during his frantic struggle towards the air he might have struck his head against the canoe. Shumari was inclined to think that the bandages on his feet might have impeded him; while Saywa thought it must have been his heavy clothes which prevented the full play of the limbs required in such a desperate situation.

All over Zinga, Mbelo, and Mowa the dismal tidings spread rapidly. "The brother of the Mundelé is lost—lost at Massassa," they cried; and, inspired by pure sympathy, they descended to Zinga, to hear how the fatal accident occurred. Good, kindly Ndala—who came accompanied by his wives, and with a true delicacy of feeling would not permit the natives to throng about me, but drove them outside the camp, where they might wonder and gossip without disturbing us—old Monango, Kapata, and tall, good-natured Itumba, and a few of the principal men, were alone admitted.

After hearing the facts, Ndala informed me there was no doubt that it was the "bad fetish" of Massassa people, and he proposed that the four kings of Zinga and the three kings of Mbelo should unite and completely destroy the Massassa people for their diabolical act. Said they, "It is not the first time an accident has happened at Massassa; for, about two months ago, one of our men, while standing on the rock, suddenly fell into the river, and was never seen again; and one of Mowa's people has also been lost there in the same way."

The suggestion that it was the fetish of Massassa which had caused this sudden and sharp calamity was natural to the superstitious and awed natives; but in a few words I informed them that I blamed no man for it.

"Say, Mundelé," asked Ndala suddenly, "where has your white brother gone to?"

"Home."

"Shall you not see him again?"

"I hope to."

"Where?"

"Above, I hope."

"Ah! we have heard that the white people by the sea came from above. Should you see him again, tell him that Ndala is sorry, and that he is angry with Massassa for taking him from you. We have heard from Mowa that he was a good, kind man, and all Zinga shall mourn for him. Drink the wine of our palms, Mundelé, and forget it. The Zinga palms are known throughout the lands of the Babwendé, and our markets are thronged with buyers. The Zinga wine will comfort you, and you will not be troubled with your sorrow."

Sympathy, real and pure sympathy, was here offered after their lights, which, though rude, was not unkind. The large crowds without spoke together in low subdued tones, the women gazed upon me with mild eyes, and their hands upon their lips, as though sincerely affected by the tragic fate of my companion.

The effect on the Wangwana was different. It had stupefied them, benumbing their faculties of feeling, of hope, and of action. From this date began that exhibition of apathetic sullenness and lack of feeling for themselves, and for their comrades, which distinguished their after-life in the cataracts. The slightest illness would cause them to lean against a rock, or crouch by the fire in the posture of despair. They never opened their lips to request help or medicine, and as they were inaccessible to solicitude for themselves, they had none to bestow on others. After this fatal day I could scarcely get a reply to my questions when anxious to know what their ailments were. Familiarity with many forms of disease, violent and painful deaths, and severe accidents had finally deadened, almost obliterated, that lively fear of death which they had formerly shown.

As I looked at the empty tent and the dejected, woe-stricken servants, a choking sensation of unutterable grief filled me. The sorrow-laden mind fondly recalled the lost man's inestimable qualities, his extraordinary gentleness, his patient temper, his industry, cheerfulness, and his tender friendship; it dwelt upon the pleasure of his society, his general usefulness, his piety, and cheerful trust in our success with which he had renewed our hope and courage; and each new virtue that it remembered only served to intensify my sorrow for his loss, and to suffuse my heart with pity and regret, that after the exhibition of so many admirable qualities and such long faithful service he should depart this life so abruptly, and without reward.

When curtained about by anxieties, and the gloom created by the almost insurmountable obstacles we encountered, his voice had ever made music in my soul. When grieving for the hapless lives that were lost, he

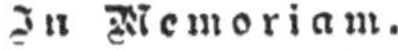

FRANCIS JOHN POCOCK.

Drowned June 3, 1877.

consoled me. But now my friendly comforter and true-hearted friend was gone! Ah, had some one but relieved me from my cares, and satisfied me that my dark followers would see their Zanjian homes again, I would that day have gladly ended the struggle, and, crying out, "Who dies earliest dies best," have embarked in my boat and dropped calmly over the cataracts into eternity.

The moon rose high above the southern wall of the chasm. Its white funereal light revealed in ghostly motion the scene of death to which I owed the sundering of a long fellowship and a firm-knit unity. Over the great Zinga Fall I sat for hours upon a warm boulder, looking up river towards the hateful Massassa, deluding myself with the vain hope that by some chance he might have escaped out of the dreadful whirlpool, picturing the horrible scene which an intense and morbid imagination called up with such reality, that I half fancied that the scene was being enacted, while I was helpless to relieve.

How awful sounded the thunders of the many falls in the silent and calm night! Between distant Mowa's torrent-rush, down to Ingulufi below, the Massessé, Massassa, and Zinga filled the walled channel with their fury, while the latter, only 30 yards from me, hissed and tore along with restless plunge and gurgle, and roaring plunged, glistering white, into a sea of billows.

Alas! alas! we never saw Frank more. Vain was the hope that by some miracle he might have escaped, for eight days afterwards a native arrived at Zinga from Kilanga, with the statement that a fisherman, while skimming Kilanga basin for whitebait, had been attracted by something gleaming on the water, and. paddling his canoe towards it, had been horrified to find it to be the upturned face of a white man.

CHAPTER XV.

Mutiny in the camp—Again among the cataracts—Frank's body found—The fall of the Edwin Arnold River—Tired out!—Wholesale desertion—More cataracts—"Good-bye, my brother, nothing can save you!"—Rushing blindly on—Saved again!—The *Jason* found.

"*June* 4.—We are all so unnerved with the terrible accident of yesterday that we are utterly unable to decide what is best to do. We have a horror of the river now, and being far apart—over eighty men being at Mowa—we are unable to communicate with each other, for the journey overland to Mowa is long and fatiguing. The natives of Zinga strongly sympathize with me, which is a consolation in my affliction.

"*June* 5.—My troubles increase. A messenger came this morning from Manwa Sera bearing the terrible news that the people have mutinied and refuse to work. They say they would prefer hoeing for the heathen to following me longer, for they say that the end of all will be death. The Mowa natives have also infected them with their silly superstitions, by talking about the Spirits of the Falls, for it appears that the late catastrophe has elicited a host of legends in connection with Massassa. Had we sacrificed a goat to the two falls, they say, the accident would never have occurred! Though Muslims by profession, my people are also heathen. But I have not myself recovered from the shock, and I judge their feelings by my own, therefore it is better they should rest where they are.

"*June* 9.—I left Zinga before dawn with Uledi and the boat's crew, travelling along the river, and took a closer view of Massassa, and the cove where they had halted their canoe. Poor, rash Frank! had he only crawled over the rocks a few yards he would have realized the impossibility of safely shooting the Massassa. The rocky projections, which raise the curling waves in mid-river, are single blocks from 10 to 40 feet high piled one above another, lying at the base of a steep cliff of Massassa. The cliff is of course impassable, as it is from three hundred to four hundred feet high. The colossal size of the blocks is a serious impediment. The falls we have had enough of, at least for the present. From Massassa I proceeded to Mowa, and reasoned with the men. They were extremely depressed, rueful of face, and apparently sunk in despair. Only Manwa Sera, the chiefs, and boat's crew seemed alive to the fact that necessity compelled us to move, before starvation overtook us. They would not be convinced that it was best to struggle on. However, I would even begin to battle with the falls once more; and after a little persuasion I succeeded in inducing the boat's crew to man one of the canoes, and to take it to the cove whither they had taken the unfortunate *Jason*, before they had been rash enough to listen to a sick man's impatience. The feat was successful; the canoe was lashed to the rocks and a guard of ten men set over it. This act seemed to encourage the Wangwana to believe that there was no danger after all as far, at any rate, as the cove. At sunset I reached Zinga again, terribly fatigued.

"*June* 10.—The full story of the sufferings I have undergone cannot be written, but is locked up in a breast that feels the misery into which I am plunged neck-deep. Oh! Frank, Frank, you are happy, my friend. Nothing can now harrow your mind or fatigue your body. You are at rest for ever and for ever. Would that I were also! While I was absent yesterday from Zinga, a man lost to all feeling, Saburi Rehani, proceeded to steal the cassava of the natives, which of course raised their ire, and for a period things were very gloomy this morning. However, a liberal payment of cloth has quenched the sulkiness of the Zingaese, and Saburi was punished. I have now three camps, one at Zinga, one at Massassa, and the other at Mowa, and I was not able to leave Zinga before noon because of Saburi's robbery. The boat's crew took another canoe down to Massassa in the afternoon, and at 5 P.M. I was obliged to clamber over the mountains, walk round Pocock Pool, and down to Zinga again, where I have just arrived, weak, fainting, and miserable.

"*June* 11.—The body of Frank was found in Kilanga basin three days ago by a native fisherman, as it was floating about, but the horrified man would not touch it. The body was on its back, the upper part nude, he having torn his shirt away to swim. It is to be regretted that the body was thus left to float a dishonoured spectacle; and Ndala, king of Zinga, also grieves that it was not brought ashore for respectful burial.

"*June* 12.—Crossed again to Massassa, and four more canoes have been brought to the cove, without accident.

"*June* 13 *and* 14.—Sick of a fever; but in the mean-time I am gratified to hear that Manwa Sera has been successful in bringing all the canoes down to Massassa, and that all the people have finally left Mowa.

"*June* 15.—At early dawn proceeded up the Zinga mountain, skirted the Pocock Pool, crossed the Edwin

FALL OF THE EDWIN ARNOLD RIVER INTO THE POCOCK BASIN.

Arnold River, and descended to Massassa. A grove covered the top of the cliff, and the axe-men were detailed to cut down branches, which those without axes conveyed to fill the deep pits between the several colossal blocks. Others were employed in fixing two rows of piles in the cove, sinking the ends between the boulders, which, when filled with brush, might enable us to draw the canoes upward.

"*June* 18.—The last three days have witnessed some

hard work. To the astonishment of the aborigines, Massassa Point has been covered from end to end, a distance of 600 yards, with brushwood, in some places 40 feet thick, and three canoes have been hauled successfully past the falls, and dropped into Pocock Basin. Leaving instructions with Manwa Sera, I manned the canoes and proceeded to Zinga by water. Mid-way, as we skirted the base of the lofty cliffs, we came to a fine fall of the Edwin Arnold River, 300 feet deep. The cliff-walls are so perpendicular, and the rush of water so great from the cascades above, that the river drops on the boulders below fully thirty feet from the cliff's base.

"*June* 10.—The canoes have all, thank Heaven! passed the dread Massassa, and are safe at Zinga, about two hundred yards above the Zinga Fall. I ventured into nearly the middle of the Pocock Pool to-day, about seven hundred yards below where Frank lost his life, and sounding I obtained 55 fathoms, or 330 feet, of water; then rowing steadily towards Edwin Arnold Fall, it slowly decreased to 35 feet, the lead striking hard against the submerged rocks."

By the 17th I observed that the river had fallen 9 feet since the third of the month, and that the Massassa was much milder than on the fatal 3rd. Zinga is, however, just as wild as at first, and it is evident that the channel of the fall is much obstructed by boulders.

It is worthy of notice that each fall is known by the natives of the opposing banks under different names. "Zinga" is only employed by the Babwendé, who occupy the table-land on the right side of the river; the Bassessé, on the left side, call it "Bungu-Bungu."

The fish-laws are very strict here. The people descend to the Zinga Fall each day about 7 A.M., and at the same time the Bassessé may be seen descending the opposite mountain, for both sides of the fall have their respective large boulders, amongst which the full swollen river rushes impetuously in narrow foamy channels, where the nets are placed. On the Zinga side, as many as thirty nets are placed, but no man may lift a net until one of the kings, or one of their sons, is present, and the half of the produce is equitably divided among the kings Ndala, Mpako, and Monango, and each king has his separate rock on which his share is laid. If the Zinga folks have had a fortunate find in their nets, they announce it by a loud shout to the Bassessé on the opposite side; and the Bassessé, on successful mornings, take care to express their luck with equal spirit and animation. The pike and cat-fish, the silurus, the water-snake and eel, and the various fish found in the African lakes and rivers, I find to be common to the Livingstone also.

Several of the boulders of the Zinga cataract are covered by a species of Podostomaceæ, which while the river covers them are green and fresh, resembling sea-weed, and affording the natives a kind of spinach; when the river recedes, the weed soon withers and becomes shrivelled up.

To-day, for the first time, I heard of the Kwango from a man who has visited Embomma, which I believe to mean the "place of the king" in the language of Babwendé, and to be synonymous with Kwikuru in Unyamwezi, and Kibuga in Uganda. They point it out as being west. They have a curious idea in their heads that I must have come from some place south of the Bakonga country, and floated down some great body of water; and, lest their superstitious heads should find something objectionable in my coming down the great river, I have been very reticent.

They call the Livingstone the Bilumbu at Nzabi, which may be interpreted "day." At Zinga they call it Mwana Kilunga, the "lord of the ocean." Mputu, though signifying sea, also means "the sea along the coast," most probably the surf. The Babwendé term for "river" is Njari.* A constant companion of the Babwendé is the haversack net, made out of the Hyphene palm fibre. I was reminded, as I looked at each native bearing this net-pouch with him, of the traveller's satchel carried by tourists in Europe.

Along the cataracts in the Babwendé country there is no game. The noise of gunpowder, more than its destructiveness, has driven the game into the lands occupied by the silent-weaponed tribes. But there is a species of small bush antelope, and the coney, which is still hunted by the natives with their dogs—animals of the normal pariah class.

"*June* 20.—As we began to lay brushwood along the tracks this morning, by which we are to haul our canoes from the Pocock Basin past the Zinga point into the basin below, the people stirred about so languidly and sullenly that I

* In the Bunda language a river is Mikoko, which would be spelt by the Portuguese Micoco. I have a suspicion that there never was a king called Micoco, that the natives meant Micoco, the great river. Hence the profound mystery attached to his locality.

asked what was the matter. One fellow, remarkable for nothing but his great size and strength, turned round and said sharply, 'We are tired, and that's what's the matter,' which opinion one-third did not hesitate to confirm. Such a spirit being most serious in these days of scant food and hard toil—men, like beasts of prey, being governed by the stomach —I invited the people together to rehearse their grievances and to describe their wrongs. They could say nothing, except that they were tired and were not going to work more. Death was in the river; a wearisome repetition of frightful labour waited for them each day on the rocks; their stomachs were hungry, they had no strength. Said I, 'And I have none, my friends, I assure you. I am as hungry as any of you. I could get meat to make me strong, but it would be robbing you. I am so tired and sorry that I could lie down smiling and die. My white brother, who was lost the other day, is far happier than I. If you all leave me, I am safe, and there is no responsibility on me. I have my boat, and it is in the river. The current is swift, the fall is only a few yards off. My knife can cut the rope, and I shall then go to sleep for ever. There are the beads; take them, do what you will. While you stay with me, I follow this river until I come to the point where it is known. If you don't stay with me, I still will cling to the river, and will die in it.' I walked away from them. One man, Safeni, the coxswain at Bumbireh, on being asked by a disaffected body of men what was best to be done, said, 'Let us pack up and be gone. We shall die anyhow, whether we stay here or whether we travel.' They were not long in following his counsel, and filed up the steep ascent to the table-land, thirty-one in number. One of the tent-boys came to announce the fact. On ascertaining that the infection was not general, I then resolved that they should not endanger their own lives or the lives of the faithful, and called Kachéché and Manwa Sera to follow and plead with them. They overtook them five miles from here, but only received a determined refusal to return, and persisted in continuing their journey. Meanwhile the faithful are at work.

"*June* 21.—Despatched Kachéché and Manwa Sera again early this morning to cut off the fugitives, to inform the chiefs in advance that my people were not to be permitted to pass them, but, if they persisted in going beyond them, to lay hands on them and bind them until I could arrive on the scene. The chiefs seconded me so well that they beat their war-drum, and the mock excitement was so great that the mutineers were halted, and I learn by my two men that they already regret having left their camp.

"*June* 22.—Again Kachéché and Manwa Sera returned to the mutineers, who were fifteen miles away from here, and, promising them pardon and complete absolution of the offence, succeeded, with the aid of the friendly chiefs, in inducing them to return, sadder and wiser men, to resume their duties, and so to enable me to triumph over these obstacles.

"*June* 23.—We commenced our work this morning, assisted by 150 Zinga natives, and by 10 A.M. had succeeded in drawing three canoes up the 200-foot steep to the level of the rocky point. The fourth canoe was the new *Livingstone*, which weighed about three tons. It was already 20 feet out of the water, and we were quite confident we should be able with 200 men to haul her up. But suddenly the rattan and *Ficus elastica* cables snapped, and with the rapidity of lightning the heavy boat darted down the steep slopes into the depths. The chief carpenter of the Expedition, who had superintended its construction, clung to it under the idea that his single strength was sufficient to stay its rapid downward descent, and he was dragged down into the river, and, unable to swim, scrambled into the canoe. Uledi sprang after the carpenter, as the men remembered that he could not swim, and, reaching the canoe, cried out to him to jump into the river and he would save him. 'Ah, my brother,' the unfortunate man replied, 'I cannot swim.' 'Jump, man, before it is too late! You are drifting towards the cataract!' 'I am afraid.' 'Well, then, good-bye, my brother; nothing can save you!' said Uledi as he swam ashore, reaching it only 50 feet above the cataract. A second more and the great canoe, with Salaam Allah in it, was swept down over the cataract, and was tossed up and down the huge waves until finally a whirlpool received it. I reckoned fifty-four during the time it was under water; then it rose high and straight out of the depths, the man still in it. Again it was sucked down, revolving as it disappeared, and in a few seconds was ejected a second time, the man still in it. A third time it was drawn in, and when it emerged again Salaam Allah had disappeared. The fleet-footed natives and the boat's crew had started overland to Mbelo Ferry, and shouted out the warning cries to the ferrymen, who were at once on the alert to save the canoe. After riding high on the crests of the waves of the Ingulufi Rapids, the *Livingstone* canoe entered the calmer waters of the crossing-place, and, in view of all gathered to witness the scene, wheeled round five times over the edge of a large whirlpool and disappeared for ever! It is supposed that she was swept against the submerged rocks beneath, and got jammed; for though there is a stretch of a mile of quiet water below the pool, nothing was seen of her up to sunset, five hours after the catastrophe. Two of the new canoes are thus lost, and

THE CHIEF CARPENTER CARRIED OVER ZINGA FALL.

another good man has perished. The Wangwana take this fatal accident as another indication of the general doom impending over us. They think the night of woe approaching, and even now, as I write, by the camp-fires they are counting up the lost and dead. Poor people! Poor me!

"*June* 24.—We were five hours engaged in hauling the *Glasgow*, our longest canoe, up a hill 200 feet, with over two hundred men. Of the smaller canoes we ran up three. It has been my policy to excite the people, with whatever tends to keep them from brooding over our losses, with wine, drums, and music, which I purchase liberally, because though apparently extravagant at such a period, it is really the most economical.

"I hear of a place called Kakongo below, where the natives intend to fight me—for the glory of it, it seems, for so far reports have all been in our favour. No native has been injured by me wilfully, neither have I permitted injury to be done them from any of my people. Strong in my innocence, and assured that they shall have the first fire, it is a matter of unconcern. If we do not fear terrible Nature in this region, we certainly shall not step aside for the vaunts or threats of savages.

"*June* 25.—At dawn of day we were up and began to lower the boat and canoes into the basin below Zinga. By night, thank God, all our flotilla was beyond the cataract. The Zingaese say there are only the Ingulufi, Mbelo, and Ntombo Mataka Falls—three more falls!—and the last, I hope, will prove to be 'Tuckey's Cataract,' with fair sailing down to the Yellala Falls; and then, with bowed heads, we will travel for the sea as only hungry men can travel.

"*June* 26.—I intrusted to Wadi Rehani and Kachéché the task of taking the goods overland to Mbelo Falls, while I passed the day at Zinga. A month ago we descended the Upper Mowa Falls; it is still in sight of me, being only three miles off. Three miles in thirty days, and four persons drowned even in this short distance!

"*June* 27.—Again I led the way this morning, round the Zinga basin, and approached the Ingulufi Rapids. We sought a channel between a few scattered boulders which stood close to shore and disparted the ever vexed river, and having examined the stream, and finding it to be mere rapids, without those fatal swirling vortices, dashed over the waves into the Mbelo basin. Reaching camp, which was at the top of a 300-foot cliff, we halted for a hermit's lunch on bananas, and, wishing to inspire once more that spirit which was almost quenched by our late accidents, at 1 P.M. I descended the cliff again by means of ladders of rattan-cane, which for the last 30 feet enabled us to reach the water-line, and embarked. Cautiously we moved along—ten men to the cane-cables at bow and stern—and step by step, with a prudence born of perfect knowledge of its dangers, we approached the Mbelo Falls. It was almost another copy of the Lady Alice Rapids: the river was just as confined; rocky islets rose to the left of us; the cliffs towered upward, dwarfing us into mere minute atoms compared to the colossal height of cliffy front and tree-clad slopes, which ran steep from the cliffy verge to the level of the table-land. The river roared as loudly, the white-brown waves were as menacing, the massive rock-fragments hung toppling over their bases. As we neared a great rock looming in front of us in the water, we saw a channel between it and the shore; and while our eyes were fixed upon that narrow thread-like stream, with the dear hope that it would enable us to triumph over the difficulty of Mbelo, the faithless stern-cable parted, the river just then gave an uneasy heave, which snapped the bow-cable, and again were we borne, on the crests of the wild waves, into mid-channel; rocks, boulders, and cliffs flying past us with incredible rapidity. There were six men in the boat besides myself, and Uledi was at the helm, calm, cool, and confident. Our feelings are, however, different to those which filled us during a similar period of danger. There are certain voices whispering, 'What will be, will be,' 'One cannot escape the inevitable,' and such like, so that the sense of danger is somewhat blunted. Those lively fears which once oppressed us we know no more. Nerve and soul have alike been deadened by oft-seen woes, oft-felt strokes of misfortune. We have wept so often we can weep no more: we have suffered so much we cannot suffer more. Thus the ridgy waves which pelt us, and their rude strength and giant force, awe us not. The cliff-walls rising in solemn majesty up to the zenith, the dark shaggy lines of trees, the fury of waters, the stern rigidness of the stupendous heights, we reck not of. 'What is to be, will be.' We are past the Mbelo Falls, and a stream, brown-black and menacing, enters the main river from behind the rock islets; we are whirled round twice by the eddying pool, precipitated into a dancing, seething, hissing cauldron, just as if the river was boiling over. A sharp angular edge of mountain cliff, as though of a fortress, is past, and away down stream we dart, racing amid noise and waves and foam, when the cold grey cliffs drop sheer down, and finally emerge in Nguru basin, borne on a slackened current; and it is then we sigh, and murmur 'Saved again!' With nothing of triumph, nothing of the flashing glitter of proud eyes, but subdued and grateful, we seek the sandy beach of Kilanga.

"Leaving four men at Kilanga in charge of the boat, I

crossed the little brook that divided the district of Kilanga from Nguru, and proceeded to meet the terror-stricken multitude, who could scarcely believe their eyes when they saw me advancing towards them. I was like one risen from the dead to them. 'Yes, we shall reach the sea, please God!' said they. 'We see the hand of God, now. But you must not tempt the wicked river any more, master. We shall do it ourselves. Better far that we die than you. You shall not go to the river again until we are beyond the falls.' Poor dear souls, they made me forgive them all. How bitter had my thoughts been lately; but this genuine expression of love and devotion healed the sickened soul, and infused new vigour into it, until I felt again that old belief that success would finally reward us."

* * * * * *

The above, faithfully transcribed from my note-book, convey, more truly than any amount of after-written descriptions, the full sense of the miserable scenes we endured during that fatal month of June 1877. Four days after my last narrow escape we succeeded, by patience, great caution, and laborious toil, in escaping past the dread Mbelo and reaching Kilanga, happily without further accident, but not without incident; for amongst the lower rocks of Nguru basin, left high and dry by the subsiding river, we discovered the *Jason*, broken in half, the two portions being about fifty feet apart; and midway between them was the almost mummied body of Jumah, the guide, lying on its face, with its arms outstretched. This Jumah was one of the two drowned with Francis Pocock on the fatal 3rd of June, and while Uledi and his comrades were wondering what had become of the two Wangwana who had so suddenly sunk out of sight, and endeavouring to right the canoe as they drifted through the Pocock Basin, he must have been clinging to one of the cables beneath it.

The last day of our stay at Mbelo was marked by the death of the poor ram, which had accompanied us ever since we left the cheerless gloom of the Uregga forests, by a fall from the cliffs

CHAPTER XVI.

Final warnings against theft—Humiliating a protectionist—Kindly tribes—Five of the Expedition abandoned to slavery for theft—Safeni goes mad from joy—Goaded to crime—Ali Kiboga's adventures—The cataract of Isangila—Only five marches from white faces!—Staunch to the death—Rum—My appeal to Embomma—The forlorn hope—The "powerful man" insults us—Struggling on—"We are saved, thank God!"—"Enough now; fall to"—My letter of thanks—Approaching civilization—Amongst whites—Boma—The Atlantic Ocean.

July 6.—Strongly impressed with the knowledge that nothing but a persevering, persistent, even impetuous advance towards the sea could now save us from the pangs of famine, we only halted two days at Kilanga. Therefore on the 6th July the goods were transported to a distance of two miles to Kinzoré, beyond the district Suki, or "Hair." Having ascertained that no rapids of a dangerous nature, during the quick recession of the flood, troubled the narrow and tortuous gap, Uledi was directed to lead the canoes past Kinzoré and camp to Mpakambendi, which enabled us to move forward next morning to join them without delay or accident.

Mpakambendi terminates the narrow, walled chasm which we had followed since leaving the Kalulu Falls, and in which we had spent 117 days—that is, from 29th March to 6th July. The distance from Mpakambendi to Ntamo along the course of the river is only 95 geographical miles, and we were 131 days effecting this journey! At Mpakambendi the defile through which the river rushes opens to a greater width, and the mountains slope away from it with a more rounded contour, and only at intervals do they drop down abrupt in cliffs. Consequently the river expands, and, being less tortured by bouldery projections and cliffy narrows, assumes somewhat of a milder aspect. This is due to the change in the character of the rocks. Above, we had horizontally stratified gneiss and sandstone with an irregular coping of granite masses, and here and there a protrusion of the darker trappean rocks. Below Mpakambendi, the river is disturbed by many protruded ledges of the softer greenish shales, which have been so pounded and battered by the river that we have merely rapids without whirlpools and leaping waves to interrupt our descent. Every other mile or so of the river shows symptoms of interruption, and its surface is here marked by thin lines of low waves, and there by foamy stretches.

From Mpakambendi to the rounded mount-shoulder on which Nsenga is situate stretches about a mile and a half of calm river, deep and majestic, and a long strip of land along the right side affords admirable camping-places or sites for fishing-stations.

The Wangwana still persisted in robbing the natives. Two were here apprehended by them for stealing the fowls and maltreating the women, and of course I had either to redeem them or leave them in the hands of those whom they had injured. We consented to redeem them, and paid so largely that it left us nearly beggared and bankrupt. Again a warning was given to them that such a course must end in my abandoning them to their fate, for they must never expect me to use force to release them from the hands of the natives, or to adopt any retaliatory measures on behalf of thieves.

Two poor souls succumbed to life's trials and weariness here—one of them from mortification supervening on ulcers; the other of chronic dysentery. This latter disease worried many of the people, and scant and poor food had reduced us all to hideous bony frames.

The Western Babwendé, from Mpakambendi to the lands of the Basundi are wilder in appearance than those farther east, and many adopt the mop head, and bore the lobes of their ears, like the Wasagara and Wagogo on the east side of the continent. Some Bakongo and Bazombo natives of Congo and Zombo were seen here as they were about to set off east for a short trading trip. It appeared to me on regarding their large eyes and russet-brown complexions that they were results of miscegenation, probably descendants of the old Portuguese and aborigines; at least, such was my impression, but if it is an erroneous one, the Bakongo and Bazombo are worthy of particular study for their good looks and clear brown complexions. They are of lower stature than the negro Babwendé, Basessé, and Bateké.

They did not seem to relish the idea of a white Mundelé

in a country which had hitherto been their market, and they shook their heads most solemnly, saying that the country was about to be ruined, and that they had never known a country but was injured by the presence of a white man. Poor aboriginal conservatives! But where is the white or the black, the yellow or the red man who does not think himself happier with his old customs than with new? The history of mankind proves how strong is the repugnance to innovations. I questioned an old growler who was rapidly beginning to win sympathizers among my Babwendé friends by asking him in their presence where he obtained his gun.

"From the Mputu" (coast), said he.

"Where did you obtain that fine cloth you wear?"

"From the Mputu."

"And those beads, which certainly make you look handsome?"

He smiled. "From the Mputu."

"And that fine brass wire by which you have succeeded in showing the beauty of your clear brown skin?"

He was still more delighted. "From the Mputu; we get everything from the Mputu."

"And wine too?"

"Yes."

"And rum?"

"Yes."

"Have the white men been kind to you?"

"Ah, yes."

"Now," said I, turning to my Babwendé friends, "you see this man has been made happy with a gun, and cloth, and beads, wire, wine, and rum, and he says the white men treat him well. Why should not the Babwendé be happier by knowing the white men? Do you know why he talks so? He wants to sell those fine things to the Babwendé himself, for about double what he paid for them. Don't you see? You are wise men."

The absurd aboriginal protectionist and conservative lost his influence immediately, and it appeared as though the Babwendé would start a caravan instantly for the coast. But the immediate result of my commercial talk with them was an invitation to join them in consuming a great gourdful of fresh palm-wine.

July 10.—On the 10th of July we embarked the goods,

and descended two miles below Mpakambendi, and reached the foot of the Nsenga Mount. The next day we descended in like manner two miles to the lofty mountain bluff of Nsoroka, being frequently interrupted by the jagged shaly dykes which rose here and there above the stream, and caused rapids.

Two miles below Nsoroka we came to Lukalu, which is a point projecting from the right bank just above the Mansau Falls and Matunda Rapids, which we passed by a side-stream without danger on the 13th. Between Matunda Rapids and Mansau Falls, we were abreast of Kakongo, that warlike district of which we had heard. But though they crossed the river in great numbers, the men of Kakongo became fast friends with us, and I was so successful with them that five men volunteered to accompany me as far as the "Njali Ntombo Mataka Falls," of which we had heard as being absolutely the "last fall." "Tuckey's Cataract," no doubt, I thought, for it was surely time that, if there was such a fall, it ought to be seen.

Below Matunda Falls, in the district of Ngoyo, are a still more amiable people than the Upper Babwendé, who share the prevalent taste for boring their ears and noses. We held a grand market at Ngoyo, at which bananas, pine-apples, guavas, limes, onions, fish, cassava bread, ground-nuts, palm-butter, earthenware pots, baskets, and nets, were exchanged for cloth, beads, wire, guns, powder, and crockery.

July 16.—On the 16th, accompanied by our volunteer guides, we embarked all hands, and raced down the rapid river a distance of three miles to the great cataract, which on the right side is called Ntombo Mataka, and on the left Ngombi Falls, or Njali Ngombi. On the right side the fall is about 15 feet, over terraces of lava and igneous rocks; on the left it is a swift rush, as at Mowa, Ntamo, Zinga, Inkisi, with a succession of leaping waves below it.

There was a large concourse of natives present, and all were exceedingly well-behaved and gentle. Three chiefs, after we had camped, advanced and offered their services, which were at once engaged, and the next morning 409 natives conveyed the canoes and boat below the fall in admirable style, though one small canoe was wrecked. They expressed as much concern about the accident as though they had been the authors of it, but I paid them even more liberally than I had contracted for, and the utmost good feeling prevailed. Indeed, the chiefs were so grateful that they offered to take the canoes themselves a distance of three miles to the sand-beaches on the right bank opposite Kinzalé Kigwala—and the offer was gladly accepted.

The Ntombo Mataka people I regarded as the politest people I had encountered in Africa, and they certainly distinguished themselves by a nobility of character that was as rare as it was agreeable.

Arrived at the beautiful camping-place below the falls, I proceeded in a canoe to a cluster of low rocky islets, to view the cataract which we had so agreeably and pleasantly passed, and it struck me at the time that this was the great cataract described by Tuckey as being above that "Farthest," which has been printed on so many charts. The cataract has a formidable appearance from the centre of the river as one looks upward, and during the rainy season the whole of the rocky dyke is covered with water, which would then give a direct fall of 20 feet. The natives of Ntombo Mataka were not aware of any more obstructions below of any importance. About five miles north-north-east of this point is the large and popular market-place of Manyanga, where the natives of Ngoyo, Kakongo, Ntombo Mataka, Ngombi, Ilemba, Kingoma, Kilanga, Kinzoré, Suki, Nguru, Mbelo, Zinga, Mowa, and Nzabi, up river, meet the natives of Ndunga, Mbu, Bakongo, and Bassessé.

July 19.—On 19th of July we cautiously descended three miles to Mpangu, on the right bank. From the slope of the table-land there is projected a line of lower hills, tawny with sere and seeding grass, and gently sloping sides, smooth shores marked by extensive lengths of sandbanks, and here and there on the lower levels a cassava garden. But though the river is much wider, the rapids are frequent, rocky projections from the schistose rocks on the right breaking the river's surface, while along the centre sweeps the mighty stream fiercely and hoarsely.

The schistose dykes which thus interrupt the river are from a few hundred yards to a mile apart, and between them, in the intermediate spaces, lie calm basins. Nor is the left bank free from them, though all the force of the river has been for ages mainly directed against it.

July 20.—We descended on the 20th to Mata river, on both sides of which the natives were sulky, and disposed to resent our approach, but no outbreak occurred to mar our peaceful progress to the sea. They would not, however, part with food except at extravagant prices. They are devoted to whitebait or minnow-catching, which they dry on the rocks for sale in the markets, and here, all day long, we found them, crouched behind the shelter of large rocky fragments with their enormous hand-nets resting close by them, whistling to the minnows. As soon as the shoal advanced about them, they swam out in a body forming line with their nets laid diagonally across in front of them to meet the shoal; and then, returning to the shore, would empty their "finds" on a large slab-like rock, amid boasts, and jests, and rude excitement. At the same time the canoes would be employed skirmishing in the deeper portions, and the crews with the handle of their hand-nets laid under their legs, paddling up and down with long silent strokes, would thus secure large hauls.

By a daring rush down river we passed the rapids of Ungufu-inchi, and, proceeding six miles along low sandy shores, and alluvial folds between low hills, we came to the rapids between Kilemba and Rubata, and were halted abreast of the Rubata Cauldron, near the village of Kibonda, which occupies the summit of a bluff opposite Elwala river on the left bank.

The natives here are given up to the cultivation of ground-nuts and cassava, and minnow-catching. Food was therefore so scarce, and so unsuitable for the preservation of working men's strength, that our sick-list was alarmingly increased. The Basundi are a most wretched, suspicious, and degraded race, quarrelsome, and intensely disposed to be affronted. I was unable to purchase anything more than a few ground-nuts, because it involved such serious controversy and chaffer as sickened the hungry stomach. The Wangwana were surprised, after their recent experiences, to meet people more extortionate than any they had yet seen, and who abated nothing of the high demands they made. One of them, unable to obtain food, proceeded to the cassava gardens and coolly began to dig up a large stock of tubers, and when warned off behaved very violently. The natives, indisposed to brook this, closed round him, and, binding him hand and foot, carried him to their village.

On hearing of it I despatched men to ascertain the truth, and they brought the chief and some of his elders to camp to obtain the price of his freedom. Unfortunately the price was so large—being four times the total value of all our store—that, despite all our attempts to induce them to lower their demands, we saw that the captive was doomed. One of my chiefs suggested that we should lay hands on the chief of Kibonda, and retain him until Hamadi, the captive, was released; but this suggestion I positively refused to entertain for one moment. We were too poor to buy his freedom, and it would have been an injustice to employ violence. He was therefore left in captivity.

July 24.—I hoped this would have stopped the Wangwana from venturing to appropriate the property of such determined aborigines; but on the 24th, after descending 3½ miles to Kalubu, another man was arrested for theft of fowls and cloth. The case was submitted to the captains and members of the Expedition, and it was explained to them, that if the man's liberty could be purchased, half of the goods were at their disposal; but that if they determined to fight for his release, they must give me warning, so that I might move down river with those who preferred to be guided by me. The captains unanimously condemned him to captivity, and their decision was gravely delivered in presence of all.

Just above Kalubu, on the right side of the river, a lofty reddish cliff stands, which, upon examination, presents many traces of igneous eruptions. From the elbow below it are visible the remains of an old cataract, and lava is so abundant that it gives quite a volcanic appearance to the scene. A lofty ridge south of Kalubu strikes towards the north-north-east, and formed a notable feature as we descended from Mata river.

July 25.—Four miles farther down brought us, on the 25th, to a little cove above Itunzima Falls, where was another furious display of the river, and a most dangerous cataract. Crossing over to the left bank, we succeeded next day in passing it, after a laborious toil of eight hours, and camped in a beautiful bend below.

At this camp we first met natives who were acquainted with the name Yellala, but they informed us that there were several great rapids below Itunzima, upon which I finally abandoned the search for "Tuckey's Cataract," and instead of it strove to ascertain if any were acquainted with the name of "Sangalla." None of them had ever heard of it; but they knew "Isangila," which we were informed was about five days' journey by water; but that no native journeyed by river, it being too dangerous.

The Wangwana, weakened by scant fare and suffering from pining vitals, were intensely affected when I announced to them that we were not far from the sea. Indeed one poor fellow—distinguished in the first volume as the coxswain of the *Lady Alice* during the adventurous circumnavigation of Lake Victoria—was so intoxicated with joy that he became outrageous in his behaviour. Still I did not suspect that this was madness, and when he advanced to me and embraced my feet, saying, "Ah, master! El hamd ul Illah! We have reached the sea! We are home! we are home! We shall no more be tormented by empty stomachs and accursed savages! I am about to run all the way to the sea, to tell your brothers you are coming!" the idea of his lunacy was far from my mind. I attributed his tears and wildness simply to excess of emotion and nervous excitement. I replied to him soothingly; but he, seizing his parrot and placing it on his shoulder, plunged into the woods. After a few seconds' reflection, it occurred to me that the man was a lunatic, and I sent three men instantly to bring him back, and to recover him by force if necessary; but after four hours' search they returned unsuccessful, and I never saw the sage Safeni more. We probably might have been able to recover him after several days' search; but valuable as he had been, and dear as he was, death by starvation threatened us all, and we were compelled to haste—haste away from the baleful region to kinder lands.

July 26.—On the 26th of July I obtained by observation south latitude 5° 9′.

From the bend below Itunzima Falls we had a straight stretch of four miles, on a river which recalled to our minds reminiscences of the quiet-flowing stream below Chumbiri. Clinging to the left, we had a glorious grey sandbank, backed by growths of wild olive and a narrow belt of forest trees, in which the tracks of game were numerous. The right bank was similar, and dome-like hills rose conspicuous in a deep fold of the retreating table-land.

We reached at the end of this course, on the left bank, a small quiet river, 30 yards wide at the mouth, entering the Livingstone between steep alluvial banks about 20 feet high. The table-land had approached the river again, and formed a high point opposite the place where the little river debouched, and, directly below it, roared and thundered another cataract. A large island rose, high, rocky, and steep, from the centre. To the right it was utterly impassable; but after examining the rapids on the left, and discovering that the main force of the stream was on the other side, we raced down the waters with all hands on board without accident.

July 28.—On the 28th we began our journey early, and discovered that the river was still much obstructed, rapids roaring at every short distance, and requiring caution and vigilance. By noon however we had passed four series without trouble. Above the islet line above Kilolo I found we had reached south latitude 5° 19′.

There are but few natures among my own race, either in Europe or America, who would not feel a curious pleasure in, and envy me the opportunity of, exploring the beautiful and endless solitudes of this region, were they but certain that they would be sustained the while by nourishing food, and be secure from fatal harm. For in all civilized countries that I have travelled in, I have observed how very large a number of people indulge this penchant for travel in such unfrequented corners and nooks of wild woodland, glen, or heath as present themselves near home. I myself was conscious that the table-land on both sides of the Livingstone, with its lofty ridges, which ran away north or south to some complicated watershed, enclosing, no doubt, some awesome glens and solemn ravines, or from whose tops I might gaze upon a world of wild beauty never seen before, presented to me opportunities of exploring such as few had ever possessed: but, alas! all things were adverse to such pleasure; we were, to use a Miltonian phrase, subject to the "hateful siege of contraries." The freshness and ardour of feeling with which I had set out from the Indian Ocean had, by this time, been quite worn away. Fevers had sapped the frame; over-much trouble had strained the spirit; hunger had debilitated the body, anxiety preyed upon the mind. My people were groaning aloud; their sunken eyes and unfleshed bodies were a living reproach to me; their vigour was now gone, though their fidelity was unquestionable; their knees were bent with weakness, and their backs were no longer rigid with the vigour of youth, and life, and strength, and fire of devotion. Hollow-eyed, sallow, and gaunt, unspeakably miserable in aspect, we yielded at length to imperious nature, and had but one thought only—to trudge on for one look more at the blue ocean.

Rounding, after a long stretch of tolerably calm water, a picturesque point, we view another long reach, and half-way on the left bank we camp. Maddened by sharp pangs of hunger, the people soon scatter about the district of Kilolo. What occurs I know not. Likely enough the wretched creatures, tormented by the insufferable insolence of the aborigines, and goaded by a gnawing emptiness, assisted themselves with the wanton recklessness of necessity, and appropriated food unpaid for. While I am seated

CAMP AT KILOLO.

among a crowd from the right bank, who have come across the river to elate me with stories of white men whom they have seen by the sea, and from whom I learn the news that there are whites like myself at Embomma, I hear shots on the cultivated uplands; and though I pretend to take no interest in them, yet a bitter, restless instinct informs me that those shots have reference to myself; and presently the people return, some with streaming wounds from oxide of copper pellets and iron fragments which have been fired at them. Uledi comes also, bearing a mere skeleton on his back, whom, with his usual daring, he has rescued from the power of the men who would shortly have made a prisoner of him; and he and the rest have all a horrible tale to tell.

"Several men have been captured by the natives for stealing cassava and beans."

"Why did you do it?"

"We could not help it," said one. "Master, we are dying of hunger. We left our beads and moneys—all we had—on the ground, and began to eat, and they began shooting."

In a very short time, while they are yet speaking, a large force of natives appears, lusty with life and hearty fare, and, being angered, dare us, with loaded guns, to fight them. A few of the men and chiefs hasten to their guns, and propose to assume the defensive, but I restrain them, and send my native friends from the right bank to talk to them; and, after two hours' patient entreaties, they relax their vindictiveness and retire.

When I muster the people next morning, that we may cross the river to Nsuki Kintomba, I discover that six men have been wounded, and three, Ali Kiboga,* Matagera, and Saburi Rehani, have been detained by the infuriated villagers. It would have been merely half an hour's quick work, not only to have released the three captives, but to have obtained such an abundance of food as to have saved us much subsequent misery, but such an act would have been quite contrary to the principles which had governed and guided the Expedition in its travels from the eastern sea. Protection was only to be given against a wanton assault on the camp and its occupants; arms were only to be employed to resist savagery; and though, upon considering the circumstances, few could blame the hungry people from appropriating food, yet we

* Some two or three months after we had left Loanda, Ali Kiboga escaped from his captivity, and after a desperate journey, during which he must have gone through marvellous adventures, succeeded in reaching Boma, whence he was sent to Kabinda, thence by the Portuguese gunboat *Tamega* to San Paulo de Loanda. After a short stay at Loanda, the United States corvette *Essex*, Captain Schley, took him to Saint Helena, and thence, through the kindness of the captain of one of Donald Currie's Cape Line steamers, he was carried gratuitously to Cape Town. Again the Samaritan act of assisting the needy and distressed stranger was performed by the agent of the Union Steamship Company's line, who placed him on board the *Kaffir*, which was bound for Zanzibar. It is well known that soon after leaving Table Bay the *Kaffir* was wrecked. From the *Cape Times*, February 19, 1878, I clip the following, in spite of its compliment to myself: "On the bow were some natives of Zanzibar. Among them was the man who had gone through Africa with Stanley. This man was supposed to have been drowned with four others. But early in the morning he was found very snugly lying under a tent made of a blanket, with a roaring fire before him. Of all the wrecked people that night there was no one who had been more comfortable than Stanley's Arab. The power of resource and the genius of the master had evidently been imparted in some degree to the man."

had but sympathy to give them in their distress. Sad and sorrowful, we turned away from them, abandoning them to their dismal fate.

The river between Kilolo and Nsuki Kintomba was about fourteen hundred yards wide, and both banks were characterized by calm little bays, formed by projected reefs of schistose rock. Just above Nsuki Kintomba a range of mountains runs north-west from some lofty conical hills which front the stream. Below a pretty cove, overhung by a white chalky cliff, in the centre of which there stood a tree-covered islet, we occupied a camp near a high and broad tract of pure white sand.

The inhabitants of the settlement on the right side were unfriendly and they had little, save ground-nuts and cassava, to sell. Whether embittered by the sterility of their country, or suffering from some wrongs perpetrated by tribes near Boma, they did not regard our advent to their country with kindly eyes by any means. Indeed, since leaving Ntombo Mataka we had observed a growing degradation of the aborigines, who were vastly inferior in manners and physical type to the Babwendé. They talked "largely," but we had been accustomed to that, and our sense of self-respect had long ago become deadened. We obtained a little food—a supply of ground-nuts and bitter cassava; otherwise we must have died.

July 30.—On the 30th of July we continued our journey along the right bank. We first passed several serrated schistose reefs; and behind these we saw a deep creek-like cove—no doubt the Covinda Cove of Tuckey.

Observing at Rock Bluffs Point that the river was ruffled by rocks, we struck again to the left bank, and, following the grove-clad bend, we saw a fine reach of river extending north-west by north, with a breadth of about eighteen hundred yards. Again we crossed the river to the right bank, and a mile from Rock Bluffs Point came to some rapids which extended across the river. We passed these easily, however, and continued on our journey under the shelter of brown stone bluffs, from fifty to eighty feet high. On the left side of the river I observed a line of rock-islets close to the shore. At the end of this long reach was a deep bend in the right bank, through which a lazy creek oozed slowly into the Livingstone. From this bend the great river ran south-south-west, and the roar of a great cataract two miles below became fearfully audible, and up from it light clouds of mist, and now and then spray showers, were thrown high into view. Towering above it, on the left, was the precipitous shoulder of a mountain ridge, the summit of which appeared crescent-shaped as we approached it from above. Picking our way towards it cautiously, close to projected reefy points, behind which are the entrances to the recesses in the mountainous bank already described, we arrived within fifty yards of the cataract of Isangila, or Tuckey's "Second Sangalla."

We drew our boat and canoes into a sandy-edged basin in the low rocky terrace, and proceeded to view the cataract of Isangila. On the left rises the precipitous shoulder of a mountain ridge, the highest summit of which may be 900 feet. On the right a naked and low rocky terrace is projected from a grassy and gently sloping shelf a mile deep, above which the table-land rises 1200 feet with steep slopes. The rocky terrace appears to be covered by the river in the flood season, but at this period it is contracted to a width of 500 yards. The fall is in the shape of a crescent, along which arise at intervals rocky protuberances of an iron-rust colour, seven in number, one of which, near the middle of the stream, is large enough to be called an islet, being probably a hundred yards in length. Near the right side there is a clear drop of 10 feet, and close below it another drop of 8 feet; on the left side the river hurls itself against the base of the cliff, and then swerves abruptly aside to a south-west-by-south direction; it bounds down the steep descent in a succession of high leaping billows, along a wild tempestuous stretch of a mile and a half in length, disparted in its course by a lofty island, below which it sweeps round into an ample sand-lined basin on the left bank, south of the cataract. To study the nature of the ground I proceeded to a point opposite this basin, and observed the river continue in a westerly course (magnetic). There are abundant traces of lava in the neighbourhood of this cataract, and the cliffs opposite have the appearance of rock subjected to the influence of a fierce fire.

After about two hours' stay here, the inhabitants of Mwato Zingé, Mwato Wandu, and Mbinda visited us, and we soon became on terms of sociable and friendly intercourse with them; but, unfortunately, they possessed nothing but ground-nuts, bitter cassava, and a few bananas. A couple of goats were purchased at a ruinous price; a handful of ground-nuts cost a necklace of beads, while cowries were worthless. Rum, gunpowder, and guns would have purchased ample supplies; but such things required a railway for transportation, and our own guns we could not part with. One chief from the left bank above the cataract came over with his little boy, a pure albino, with blue eyes, curly white hair, and a red skin, of whom he appeared to be very proud, as he said he was also a little Mundelé. The old chief's hands were bleached in the palms, and in various parts of the body, proving the origin of the peculiar disease.

We received the good news that Embomma was only five days' journey, rated thus:—

From	Isangila	to	Inga	1 day.
,,	Inga	,,	Boondi	,,
,,	Boondi	,,	Ntabo	,,
,,	Ntabo	,,	Bibbi	,,
,,	Bibbi	,,	Embomma	,,

We heard also that there were three great cataracts below Isangila, and "any number" of intermediate "Mputu-putuputu" rapids. The cataracts were Nsongo Yellala, a larger one than either Isangila, Yellala, or Ngufu.

There was not the slightest doubt in my mind that the Isangila cataract was the second Sangalla of Captain Tuckey and Professor Smith, and that the Sanga Yellala of Tuckey and the Sanga Jelalla of Smith was the Nsongo Yellala, though I could not induce the natives to pronounce the words as the members of the unfortunate Congo Expedition of 1816 spelled them.*

As the object of the journey had now been attained, and the great river of Livingstone had been connected with the Congo of Tuckey, I saw no reason to follow it farther, or to expend the little remaining vitality we possessed in toiling through the last four cataracts.

* I ascertained, upon studying carefully the accounts of the Congo Expedition of 1816, that Professor Smith's account in many respects is much more reliable than Captain Tuckey's. Professor Smith gives the river above Isangila a general width of about one English mile, which is quite correct, and at a place which the officers reached on the 8th September, 1816, he estimates the width to be about half a Danish mile, which Captain Tuckey has unaccountably extended to about four or five English miles, that is to say, from 6640 to 8800 yards! Captain Tuckey, according to Stanford's Library Map of 1874, places the second Sangalla by dead reckoning in east longitude 14° 36′, south latitude 4° 59′, which is very far from being its position. On July 28, 1877, I obtained south latitude 5° 19′ by observation. Captain Tuckey is, however, more reliable in his orthography than the botanist of his Expedition. Both gentlemen have unaccountably passed the largest fall, viz., Nsongo Yellala, with but a mere word of mention.

I announced, therefore, to the gallant but wearied Wangwana that we should abandon the river and strike overland for Embomma. The delight of the people manifested itself in loud and fervid exclamations of gratitude to Allah! Quadruple ration-money was also distributed to each man, woman, and child; but owing to the excessive poverty of the country, and the keen trading instincts and avaricious spirit of the aborigines, little benefit did the long-enduring, famine-stricken Wangwana derive from my liberality.

July 31.—Fancy knick-knacks, iron spears, knives, axes, copper, brass wire, were then distributed to them, and I emptied the medicine out of thirty vials; and my private clothes-bags, blankets, waterproofs, every available article of property that might be dispensed with, were also given away, without distinction of rank or merit, to invest in whatever eatables they could procure. The 31st of July was consequently a busy day, devoted to bartering, but few Wangwana were able to boast at evening that they had obtained a tithe of the value of the articles they had sold, and the character of the food actually purchased was altogether unfit for people in such poor condition of body.

At sunset we lifted the brave boat, after her adventurous journey across Africa, and carried her to the summit of some rocks about five hundred yards north of the fall, to be abandoned to her fate. Three years before, Messenger of Teddington had commenced her construction; two years previous to this date she was coasting the bluffs of Uzongora on Lake Victoria; twelve months later she was completing her last twenty miles of the circumnavigation of Lake Tanganika, and on the 31st of July, 1877, after a journey of nearly 7000 miles up and down broad Africa, she was consigned to her resting-place above the Isangila Cataract, to bleach and to rot to dust!

* * * * * *

Aug. 1.—A wayworn, feeble, and suffering column were we when, on the 1st of August, we filed across the rocky terrace of Isangila and sloping plain, and strode up the ascent to the table-land. Nearly forty men filled the sick list with dysentery, ulcers, and scurvy, and the victims of the latter disease were steadily increasing. Yet withal I smiled proudly when I saw the brave hearts cheerily respond to my encouraging cries. A few, however, would not believe that within five or six days they should see Europeans.

They disdained to be considered so credulous, but at the same time they granted that the "master" was quite right to encourage his people with promises of speedy relief.

So we surmounted the table-land, but we could not bribe the wretched natives to guide us to the next village. "Mirambo," the riding-ass, managed to reach half-way up the table-land, but he also was too far exhausted through the miserable attenuation which the poor grass of the western region had wrought in his frame to struggle further. We could only pat him on the neck and say, "Good-bye, old boy; farewell, old hero! A bad world this for you and for us. We must part at last." The poor animal appeared to know that we were leaving him, for he neighed after us—a sickly, quavering neigh, that betrayed his excessive weakness. When we last turned to look at him he was lying on the path, but looking up the hill with pointed ears, as though he were wondering why he was left alone, and whither his human friends and companions by flood and field were wandering.

After charging the chief of Mbinda to feed him with cassava leaves and good grass from his fields, I led the caravan over the serried levels of the lofty upland.

At the end of this district, about a mile from Mwato Wandu, we appeared before a village whose inhabitants permitted us to pass on for a little distance, when they suddenly called out to us with expostulatory tones at an almost shrieking pitch. The old chief, followed by about fifty men, about forty of whom carried guns, hurried up to me and sat down in the road,

In a composed and consequential tone he asked, "Know you I am the king of this country?"

I answered mildly, "I knew it not, my brother."

"I am the king, and how can you pass through my country without paying me?"

"Speak, my friend; what is it the Mundelé can give you?"

"Rum. I want a big bottle of rum, and then you can pass on."

"Rum?"

"Yes, rum, for I am the king of this country!"

"Rum!" I replied wonderingly.

"Rum; rum is good. I love rum," he said, with a villainous leer.

Uledi, coming forward, impetuously asked, "What does this old man want, master?"

"He wants rum, Uledi. Think of it!"

"There's rum for him," he said, irreverently slapping his Majesty over the face, who, as the stool was not very firm, fell over prostrate. Naturally this was an affront, and I reproved Uledi for it. Yet it seemed that he had extricated us from a difficult position by his audacity, for the old chief and his people hurried off to their village, where there was great excitement and perturbation, but we could not stay to see the end.

Ever and anon, as we rose above the ridged swells, we caught the glimpse of the wild river on whose bosom we had so long floated. Still white and foaming, it rushed on impetuously seaward through the sombre defile. Then we descended into a deep ravine, and presently, with uneasy throbbing hearts, we breasted a steep slope rough with rock, and from its summit we looked abroad over a heaving, desolate, and ungrateful land. The grass was tall and ripe, and waved and rustled mournfully before the upland breezes. Soon the road declined into a valley, and we were hid in a deep fold, round which rose the upland, here to the west shagged with a thin forest, to the north with ghastly sere grass, out of which rose a few rocks, grey and sad. On our left was furze, with scrub. At the bottom of this, sad and desolate, ran a bright crystal brook. Up again to the summit we strove to gain the crest of a ridge, and then, down once more the tedious road wound in crooked curves to the depth of another ravine, on the opposite side of which rose sharply and steeply, to the wearying height of 1200 feet, the range called Yangi-Yangi. At 11 A.M. we in the van had gained the lofty summit, and fifteen minutes afterwards we descried a settlement and its cluster of palms. An hour afterwards we were camped on a bit of level plateau to the south of the villages of Ndambi Mbongo.

The chiefs appeared, dressed in scarlet military coats of a past epoch. We asked for food for beads. "Cannot." "For wire?" "We don't want wire!" "For cowries?" "Are we bushmen?" "For cloth?" "You must wait three days for a market! If you have got rum you can have plenty!!" Rum! Heavens! Over two years and eight months ago we departed from the shores of the Eastern Ocean, and they ask us for rum!

Yet they were not insolent, but unfeeling; they were not rude, but steely selfish. We conversed with them sociably enough, and obtained encouragement. A strong healthy man would reach Embomma in three days. Three days! Only three days off from food—from comforts—luxuries even! Ah me!

Aug. 2.—The next day, when morning was greying, we lifted our weakened limbs for another march. And such a march!—the path all thickly strewn with splinters of suet-coloured quartz, which increased the fatigue and pain. The old men and the three mothers, with their young infants born at the cataracts of Massassa and Zinga, and another near the market town of Manyanga, in the month of June, suffered greatly. Then might be seen that affection for one another which appealed to my sympathies, and endeared them to me still more. Two of the younger men assisted each of the old, and the husbands and fathers lifted their infants on their shoulders and tenderly led their wives along.

Up and down the desolate and sad land wound the poor, hungry caravan. Bleached whiteness of ripest grass, grey rock-piles here and there, looming up solemn and sad in their greyness, a thin grove of trees now and then visible on the heights and in the hollows—such were the scenes that with every uplift of a ridge or rising crest of a hill met our hungry eyes. Eight miles our strength enabled us to make, and then we camped in the middle of an uninhabited valley, where we were supplied with water from the pools which we discovered in the course of a dried-up stream.

Our march on the third day was a continuation of the scenes of the day preceding until about ten o'clock, when we arrived at the summit of a grassy and scrub-covered ridge, which we followed until three in the afternoon. The van then appeared before the miserable settlement of Nsanda, or, as it is sometimes called, Banza (town) N'sanda N'sanga. Marching through the one street of the first village in melancholy and silent procession, voiceless as sphinxes, we felt our way down into a deep gully, and crawled up again to the level of the village site, and camped about two hundred yards away. It was night before all had arrived.

Aug. 4.—After we had erected our huts and lifted the tent into its usual place, the chief of Nsanda appeared, a youngish, slightly made man, much given to singing, being normally drunk from an excess of palm-wine. He was kindly, sociable—laughed, giggled, and was amusing. Of course he knew Embomma, had frequently visited there, and carried thither large quantities of *Nguba* ground-nuts, which he had sold for rum. We listened, as in duty bound, with a melancholy interest. Then I suddenly asked him if he would carry a *makanda*, or letter, to Embomma, and allow three of my men to accompany him. He was too great to proceed himself, but he would despatch two of his young men the next day. His consent I obtained only after four hours of earnest entreaty. It was finally decided that I should write a letter, and the two young natives would be ready next day. After my dinner—three fried bananas, twenty roasted ground-nuts, and a cup of muddy water, my usual fare now—by a lamp made out of a piece of rotten sheeting steeped in a little palm-butter I wrote the following letter :—

"Village of Nsanda, *August* 4, 1877.

"*To any Gentleman who speaks English at Embomma.*

"DEAR SIR,

"I have arrived at this place from Zanzibar with 115 souls, men, women and children. We are now in a state of imminent starvation. We can buy nothing from the natives, for they laugh at our kinds of cloth, beads, and wire. There are no provisions in the country that may be purchased, except on market days, and starving people cannot afford to wait for these markets. I, therefore, have made bold to despatch three of my young men, natives of Zanzibar, with a boy named Robert Feruzi, of the English Mission at Zanzibar, with this letter craving relief from you. I do not know you; but I am told there is an Englishman at Embomma, and as you are a Christian and a gentleman, I beg you not to disregard my request. The boy Robert will be better able to describe our lone condition than I can tell you in this letter. We are in a state of the greatest distress; but if your supplies arrive in time, I may be able to reach Embomma within four days. I want three hundred cloths, each four yards long, of such quality as you trade with, which is very different from that we have; but better than all would ten or fifteen man-loads of rice or grain to fill their pinched bellies immediately, as even with the cloths it would require time to purchase food, and starving people cannot wait. The supplies must arrive within two days, or I may have a fearful time of it among the dying. Of course I hold myself responsible for any expense you may incur in this business. What is wanted is immediate relief; and I pray you to use your utmost energies to forward it at once. For myself, if you have such little luxuries as tea, coffee, sugar, and biscuits by you, such as one man can easily carry, I beg you on my own behalf that you will send a small supply, and add to the great debt of gratitude due to you upon the timely arrival of the supplies for my people. Until that time I beg you to believe me,

"Yours sincerely,

"H. M. Stanley,

"**Commanding Anglo-American Expedition for Exploration of Africa.**

"P.S.—You may not know me by name; I therefore add, I am the person that discovered Livingstone in 1871. —H. M. S."

I also wrote a letter in French, and another in Spanish as a substitute for Portuguese, as I heard at Nsanda that there was one Englishman, one Frenchman, and three Portuguese at Embomma; but there were conflicting statements, some saying that there was no Englishman, but a Dutchman. However, I imagined I was sure to obtain provisions—for most European merchants understand either English, French, or Spanish.

The chiefs and boat's crew were called to my tent. I then told them that I had resolved to despatch four messengers to the white men at Embomma, with letters asking for food, and wished to know the names of those most likely to travel quickly and through anything that interposed to prevent them; for it might be possible that so small a number of men might be subjected to delays and interruptions, and that the guides might loiter on the way, and so protract the journey until relief would arrive too late.

The response was not long coming, for Uledi sprang up and said, "Oh, master, don't talk more; I am ready now. See, I will only buckle on my belt, and I shall start at once, and nothing will stop me. I will follow on the track like a leopard."

"And I am one," said Kachéché. "Leave us alone,

master. If there are white men at Embomma, we will find them out. We will walk, and walk, and when we cannot walk we will crawl."

"Leave off talking, men," said Muini Pembé, "and allow others to speak, won't you? Hear me, my master. I am your servant. I will outwalk the two. I will carry the letter, and plant it before the eyes of the white men."

"I will go too, sir," said Robert.

"Good. It is just as I should wish it; but, Robert, you cannot follow these three men. You will break down, my boy."

"Oh, we will carry him if he breaks down," said Uledi. "Won't we, Kachéché?"

"Inshallah!" responded Kachéché decisively. "We must have Robert along with us, otherwise the white men won't understand us."

Aug. 5.—Early the next day the two guides appeared, but the whole of the morning was wasted in endeavouring to induce them to set off. Uledi waxed impatient, and buckled on his accoutrements, drawing his belt so tight about his waist that it was perfectly painful to watch him, and said, "Give us the letters, master! we will not wait for the pagans. Our people will be dead before we start. Regard them, will you! They are sprawling about the camp without any life in them. Goee—Go-ee—Go-ee." Finally, at noon, the guides and messengers departed in company.

Meanwhile a bale of cloth and a sack of beads were distributed, and the strongest and youngest men despatched abroad in all directions to forage for food. Late in the afternoon they arrived in camp weakened and dispirited, having, despite all efforts, obtained but a few bundles of the miserable ground-nuts and sufficient sweet potatoes to give three small ones to each person, though they had given twenty times their value for each one. The heartless reply of the spoiled aborigines was, "Wait for the zandu," or market, which was to be held in two days at Nsanda; for, as amongst the Babwendé, each district has its respective days for marketing. Still what we had obtained was a respite from death; and, on the morning of the 5th, the people were prepared to drag their weary limbs nearer to the expected relief.

Our route lay along the crest of a ridge, until we arrived at a narrow alluvial valley, in which the chief village of the Nsanda district is situate, amidst palms, ground-nut, and cassava gardens, and small patches of beans, peas, and sweet potatoes. From this valley we ascended the grassy upland, until we came to what we might call Southern Nsanda. We had proceeded about two hundred yards beyond it when a powerful man, followed by a large crowd, advanced toward us, and, like him near Mwato Wandu, demanded to know why we passed through without payment.

"Payment! Payment for what? Look at my people; they are skin and bone. They are dying for want of food in your country. Brother, stand off, or these men will be smelling food for themselves, and I would not stop them."

He became outrageous; he called for his gun; his followers armed themselves. Observing matters getting serious, I disposed as a precautionary measure twenty men as skirmishers in front of the road and ten in rear, leaving the goods and sick people in the centre. Word was then given to the powerful man that they had better not shoot, for our people were angry, and were very different from any they had seen, and nothing could stop them if they began; and it was possible they might eat every soul in Nsanda. I observed that the last sentence had a potent effect; the angry demonstrations were followed by a loud consultation; the loud consultation subsided into whispers, and soon the "powerful man" said "Enough," and we advanced towards each other, laughed, and shook hands heartily. At this juncture appeared the chief of the central village, who had furnished us with guides, and he, upon hearing of the intended injury to the Mundelé, insisted upon the "powerful man" bringing forth a gourd and jug and wash-basin full of palm-wine, and sealing our friendship by a "drink all round;" which was done, and I promised to send the "powerful man" a present of a bottle of rum from Embomma.

At 3 P.M., after a march of twelve miles, the van of the Expedition descended the slope of the high wood-covered ridge of Ikungu, whence the populous valley of Mbinda lay revealed. Halfway down the slope we camped, being in view of eighteen villages. The entire population of Mbinda—the valley, or basin, derives its name from the south-eastern ridge, which is called Mbinda—I roughly estimated at being about three thousand souls. Each of these villages bears a different name, but the entire number is under three chiefs, who are styled "kings," and are extremely absurd in their pomposity. The people are sufficiently amiable, but terribly extortionate and grasping, and so niggardly and close in trade that the Wangwana became more and more weakened. Festishism is carried to an extraordinary extent. Idols of wood, tolerably well carved, are numerous, and the various ceremonies practised by these people would fill a volume. Some hideous and ghostly objects, with chalked bodies, wearing skirts of palm-leaves or grass, hovered about at respectful distance, and I was told by the chief of Nsanda that they had been lately circumcised. Ground-nuts are the chief produce here, as well as of all the region from Manyanga of the Babwendé, because they are in demand by the merchants of Embomma. By means of the markets held alternately in each district, the ground-nuts are being brought from immense distances. But while their cultivation retards exploration, it proves that the

MBINDA CEMETERY.

natives are willing to devote themselves to any branch of agriculture that may be profitable. In former days the slave and the ivory-trade supported a vast portion of this region, but perceiving that slaves are not now in demand, and ivory not abundant enough to be profitable, the natives have resorted to the cultivation of ground-nuts for the supply of the Europeans at Embomma, palms for the sake of their intoxicating juice, and only a few small patches of beans, vetches, sweet potatoes, &c., for home consumption.

Close to our camp was a cemetery of a village of Mbinda. The grave-mounds were neat, and by their appearance I should judge them to be not only the repositories of the dead, but also the depositories of all the articles that had belonged to the dead. Each grave was dressed out with the various mugs, pitchers, wash-basins, teapots, kettles, glasses, gin, brandy, and beer bottles, besides iron skillets, kettles, tin watering-pots, and buckets; and above the mound thus curiously decorated were suspended to the branch of a tree the various net haversacks of palm-fibre in which the deceased had carried his ground-nuts, cassava bread, and eatables. The various articles of property thus exhibited, especially the useful articles, had all been purposely rendered useless, otherwise I doubt if, with all their superstition, thieves could have been restrained from appropriating them.

Aug. 6.—On the 6th we roused ourselves for a further effort, and after filing through several villages separated from each other by intervals of waste land, we arrived at 9 A.M. near Banza Mbuko. Haggard, woe-begone invalids, with bloated faces, but terribly angular bodies, we sought a quiet spot a mile beyond the outermost village of the settlement. Mbinda's wooded ridge was in view, and Ikungu's bearded summits were fast receding into distance and obscurity. Banza Mbuko seemed prosperous; the inhabitants appeared to be well fed, but, as though we were denizens of another world, nothing of warm sympathy could I detect in the face of any one of all those that gazed on us. Ah! in what part of all the Japhetic world would such a distressed and woful band as we were then have been regarded with such hard, steel-cold eyes? Yet not one word of reproach issued from the starving people; they threw themselves upon the ground with an indifference begotten of despair and misery. They did not fret, nor bewail aloud the tortures of famine, nor vent the anguish of their pinched bowels in cries, but with stony resignation surrendered themselves to rest, under the scant shade of some dwarf acacia or sparse bush. Now and then I caught the wail of an infant, and the thin voice of a starving mother, or the petulant remonstrance of an older child; but the adults remained still and apparently lifeless, each contracted within the exclusiveness of individual suffering. The youths, companions of Uledi, and the chiefs, sat in whispering groups, removed from the sick and grieving, and darkly dotted the vicinity of the tent; the childless women were also seen by twos and threes far apart, discussing, no doubt, our prospects, for at this period this was the most absorbing topic of the camp.

Suddenly the shrill voice of a little boy was heard saying, "Oh! I see Uledi and Kachéché coming down the hill, and there are plenty of men following them!"

"What!—what!—what!" broke out eagerly from several voices, and dark forms were seen springing up from amongst the bleached grass, and from under the shade, and many eyes were directed at the whitened hill-slope.

"Yes; it is true! it is true! La il Allah il Allah! Yes; el hamd ul Illah! Yes, it is food! food! food at last! Ah, that Uledi! he is a lion, truly! We are saved, thank God!"

Before many minutes, Uledi and Kachéché were seen tearing through the grass, and approaching us with long springing strides, holding a letter up to announce to us that they had been successful. And the gallant fellows, hurrying up, soon placed it in my hands, and in the hearing of all who were gathered to hear the news I translated the following letter:—

"EMBOMMA, "6.30 A.M.,
"ENGLISH FACTORY. "BOMA, *6th August*, 1877.

"H. M. STANLEY, Esq.

"DEAR SIR,

"Your welcome letter came to hand yesterday, at 7 P.M. As soon as its contents were understood, we immediately arranged to despatch to you such articles as you requested, as much as our stock on hand would permit, and other things that we deemed would be suitable in that locality. You will see that we send fifty pieces of cloth, each 24 yards long, and some sacks containing sundries for yourself; several sacks of rice, sweet potatoes, also a few bundles of fish, a bundle of tobacco, and one demijohn of rum. The carriers are all paid, so that you need not trouble yourself about them. That is all we need say about business. We are exceedingly sorry to hear that you have arrived in such piteous condition, but we send our warmest congratulations to you, and hope that you will soon arrive in Boma (this place is called Boma by us, though on the map it is Em-bomma). Again hoping that you will soon arrive, and that you are not suffering in health,

"Believe us to remain,

"Your sincere friends,

"HATTON & COOKSON.

(*Signed*) "A. DA MOTTA VEIGA.
"J. W. HARRISON."

Uledi and Kachéché then delivered their budget. Their guides had accompanied them halfway, when they became frightened by the menaces of some of the natives of Mbinda, and deserted them. The four Wangwana, however, undertook the journey alone, and, following a road for several hours, they appeared at Bibbi after dark. The next day (the 5th), being told by the natives that Boma (to which Embomma was now changed) was lower down river, and unable to obtain guides, the brave fellows resolved upon following the Congo along its banks. About an hour after sunset, after a fatiguing march over many hills, they reached Boma, and, asking a native for the house of the "Ingreza" (English), were shown to the factory of Messrs. Hatton and Cookson, which was superintended by a Portuguese gentleman, Mr. A. da Motta Veiga, and Mr. John W. Harrison, of Liverpool. Kachéché, who was a better narrator than Uledi, then related that a short white man, wearing spectacles, opened the letter, and, after reading awhile, asked which was Robert Feruzi, who answered for himself in English, and, in answer to many questions, gave a summary of our travels and adventures, but not before the cooks were set to prepare an abundance of food, which they sadly needed, after a fast of over thirty hours.

By this time the procession of carriers from Messrs. Hatton and Cookson's factory had approached, and all eyes were directed at the pompous old "capitan" and the relief caravan behind him. Several of the Wangwana officiously stepped forward to relieve the fatigued and perspiring men, and with an extraordinary vigour tossed the provisions—rice, fish, and tobacco bundles—on the ground, except the demijohn of rum, which they called pombé, and handled most carefully. The "capitan" was anxious about my private stores, but the scene transpiring about the provisions was so absorbingly interesting that I could pay no attention as yet to them. While the captains of the messes were ripping open the sacks and distributing the provisions in equal quantities, Murabo, the boat-boy, struck up a glorious loud-swelling chant of triumph and success, into which he deftly, and with a poet's licence, interpolated verses laudatory of the white men of the second sea. The bard, extemporizing, sang much about the great cataracts, cannibals, and pagans, hunger, the wide wastes, great inland seas, and niggardly tribes, and wound up by declaring that the journey was over, that we were even then smelling the breezes of the western ocean, and his master's brothers had redeemed them from the "hell of hunger." And at the end of each verse the voices rose high and clear to the chorus—

> "Then sing, O friends, sing; the journey is ended;
> Sing aloud, O friends, sing to this great sea."

"Enough now; fall to," said Manwa Sera, at which the people nearly smothered him by their numbers. Into each apron, bowl, and utensil held out, the several captains expeditiously tossed full measures of rice and generous quantities of sweet potatoes and portions of fish. The younger men and women hobbled after water, and others set about gathering fuel, and the camp was all animation, where but half an hour previously all had been listless despair. Many people were unable to wait for the food to be cooked, but ate the rice and the fish raw. But when the provisions had all been distributed, and the noggin of rum had been equitably poured into each man's cup, and the camp was in a state of genial excitement, and groups of dark figures discussed with animation the prospective food which the hospitable fires were fast preparing, then I turned to my tent, accompanied by Uledi, Kachéché, the capitan, and the tent-boys, who were, I suppose, eager to witness my transports of delight.

With profound tenderness Kachéché handed to me the mysterious bottles, watching my face the while with his sharp detective eyes as I glanced at the labels, by which the cunning rogue read my pleasure. Pale ale! Sherry! Port wine! Champagne! Several loaves of bread, wheaten bread, sufficient for a week. Two pots of butter. A packet of tea! Coffee! White loaf-sugar! Sardines and salmon! Plum-pudding! Currant, gooseberry, and raspberry jam!

The gracious God be praised for ever! The long war we had maintained against famine and the siege of woe were over, and my people and I rejoiced in plenty! It was only an hour before we had been living on the recollections of the few pea-nuts and green bananas we had consumed in the morning, but now, in an instant, we were transported into the presence of the luxuries of civilization. Never did gaunt Africa appear so unworthy and so despicable before my eyes as now, when imperial Europe rose before my delighted eyes and showed her boundless treasures of life, and blessed me with her stores.

When we all felt refreshed, the cloth bales were opened, and soon, instead of the venerable and tattered relics of Manchester, Salem, and Nashua manufacture, which were hastily consumed by the fire, the people were reclad with white cloths and gay prints. The nakedness of want, the bare ribs, the sharp protruding bones were thus covered; but months must elapse before the hollow sunken cheeks and haggard faces would again resume the healthy bronze colour which distinguishes the well-fed African.

My condition of mind in the evening of the eventful day which was signalized by the happy union which we had made with the merchants of the west coast, may be guessed by the following letter:—

"BANZA MBUKO, *August* 6, 1877.

"MESSRS. A. DA MOTTA VEIGA AND J. W. HARRISON,
EMBOMMA, CONGO RIVER.

"GENTLEMEN,

"I have received your very welcome letter, but better than all, and more welcome, your supplies. I am unable to express just at present how grateful I feel. We are all so overjoyed and confused with our emotions, at the sight of the stores exposed to our hungry eyes—at the sight of the rice, the fish, and the rum, and for me—wheaten bread, butter, sardines, jam, peaches, grapes, beer (ye gods! just think of it—three bottles pale ale!) besides tea and sugar—that we cannot restrain ourselves from falling to and enjoying this sudden bounteous store—and I beg you will charge our apparent want of thankfulness to our greediness. If we do not thank you sufficiently in words, rest assured we feel what volumes could not describe.

"For the next twenty-four hours we shall be too busy eating to think of anything else much; but I may say that the people cry out joyfully, while their mouths are full of rice and fish, 'Verily, our master has found the sea, and his brothers, but we did not believe him until he showed us the rice and the pombé (rum). We did not believe there was any end to the great river; but, God be praised for ever, we shall see white people to-morrow, and our wars and troubles will be over.'

"Dear Sirs—though strangers, I feel we shall be great friends, and it will be the study of my lifetime to remember my feelings of gratefulness, when I first caught sight of your supplies, and my poor faithful and brave people cried out, 'Master, we are saved!—food is coming!' The old and the young—the men, the women, the children—lifted their wearied and worn-out frames, and began to chant lustily an extemporaneous song, in honour of the white people by the great salt sea (the Atlantic) who had listened to their prayers. I had to rush to my tent to hide the tears that would issue, despite all my attempts at composure.

"Gentlemen, that the blessing of God may attend your footsteps whithersoever you go is the very earnest prayer of

"Yours faithfully,

"Henry M. Stanley,

"Commanding Anglo-American Expedition."

Aug. 7.—At the same hour on the morning of the 7th that we resumed the march, Kachéché and Uledi were despatched to Boma with the above letter. Then surmounting a ridge, we beheld a grassy country barred with seams of red clay in gullies, ravines, and slopes, the effects of rain, dipping into basins with frequently broad masses of plateau and great dyke-like ridges between, and in the distance south-west of us a lofty, tree-clad hill-range, which we were told we should have to climb before descending to N'lamba N'lamba, where we proposed camping.

Half an hour's march brought us to a market-place, where a tragedy had been enacted a short time before the relief caravan had passed it the day previous. Two thieves had robbed a woman of salt, and, according to the local custom which ordains the severest penalties for theft in the public mart, the two felons had been immediately executed, and their bodies laid close to the path to deter others evilly disposed from committing like crimes.

At noon we surmounted the lofty range which we had viewed near Banza Mbuko, and the aneroid indicated a height of 1500 feet. A short distance from its base, on two grassy hills, is situate N'lamba N'lamba, a settlement comprising several villages, and as populous as Mbinda. The houses and streets were very clean and neat; but, as of old, the natives are devoted to idolatry, and their passion for carving wooden idols was illustrated in every street we passed through.

Aug. 8.—On the 8th we made a short march of five

GROUP OF MR. STANLEY'S FOLLOWERS AT KABINDA, WEST COAST OF AFRICA, JUST AFTER CROSSING THE "DARK CONTINENT."

[*To face page* 376.

(From a photograph by Mr. Phillips, of Kabinda.)

miles to N'safu, over a sterile, bare, and hilly country, but the highest ridge passed was not over 1100 feet above the sea. Uledi and Kachéché returned at this place with more cheer for us, and a note acknowledging my letter of thanks.

In a postscript to this note, Mr. Motta Veiga prepared me for a reception which was to meet me on the road halfway between N'safu and Boma; it also contained the census of the European population, as follows:—

"Perhaps you do not know that in Boma there are only eleven Portuguese, one Frenchman, one Dutchman, one gentleman from St. Helena, and ourselves (Messrs. Motta Veiga and J. W. Harrison), Messrs. Hatton and Cookson being in Liverpool, and the two signatures above being names of those in charge of the English factory here."

Aug. 9.—On the 9th of August, 1877, the 999th day from the date of our departure from Zanzibar, we prepared to greet the van of civilization.

From the bare rocky ridges of N'safu there is a perceptible decline to the Congo valley, and the country becomes, in appearance, more sterile—a sparse population dwelling in a mere skeleton village in the centre of bleakness. Shingly rocks strewed the path and the waste, and thin sere grass waved mournfully on level and spine, on slope of ridge and crest of hill; in the hollows it was somewhat thicker; in the bottoms it had a slight tinge of green.

We had gradually descended some five hundred feet along declining spurs when we saw a scattered string of hammocks appearing, and gleams of startling whiteness, such as were given by fine linen and twills.

A buzz of wonder rang along our column.

Proceeding a little farther, we stopped, and in a short time I was face to face with four white—ay, truly white men!

As I looked into their faces, I blushed to find that I was wondering at their paleness. Poor pagan Africans—Rwoma of Uzinja, and man-eating tribes of the Livingstone! The whole secret of their wonder and curiosity flashed upon me at once. What arrested the twanging bow and the deadly trigger of the cannibals? What but the weird pallor of myself and Frank! In the same manner the sight of the pale faces of the Embomma merchants gave me the slightest suspicion of an involuntary shiver. The pale colour, after so long gazing on rich black and richer bronze, had something of an unaccountable ghastliness. I could not divest myself of the feeling that they must be sick; yet, as I compare their complexions to what I now view, I should say they were olive, sunburnt, dark.

Yet there was something very self-possessed about the carriage of these white men. It was grand; a little self-pride mixed with cordiality. I could not remember just then that I had witnessed such bearing among any tribe throughout Africa. They spoke well also; the words they uttered hit the sense pat; without gesture, they were perfectly intelligible. How strange! It was quite delightful to observe the slight nods of the head; the intelligent facial movements were admirably expressive. They were completely clothed, and neat also; I ought to say immaculately clean. Jaunty straw hats, coloured neck-ties, patent-leather boots, well-cut white clothes, virtuously clean! I looked from them to my people, and then I fear I felt almost like being grateful to the Creator that I was not as black as they, and that these finely-dressed, well-spoken whites claimed me as friend and kin. Yet I did not dare to place myself upon an equality with them as yet; the calm blue and grey eyes rather awed me, and the immaculate purity of their clothes dazzled me. I was content to suppose myself a kind of connecting link between the white and the African for the time being. Possibly familiarity would beget greater confidence.

They expressed themselves delighted to see me; congratulated me with great warmth of feeling, and offered to me the "Freedom of Boma!" We travelled together along the path for a mile, and came to the frontier village of Boma, or Embomma, where the "king" was at hand to do the honours. My courteous friends had brought a hamper containing luxuries. Hock and champagne appeared to be cheap enough where but a few hours previous a cup of palm-wine was as precious as nectar; rare dainties of Paris and London abundant, though a short time ago we were stinted of even ground-nuts. Nor were the Wangwana forgotten, for plenty had also been prepared for them.

My friends who thus welcomed me amongst the descendants of Japhet were Mr. A. da Motta Veiga, Senhores Luiz Pinto Maroo, João Chaves, Henrique Germano Faro, and Mr. J. F. Müller, of the Dutch factory. They had brought a hammock with them, and eight sturdy, well-fed bearers.

THE RECUPERATED AND RECLAD EXPEDITION AS IT APPEARED AT ADMIRALTY HOUSE, SIMON'S TOWN, AFTER OUR ARRIVAL ON H.M.S. 'INDUSTRY.'

[*To face page* 358.

They insisted on my permitting them to lift me into the hammock. I declined. They said it was a Portuguese custom. To custom, therefore, I yielded, though it appeared very effeminate.

It was a gradual slope through a valley, which soon opened into a low alluvial plain, seamed here and there with narrow gullies, and then over the heads of the tall grass as I lay in the hammock I caught a glimpse of the tall square box of a frame-house, with a steep roof, erected on rising ground. It brought back a host of old recollections; for everywhere on the frontiers of civilization in America one may see the like. It approached nearer and larger to the view, and presently the hammock was halted by whitewashed palings, above which the square two-storied box rose on piles with a strangeness that was almost weird. It was the residence of those in charge of the English factory.

Looking from the house, my eyes rested on the river. Ah! the hateful, murderous river, now so broad and proud and majestically calm, as though it had not bereft me of a friend, and of many faithful souls, and as though we had never heard it rage and whiten with fury, and mock the thunder. What a hypocritical river! But just below the landing a steamer was ascending—the *Kabinda*, John Petherbridge, master. How civilization was advancing on me! Not a moment even to lie down and rest! Full-blooded, eager, restless, and aggressive, it pressed on me, and claimed me for its own, without allowing me even the time to cast one retrospective glance at the horrors left behind. While still overwhelmed by the thought, the people of the Expedition appeared, pressing forward to admire and gaze wide-eyed at the strange "big iron canoe," driven by fire on *their* river; for there were several Wanyamwezi, Waganda, and east coast men who would not believe that there was anything more wonderful than the *Lady Alice*.

Our life at Boma,* which lasted only from 11 A.M. of the 9th to noon of the 11th, passed too quickly away; but throughout it was intensest pleasure and gaiety.

There are some half-dozen factories at Boma, engaging the attention of about eighteen whites. The houses are all constructed of wooden boards, with, as a rule, corrugated zinc roofs. The residences line the river front; the Dutch,

* There were three little banquets given me at Boma, and I do believe everybody toasted me, for which I felt very much obliged.

French, and Portuguese factories being west of an isolated high square-browed hill, which, by-the-bye, is a capital site for a fortlet; and the English factory being a few hundred yards above it. Each factory requires an ample courtyard for its business, which consists in the barter of cotton fabrics, glass-ware, crockery, iron-ware, gin, rum, guns and gunpowder, for palm-oil, ground-nuts, and ivory. The merchants contrive to exist as comfortably as their means will allow. Some of them plant fruits and garden vegetables, and cultivate grape-vines. Pine-apples, guavas and limes may be obtained from the market, which is held on alternate days a short distance behind the European settlement.

Though Boma is comparatively ancient, and Europeans have had commercial connections with this district and the people for over a century, yet Captain Tuckey's description of the people, written in 1816—their ceremonies and modes of life, their suspicion of strangers and intolerance, their greed for rum and indolence, the scarcity of food—is as correct as though written to-day. The name "Boma," however, has usurped that of "Lombee," which Captain Tuckey knew; the *banza* of Embomma being a little distance inland. In his day it was a village of about one hundred huts, in which was held the market of the banza, or king's town.

The view inland is dreary, bleak, and unpromising, consisting of grassy hills, and of a broken country, its only boast the sturdy baobab, which relieves the nakedness of the land. But—fresh from the hungry wilderness and the land of selfish men, from the storm and stress of the cataracts, the solemn rock defiles of the Livingstone, and the bleak table-land —I heeded it not. The glowing warm life of Western civilization, the hospitable civilities and gracious kindnesses which the merchants of Boma showered on myself and people, were as dews of Paradise, grateful, soothing, and refreshing.

Aug. 11.—On the 11th, at noon, after a last little banquet and songs, hearty cheers, innumerable toasts, and fervid claspings of friendly hands, we embarked. An hour before sunset the "big iron canoe," after a descent of about thirty-five miles, hauled in-shore, on the right bank, and made fast to the pier of another of Hatton and Cookson's factories at Ponta da Lenha, or Wooded Point. Two or three other Portuguese factories are in close neighbourhood to it, lightening the gloom of the background of black mangrove and forest.

1. Wife of Murabo.
2. ,, Robert.
3. ,, Mana Koko.
4. Half caste of Gambaragara, whom Wadi Rehani married.
5. Zaidi's wife.
6. Wife of Wadi Baraka.
7. Wife of Manwa Sera.
8. ,, Chowpereh.
9. ,, Mului Pembé.
10. Wife of Muscati.
11. ,, Chiwonda.
12. ,, Mutta.

[To face page 360.

After a very agreeable night with our hospitable English host, the *Kabinda* was again under way.

The puissant river below Boma reminded me of the scenes above Uyanzi; the colour of the water, the numerous islands, and the enormous breadth recalled those days when we had sought the liquid wildernesses of the Livingstone, to avoid incessant conflicts with the human beasts of prey in the midst of Primitive Africa, and at the sight my eyes filled with tears at the thought that I could not recall my lost friends, and bid them share the rapturous joy that now filled the hearts of all those who had endured and survived.

A few hours later and we were gliding through the broad portal into the Ocean, the blue domain of civilization!

Turning to take a farewell glance at the mighty River on whose brown bosom we had endured so greatly, I saw it approach, awed and humbled, the threshold of the watery immensity, to whose immeasurable volume and illimitable expanse, awful as had been its power, and terrible as had been its fury, its flood was but a drop. And I felt my heart suffused with purest gratitude to Him whose hand had protected us, and who had enabled us to pierce the Dark Continent from east to west, and to trace its mightiest River to its Ocean bourne.

AT REST: MY QUARTERS AT KABINDA BY THE SEA.

(From a photograph by Mr. Phillips.)

CONCLUSION.

Kabinda—San Paulo de Loanda—Simon's Bay—Cape Town—Natal—Zanzibar—Joy of the returned—The martyrs to geography—Reverie—Laus Deo!

Aug. 12–20.—After steaming northward from the mouth of the Congo for a few hours, we entered the fine bay of Kabinda, on the southern shores of which the native town of that name in the country of Ngoyo is situate. On the southern point of the bay stands a third factory of the enterprising firm of Messrs. Hatton and Cookson, under the immediate charge of their principal agent, Mr. John Phillips. A glance at the annexed photograph will sufficiently show the prosperous appearance of the establishment, and the comfortable houses that have been constructed. The Expedition received a cordial welcome from Messrs. Phillips, Wills, Price, and Jones, and I was housed in a cottage surrounded by gardens and overlooking the glorious sea, while the people were located in a large shed fronting the bay.

The next morning, when I proceeded to greet the people, I discovered that one of the Wangwana had died at sunrise; and when I examined the condition of the other sufferers it became apparent that there was to be yet no rest for me, and that to save life I should have to be assiduous and watchful. But for this, I should have surrendered myself to the joys of life, without a thought for myself or for others, and no doubt I should have suffered in the same degree as the Wangwana from the effects of the sudden relaxation from care, trouble, or necessity for further effort. There were also other claims on my energies: I had to write my despatches to the journals, and to re-establish those bonds of friendship and sympathetic communion that had been severed by the lapse of dark years and long months of silence. My poor people, however, had no such incentives to rouse themselves from the stupor of indifference, as fatal to them as the cold to a benighted man in a snowy wilderness. Housed together in a comfortable, barrack-like building, with every convenience provided for them, and supplied with food, raiment, fuel, water, and an excess of luxuries, nothing

EXPEDITION AT KABINDA.

(*From a photograph by Mr. Phillips.*)

remained for them to do; and the consequence was, that the abrupt dead-stop to all action and movement overwhelmed them, and plunged them into a state of torpid brooding from which it was difficult to arouse them.

The words of the poet—

> "What's won is done: Joy's soul lies in the doing"—

or, as Longfellow has it—

> "The reward is in the doing,
> And the rapture of pursuing
> Is the prize"—

recurred to me, as explaining why it was that the people abandoned themselves to the dangerous melancholy created by inactivity. I was charmed by it myself; the senses were fast relapsing into a drowsy state, that appeared to be akin to the drowsiness of delirium. No novel or romance interested me, though Mr. Phillips's cottage possessed a complete library of fiction and light reading. Dickens seemed rubbish, and the finest poems flat. Frequently, even at meals, I found myself subsiding into sleep, though I struggled against it heroically; wine had no charm for me; conversation fatigued me. Yet the love of society, and what was due to my friendly hosts, acted as a wholesome restraint and a healthy stimulant; but what had the poor, untutored black strangers, whose homes were on the east side of the continent, to rouse them and to stimulate them into life?

"Do you wish to see Zanzibar, boys?" I asked.

"Ah, it is far. Nay, speak not, master. We shall never see it," they replied.

"But you will die if you go on in this way. Wake up—shake yourselves—show yourselves to be men."

"Can a man contend with God? Who fears death? Let us die undisturbed, and be at rest for ever," they answered.

Brave, faithful, loyal souls! They were, poor fellows, surrendering themselves to the benumbing influences of a listlessness and fatal indifference to life! Four of them died in consequence of this strange malady at Loanda, three more on board H.M.S. *Industry*, and one woman breathed her last the day after we arrived at Zanzibar. But in their sad death, they had one consolation, in the words which they kept constantly repeating to themselves—

"We have brought our master to the great sea, and he has seen his white brothers, La il Allah, il Allah!—There is no God but God!" they said—and died.

It is not without an overwhelming sense of grief, a choking in the throat and swimming eyes, that I write of those days, for my memory is still busy with the worth and virtues of the dead. In a thousand fields of incident, adventure, and bitter trials they had proved their staunch heroism and their fortitude; they had lived and endured nobly. I remember the enthusiasm with which they responded to my appeals; I remember their bold bearing during the darkest days; I remember the Spartan pluck, the indomitable courage with which they suffered in the days of our adversity. Their voices again loyally answer me, and again I hear them address each other upon the necessity of standing by the "master." Their boat-song, which contained sentiments similar to the following:—

"The pale-faced stranger, lonely here,
In cities afar, where his name is dear,
Your Arab truth and strength shall show;
He trusts in us; row, Arabs, row"—

despite all the sounds which now surround me, still charms my listening ear.

Aug. 21–*Sept.* 27.—The Expedition, after a stay of eight days at Kabinda, was kindly taken on board the Portuguese gunboat *Tamega*, Commander José Marquez, to San Paulo de Loanda. The Portuguese officers distinguished themselves by a superb banquet, and an exhibition of extraordinary courtesy towards myself and great sympathy towards my followers. Two gentlemen, Major Serpa Pinto and Senhor José Avelino Fernandez, who were on board, extended their hospitalities so far as to persuade me to accompany them to their residence in the capital of Angola. To house the 114 Wangwana who accompanied me was a great task on the liberality of these gentlemen, but the Portuguese Governor-General of Angola nobly released them and myself from all obligations, and all the expenses incurred by us from the 21st of August to the 27th of September were borne by the colony. One of the first acts of Governor-General Albuquerque was to despatch his aide-de-camp with offers of assistance, money, and a gunboat to convey me to Lisbon, which received, as it deserved, my warmest thanks. The Portuguese Commodore gave a banquet to the Portuguese explorers, Major Serpa Pinto, Commander Brito Capello, and Lieutenant Roberto Ivens, who were about setting out for the exploration of the Kunené or Nourse river, as far as Bihé, thence to Lake Nyassa and Mozambique, and upon the festive occasion they honoured me. The Board of Works at Loanda also banqueted us royally; as also did Mr. Michael Tobin, the banker, while Mr. Robert Newton was unceasing in his hospitalities.

The Government hospital at Loanda was open to the sick strangers; Doctor Lopez and his assistants daily visited the sick ward of our residence, and a trained nurse was detailed to attend the suffering. Pure Samaritanism animated the enthusiastic Senhor Capello, and free unselfish charity inspired my friend Avelino Fernandez to watch and tend the ailing, desponding, and exhausted travellers.

With a generosity unequalled, Serpa Pinto distributed a large sum of money among them, that they might be enabled to suit their sick cravings as they pleased in the markets.

Nor must the English officers of the Royal Navy be forgotten for their chivalrous kindness. I shall ever remember Captain Maxwell Heron, of H.M.S. *Seagull*, and Captain D. Hopkins, British Consul, as my friends; and so also Captain John Childs Purvis, of H.M.S. *Danae*, who, when I was wondering whether I should be compelled to lead the Wangwana across the continent to their homes, solved my doubts and anxieties by offering the Expedition a passage to Cape Town in H.M.S. *Industry*, Commander R. C. Dyer. The offer of the Portuguese Governor-General to convey me in a gunboat to Lisbon, and the regular arrivals of the Portuguese mail steamers, were very tempting, but the condition of my followers was such that I found it impossible to leave them. I resolved therefore to accompany them to the Cape of Good Hope.

The cordial civilities that were accorded to us at Loanda were succeeded by equally courteous treatment on board the *Industry*. Her officers, Captain Dyer, Assistant-Surgeon William Brown, and Paymaster Edwin Sandys, assisted me to the utmost of their ability in alleviating the sufferings of the sick and reviving the vigour of the desponding. But the accomplished surgeon found his patients most difficult cases. The flame of life flickered and spluttered, and to fan it into brightness required in most of the cases patience and tact more than medicine. Yet there was a little improvement in them, though they were still heavy-eyed.

Oct. 21–*Nov.* 6.—Upon arriving at Simon's Bay, Cape of Good Hope, on the 21st of October, I was agreeably surprised by a most genial letter, signed by Commodore Francis William Sullivan, who invited me to the Admiralty House as his guest, and from whom during the entire period of our stay at the Cape we met with the most hearty courtesy and hospitality. He had also made preparations for transporting the Expedition to Zanzibar, when a telegram from the Lords of the British Admiralty was received, authorizing him to provide for the transmission of my followers to their homes, an act of gracious kindness for which I have recorded elsewhere my most sincere thanks.

Had we been able to accept all the invitations that were showered upon us by the kind-hearted colonists of South Africa, from Cape Town to Natal, it is possible we might still be enjoying our holiday at that remote end of Africa, but her Majesty's ship could not be delayed for our pleasure and gratification. But during the time she was refitting, the authorities of Cape Town and Stellenbosch, through the influence of Lady Frere, Commodore Sullivan, and Captain Mills, Colonial Secretary, exerted themselves so zealously to gratify and honour us, that I attribute a large share of the recovery in health of my followers to the cordial and unmistakable heartiness of the hospitalities they there enjoyed. Here the Wangwana saw for the first time the "fire-carriage," and, accompanied by Commodore Sullivan, the Dean of Cape Town and several of the leading residents of the Cape, the Expedition was whirled to Stellenbosch at the rate of thirty miles an hour, which, of all the wonders they had viewed, seemed to them the most signal example of the wonderful enterprise and superior intelligence of the European. Lady Frere and Commodore Sullivan devised several entertainments for the Wangwana; and the "Great Lady," as they called Lady Frere, presented men, women, and children with many useful souvenirs of their visit to the Governor's palace. The Prime Minister, Mr. Molteno, in the name of the colony, re-clothed them with comfortable "jerseys," which were suitable and necessary in the cold and raw climate. A special evening was devoted to them at the theatre, at which the acrobats received thunderous applause, the most hearty that was probably ever accorded them. Nor must I forget the credit due to the journalists of the metropolis of Cape Colony, who with unanimous cordiality tendered me and mine honours such as are worthy of being treasured. But there was one illustrious figure absent from the festive occasions to which his presence would have given *éclat*—I mean Sir Bartle Frere. I should have been glad to have thanked him for the kindness he has uniformly shown to me, and for his chivalrous defence of me while absent, and to have shown my followers the sterling friend of that pious hero whose bones many of them assisted to carry from the distant camp on Lake Bemba to the Indian Ocean.

I ought not to omit describing a little episode that occurred soon after our arrival in Simon's Bay. For the first three days after landing at Simon's Town, blustering gales prevented me from returning to the ship. The people thereupon became anxious, and wondered whether this distant port was to terminate my connection with them. On returning to the ship, therefore, I found them even more melancholy than when I had left them. I asked the reason.

"You will return to Ulyah" (Europe), "of course, now."

"Why?"

"Oh, do we not see that you have met your friends, and all these days we have felt that you will shortly leave us?"

"Who told you so?" I asked, smiling at the bitterness visible in their faces.

"Our hearts; and they are very heavy."

"Ah! And would it please you if I accompanied you to Zanzibar?"

"Why should you ask, master? Are you not our father?"

"Well, it takes a long time to teach you to rely upon the promise of your father. I have told you, over and over again, that nothing shall cause me to break my promise to you that I would take you home. You have been true to me, and I shall be true to you. If we can get no ship to take us, I will walk the entire distance with you until I can show you to your friends at Zanzibar."

"Now we are grateful, master."

I observed no sad faces after this day, and Captain Dyer and his officers noticed how they visibly improved and brightened up from this time.

On the 6th of November H.M.S. *Industry* was equipped and ready for her voyage to Zanzibar. To the last moment the gallant commodore was consistent in his kindness, and the blue-jackets of the *Active* cheered us heartily as we steered out of Simon's Bay. On the twelfth of the month the *Industry* dropped anchor in the harbour of Natal to coal, and until the fourteenth the Natal press and the mayor of the city of D'Urban contributed generously to the courtesies and genial memories we retain of the rising and prosperous states of South Africa.

Fourteen days afterwards the palmy island of Zanzibar rose into sight, and in the afternoon we were bearing straight for port.

As I looked on the Wangwana, and saw the pleasure which now filled every soul, I felt myself amply rewarded for sacrificing several months to see them home. The sick had, all but one, recovered, and they had improved so much in appearance that few, ignorant of what they had been, could have supposed that these were the living skeletons that had reeled from sheer weakness through Boma.

The only patient who had baffled our endeavours to restore her to health was the woman Muscati, unfortunate Safeni's wife. Singular to relate, she lived to be embraced by her father, and the next morning died in his arms, surrounded by her relatives and friends. But all the others were blessed with redundant health—robust, bright, and happy.

And now the well-known bays and inlets, and spicy shores and red-tinted bluffs of Mbwénni, enraptured them. Again they saw what they had often despaired of seeing: the rising ridge of Wilezu, at the foot of which they knew were their homes and their tiny gardens; the well-known features of Shangani and Melindi; the tall square mass of the Sultan's palace. Each outline, each house, from the Sandy Point to their own Ngambu, each well-remembered bold swell of land, with its glories of palm and mango-tree, was to them replete with associations of bygone times.

The captain did not detain them on board. The boats were all lowered at once, and they crowded the gangway and ladder. I watched the first boat-load.

To those on the beach it was a surprise to see so many white-shirted, turbaned men making for shore from an English man-of-war. Were they slaves—or what? No; slaves they could not be, for they were too well dressed. Yet what could they be?

The boat-keel kissed the beach, and the impatient fellows leaped out and upwards, and danced in ecstasy on the sands of their island; they then kneeled down, bowed their faces to the dear soil, and cried out, with emotion, their thanks to Allah! To the full they now taste the sweetness of the return home. The glad tidings ring out along the beach, "It is Bwana Stanley's expedition that has returned."

Then came bounding toward them their friends, acquaintances, countrymen, demanding ever so many questions, all burning to know all about it. Where had they been? How came they to be on board the man-of-war? What had they seen? Who was dead? Where is So-and-so? You have gone beyond Nyangwé to the other sea? Mashallah!

The boats come and go.

More of the returned braves land, jump and frisk about, shake hands, embrace firmly and closely; they literally *leap* into each other's arms, and there are many wet eyes there, for some terrible tales are told of death, disaster, and woe by the most voluble of the narrators, who seem to think it incumbent on them to tell all the news at once. The minor details, which are a thousand and a thousand, shall be told to-morrow and the next day, and the next, and for days and years to come.

The ship was soon emptied of her strange passengers. Captain Sullivan, of the *London*, came on board, and congratulated me on my safe arrival, and then I went on shore to my friend Mr. Augustus Sparhawk's house. We will pass over whatever may have transpired among the reunited friends, relatives, acquaintances, &c., but I will give substantially what Mabruki, a stout, bright-eyed lad, the Nestor of the youths during the expedition, related of his experiences the next day.

"Well, Mabruki, tell me, did you see your mother?" Mabruki, knowing I have a lively curiosity to know all about the meeting, because he had been sometimes inclined to despair of seeing poor old "mamma" again, relaxes the severe tightness of his face, and out of his eyes there gushes such a flood of light as shows him to be brimful of happiness, and he hastens to answer, with a slight bob of the head—

"Yes, master."

"Is she quite well? How does she look? What did she say when she saw her son such a great strong lad? Come, tell me all about it."

"I will tell you—but ah! she is old now. She did not know me at first, because I burst open the door of our house, and I was one of the foremost to land, and I ran all the way from the boat to the house. She was sitting talking with a friend. When the door opened she cried out, 'Who?'

"'Mi-mi, ma-ma. It is I, mother. It is I—Mabruki, mother. It is I, returned from the continent.'

"'What! Mabruki, my son!'

"'Verily it is I, mother.'

"She could scarcely believe I had returned, for she had heard no news. But soon all the women round about gathered together near the door, while the house was full, to hear the news; and they were all crying and laughing and talking so fast, which they kept up far into the night. She is very proud of me, master. When the dinner was ready over twenty sat down to share with us. 'Oh!' they all said, 'you are a man indeed, now that you have been farther than any Arab has ever been.'"

Four days of grace I permitted myself to procure the thousands of rupees required to pay off the people for their services. Messages had also been sent to the relatives of the dead, requesting them to appear at Mr. Sparhawk's, prepared to make their claims good by the mouths of three witnesses.

On the fifth morning the people—men, women, and children—of the Anglo-American Expedition, attended by hundreds of friends, who crowded the street and the capacious rooms of the Bertram Agency, began to receive their well-earned dues.

The women, thirteen in number, who had borne the fatigues of the long, long journey, who had transformed the stern camp in the depths of the wilds into something resembling a village in their own island, who had encouraged their husbands to continue in their fidelity despite all adversity, were all rewarded.

The children of the chiefs who had accompanied us from Zanzibar to the Atlantic, and who, by their childish, careless prattle, had often soothed me in mid-Africa, and had often caused me to forget my responsibilities for the time, were not forgotten. Neither were the tiny infants—ushered into the world amid the dismal and tragic scenes of the cataract lands, and who, with their eyes wide open with wonder, now crowed and crooned at the gathering of happy men and elated women about them—omitted in this final account and reckoning.

The second pay-day was devoted to hearing the claims for wages due to the faithful dead. Poor faithful souls! With an ardour and a fidelity unexpected, and an immeasurable confidence, they had followed me to the very death. True, negro nature had often asserted itself, but it was after all but human nature. They had never boasted that they were heroes, but they exhibited truly heroic stuff while coping with the varied terrors of the hitherto untrodden and apparently endless wilds of broad Africa.

The female relatives filed in. With each name of the dead, old griefs were remembered. The poignant sorrow I felt—as the fallen were named after each successive conflict in those dark days never to be forgotten by me—was revived. Sad and subdued were the faces of those I saw, as sad and subdued as my own feelings. With such sympathies between us we soon arrived at a satisfactory understanding. Each woman was paid without much explanation required—one witness was sufficient. There were men, however, who were put to great shifts. They appeared to have no identity. None of my own people would vouch for the relationship; no respectable man knew them. Several claimed money upon the ground that they were acquaintances; that they had been slaves under one master, and had become freemen together on their master's death. Parents and true brothers were not difficult to identify. The settlement of the claims lasted five days, and then—the Anglo-American Expedition was no more.

Dec. 13.—On the 13th of December the British India Steam Navigation Company's steamer *Pachumba* sailed from Zanzibar for Aden, on board which Mr. William Mackinnon had ordered a state room for me. My followers through Africa had all left their homes early that they might be certain to arrive in time to witness my departure. They were there now, every one of them arrayed in the picturesque dress of their countrymen. The fulness of the snowy dishdasheh and the amplitude of the turban gave a certain dignity to their forms, and each sported a light cane. Upon inquiring I ascertained that several had already purchased handsome little properties—houses and gardens—with their wages, proving that the long journey had brought, with its pains and rough experience, a good deal of thrift and wisdom.

When I was about to step into the boat, the brave, faithful fellows rushed before me and shot the boat into the sea, and then lifted me up on their heads and carried me through the surf into the boat.

We shook hands twenty times twenty, I think, and then at last the boat started.

I saw them consult together, and presently saw them run down the beach and seize a great twenty-ton lighter, which they soon manned and rowed after me. They followed me thus to the steamer, and a deputation of them came on board, headed by the famous Uledi, the coxswain; Kachéché, the chief detective; Robert, my indispensable factotum; Zaidi, the chief, and Wadi Rehani, the storekeeper, to inform me that they still considered me as their master, and that they would not leave Zanzibar until they received a letter from me announcing my safe arrival in my own country. I had, they said, taken them round all Africa to bring them back to their homes, and they must know that I had reached my own land before they would go to seek new adventures on the continent, and—simple, generous souls!—that if I wanted their help to reach my country they would help me!

They were sweet and sad moments, those of parting. What a long, long and true friendship was here sundered! Through what strange vicissitudes of life had they not followed me! What wild and varied scenes had we not seen together! What a noble fidelity these untutored souls had exhibited! The chiefs were those who had followed me to Ujiji in 1871; they had been witnesses of the joy of Livingstone at the sight of me; they were the men to whom I entrusted the safeguard of Livingstone on his last and fatal journey, who had mourned by his corpse at Muilala, and borne the illustrious dead to the Indian Ocean.

And in a flood of sudden recollection, all the stormy period here ended rushed in upon my mind; the whole panorama of danger and tempest through which these gallant fellows had so staunchly stood by me—these gallant fellows now parting from me. Rapidly, as in some apocalyptic vision, every scene of strife with Man and Nature through which these poor men and women had borne me company, and solaced me by the simple sympathy of common suffering, came hurrying across my memory; for each face before me was associated with some adventure or some peril, reminded me of some triumph or of some loss. What a wild, weird retrospect it was, that mind's flash over the troubled past! So like a troublous dream!

And for years and years to come, in many homes in Zanzibar, there will be told the great story of our journey, and the actors in it will be heroes among their kith and kin. For me, too, they are heroes, these poor ignorant children of Africa, for, from the first deadly struggle in savage Ituru to the last staggering rush into Embomma, they had rallied to my voice like veterans, and in the hour of need they had never failed me. And thus, aided by their willing hands and by their loyal hearts, the Expedition had been successful, and the three great problems of the Dark Continent's geography had been fairly solved.

LAUS DEO!

APPENDIX.

SIMPLE RULES FOR PRONOUNCING AFRICAN WORDS.

The letter *u*, when beginning or ending a word, is sounded like *oo*, or the French *ou*, thus: Uchungu—Ouchungou, or Oochungoo.

„ „ *a*, whether at the commencement, middle, or termination of a word, sounds like *ah*, thus: Asama, or Ahsahmah.

„ „ *e*, either commencing or terminating a word, as in the Yoruba word éwuré, sounds like ehwureh.

„ „ *i*, when beginning a word, as in the Kinyamwezi term ifisi, sounds like *i* in the English words if, is, it, in, ill; when it terminates the word, *i* has the shortened sound of *ee*; thus, ifisi, with a phonetical exactitude, would be spelled ifeesee.

The consonant M used as a prefix, as in Mtu, has a shortened sound of Um. The South African colonists, I observe, invariably spell this abbreviated sound as Um, as in Umtata, Umgeni, Umzila, which travellers in Equatorial Africa would spell Mtata, Mgeni, Mzila.

The prefix Ki, as in Ki-Swahili or Ki-Sagara, denotes language of Swahili or Sagara. The prefix U represents country; Wa, a plural, denoting people; M, singular, for a person, thus:—

U—Sagara. Country of Sagara.
Wa—Sagara. People of Sagara.
M—Sagara. A person of Sagara.
Ki—Sagara. Language of Sagara, or after the custom, manner, or style of Sagara, as English stands in like manner for anything relating to England.

English.	Ki-Swahili.	Ki-Sagara.	Ki-Gogo.	Ki-Nyamwezi.	Ki-Sukuma.	Ki-Nyambu.	Ki-Ganda.
One	moyyi	mwe	limonga	solo	limo	nyimo	emu
Two	mbiri	wawiri	megetch	biri	iwiri	ziviri	mbiri
Three	tato	watato	madato	tato	idato	sato	sato
Four	ena	ena	maena	ena	ena	nyinch	nya
Five	tano	tano	mahano	tano	tano	nysano	tano
Six	seta	seta	tandato	mkaga	tandato	mkaga	mkaga
Seven	saba	mfungati	mpungata	musamvu	mpungati	musamvu	musamvu
Eight	nani	minana	mnani	mnanch	nani	mnana	mnana
Nine	kenda	kenda	mikenda	sienda	kenda	mwenda	mwenda
Ten	kumi	kumi	kumi	ikumi	ikumi	chumi	kumi
Eleven	kumi na moyyi	kumi na mwe	kumi na monga	kumi na imwe	kumi na limo		kumi n'emu
Twelve	kumi na mbiri	kumi na awiri	kumi na megetch	kumi na wiri	kumi ne wiri		kumi n'mbiri
Thirteen	kumi na tato	kumi na watato	kumi na madato	kumi na sato	kumi ne idato		kumi na sato
Fourteen	kumi na ena	kumi na ena	kumi na maena	kumi na ind	kumi na ena		kumi na n'ya
Fifteen	kumi na tano	kumi na tano	kumi na mahano	kumi ni tano	kumi ni tano		kumi na tano
Sixteen	kumi na seta	kumi na seta	kumi na tandato	kumi na mukaga	kumi na tandato		kumi na mkaga
Seventeen	kumi na saba	kumi na fungati	kumi na mpungata	kumi na musamvu	kumi na mpungati		kumi na musamvu
Eighteen	kumi na nani	kumi na minana	kumi na mnana	kumi na mnanch	kumi ni nani		kumi na mnana
Nineteen	kumi na kenda	kumi na kenda	kumi na kenda	kumi na sienda	kumi na kenda		kumi na mwenda
Twenty	makumi-mawiri	mirongo-nawiri	makumi-megetch	makumi-awiri	makumi-awiri	machumi-nawiri	kumi na wiri
Thirty	makumi-matato	mirongo-midato	kumi megetch na monga	makumi-asato	makumi-adato		kumi asato
Forty	makumi-maena	mirongo-maena	kumi megetch na megetch	makumi-aena	makumi aena		kumi aana
Fifty	makumi-matano	mirongo-mitano	kumi megetch na madata	makumi-atano	makumi atano		kumi atano
Sixty	makumi-seta	mirongo-seta	makumi-tandato	makumi-mkaga	makumi atandato		n'kaga
Seventy	makumi-saba	mirongo-fungati	makumi-mpungata	makumi-musamu	pungati		samvu
Eighty	makumi-manani	mirongo-minana	makumi-mnana	makumi-mnanch	na minani		kinana
Ninety	makumi-kenda	mirongo-kenda	makumi-n'kenda	makumi-sienda	na kenda		kenda
Hundred	mia	mirongo-kumi	igana	igana	igana	igana	kikumi
Man	mtu	mutu	muntu	muntu	munhu	muntu	muntu
Woman	mwana-mke	mdereh	mchekuru	mukima	kima	mukazi	m'kazi
Cow	n'gombe	n'gombe	n'gombe	n'gombe	n'gombe	ente	n'te
Dog	m'bwa	suku	dibwa	m'bwa	m'bwa	m'bwa	m'bwa
Goat	m'buzi	mpeneh	mpeneh	m'buzi	m'buri	m'buzi	n'buzi
Sheep	kondoe	nhoro	n'koro	kolo	n'holo	ntama	n'diga
Foot	m'gu	wyu	kigereh	lugeri	lugeri	kirengi	kigeri
Finger	kidori	kidori	kahla	liala	liala	rukumu	n'garu
Head	kichwa	mutwi	litwe	itwe	m'twe	mutwe	m'twe
Stool	kiti	ligoda	kigoda	iteweh	isumbi	ntewi	n'tewi
Box	b'weta		mtundu	iweta	iweta	terekero	bweta
Canoe	m'tumbwi			bwato	wato	amato	ryato
Paddle	kafi			msaba	ngyehi	ngassi	n'kassi
Tree	m'ti	mutti	biki	mutti	m'ti	mutti	mutti
House	nyumba	nyumba	n'ganda	numba	numba	eushu	myu
Arrow	m'shari	muvi	n'songa	wambi	songa	mwambi	kasari
Gourd	kibuyu	nhungu	toma	sikondo	suba	kisisi	kitta
Knife	kisu	magi	mwereh	keri	lushu	mwiyu	kambi
Bow	uta, or mpindi	uta	pindi	ntta	uta	uta	mtego
Spear	m'kuki	mgoha	mgoha	sumo	kima	ichumo	fumo
Chicken	kuku	nguku	nguku	koko	ngoko	enguku	n'koko
Pool	ziwa	didimazi	irambo	iziwa	irambo	kesero	kidiwa
Small Lake	kiziwa						kiyanja-anja
Large Lake	ziwa	ziwa		irambo	niyanza	niyanja	nyanja ngazi
River	m'toni	m'korongo	mongo	mongo	mongo	hamuga	mug-ga
Water	maji	maji	marenga	minzi	minzi	madzi	mazi

Fire	moto	moto	moto	muriro	mot	muriro	muriro
Air	baridi	mbeho	mbeho	mtaka	mbeho	rugolye	mpewo
Smoke	moshi	mosi	llosh	llonsi	llochi	moshi	mukka
Sun	jiwa	jiwa	izuwa	izlowa	rimi	enzuwa	njiwa
Moon	mwezi	mrengi	mrengi	mwezi	mwezi	hwezi	mwezi
Stars	niota	nirezi	ntondwa	sonda	sonda		m'yenyi
Sky	wingu	vundeh	vundeh	irundi	irundeh	vireli	bireh
Rain	mvuhha	mvula	tonya	mvula	mbula	enzura	nkuva
Lion	simba	simba	simba	simba	simba	ntari	porogoma
Leopard	chuwi	chuwi	nsuwi	ngwi	suwi	engo	ngo
Hyena	fisi	visi	biti	ifisi	iviti	mpisi	mpisi
Fish	sumaki	somba	chomba	somba	somba	nswi	chakulira
Meat	nyama	nyama	nyama	nama	nama	ehnyama	nyama
Bird	ndegeh	ndegeh	ndegeh	noni	noni	kibungu	nyonni
Country	in-chi	kirunga	hasi	siaro	chalo	itaka	ikaro
Mountain	mlima	kigongo	ituada	itunda	itunda	arusosyi	rusosyi
Hill	kirima	kirima	kigongo	vigongo	vigongo	kavanga	kusosyi
Plain	bondeh, or m'buga	ruanja	nika	miwondeh	mbuga	ruweyah	rusenyi
Food	chakula	ugali	uhemba	ugali	ugali	vyakulya	mer-reh
Stick	fimbo	m'hando	muranga	muranga	mlanga	n'koni	muggo
Cloth	n'guo	suke	mwenda	mwenda	mwenda	mwenda	rugoyi
Potatoes	viazzi	mhoka	ninmbu	kafu	numbu	vijumba	rumondeh
Banana	n'dizi	n'howo	matokeh	matokeh	madogeh	kitokeh	tokeh
Salt	chumvi	munyu	munyu	mwenu	munu	munyu	munyu
Flour	oonga	usagi	usagi	ufuma	usu	usu	usano
Farm	shamba	mugunda	mlegeheh	migunda	m'gunda	dimiro	rusuko
Road	injia	njia	njira	n'zira	n'zira	mubanda	kuvo
Stone	jiweh	dibwé	dibwé	igwé	iweh	ivareh	jinja
Island	kisiwa					kizinga	kisinga
Eye	gicho	gicho	diso	diso	diso	riso	diso
Nose	pua	pua	mpula	nindo	nindo	nindo	nindo
Mouth	kinwa	lulaka	kinwa	mulomo	m'lomo	anunwa	kamwa
Teeth	jino	meno	meno	lino	lino	hamyeno	dinyo
Lips	m'domo	mulomo	m'lomo	mulomo	iromo	minwa	mumwa
Ears	muskio	gutwi	makutu	matwi	matwi	matwi	kutu
Hair	n'yuweri	n'weri	muwiri	misasi	uvwiri	hysokeh	ruviri
Tongue	urimi	lulimi	lulimi	lulimi	ulimi	harurimi	dilmi
Hand	m'kono	ganja	muoko	kuoko	kono	akibatu	kibatu
Hide	ngozi	kwaru	nchingo	ndiri	diri	ruhu	diva
Leaf	jani	jani	mahanzi	mawasi	maswa	ikivavi	karagara
Day	mchana	hamisi	kinguru	siku	siku	musana	misana
Night	usiku	kiro	kiro	ufuku	uziku	chiro	kiro
Walk	kutembea	kudowara	kudowala	kwiumba	kwiumba	kuvunga	kuchara
Run	kukimbia	kutijla	kumaaka	kwiruka	kupera	kwiruka	kuduna
Jump	kuruka	kujumba		kuguluka	kuguluka	yaguruka	kuvuka
Sleep	kulala	kugona	kugona	kulala	kulala	kuviyama	kwevaka
Dream	ku-otta	njozi	nalota	nalotera	nalotera	naroscreh	kulota
Darkness	jiza	finji	kutitu	lizima	giti	kwagwiteh	kizi-kiza
Thanks	kushukuru					nepanzi	twiyanzi
Father	baba	baba	tata	tata	bava	tata	kitangi
Mother	mama	mye-yi	ya ya	mayu	mayu	maweh	n'yabo
Brother	ndugu	ndugu	ndugu	ndugu	ndugu	mrumuna	mganda
Dead	kufa	usira	sakapa	kufwa	kufwa	ukavireh	afudeh
No	akuna	kuduhu	kuliza	wengo	kuduhu	nangu	nedda
Yes	ndio	mboga	vivyo	kwa-kwené	osheneh	mpaho	hotyo
Good day	yambo	mbukwa	mbukwa	uhoro	mwadira, or angaruka	usivireji, or mirembe	utyano

These seven columns are original, collected by myself.

ENGLISH.	KI-JIJI.	KI-GUHA.	WEST MANYEMA.	MARUNGU, URUNGU, UEMBA, AND UFIPA.	KI-BISA.	INTERIOR UNYORO.	EAST MANYEMA.
One	mwé	imo	omosa	kimwé	imo	chimwé	jumo
Two	wawiri	wawiri	babiri	fiwiri	siviri	biri	mabiri
Three	watatu	wasato	wasato	vitato	sitato	asato	basatua
Four	wa-ena	waana	wanachi	vineh	sineh	ina	bana
Five	wa-tano	wa-tano	watano	vitano	sisano	itano	batano
Six	watandatu	mutanda	mutuba	vitandato	mtanda	mkaga	mutuwa
Seven	ndwi	musambo	musambo	mtanda	mfungati	musanju	musambo
Eight*	minani	muwanda	muhanda	mnaneh	kinani	mnana	mu-anda
Nine	kienda	kitema	ketema	kampusyo	mwenda	mwenda	kitema
Ten	wachumi	kumi	ikumi	sumi	irikumi	ichumi	nikumi
Eleven	chumi na mwé	..	ikumi na nundomo	..	ikumi narrimo	ichumi na rimo	kumi na yumo
Twelve	chumi na wiri	..	ikumi na wawiri	..	kumi na subiri	ichumi na ziviri	kumi na wawiri
Thirteen	chumi na watatu	..	ikumi na wasato	..	kumi na sitato	ichumi na isato	kumi na wasato
Fourteen	..	..	ikumi na wanachi	..	kumi na sineh	ichumi na ina	kumi na wana
Fifteen	..	..	ikumi na watano	..	kumi na sisano	ichumi na itano	kumi na watano
Sixteen	..	..	ikumi na mutuba	..	kumi na mtanda	ichumi na mkaga	kumi na mtuwa
Seventeen	..	..	ikumi na musambo	..	kumi na fungati	ichumi na musanju	kumi na musambo
Eighteen	..	..	ikumi na muhanda	..	kumi na kinani	ichumi na mnana	kumi na mnanda
Nineteen	..	..	ikumi na kitema	..	kumi na mwenda	ichumi na mwenda	kumi na kitema
Twenty	..	makumi mawiri	makumi awiri	..	a makumi naviri	makumi awiri	makumi-awari
Thirty	..	..	..	..	a makumi yatato	makumi asato	..
Forty	..	..	..	..	a makumi macua	..	..
Fifty	..	..	..	..	a makumi amasano	..	..
Sixty	..	..	..	..	a makumi mtanda	..	..
Seventy	..	..	..	..	a makumi fungati [maneh	..	..
Eighty	..	..	..	..	a makumi ukumaneh-uku-	..	..
Ninety	..	..	..	..	a mukumi mwenda	..	..
Hundred	igana	lukama	lukama	..	ikikumi	igana	lukama
Man	muntu	muntu	mundu	muntu	muntu	muntu	mbandu
Woman	m'goreh	m'kazyana	mkazi	mwanakazi	mwanakazi	mkazi	mkazi
Cow	inka	..	n'gombé	vingombé	ingombé	n'té	n'gombé
Dog	m'bwa	imbwa	imbwa	kabwa	kabwa	m'bwa	imbwa
Goat	m'pench	mbusi	m'buzi	m'buzi	m'buzi	m'buri	mbuzi
Sheep	n'tama	mkoko	mkoko	mikoko	impanga	n'tama	mukoko
Foot	maguru	koguru	maholu	magassa	amoru	virengi	ma-ulu
Finger	urutoké	minwé	misani	kiara	munwé	rukumu	minwé
Head	mutwé	kitwi	mutwi	kitwé	mutwé	mutwi	muswé
Stool	n'teweh	kiwala	kibara	n'teweh	kipuna	antewi	kikala
Box	..	..	kirindo	n'fua	..	terekera	kirindo
Canoe	uwato	mbwato	bwato	uwato	bwato	awato	wato
Paddle	mageli	magafi	ngafi	mikingi	inkafi	n'kassi	ngafi
Tree	iwitti	mutti	mutti	fimutti	umutti	ekiti	mutyo
House	nzu	siho	ndabu	nganda	nganda	enzu	kendeh
Arrow	myambi	misari	masoma	mifwi	mufwi	mwambi	masoma
Gourd	kisawo	kiasa	kiasa	nsupa	nsupa	kisisi	kisawa
Knife	n'tambi	luheté	rubahu	mwereh	mwereh	kyeyu	luweteh
Bow	muwheto	utawako	uta	uta	uvuta	mtego	butta
Spear	chumo	fumu	itumo	fumo	ifumo	chumo	fumu
Chicken	n'koko	n'guku	n'goko	n'goko	ingoko	engoko	solo
Pool	kitanga	kiziwa	kiziwa	kirambi	kirambeh	viasero	kiziwa
Small Lake	kitanga	..	..	..	..	..	..
Large Lake	tanganika	nduyi	luchi	kimumana	umumana	niyanza	lugi
River	mugezi	mututo	luchi	mulonga	muronga	hamwiga	amema

Water	na-mazi	mema	machi	amenzi	amenzi	mansi	mema
Fire	muchanwa	muriro	tuya	muriro	muriro	muriro	muriro
Air	mbelo	masika	masika	ukupema	ukupema	vikoi	masika
Smoke	mumusi	mosi	muki	ikiunsi	ikunzi	mwik a	mozi
Sun	izuwa	yuwa	juwa	akazua	akasua	rizowa	muminya
Moon	nkwezi	mwesi	sungi	mwezi	mwezi	kwezi	mwango
Stars	masata	kangemo gemo	kangamina	ntanda	intanda	hamunyoni	kangomina
Sky	ijuru	yulu	ijulu	mavimbi	mavimbi	harugaru	nikuni
Rain	mvula	vula	mbula	infula	n'fula	euzula	vula
Lion	n'tari	ntambwé	ndambwé	msimba	kalamo	ntari	ndambwi
Leopard	ngwé	ningé	ingwé	kabwima	mbwiri	engo	ningwi
Hyena	fisi	kimbwi	kimbwi	kimbwi	ikimbwi	mpissi	gimbwi
Fish	nsiwi	nyama na mema	nyama-chi machi	isawi	nswi	nehwi	nyama na mema
Meat	nyama	nyama	nyama	inama	inama	nyama	nyama
Bird	uzewa	nkoni	koni	floni	ifijoni	kinoni	tuni
Country	insi	mwaro	musengeh	ikaro	ikaro	ensi	kibaro
Mountain	musosyi	ninguru	ngulu	mpiri	urupiri	arusosyi	ulyangulu
Hill	musosyi	mutenda	mukuna	utupiri	utulima	akasosyi	ulyamngongo
Plain	nika	lungu	kungu	mwirungu	mwirongu	aruseni	lilungu
Food	viribwa	viriasi	viribwa	uwali	ubwari	vyakulya	virirwa
Stick	n'koni	kakoi	fimbo	kamama	uwembea	n'koni	miti
Cloth	mwenda	mariwa	kiramba	nsaro	nsaro	mienda	nguo
Potatoes	virumbu	virumbu	kasenga	ifumbu	ifiumbu	vitakuli	bihama
Banana	tokeh	matokeh	n'doso	mikondeh	mikondeh	kitokeh	ma-ondeh
Salt	munyu	munyu	musiki	mikereh	mikeri	munyu	mungwa
Flour	ufu	ushych	bunga	uvunga	uvunga	buro	vunga
Farm	mrima	mavala	ishio	mavala	amavala	lunimiro	makunda
Road	njira	tuchira	injila	munsira	inzira	mulunda	munzira
Stone	iwuyeh	dibwé	dibwé	iribwé	iribwé	ivuri	mabwé
Island	kirira	..	..	kisera	kisinziri	..	..
Eye	amaso	liso	diso	ameuso	iriuso	hariso	meso
Nose	izulu	mohembé	mohembé	mona	umona	hamindo	muwembeh
Mouth	kanwa	kukanwa	kanwa	akanwa	akanwa	hamunwa	kanywa
Teeth	amenyo	meno	mino	ameno	ameno	hamano	meno
Lips	munwa	miromo	molomo	miromo	mulomo	hamuromo	mulomo
Ears	ngutwi	makutwi	magutwi	amatwi	amatwi	amatwi	makusweh
Hair	uzwiri	n'yuweri	suki	musisi	musisi	isokeh	n'weli
Tongue	uru-rimi	ulim	lulimi	ululimi	ulurimi	harurimi	durimi
Hand	kiganza	m'kono	maboko	minwé	amaboko	haruwatu	maboko
Hide	muwiri	kisewa	kesewa	kiganda	impapa	haru	kisewa
Leaf	muvavi	mejani	gani	mavula	ifijani	ikivavi	tubizi
Day	izuwa	juwa	juwa	chingulo	akazua	m'sanu	juwa
Night	uchugo	ufuku	utu	uvusiku	avasiku	hakiro	mufuku
Walk	kugenda	mukwenda	kwenda	kwangala	kutandala	kuunga	kusumuka
Run	asimba	washuka	lubila	uriviro	uriviro	eyeruka	luvilo
Jump	takwiruka	kutambuka	kusuluka	kiruka	ukukiruka	uguruka	watambuka
Sleep	alaly-yeh	nakarala	kusama	kusendama	kusendama	kuvyama	jenala-canga
Dream	kulota	kulota	kulota	virodo	viroto	ndosireh	falota
Darkness	..	mufito	ikunyi	nfinsi	nfinsi	liala ula	nikunyi
Thanks	wakora	ki-ini	chuwo, woloko	nyikuta	nyikuta	wintusi	ngahyi
Father	data	tutu	utata	tata	tata	tata	nitutu
Mother	mama	nana	nené	yangu	ma-yo	maweh	yeh-yi
Brother	mwen-eweh	mukingu wani	motaaneh	mwyeki	munangi	munu muna	mwina
Dead	afwieh	ukufa	kukwa	infwa	ukufa	iwafwa	wafwa
No	ataych	n-ha	kusikiendo	yo	tapari	n'ga	utoko
Yes	ayé	eh	wowo	eh	eh	niho	eh
Good day	..	ayn-muga	bakwenu	mapola	mapola	ulije-liota	utengo

ENGLISH.	KI-YAU.	KI-NYASSA.	MAFITTÉ OR WATUTA.	KI-RORI.	BAREGGA.	KI-KUSU.	KI-YANZI.	KI-BWENDÉ.
One	jumo, or yumpepeh	kimodzi	..	..	chamojé	kechi	mosych	mosi
Two	wawiri	vi-wiri	..	..	ibi	kipeh	mwé	miolé
Three	watatu	vitatu	..	..	isato	isato	siti	mitato
Four	mecheché	vinyé	..	..	inya	kenem	ina	miya
Five	msano	visano	..	..	koloko	kiano	mitano	vitano
Six	musano na jumo	visano na kimodzi	..	..	mutuba	usha-malo	mtuba	misamba
Seven	musano na wiri	visano na vi-wiri	..	..	..	sambeli	musamvu	sambwari
Eight	musano na watatu	visano na vitatu	..	..	chinana	inanem	mwambi	nana
Nine	musano na mecheché	visano na vinyé	..	..	..	di-vwa	lwa	vwa
Ten	ikumi	chikumi	..	..	ikama	vu-um	kumi	kumi
Eleven	..	pambula na modzi	..	..	..	vu-ndomo	..	..
Twelve	..	pambula na zivirf	..	..	..	vu-nduafé	..	..
Thirteen	..	pambula na sitato	..	..	..	vu-ndasato	..	..
Fourteen	..	pampula na sineh	..	..	..	vu-ndanem	..	..
Fifteen	..	pambula na isano	..	..	..	vu-nda-atano	..	..
Sixteen	..	pambula isano na imodzi	..	..	..	vu-nda-asamalo	..	..
Seventeen	..	..	..	..	..	vu-nda-sambeli	..	..
Eighteen	..	..	..	..	..	vu-nda-inanem	..	..
Nineteen	..	..	..	..	..	vu-nda-divwa	..	..
Twenty	makumi gaviri	makumi mawiri	..	..	..	um-apé	..	kumi miolé
Thirty	makumi gatato	makumi madatu	..	..	..	um-asato	..	kumi mitato
Forty	makumi mecheché	makumi manyé	..	..	..	u-m-amem	..	kumi miya
Fifty	makumi musano	makumi asano	..	..	..	u-m-atano	..	..
Sixty	makumi musano na rimo	..	..	..	..	u-m-asamalo	..	..
Seventy	makumi musano na wawiri	..	..	..	..	u-m-asambeli	..	..
Eighty	..	..	..	..	..	u-ma-inanem	..	..
Ninety	..	..	..	..	..	u-m'difwa	..	..
Hundred	makumi mikumi	..	..	..	..	lukama	..	mukama
Man	mundu	muntu	muntu	munhu	mutu	untu	mutu	muntu
Woman	wakongweh	mkazi	wakazi	mudara	mukazi	omoto	m'kali	mikento
Cow	ngombé	ngombé	zinkomo	ingombé	..	..	..	n'gombi
Dog	m'bwa	garu	inja	m'bwa	m'bwa	mvwa	m'bwa	m'bwa
Goat	mbuzi	mbuzi	imbuzi	mpeneh	mburi	mburi	ntawa	kombo
Sheep	kondolo	dira	pereh	nkhoro	memé	oguko	memé	memé
Foot	makongolo	mwendo	imiendo	miguru	tindé	igulu	likuru	utambi
Finger	kahla	kahla	nikidori	kidori	numi	beo	musi	m'lembo
Head	m'twé	mutu	rikanda	mutwé	mutchwi	utwó	mpu	n'tu
Stool	kitengu	mpando	ligoda	kigoda	kitumbi	uti	..	..
Box	ibweta	..	likala	ifiyo	..	..	..	..
Canoe	wato	bwato	uwato	ruwato	mato	wato	mato	matungu
Paddle	mparisiro	n'kafi	inkafi	rukhafi	nkafi	kafi	..	nkafi
Tree	mtera	mtengo	mtera	ripiki	kiti	iti	muiti	mutti
House	niumba	niumba	inyumba	iritembé	nyumba	lum	..	manzu
Arrow	mpamba	mpariro	mpvvi	misari	..	lole	..	..
Gourd	ngembo	chigubu	chigugu	lunguru	kikuru	ohombo	..	..
Knife	kipula	chipula	mageh	magi	obeo	lukula	blereh	mbelé
Bow	ukunjeh	uta	intʇa	kiwutta	..	uta	..	mikeleh
Spear	lipanga	ntungo	mkondo	mharara	tumu	likonga	ikongo	wiyongé
Chicken	n'guku	n'kuku	inkuku	inkuku	koko	koko	nsusu	nsusu
Pool	itamanda	tawareh	..	masiwa	..	ijuwa	..	..
Small Lake	..	..	..	..	..	irnwa	..	..
Large Lake	..	niyanja	inyanja	inyanja	..		..	..
River	luzulo	msinjeh	mfureni	mhkhogo	ikingi	okeli	ibari	njali

Water	mesi	madzi	magassi	merenga	myé	ashi		maza
Fire	moto	moto	mubasso	moto	kasa	njo		tia
Air	mbepo	mpepo	impepo	impepo				
Smoke	liosi	motsi	iriosi	mosi	muki	oringa		
Sun	lyua	udzua	idzua	irijua	jowa	ouya	ikanga	ntangu
Moon	mwezi	mwezi	inyanga	mwesi	meri	weri	nsungi	ngonda
Stars	ndondwa	ntondwa	n'kanyesi	vinyota	kendi-kendi	toto		
Sky	liundeh	mitambo	iikuturuka	irivingu	itu-kutcha	i-ubenvula		s'iu
Rain	ula	mvula	imvula	imfura	mbura	mvula		mavula
Lion	lisimba	mkango	kawangu	nyerupara		kimbungu		
Leopard	kisuwi	n'yalugwé	idumo	nduma	kengé	kom		ngo
Hyena	litunu	fissi	ifisi	nfisi		tambwé		
Fish	somba	nsomba	sinjoka	nswi	mfi	lusi		mbisi
Meat	nyama	nyama	in'yama	in'yama	nyama	nyama		mbisi
Bird	kigijuni	balameh	nyama zani	inyuni	kokombiri	filu		
Country	kirambo	dziko	isi	inhi	kanda	welu		n'si
Mountain	itumbi	piri	ilgomo	vidunda	keoma	nkunji		izuru
Hill	katundulima	kapiri	kagomo	kidunda		selemoto	mbenga	
Plain	irambo	dambo	kuridambo	imbuga	itondo	osuwé		batto
Food	chakulya	chakudya	chigesa	ugali	mata	uma		ulya
Stick	ngolombeh	ndodo	intonga	n'kwegu	cheti	yanga		mukawa
Cloth	nguo	nsaro	zinyula	mwenda	nturu	ukisi		
Potatoes	batata	batata	chimungurwé	madulé		kilunga		chikwa
Banana	magombo	ntochi	zinkho	nkho	mama	likondo		makondé
Salt	getch	mchereh	mkireh	munyu	mu-u	luwebo		mungwa
Flour	ntandi	ufa	mpupu	utini	umata	okula		muyaka
Farm	mgunda	munda	kunduda	migunda		ikambwa		kugata
Road	itala	n'jira	injira	inzira	ingeya	ugulu		makanga
Stone	liganga	mwala	diranga	ijua	i-wé	div-weh	ibwa ; pl. maba	
Island	kirumba	kirumba	rizinga	irisiwa	kititi	kisiwa		
Eye	liso	diso	meso	amcho	liso	chu	liso	diso
Nose	lupula	mpuno	impuno	impura	moemid	ulu	juru	mbombo
Mouth	pakanwa	kamwa	ikamwa	rumiro	kama	uniwa	munya	nwa
Teeth	dino	dzino	imeno	meno	meno	wyenyu		meno
Lips	ngomo	mlomo	mlomo	muromo	mitutu	elomo		
Ears	mapikaniro	kutu	makutu	burukutu	kuta	atum	itoi	kutu
Hair	umbo	sitsi	zifwiri	n'yeri	mbi	divu	nsueh	suki
Tongue	lulimi	dilimi	lulimi	urumiri	chiami	lalim		
Hand	mkono	dzanja	nimikono	mavokho	makasa	lani	liboko	moko
Hide	lipendeh	n'guo	kisango	nkwembi	okowa	lowa		
Leaf	masamba	samba	inyasi	risori		adilu	ikuku	mkobo
Day	musi	mtzana	diranga	pamunsi	utukutcha	kososi		biiumbu
Night	kiro	usiku	usiku	pakiro	utagwyra	u-chu		
Walk	kwenda-genda	kwienda-enda	kusasira	gendanga	itungu	seteta		
Run	ku-utuka	kutamanga	kujujima	ruviro	okobé	luwango		
Jump	usumba	kulumpa	ulapora	kurukha	ky-yé	tamba		
Sleep	ugona	kugona	kugona	kwigona	kulama	jetama	ngori	
Dream	nsagamira	kulota	zindoto	sindoto		dotalo		
Darkness	kipi	m'dima	mudima	ndisisa				
Thanks	kulomba-mulungu							
Father	atati	atatch	nvava	uheso	moma	ya-oneh	tara	tata
Mother	amau	amai	himama	nineso	inawé	mboneh	mama	mama
Brother	mpwanga	mpwanga	mana-kwetu	lukholo	meya	kadiwem	ndu	ndugu
Dead	awireh	kufa	afireh	afwireh	kukinduka	utuvweh	afua	
No	ngwamba	parijeh	paribé	pasiri		kwapa		
Yes	yereyo	kodi	ye-u	nipereré		lumbweh		
Good day	kivera	ulumoyo	tu-koneh	ajageh		we-mweh		

English.	Kakongo and Kabinda.*	Ki-Rua.*	M'Fan (Usseydas).†	Ukanda.†	Adumas.†	Ukoa, or M'Bongo.†	Kafir.‡
One	bosa	kamo	fo	moti	mo	boko	nyé
Two	kwali	tuwili	beji	bali	yoli	wuma	bilé
Three	tato	tusatu	la	eato	eato	motadi	tatu
Four	n-na	tuna	nal	na	na	kongoli	né
Five	tano	tutano	tané	ota	bitano	mongobi	hlané
Six	sambanu	tusamba	kamé	motoba	samon	diata	itatisitupa
Seven	sambwali	tusambalawili	jenyoi, or jonyoi	napo	somnbo	mendjeiba	kombisa
Eight	na-na	mwanda	wonum	enana	pommbo	koeu dnjeila	ishiyangalobilé
Nine	ev-wa	kitema	elon	buka	liboi	monkonyolo	isishiyangalobilé
Ten	ikumi	di kumi, or kikwi	ayomi	djema	eomi	monkoumokoi	ishumi
Eleven		di kumi na kamo		edjima moti	eomi na l'no		ishumi li-na-nyé
Twelve		di kumi na tuwili			eomi na jolé		ishumi li-nabilé
Thirteen							ishumi li-nesitatu
Fourteen							ishumi li-na-ni
Fifteen							ishumi li-nenhlanu
Sixteen							ishumi li-ne-tatisitupa
Seventeen							ishumi li-na-kombisa
Eighteen							ishumi li-na-shiyangalobilé
Nineteen							ishumi li-na-isishiyangalobilé
Twenty	makumi-wali	vikwi viwili					amashumi amabilé
Thirty	makumi-tato	vikwi visatu					amashumi amatatu
Forty	makumi-na						amashumi amané
Fifty	makumi-tano						amashumi amahlanu
Sixty	makumi-sambanu						amashumi atatisitupa
Seventy	lusambwala-n'kama						amashumi akombisa
Eighty	lunana-n'kama						amashumi ashiyangalobilé
Ninety	luvwala-n'kama						amashumi isishiyangalobilé
Hundred	n'kama	katwa	kama (?)	kama (?)	kama (?)		ikulu
Man	muntu	muntu	efan voklé	momei neto	libolu (?)	mflumé	indoda
Woman	m'chento	mkazi	munga	mento	kason, or kasa	beito	umfazi
Cow	n'gombi	n'gombé	nfa	djoma	maré	gongné	inkomo
Dog	m'bwa	m'bwa	m'vu	m'fa	m'buandi	buandé (?)	inja
Goat	n'kombo	mbuzi	golé kaba	kaba moi	laba	bodi	imbuzi
Sheep	me-mé	mkoko	galé toma	doplo	monka dombé		imvu
Foot	kulu	uswaya	akulubo	winhé	litambi	dibombo	inyawo
Finger	nzala	mluwé	onu, or unu	mon shalei	monlembo	malomé	umunwé
Head	m'tu	kutwé					ikanda, or inhloko
Stool							isihlalu
Box	bubulu	kipōwu	evora	egala, or egara	egara		umpongolo
Canoe	bwato	wato	bia	bongo	bongo	boielo	umkumbana
Paddle	chiela	kwuho	oka	yokabi	ikapi		ipini
Tree	mti	chiti	ili	eteltei	mouté	kananya	umuti
House	bwala	mzuo	n'dar	daka	jo	dongu	intlu
Arrow		mikétu	m'boyé	manbanjei			umcibityelo
Gourd		mungu					iselwa
Knife	mbelé	lupété	aukan	vekuma	beidi	m'beidi (?)	umkwa
Bow		uta	ekulora m'bei		munayé		umcibityelo
Spear		mkové	muku	gonga	ikongo		umkonto
Chicken	nsusu		ku, or n'ku	susu	kuba dsudsu (?)	kuba	inyané
Pool							isiziba
Small Lake		ru-wa					umsinga
Large Lake							
River	nzali	luwi	lo	bulomebé	bagui-dali-dsali		umfula

COMPARATIVE TABLE OF AFRICAN LANGUAGES 383

Water	mlangwa, or mazzi	méma	majime osi	mamngi	manba	mandiba	amanzi
Fire	mbazu	miriro	doit	bibn	m'bao	isako	umlilo
Air	mpemo			pejiel	teino (wind)		umoya
Smoke	muisi						umusi
Sun	ntangu	minyia	viel	konmbé	vadu	cimojo	ilanga
Moon	ngonda	kwési					inyanga
Stars		kauyenya					ikanyezi
Sky	li-ilu						izulu
Rain	mvula	mvula					imvula
Lion	chingumbu	tambu					igonyama
Leopard	ngo	ngé	n'zé	jeigo	ebabi	bongonjo	ingwé
Hyena		kumungu	zoé				impisi
Fish	mfu	mwita wa luwi	béluné		inzanga		inhlanzi
Meat	mbizi		vité	numa	bolu	beseibo	inyama
Bird		nguni					inyoni
Country		n shi					ilizwé
Mountain	mula						umango
Hill		m'kuna					ithaba
Plain	ntando						itafa
Food	bilya	wulio, or viliwa	vité	niuma	bolu	beseibo	ukuhla
Stick	mpu						uluti
Cloth		mbwisha					indwangu
Potatoes	mbala	kutungu	amon-a	fagola	fanetel	flello	amazembané
Banana	ntutu	makondé	isu-ikomé	motabo	icomako	monbungel	ukova
Salt	nsalo	mwépu	ny fu	vianga			momunya
Flour	falinya	ukula					impupu
Farm		kurimi					ilizwé
Road	nzili	mishinda					indlela
Stone	(pl.) manya : lilanya (s.)	uivé					ilityé
Island							isihlenga
Eye	lieso	masa	dicé	incho	disu	di-so (?)	iliso
Nose	i-ilu	mlona	dji	pumbo	jolo	mukomba	impumlo
Mouth	mumo	makanu					umlomo
Teeth	meno	néno					amazinyo
Lips							ndebé (s.)
Ears	ukutu	matwi					inhlebé (pl.)
Hair	lenjé	mwéné					unwelé
Tongue	lulaka						ulimi
Hand	koko		akluoa	misabi	ekoka	kaka	isanhla
Hide	m'kandi						isikumba
Leaf	ntiti						iqabi
Day	lumbo	mfuko					ilanga
Night	bwilo	cholwa					ubusuku
Walk	llata	kanunga					hamba
Run		euda uviro	amana	otsi-i	esili, or tili	avolé	gijima
Jump							gqita
Sleep	lala	lala					ubutongo
Dream							ipupa
Darkness							ubumnyama
Thanks	ntondesi						nkunaneka
Father	tata	tata	tara	teita	tata		baba
Mother	mama	lolo	mané	l-ya	gu		mamé
Brother	nkomba	tula					umné
Dead	ufwiré				(more ")		abafeleyo
No	vé	vitun	koko	geilé	abial, or ubiki ("no		ca : ai : qa
Yes	ngeté		niu	bni-ein	mezail	andéké-oié	ewe : yebo
Good day	keba-bota		bolo	ntehi koié	maso koi	chika	valiseia

* The first two columns are original, collected by myself.

† These four are kindly furnished by M. Ed. Marche, of the Ogowai Exploration, conformed to the English system by myself. ‡ Furnished by Rev. Robert Moffat.

ENGLISH.	SECHWANA.*	JALIF.	SÚSÍ.	TIMANÍ.	MANDINGO.	SOKNA AND TUARIK.	BORNU.
One	ñwé	ben	kiring	pen		idgen	tilo
Two	peri	yar	far-ing	prung		sunn	andi
Three	tharo	niet	shuk-ing	tisas		shard	yaskú
Four	nné	nianett	nari	páuli		erbar (Ar.)	daigú
Five	tlhano	gurum	shuli	tomát		(All the numbers above three are the same as in Arabic.)	ngú
Six	thataro	gurum ben	shinlé	rokin			araskú
Seven	shupa	gurum yar	shulifiring	dayring			tuller
Eight	gohèra meberi	gurum niet	shulimashukung	daysas			oskú
Nine	gohéra o lé moñué	gurum niant	shulinuang	dayoga			lekár
Ten	leshomé	fué	fuang	tofot			maigú
Eleven	leshomé lé moco o lé moñué						
Twelve	leshomé lé moco mé beri						
Thirteen	leshomé lé moco meraro						
Fourteen	leshomé lé moco mené						
Fifteen	leshomé lé moco metlhano						
Sixteen	leshomé lé moco meratharo						
Seventeen	leshomé lé moco é shupa						
Eighteen	leshomé lé moco é hèra meberi						
Nineteen	leshomé lé moco é hèra o lé moñué						
Twenty	mashomé maberi	nill	mawhinia	tofot marung			
Thirty	mashomé mararo	fanever	tongasifukúng	tofot masas			maigú lata maigú
Forty	mashomé mané	nianet fué	tonganana	tofot manlu			
Fifty	mashomé matlhano	guaum fué	tóngashulang	tofot tomat			
Sixty	mashomé maratharo	guaum ben fué	tongashini	tofot rokin			
Seventy	mashomé é shupa	guaum yar fué	tongashulifring	tofot dayring			
Eighty	mashomé a hèra maheri	guaum niet fué	tongashulimashakung	tofot daysas			
Ninety	mashomé a hèra o lé moñué	guaum nianet fué	tongashulimanáné	tofot danygah			
Hundred	sekholu	temer	kiné	tofot tofot			farrú
Man	monona	gour			mo, or fato	mar	kúa
Woman	mosari	diguen			moosea	tamtüt	mata
Cow	khomo é namagari		ninkgeginé			lebgurr	fai
Dog	ncha					edé	
Goat	porl	phas	shi			teaghsi	
Sheep	àku	zedré	juhé			tile, or utus	
Foot	lonao				(pl.)	sishkunt	shié
Finger	monuana	baram (pl.)			boalla ronding		
Head	tlogo	bop	hung hungji		run	ighrof	kela
Stool	serulo						
Box	lethulé						
Canoe	mokoro						
Paddle	sehuri						
Tree	setlhari	garallun					
House	ntlo		bankhi			sashka	
Arrow	mochwi						
Gourd	sego						
Knife	thipa		finé			uzal	
Bow	bora						
Spear	lerumo					tagarit (*jerid*)	
Chicken	kokouna						
Pool	mogobé						
Small Lake	letsa						
Large Lake	letsa-yé-legolu						
River	molapo (or "a valley")						
Water	metsé	dok			gi	aman	aukl

Fire	molelo					isghráran, and tims.	kanno
Air	pheho						
Smoke	mosi						
Sun	letsatsi	burham safara	shugé		till	sefúkt	kú
Moon	nueri	burham lion	kigé		koro	tajiri	kengál
Stars	dinaleri					eráu	shilluga
Sky	legorimo						
Rain	pula						
Lion	tau						
Leopard	nkué		shuko shé				
Hyena	phiri						
Fish	tlapi	quieum				khút (Ar.)	boné
Meat	nama					aksúm (*flesh*, tagilla)	
Bird	nonyané					azdiah	ongúdo
Country	lehatsé						
Mountain	thaba						
Hill	thabana						
Plain	motlhaba						
Food	liyo						
Stick	tsamma					tagaghrit	
Cloth	letsela, khai					melf (Ar.)	
Potatoes	makhuilé						
Banana							
Salt	lechoai					tisaut	
Flour	bopi					aruna	
Farm	tsimo						
Road	tsela		kirá				
Stone	leinchué					teghrúghan	kau
Island	sekiri						
Eye	leitlo					tiat	shim (pl.)
Nose	nko	bauané	nieué		uung	laksham	keusha
Mouth	molomo	guémin	dé		da	eemi	
Teeth	meno	guene					timmi
Lips	melomo						
Ears	ditsebé					tamazúkh	
Hair	moriri	cayor				zaú	kondoli
Tongue	lolemé	lamin	nlug ningjé		ning		
Hand	seatla	baram			boalla, ronding	fús	moskú
Hide	letlalo					illam (leather or skin)	
Leaf	tsebé						
Day	letsatsi		hi			azill	kú
Night	bosigo		qué			yetti	lúné
Walk	sepela					achel	
Run	taboga		gee fé			uzzel, or azzil	
Jump	tlola		tubang fé				
Sleep	robala						kúnem
Dream	lora						
Darkness	lehihi						
Thanks	maleboga	guérum ualá					
Father	rara	ball	taffé		fa		abbah
Mother	ma	dé	inga		ba		yané
Brother	mokauleñue	rak gour	tarahunjla		ba dingkea	nitta	
Dead	shulé					utima	nowé
No	nya	dhiett					
Yes	è	ouau					
Good day	salaseutlé	dhuarakio		currea			

* Furnished by Rev. Robert Moffat.—The other six columns from various authors.

ENGLISH.	SAKATÚ.	TIMBUCTOO.	SOUDAN, OR HAUSA.	TIBBU.	HOTTENTOT.	YORUBA.*	MAKUA.
One			daya	trono	ko-isé	eni : okan	
Two			bin	chew	ka-msé	edzi	
Three			okú	agozu	arusé	eta	
Four			fúdú	tuzzao	gna-to-i	erin : merin	
Five			biat	fo	metuka	arun	
Six			shidda	dessi	krubi	efa	
Seven			bokkoi	tútúsú	gna tigna	edźé	
Eight			tokkos	usú	gulnka	edźo : medźo	
Nine			tara	issi	tuminkma	esan	
Ten			goma	mordum	gomatsé	èwa	
Eleven			goma shadaya			okanlá	
Twelve			goma bin			edźilá	
Thirteen			goma okú			etalá	
Fourteen			goma fúdú			erinlá	
Fifteen			goma biät			eedógun	
Sixteen			goma shidda			erindilógun	
Seventeen			goma bokkoi			etadilógun	
Eighteen			goma tokkos			èdźidilógun	
Nineteen			goma tara			ókandilógun	
Twenty			asherin			ogún	
Thirty			thalatin			ogbón	
Forty			(and so on to			ogodźi : òdźi	
Fifty			100, as in			ádota	
Sixty			Arabic.)			ogota : ota	
Seventy						ádorin	
Eighty						ogorin : orin	
Ninety						ádorun	
Hundred			dari			ogorun : orun	
Man	efillo	ahinda		naih	kupp	okonri : ènia	mo-lù-mé
Woman	debbo	aflutú		adi		obíri : obinri	mut-té-á-na
Cow	nagga	abari	sania	farr	gós : góossa	malú	
Dog	kutúrú		karré		arikié : tutu : tup	adzá	ma-la-po-a (im-pum- [pes at Dos Santos)
Goat	bäia	eggshi				ake : èkiri : ewure : oruko	
Sheep	baldú	taili		hadinni	gona	águtan	
Food	koiuka	edthi				èse	
Finger	honedú (pl.)	beddi (pl.)	fershi (pl.)			íka	
Head	hora	agodi		dafú		eri : ori	mú-rú
Stool					nenamhop	aga : akpotí	
Box			sandúk		geip	akpoti : ago : bata	
Canoe						fatẹ̀le, òko, okpere	
Paddle						adźe : walami	
Tree	barkihl	esheri				igi	ft-tu-va (maturi at [Dos Santos)
House	ura	bactú			geihep : omma	ilé	é-mú-ba
Arrow	lebbo		kibbia			ofa	é-ta-ra (pl.)
Gourd						ademo : aha : àgbé : agbedzolo : akpala : [ato : igbodzé : igba	
Knife	lab.				nórap	obé	
Bow						orun	mùr-ra
Spear	ghembirri					esin ; òko	lé va ga
Chicken	gertúka		kazá	kokaiya		adire : adié	
Pool						àbata	
Small Lake						}adagun	
Large Lake							
River	lana	bori				òdo : ikpa òdo	ú-ré-ah

Water	ghium	ami			kamma	omi : òdo	ma-zé
Fire	ceta	ofi	uta	nuf	ci : elp : neip	ina	múr-ro
Air				al		afẹfẹ : ẹfufu	
Smoke						efi : fìn : efin	
Sun	maanga	offiti		túggü		òrun	czù-a
Moon	laighroo	hitti		aowrí		oṡukpa : oṡu	má-ré
Stars	caudié					irawọ (sing.)	tau-d'wa
Sky						orun	
Rain	gbium ghiwondi					édzi : òdżo	
Lion	jagerri				káma	kéniú	
Leopard						ekun : dzakumó ogidan	
Hyena						kortko : ikoriko	kezúmba
Fish			kívi			edża	o'pah [Dos Santos)
Meat	ulri	taasú	náma	yimmi	kop	ẹran : oṡeṡé	emá ma (*inhama* at
Bird	súdu		súnsu	wúggbé		eiyẹ	nú né
Country			gori			ile ilu	
Mountain						òkẹ	ma-go
Hill						òke : okiti èbé	
Plain						kpẹtẹlè	
Food						ondżẹ : idżẹ : dzidzẹ : fẹdżẹfẹdżé	
Stick	leddi	esheri		aka		igi	
Cloth						aṡo	
Potatoes						kukunduku	
Banana						ogẹdé	
Salt				gilailli		iyo : orẹrẹ	maka
Flour	klandi					èlubo : iyẹfun	
Farm					komma	oko	
Road					kudu	ọna : ikpa-óna	é-pé-ro
Stone	búddi			aai		okuta : okó	
Island						adadò : idado : erekuṡu	
Eye	gitta	aiti	iddo	soaa	mu (s.), mum (pl.)	odżú	mé-to (pl.)
Nose	hinari	hoshti		scha	koyp	imọ	
Mouth	kondúkkú	fetti		iehi		ẹnu	ya-mí
Teeth	nia				kom (sing.)	akoko : ehin : eyin (all sing.)	
Lips						eté (sing.)	
Ears	leppi		kúnneh			etí (sing.)	né-á-ro (s.)
Hair						iron	ká-rá-ré
Tongue						ahón : awọn	
Hand	jungo	akhúd		awana		owọ́	
Hide						áwọ : bata	
Leaf						ewé	
Day	hansi		rana			ídzọ́ : odzọ	
Night	ghem					òru	
Walk	jiadü	kaedodi				rin	
Run	endogga				susé kon (run away)	sá : salọh : saré : súré	
Jump						be : fò	
Sleep	fokadaan	auti	bershi (asleep)		om	idzika : odzúorùn : orún	a-rú-bá
Dream						alá : odzuala : odzuran	
Darkness						biri : biribiri : okun : okunkun	
Thanks	allah imoghul					okpé	
Father	babama	abbi			ambup : tikkop	babá : oba	sé-té
Mother	imáma [(younger b.)	emmi			andes : tissos	abiamo : iyá : yeyé iyè	má-má
Brother	maúna (elder b.) ; mlula	katl	kani		karup : ticak-wa	ará : arakouri : abúro egbon	mo-rú-ko
Dead						kú : daké : okú wo	o-kú-ah
No						kinidbżẹbẹ : kurumu : nadwo : an	
Yes						behe-ni : ẹyi : hẹ : hẹrji : ohan	
Good day					dabé : da-beté	adziré : akuoro (*good morning*)	

The first five columns from books.

* According to Rev. Mr. Bowen, American Missionary.

English.	Motjao.	Somáli.	Hurrur.	Galla.	Adaiel.	Danakil.
One		k'ow	a-had	to ko	see Danakil	inni-ké
Two		lebba	ko-út ; koté	lum-ma		lum-meh
Three		sud-dé	shisté	sed-dé		sud-dé-o
Four		af-fur	har-rut	af-fúr		fé-ré
Five		shan	ham-míst	shun		ko-no-zou
Six		l'éh	sedíst	ja		lé-hé-zé
Seven		t'dub-ba	sáté	toor-bah		mel-hé-né
Eight		sé deid	sát	sed-dét		bá-há-ra
Nine		sug-gál	zeytan	sug-gul		sé-ga-la
Ten		tubbáu	assir	kú-dun		thub-ban
Eleven		kow-é-tub-báu	assé á had	kúda-tok		thubban-ketea
Twelve		lebbé-a-tub báu	assé á kót	kuda-lum-ma		thubban ké lunemeh
Thirteen		sud-dé-a-tub-báu	etc. etc.	etc. etc.		etc. etc.
Fourteen		etc. etc.				
Fifteen						
Sixteen						
Seventeen						
Eighteen						
Nineteen						
Twenty		leh-bah-tun	kú-é-ya			lubba-tanna
Thirty		sud-dun	sassa			sud-dum
Forty		affar-tun	er-bah			moro-tum
Fifty		shan-é-tun	hem-sa			kum-tum
Sixty		leh-tun	sis-sah			la-tum-ma
Seventy		t'dub-ba-tun	sa-tes-sir			melhin-a-tumma
Eighty		sedeit-tun	su-tes-sir			bahar-tumma
Ninety		suggal-tun	they-tá-neh			sega-la-tumma
Hundred		bogal	buk-ka-la			ból
Man	ma-lop-wa-nah	ningba	abbok	ná má	adma	ka-bunt
Woman	mé-kou-gwé	maak-ta	edok : I'doatch	né té	bar-ra	ak-bo-eta
Cow		lo	laám	sou-a	la	la
Dog	um-pu-a	a-é	búché	sir-ré	kub-ba	kúta
Goat		ar-ré	dow	rée	dubbila	illa
Sheep			tai	holá	murrú	merwa
Foot		og		fá-na		
Finger				koba		
Head	mu-ta-wé	mud-dah	rús	má-tá	mú-l-ya	am-mo
Stool						
Box						
Canoe						
Paddle						
Tree	meré		buf-fo	mo-u-ka		al-eh
House	a-um-ba	fé-ras	gáal : gar			arré : bura
Arrow	im-pam-ba (pl.)		in nach (pl.)			
Gourd						
Knife						gil-lé
Bow	o-kú-á-zé		dé-gan			
Spear	le-pán-gá	war-rum				
Chicken						
Pool						
Small Lake						
Large Lake						
River			zer	leg-ga		we'ah
Water	mé-ze	hé-yú	mé	besham	li	le'h

Fire	mo-to	doh	is-sat	é-bid-deh	gi-rá	gira
Air			dúf	bú-bé	ar-hú	a-hy-ta, or sako
Smoke		kaik (also used for *tobacco*)	sun	du-gé		
Sun	d'yúva	ghurrah	eer	addu	a-i-ro	ay-é-ro
Moon	múci-zé	tai ya	werhé	djé-á : ba-té	al-sa	alsa : berra
Stars	to-u'n-du-wa	hed-du-go	sú-wi (sing.)	ur-jé : té-yu (sing.)	ur-túk-ta (sing.)	é-túk-ta : arra
Sky			sem-mé			ambu-ré
Rain						
Lion			ze-nab	ko-ba : bo-kí-ré	rú-bu	róbé
Leopard						
Hyena						
Fish	dé tu no	werrá bé	wé-rá-bah			
Meat	sóm-bah		tu-lum	búr-tú-mé	kul-lum	cul-lum
Bird	né ya mah	il-lib	busser			nado
Country	nú né	shim beir	úf, or alaté	shimberrs-tillé	kin-kro	kimbeir
Mountain	matúm-bé	bo ro	sa-ré	gá-rá	al-li	al-la
Hill						
Plain		bú'n-a	a-go-bar	dud-da		
Food						
Stick						
Cloth						
Potatoes						
Banana						
Salt	jé-té	us-sub-bo		ussú		
Flour						
Farm						
Road	é-tal-la			ugah		
Stone		lug-kah	ún	da-ga : hegga	da-a	dáta : é-ya
Island						
Eye	mé-zo (pl.)	fil (pl.)	ain	hed-ja		in-té (pl.)
Nose		san	úf	fun-yán		san-na
Mouth	oun-wa	off	aóf	af-fan		af-fa
Teeth		fil-luk	sin	il-kaé		bu-dé-na
Lips			luf-luf			wog-gu-ba
Ears	ma-kút-wé (s.)	deg	u'thun (sing.)	gúra (sing.)		ai-té (sing.)
Hair	húm-po	te-mo	tche-gur	re-fen-sa		do-gur-ta
Tongue		ar-rub	ar-rát	ar-rub-ba		ar-rub-ba
Hand						gub-ba
Hide			goga	it-til-lé	caf-té	
Leaf						
Day			oj	er-ra		at-hu : assaak
Night			mis-sheit	ul-kun		bher-ra
Walk						
Run						
Jump						
Sleep	a-gó-né	sé-oh'				
Dream						
Darkness						
Thanks						
Father	at té-a-té	ab-bai : ilba-á	ou	ab-bo	yí abba	ab-ba
Mother	a má vo	oyù	ae, or éé	bo-lé-sa : addir	yi no	yin-na
Brother	allúmbo	wel-lal		o-bo-la		ina
Dead	ou-wi-ré					rub-bé
No						
Yes						
Good day						

These six are quoted from Henry Salt, the Abyssinian traveller.

English	Arkiko (Abyssinia).	Shiho (Abyssinia.)	Adareb and Bisharm.	Darfúr.	Amháric.
One	anté	inek	en-gat	dik	and
Two	killi	lamma	ma-lúb	ou	quillet
Three	sé-lass	adda	mlh	ees	sost
Four	ubah	af-fur	ud-dig	ougal	ar-rut
Five	amús	kón	ib	os	au-mist
Six	sús	léh	sug-gúr	sitta-sún-dik	sé-dist
Seven	subhú	mel-hén	ser-é-máb	subha	sub-hat
Eight	thé-man	bahr	sum-hai	themaníar	sé-mint
Nine	tsé	sug-gal	ahed-ig	tissé	zetti
Ten	as-sur	tum-mun	tum-mún	ashurer : weja	assir
Eleven	assur-anté	in-ket-kit-a-mum	tum-nug-gir		assir and
Twelve			tum n'mal lúb		etc. etc.
Thirteen			etc. etc.		
Fourteen					
Fifteen					
Sixteen					
Seventeen					
Eighteen					
Nineteen					
Twenty	assera	lam-mat-an	tug-gúg	wing-on	háh
Thirty	selassa	zez-zan		wing-ees	selassa
Forty	erbah	me-ro-tun		wing-ougeval	erbah
Fifty	com-sa	kun-tun		etc. etc.	com-sa
Sixty	sissa	la-hé-tun			sit-sa
Seventy	sub-ha	mel-hen-tummum			sub-hah
Eighty	thé-má-ni-yah	bahr-tum-mum			semániyah
Ninety	fissal	bolé-sugga-la			zetté nah
Hundred	metę	ból		mea	mé to
Man	nas	é-üté	gál-tuk	dwo-tók	wónd
Woman	esit	nú-ma	tu-kut	yau-quó	sét
Cow	whud	la	o-sha	o-o	laam : freda
Dog	kulp	kerré	wo-yas	assa	wi-sha
Goat	tullé	la	to-nai	de-u	fé-el
Sheep	mud-uf	edo-é-dutta	o-na	doháh'-fun	bug
Foot					schamá-ig-gér
Finger			té-bal-lé (pl.)	to-ring-a	sat (pl.)
Head	ras	am-mo	ig-gré-má	tab-bo	ros
Stool					
Box					
Canoe					
Paddle					
Tree	it-chet	in-kia-ra		ku-ru	záf
House	bit	az-ré	o-gu		beit : a-dé rash
Arrow					
Gourd					
Knife			wan-ja		
Bow					
Spear		ma-ha-ré	tof-nah		
Chicken	dur-ho	dur-ho	ad-di-ro		
Pool					
Small Lake					
Large Lake					
River				mud-dil : lo-long	bahr

Water	mi	lé	o-yum	ké-ro	wá-há
Fire	es-saat	gé-ra	to-né		a'sat
Air	né fas	a-ha		do-lah	né-fás
Smoke					
Sun	tsal	al-ro	to-in	dú-lé	tsaí
Moon	wer-hé	al-sa	té-dál	do al	tckerka
Stars	kó-kub	lt-túk	hal-ek	wir-ré	quo-kub (sing.)
Sky	as-tur	ar-ran		jou-il	
Rain	zé-nab	rób			zinám
Lion	i-ut	lu-bok	wó-ad-dé	mú-rú	anbassa
Leopard	hum-mum	ar-ré-é-tun	wo-é-am	ja-ra	
Hyena	ke-rai	man-qu-la	keral	to-ro	
Fish	as-sur	as-sur	wa-assu		as-sa
Meat					
Bird	ou-af	al-lúm	kelai		wóf
Country					
Mountain				fúgú	tarara
Hill	dubr	kur-ma	or-ba		amba
Plain	gá-dúm	dug-gé		ju-da	mé-da
Food					
Stick					
Cloth					
Potatoes					
Banana					
Salt	igger	é-ba	mi-luk		
Flour					
Farm					
Road	gubbé'	ar-ra			
Stone	bau-net	dak	owi	dé-do	dengea
Island					
Eye	en	in-té	té-lé-lé (pl.)	nú mé (pl.)	afu
Nose	auf	san	og-nuf	dár-mé	af-int-cha
Mouth	af	af		n-do	af
Teeth	i-nob	é-kok	o-yuf	dug-gé	ters
Lips			am-bá-ro		
Ears	iz-un (sing.)	o-qua (sing.)	on-gué-loh	delo	djó-ro
Hair			ta-mo	nú-lú-eng-lr	tsé-gur
Tongue			mé-dá-bo		mel-as
Hand				dou-ga-suru (*right*); dong-ogu-[ro (*left*)	edje-kind (also *arm*)
Hide					corvetté
Leaf					
Day	um-mel		om-bé		kán
Night	la-lé	ber	ou-ad		memfak-lé-lit (midnight)
Walk					
Run					
Jump					
Sleep					
Dream					
Darkness					
Thanks					
Father				ablú	abaté
Mother				um-mé	enaté
Brother		nah-ba-sal			wan-dim-é (pl.)
Dead					
No					
Yes					
Good day					

From Salt.

ALTITUDES ABOVE OCEAN LEVEL OF THE FOLLOWING IMPORTANT POSITIONS, COMPUTED FROM THE FORMULA ACCORDING TO REGNAULT'S TABLES, BY SELWYN SCHOFIELD SUGDEN, NAVIGATING LIEUTENANT, ROYAL NAVY.

Dates.	Places.	Boiling-point No. 1.	Boiling-point No. 2.	Boiling-point No. 3.	Air Temperature, Fahr.	Result with Thermometer No. 1, Uncorrected.	Result with Kew Observatory Corrections.	
1877 Aug. 18	30 feet above the ocean at Kabinda .. .. .. — Boiling point: Corrected .. .. 212°·0′; Uncorrected .. .. 212·6; Temp. air, Fahr. .. 75·0							
1875						feet.	feet.	
March 3	Kagehyi, 30 feet above Lake Victoria level	205°·6	205°·5	° ′ ..	80°·	3526*	4247	* Altitudes of Lake Victoria.
,, 6	Kagehyi, Lake Victoria level	205·75	..	..	81·	3464*	4184	
,, 11	End of Speke Gulf, on islet 5 feet above lake level	205·68	..	..	80·	3461*	4240	
,, 16	North end of Majita, Bird Rocks, 10 feet above lake level	205·75	..	..	83·	3471*	4192	
,, 21	Bridge Island, lake level	205·8	..	..	79·	3400*	4119	
,, 26	Island near Namungi, 2 feet above lake level	205·85	..	..	80·	3403*	4122	
April 12	Ulagalla, Mtesa's capital	205·45	..	..	82.	3643	4366	
,, 21	Dumo, Lake Victoria level	205·85	..	..	81·	3478*	4126	* Altitudes of L. Victoria.
May 1	Refuge Island, 10 feet above lake	205·75	..	..	84·	3474*	4196	
Oct. 20	Ripon Falls, outlet of Lake Victoria, lake level	205·9	..	..	87·	3369*	4093	
Dec. 27	Wakassi river, Uganda, on Katonga river	205·8	..	..	77·	3394	4111	
	Mean level of Lake Victoria	..	..	..	..	..	4185	
1876								
Jan. 9	Uzimba, Muta-Nzigé lake	204·8	204·8	204·85	83·	4000	4724	
,, 10	West Benga, Unyoro	204·0	..	..	84·	4477	5202	
May 19	Malagarazi river, Uvinza Ferry, near Ugaga	206·4	..	..	91·	3085	3811	
June 3	Lake Tanganika, at Ujiji	207·8	..	..	76·	2228	2912	Altitudes of Lake Tanganika.
,, 4	,, ,, ,, ... (A.M.)	207·8	..	..	76·	2228	2942	
,, 4	,, ,, ,, ... (A.M.)	208·1	..	..	73·	2046	2698	
,, 4	,, ,, ,, ... (A.M.)	207·8	..	..	84·	2244	2904	
,, 4	,, ,, ,, ... (P.M.)	208·0	208·1	..	80·	2120	2719	
,, 5	,, ,, ,, ... (P.M.)	..	207·9	207·9	81·	..	..	
,, 5	,, ,, ,, ...	207·9	..	..	70·	2156	2807	
		208·2	207·9	207·9	80· / 81·	2001	2604	

„	13	„ „ Kabogo cape	207·9	..		70·	2156	2807	Altitudes of Lake Tanganika.
„	20	„ „ Kabogo Island	208·2	..		75·	1994	2648	
„	24	„ „ Kipendi Point	208·2	..		85·	2014	2675	
„	30	„ „ Kirungwé cape	208·0	..		74·5	2110	2701	
July	2	„ „ Extreme south end of lake	207·9	..		82·	2182	2840	
„	2	„ „ „ „ „	207·9	..		81·5	2180	2837	
„	5	„ „ Rufuvu river	208·1	..		83·	2066	2667	
„	9	„ „ Mapota	208·1	..		70·	2041	2784	
„	9	„ „ „	208·1	..		75·	2051	2799	
„	11	„ „ Mamwendé	208·0	..		75·	2110	2706	
„	15	„ „ Lukuga river (mouth of)	208·0	..		78·	2115	2713	
Nov.	2	Nyangwé, Livingstone river	209·1	..		79·	1480	2077	
„	29	Mburri's, on Livingstone river	209·6	..		82·	1192	1791	
Dec.	31	At confluence of Lowwa and Livingstone rivers	209·7	..		79·	1132	1729	
1877									
Jan.	20	Above Wana-Rukura, Stanley Falls	209·9	209·8	209·0	80·	1019	1614	
„	27	Below Wenya village, Stanley Falls	210·0	..	..	88·	968	1511	
Feb.	16	20 miles south of Mangala country	210·2	..	..	86·	850	1392	
„	28	Bolobo, latitude 2° 12′ s.	210·7	..	..	76·	554	1089	
March	14	Stanley Pool, above Livingstone Falls	210·6	210·55	210·6	76·	611	1147	
April	11	1 mile above Cataract river, or Round Island Rapids, Livingstone Falls	210·8	..	..	93·	505	1050	
July	10	Mbewa, below Kionzo Rapids, Livingstone Falls	211·4	..		84·	154	692	

Kew Observatory Corrections.

Thermometer No. 1.		Thermometer No. 2.		Thermometer No. 3.	
°	° ′	°	° ′	°	° ′
200 ..	− 1·10	200 ..	− 0·40	200 ..	− 0·15
205 ..	− 0·90	205 ..	− 0·45	205 ..	− 0·20
212 ..	− 0·60	212 ..	− 0·45	212 ..	− 0·20

Given at Kew, February 1878.

(Signed) G. M. Whipple,
Superintendent.

POSITIONS OF THE FOLLOWING PLACES.

Dates.	Places.	Longitudes.	D.R. or Observation.	Latitudes.	D.R. or Observation.
1874.					
Dec. 13	Mpwapwa, Usagara	36° 26′ E.	Obs.	6° 17′ S.	Obs.
" 15	Chunyu	36 21 "	"	6 14 "	"
" 18	Chikombo, Ugogo	36 4 "	"	6 8 "	D.R.
" 31	Mukondoku, Ugogo	35 14 "	"	6 16 "	Obs.
1875.					
Jan. 9	Uveriveri	35 2 "	"	5 36 "	"
" 15	Suna	35 11 "	"	5 20 "	D.R.
" 22	Vinyata	35 2 "	"	4 50 "	"
" 30	Mgongo Tembo	34 34 "	"	4 44 "	Obs.
Feb. 3	Verge of Luwamberri Plain ..	34 12 "	"	4 37 "	D.R.
" 11	Mombiti Usukuma	33 58 "	"	4 0 "	Obs.
" 18	Usiha, E...	33 48 "	"	3 38 "	D.R.
" 24	S. Usmau	33 27 "	"	2 50 "	"
" 25	Gambachika	33 17 "	"	2 33 "	Obs.
Mar. 7	Kagehyi, Lake Victoria	33 14 "	"	2 21 "	"
" 9	Natwari Island	33 28 "	"	2 23 "	D.R.
" 10	Bay south of Iramba	33 29 "	"	2 20 "	"
" 11	Speke Gulf	33 54 "	"	2 15 "	"
" 18	Igengi	33 43 "	"	1 28 "	"
" 19	Island in Urieri Bay	33 49 "	"	1 27 "	"
" 20	Shirati	34 17 "	"	1 9 "	"
" 22	Twin Islands	34 37 "	"	0 28 "	Obs.
" 25	Ngevi Island	34 10 "	"	0 10 N.	"
" 28	Mombiti	33 47 "	"	0 12 "	"
April 2	Buka	32 58 "	"	0 12 "	D.R.
" 10	Mtesa's Camp	32 41 "	"	0 21 "	"
" 17	Usavara	32 37 "	"	0 16 "	Obs.
" 17	S. extremity of Murchison's Bay	..	..	0 5 "	"
" 20	Cape Bujaju, N. side	..	..	0 14 S.	"
Nov. 17	Nakavija	32 18 E.	Obs.	0 9 N.	"
" 19	Jumba's Cove	32 7 "	"	0 5 S.	"
April 21	Dumo	31 49 "	"	0 33 "	D.R.
" 22	Isangu	31 45 "	"	0 40 "	"
" 23	Bugavu	..	..	0 56 "	Obs.
	Weza	31 57 E.	Obs.	1 2 "	D.R.
" 24	6 miles S. of Kagya	31 58 "	"	1 9 "	Obs.
	Makongo, Uzongora	31 57 "	"	1 15 "	D.R.
" 25	Musira Island, N. side	31 57 "	"	1 17 "	Obs.
" 30	Refuge Island	..	..	2 8 "	"
May 2	E. end of Komeh Island ..	32 41 E.	Obs.	2 8 "	"
" 4	S. end of Wiru	33 1 "	"	2 7 "	"
" 8	Kagehyi	33 14 "	"	2 21 "	"
Dec. 13	Musovorva	31 28 "	"	0 2 N.	"
" 14	Myembé-Gambui	31 31 "	"	0 5 "	D.R.
" 16	Ruwewa	31 29 "	"	0 9 "	"
" 27	W. of Wakassi river	31 13 "	"	0 10 "	"
1876.					
Jan. 4	Ruoko, Unyoro	30 51 "	"	0 3 "	"
" 7	W. Benga	30 37 "	"	0 5 "	"

POSITIONS OF THE FOLLOWING PLACES—*continued.*

Dates.		Places.	Longitudes.		D.R. or observation.	Latitudes.		D.R. or Observation.
1876.								
Jan.	10	Uzimba	30°	17′ E.	Obs.	0°	7′ S.	D.R.
„	21	Kitera, Uganda	31	30 „	„	0	13 N.	„
„	23	Kissosi (West Base)	31	37 „	„	0	7 „	„
Feb.	5	Karugawa, or Charugawa ..	31	22 „	„	0	57 S.	„
Mar.	2	Rumanika's lake, E. side Windermere	31	0 „	„	1	39 „	Obs.
„	7	Village of Kazinga		..	..	1	38 „	„
„	8	2½ miles N. of Kazinga on river		..	..	1	40 „	„
„	10	2 miles N. of Unyamubi Island	30	59 E.	Obs.	1	53 „	„
„	11	Lake Ihema	30	49 „	„	1	50 „	„
„	12	Kazinga, Lake Windermere ..	31	0 „	„	1	38 „	„
„	28	South extreme central arm of Uhimba	30	55 „	„	2	6 „	„
April	3	Marurama, or Kafurra's	31	2 „	„	2	27 „	D.R.
June	5	Ugoy or Ugoi, Ujiji	30	7 „	„	4	55 „	„
„	15	3½ miles S. of Sigunga Island	30	32 „	„	5	33 „	Obs.
„	16	Southern beach of Urimba ..	30	37 „	„	5	48 „	„
„	18	Karinzi Point	30	19 „	„	6	0 „	D.R.
„	19	Ulambula	30	28 „	„	6	21 „	„
„	20	Kabogo Island	30	26 „	„	6	25 „	Obs.
„	21	1 mile off Rugufu, E. by S. from Ponda's	30	38 „	„	6	30 „	D.R.
„	23	Conical Hill, Ruhinga, S.E. by S.	30	51 „	„	6	45 „	„
„	24	W. of Karema	31	5 „	„	6	55 „	Obs.
„	25	Kipendi Point	31	2 „	„	7	0 „	„
„	26	Mpimbwé cape	30	57 „	„	7	2 „	„
„	27	Mwekavanga	31	0 „	„	7	32 „	„
„	28	From Mtosi to Msamba Island	31	10 „	„	7	43 „	„
„	29	Wampembé	31	12 „	„	7	52 „	D.R.
„	30	From Zinga river	31	14 „	„	7	55 „	Obs.
July	1	Kirungwé cape	31	18 „	„	8	13 „	„
„	2	Kantamba Point	31	25 „	„	8	28 „	„
„	3	From Still Cove	31	27 „	„	8	35 „	„
„	4	Kapata river, S. end of Lake Tanganika	31	22 „	„	8	47 „	„
„	5	From Mwangala	31	13 „	„	8	45 „	„
„	6	From Umisepa	31	3 „	„	8	32 „	„
„	7	Rufuvu river	30	58 „	„	8	32 „	D.R.
„	8	Kasawa Point	30	53 „	„	8	22 „	Obs.
„	9	Mapota	30	36 „	„	7	55 „	„
„	11	Kaweré	30	33 „	„	7	41 „	„
„	13	Mount Murumbi		..	..	6	55 „	„
„	14	10 miles S. of Muganza	29	48 E.	Obs.	6	37 „	„
„	15	South of Mirembwé cape ..		..	..	6	8 „	„
„	16	Mouth of Lukuga river	29	36 E.	Obs.	5	55 „	D.R.
„	20	Kirindi Island	29	50 „	„	5	44 „	Obs.
„	22	3 miles N. of Kawasindi Island	29	33 „	„	5	27 „	„
„	23	Mkizamba, Goma		..	..	5	12 „	„
„	24	6 miles S. of Musama	29	21 E.	Obs.	4	56 „	„
„	25	3 miles N. of Kaganza	29	22 „	„	4	35 „	D.R.
„	26	3 miles S. of Kiukwe	29	31 „	„	4	34 „	..
		E. side of Ubwari	29	28 „	„	4	3 „	Obs.

Positions of the following Places—*continued.*

Dates.	Places.	Longitudes.	D.R. or observation.	Latitudes.	D.R. or Observation.
1876.					
	Kikamba	29° 30′ E.	Obs.	4° 22′ S.	D.R.
July 27	Opposite Kiunzu	29 21 "	"	..	..
" 29	Kioga	29 50 "	"	4 10 S.	D. R.
Aug. 2	Ugoy, Ujiji	30 9 "	"	4 54 "	"
" 28	Mouth of Malagarazi river, Lake Tanganika	30 27 "	"	5 15 "	"
Sept. 3	M'schazy Haven	30 20 "	"	5 27 "	"
" 14	Arab crossing-place	29 48 "	"	5 48 "	"
" 25	Mulolwa's	29 5 "	"	5 33 "	"
" 28	Kumbila	28 42 "	"	5 13 "	"
" 29	Walumbu	28 38 "	"	5 7 "	"
Oct. 1	Kajunju	28 30 "	"	5 2 "	"
" 2	Kagongwé	28 22 "	"	4 53 "	"
" 5	Uhombo	28 9 "	"	4 43 "	"
" 8	Ka-Bambarré	27 55 "	"	4 32 "	Obs.
" 15	Kabungwé	27 19 "	"	4 36 "	D.R.
" 17	Mpungu	26 50 "	"	4 48 "	"
" 20	Mwana Mamba	26 34 "	"	4 31 "	"
" 25	Benangongo	26 24 "	"	4 22 "	"
" 26	Kankumba	26 17 "	"	4 20 "	"
" 27	Nyangwé	26 16 "	"	4 15 "	Obs.
Nov. 8	Mpotira	26 25 "	"	4 6 "	D.R.
" 9	Kianga	26 18 "	"	4 0 "	"
" 12	Mirimo	26 17 "	"	3 50 "	"
" 14	Wané Kamankua	26 5 "	"	3 48 "	"
" 16	Wané Kirumbu	26 0 "	"	3 42 "	"
" 18	Kampunzu	25 53 "	"	3 37 "	"
" 19	Rukombeh's crossing, Livingstone river	..	"	3 34 "	Obs.
" 24	Mouth of Ruiki river	25 33 "	Obs.	3 26 "	D.R.
" 27	N.E. bend confluence of little river S. of Hilly Ridge ..	25 32 "	"	3 20 "	"

INDEX.

LONDON: PRINTED BY WILLIAM CLOWES AND SONS, LIMITED, STAMFORD STREET AND CHARING CROSS.

www.ingramcontent.com/pod-product-compliance
Lightning Source LLC
Chambersburg PA
CBHW022113300426
44117CB00007B/691

* 9 7 8 3 7 4 4 7 6 0 0 8 9 *